THE JEW OF MALTA
AND
THE MASSACRE AT PARIS

EDITED BY

H. S. BENNETT, M.A.
UNIVERSITY LECTURER IN ENGLISH, EMMANUEL COLLEGE, CAMBRIDGE

v. 3

GORDIAN PRESS, INC.
NEW YORK, MCMLXVI

Originally Published 1931
Reprinted 1966

Published by Gordian Press, Inc., by
arrangement with Methuen and Co. Ltd., London
Library of Congress Catalog Card No. 66-23027

Printed in the U.S.A. by
EDWARDS BROTHERS, INC.
Ann Arbor, Michigan

PREFACE

THE two plays contained in this volume have not received as much attention from the editors as have *Faustus* and *Edward II*, so that the general purpose of this edition of Marlowe's works, which is to annotate each play on a much fuller scale than was possible in former editions, finds ample scope in dealing with *The Jew of Malta*, and even more so with *The Massacre at Paris*. The General Editor in his Preface to *The Life of Marlowe* has dealt with the question of modernization of spelling, and this modernization necessarily involves questions of punctuation : here it only remains to add that where possible old forms such as *consait* (conceit) have been retained, and if rejected have been recorded in the textual notes. The difficult problem of Act and Scene division and the location of scenes has given much trouble, and I have tried to suggest in my notes the reasons which have led me to believe that the plays were acted on the Elizabethan stage with such scene changes as I have indicated. Previous editors have either fought shy of this task altogether, or have had so rudimentary a conception of the working of the Elizabethan stage as to render their observations useless.

While this volume has been under preparation I have been privileged to receive the help of several eminent scholars, and I am more than sensible of their kindness in answering my queries. Dr. F. S. Boas, Sir E. K. Chambers, Dr. W. W. Greg and Dr. R. B. McKerrow have all been good enough to enlighten me on special points, while my colleague, Mr. Aubrey Attwater, of Pembroke College, has allowed me to make use of his wide scholarship on many occasions. Professor J. le Gay Brereton, of the University of Sydney, most kindly sent me a mass of suggestions and emendations, while Professor C. F. Tucker Brooke generously placed at my disposal all his collected material on these two plays. Finally I must express my gratitude to the General Editor of the series : Professor Case has taken the most generous view of his duties, and again and again has found the solution to my difficulties and added illustrations and parallels where my own reading failed me.

Emmanuel College,　　　　　　　　　　　　　H. S. B.
　　Cambridge,
　　　　January 1931

CONTENTS

ABBREVIATIONS USED IN COLLATIONS, ETC.

O   .   The octavo edition of *The Massacre*. N.D. See *Introduction III* and *Appendix B*.

Q   .   The quarto edition of *The Jew*. 1633. See *Introduction III* and *Appendix B*.

Reed   .   Dodsley's *Select Old Plays*, 2nd edition, ed. I. Reed, 1780. See *Appendix B. Sect. II*.

Coll.   .   Dodsley, 3rd edition, ed. J. P. Collier, 1825. See *Appendix B, etc.*

Rob.   .   Robinson's edition of 1826. See *Appendix B, etc.*

Dyce[1]   .   Dyce's first edition of 1850. See *Appendix B, etc.*

Dyce[2]   .   Dyce's revised edition of 1858, etc. See *Appendix B, etc.*

Cunn.   .   Cunningham's edition of 1870, etc. See *Appendix B, etc.*

Bull.   .   Bullen's edition of 1885. See *Appendix B, etc.*

Ellis   .   Mermaid edition (ed. by H. Ellis), 1887, etc. See *Appendix B, etc.*

Wag.   .   A. Wagner's edition of 1889. See *Appendix B, etc.*

T. Brooke   .   Tucker Brooke's edition of 1910. See *Appendix B, etc.*

Greg   .   Malone Society's edition of *The Massacre at Paris*, ed. W. W. Greg, 1929. See *Appendix B, etc.*

Ed.   .   The present edition.

O.E.D.   .   *The New Oxford English Dictionary*.

The term *Q, etc.* means that all editions subsequent to the Quarto follow its reading.

The term *Rob. to Bull.* means that all the editors from Robinson to Bullen are in agreement as to a reading.

THE JEW OF MALTA

INTRODUCTION

I

EARLY HISTORY OF THE PLAY

THE earliest known reference to the *Jew of Malta* is an entry in the diary of Philip Henslowe on the 26 of February, 1592. There we read 'Rd. at the Jewe of malltuse the 26 of febrearye, 1591 (i.e. 1592. New Style) 1ˢ.'[1] It was then performed by Lord Strange's company, who continued to present it in their repertoire until the February of the following year. Of its history prior to this we know nothing; but, as Henslowe does not mark it as new when he first enters it, we must assume it was written some time before (see p. 5). Undoubtedly it was a very popular play : Strange's men performed it ten times between February 1592 and the closing of the theatres owing to the Plague in July 1592. Moreover, only one other play in their repertoire drew larger audiences—*Titus and Vespasian*—and the receipts as noted in Henslowe's *Diary* show that he received on an average £2 8s. 6d. for the seven performances of *Titus*, and £2 3s. 6d. for the ten performances of *The Jew*. We can better estimate the comparative popularity this implies if we remember that throughout this period the average receipts by Henslowe are calculated at £1 14s. (Chambers : *The Elizabethan Stage*, II, 122, 23). When the theatres opened again, Strange's men presented it with success three times between the first of January and the first of February 1593. After that we lose sight of it

---

[1] Henslowe's *Diary*, ed. W. W. Greg, Pt. I, p. 13.

1

again for little more than a year, when we find it given by
Sussex' men on the 4th February 1594, and so by various
companies—the Queen's & Sussex' in conjunction, the
Admiral's, and then by the Admiral's or the Chamberlain's
—until the 25th June 1594 when it comes into the permanent possession of the Admiral's men. Thus it would appear
probable that the play was the property of Henslowe, who
was accustomed to loan it to any company that might be
making use of his theatre at the moment. From the 25th of
June, however, until the following December the Admiral's
men presented it constantly ; and again in 1596 between
the 9th of January and the 23rd of June they gave eight
performances. This gives us a total of 36 performances
between February 1592 and June 1596—a number equalled
by no other play of Marlowe's, as far as we know, although
it must be remembered that we have no record of *Edward II*
or *Dido*, as these did not belong to Henslowe.

After this we again lose sight of the play until 1601, when
it was revived. By this time Henslowe had ceased to carry
on his record in such detail, so that we cannot tell how
successful the revival proved to be, nor for how long it continued in the repertoire. There are two brief entries only
which give us clues : First, ' Lent unto Robart Shawe and
Mr. Jube the 19 of Maye 1601 to bye divers thinges for
the Jewe of Malta the some of . . . . . . V^{li}.'   And just
below, the next entry reads, ' lent mor to the littell tayller
the same daye for more thinges for the Jewe of Malta some
of X^{s} ' (Henslowe's *Diary*, I, 137). No more is known of *The
Jew* until 1632, when Nicholas Vavasour entered at Stationers' Hall ' A Tragedy called the Jew of Malta ' (Arber's
Transcript, IV, 288). This was on November 20th ; and,
in 1633, he published the Quarto, with the following title-
page :

The Famous | TRAGEDY | OF | THE RICH IEW | OF
MALTA. | As it was playd | before the King and |
Queene, in His Majesties | Theatre at *White-Hall*, by Her

Majefties | Servants at the *Cock-pit*. Written by Christopher Marlo. | (Device) | London ; | Printed by I.B. for *Nicholas Vavasour*, and are to be sold | at his Shop in the Inner-Temple, neere the | Church. 1633.[1]

The play had been brought forward and presented both at the Court and at the Cockpit with Prologues and Epilogues by Thomas Heywood. Whether this was actually in 1633 or slightly earlier is not known, as our only evidence is derived from the Quarto of that year. To the earlier history of the text and to this Quarto we must now turn.

The Stationers' Register for May 17th, 1594, reads ' The famouse tragedie of the Riche Jewe of Malta '. *Nicholas Ling and Thomas Millington*. The previous day had seen John Danter obtaining a licence for ' a ballad intituled the murtherous life and terrible death of the riche jew of Malta ' (Arber's *Transcript*, II, 650). Here again we are disappointed, for no copy of either of these productions has come down to us. The disappearance of a broadsheet is not difficult to understand ; a flimsy thing at best and of ephemeral interest. A printed book—even a cheap theatrical quarto—is another matter, and it is difficult to explain how it has disappeared—always assuming it was ever issued. Of course it may well be that its very popularity saw it so eagerly conned and thumbed that finally it fell to pieces in the readers' hands. We know how popular the play was, and also how high the Elizabethan temper rose in its hatred of Jews about this time, and these facts would all help to increase the demand for the sight of a copy. At the same time, however, it must be noted that they also make it the more difficult to believe that Ling and Millington, after taking the trouble to enter the play as their property, proceeded no further. Certainly difficulties may have arisen with the Admiral's men about this time, for it is in the June of this year that we find them assuming proprietorship over the play to the

---

[1] For full collation, see Appendix B.

exclusion of others, whereas between February and June 1594, as we have seen, *The Jew* was acted by various companies, one after the other. Does this indicate that the players in this instance, as in others of which we have record, disliked the idea of publication as harmful to their interests, and managed to arrange for its non-appearance ? We have at present no means of answering such questions. All we can note is the undoubted fact that no copy is known at present, despite the difficulty we have in believing that so popular a play was never printed until some forty years after its first production.

Heywood's Epistle Dedicatory of 1633 speaks of it as ' now being *newly* brought to the Presse ', and this may infer that there had been an earlier edition, but the use of the word ' newly ' in such a connection is too doubtful to allow of any certainty. Professor Tucker Brooke points out (Marlowe, *Works*, 1910, p. 142) that in the 1592 *Faustbook*, the phrase ' Newly imprinted ' is followed by ' and in convenient places imperfect matter amended ' showing that it was not the *editio princeps*, while on the other hand, when we read on the title-page of *Tamburlaine*, 1590, ' Now *first*, and *newlie* published ', it does in fact mean the first impression.[1]

II

THE DATE OF THE PLAY

THE dating of *The Jew of Malta* is dependent on two facts : first the allusion in line 3 of the Prologue to the death of the Duke of Guise shows that the play (or parts of it) were written subsequent to December 23rd, 1588, and secondly the entry in Henslowe's *Diary* for February 26th, 1592, tells us that it was part of the repertoire of Lord Strange's men at that date. A. Wagner in his edition of the play has argued that the reference to the Guise, as it

---

[1] For further discussion, see Notes on p. 25.

occurs in the Prologue only, is not evidence as to the whole play. He suggests that the Prologue may have been written later, since its object is to prepare the audience for the play. He thinks the play may have been written before 1588, and that it was probably produced in 1588. This seems a little arbitrary : there is no sufficient reason to divorce the Prologue from the rest of the play, and we may accept the general opinion of the editors that *The Jew* was written about 1589–90. In the first place we have seen that the play was in the repertoire of Strange's men in February, 1592, and was not marked as being new at that time in Henslowe's list. The allusion to the Duke of Guise suggests that his assassination was fairly recent, and that the dramatist was making use of something that was current gossip. Further, the impetuous violence of the plot seems to argue for its comparative earliness in the Marlowe canon. *Tamburlaine* was written by 1588, and there seems nothing to gainsay our placing *The Jew* in the next year, or very shortly after.

III

THE FIRST KNOWN EDITION

THE Quarto of 1633 on which we have to rely for our text is, like many other play-books of the period, a poor piece of work from a typographical point of view. It contains many errors arising from ignorance, and more arising from carelessness ; and, as is commonly found, the compositor has little understanding of the differences between prose and verse, and often breaks up prose passages, or runs on verse passages, at his discretion. But, apart from the evils incident on the fact that in general it was not the best Elizabethan printers who troubled to obtain and publish contemporary plays, we are constantly hampered and bewildered by faults and obscurities which must not be attributed to the printer, but rather to the steady degenera-

2

tion which plays suffered as they passed through years of the corrupting mechanism of the repertory system. Those who have watched repertory actors over any length of time come to know that they have certain tricks : that one collocation of words, or certain adjectives or phrases come more easily to them than do others. When memory fails they gag from half-remembered passages and phrases : and if this be so with actors dealing with Elmer Rice one week and Shakespeare the next, with the most advanced experimental use of language in one play and with a normal diction in another, how much must it have been exaggerated and encouraged in actors using for the most part a very definitely rhythmic verse day after day ? Clichés and phrases must have come easily to them, and one line often recalled a similar line in another play, and in moments of stress who shall say that no confusion or interchange ever took place ?

But these changes are insignificant in the face of the greater problems presented by the present text of the play. We have seen that after it dropped out in 1596, it was revived by Henslowe in 1601, and again about 1632 by Heywood who humbly craves pardon for presenting something ' writ many years agone '. Were these two revivals merely revivals, or did they lend occasion for an overhauling of the play ? Professor Tucker Brooke thinks ' the extant text incorporates the results of at least two separate revisions : the first carried out before the revival of 1601 . . . the second that which must have been necessary before so old a work could be presented at Court or at the Cockpit '. It is not improbable, he adds, that Heywood altered the play for performance at Court. We can say nothing as to a possible revision in 1601, though it is worth remarking that an inventory of the properties of the Admiral's men, dated the 10th March, 1598, includes the item ' j cauderm for the Jewe '. It is clear from this that the final scene has not been vitally tampered with in any revision (*Henslowe Papers*, ed. W. W. Greg, p. 118). For the revision of 1632 the evidence is slender but worth consideration. Mr. Fleay in his *Biographical Chronicle of the English Drama* (I, 298 ; II, 61, 2) long ago pointed out that there is a similarity between the Friars' scenes (IV, ii, iii) and certain incidents in the minor plot of Heywood's play *The Captives*.

As Heywood certainly wrote the Prologues and Epilogues to the play when he ' usher'd it unto the Court, and presented it to the Cock-pit,' it is necessary to investigate this similarity in the hope of finding a clue that will enable us to say definitely whether these scenes are an interpolation by Heywood. First as to the story : two probable sources suggest themselves, with others far less possible in the background, namely an English jest-book story and an Italian *novella*. The English story has for title-page ' Heere beginneth a mery Iest of Dane Hew Munk of Leicester, and how he was foure times slain and once hanged '. This is undated, but was almost certainly produced before 1584, since no book printed by the same publisher is known to have been issued after this date. The Italian *novella* is the first of a series of fifty stories by Masuccio di Salerno and was first printed in 1476 at Naples (Koeppel, *Archiv für das Studium der Neueren Sprachen und Litteraturen*, xcvii, 323 ff.). Either of these contain material that could have given the author of the Friars' scenes (IV, ii and iii) the idea he develops there, but the vital difference which we must notice is the fact that the jest-book story concerns a monk and his abbot, while the *novella* tells of the quarrel of two friars. When we come to consider the evidence existing by which we may determine whether either of these sources were known to Marlowe or Heywood the scales are unevenly weighted, for we have no information whatsoever about Marlowe. He may, or may not, have seen both or either of these books. We do not know. Heywood's reading is another matter : he had certainly read Masuccio either in original or in translation, as the most recent editor of *The Captives* shows in detail (A. C. Judson, *The Captives*, p. 20), and further he had made use of the material of the *novella* in a story called ' The Faire Ladie of Norwich ' which he included in his Γνναιχεῖον or *Nine Books of Various History concerning Women* (1624, p. 253 ff.). Now in both his stories we find two friars as in the *novella*, and not a monk and an abbot as in the jest-book. This has not been noticed by Mr. Judson, but it is certainly strongly corroborative of his thesis. On the other hand to support the theory that Marlowe wrote these scenes, we have to believe either that he read the jest-book, and changed his characters ; or, that he could have seen the Italian, or a French translation. Until we know more of Marlowe's reading than is at present available the problem cannot be carried much further.

Not only these scenes, but others have been suspected. Mr. Fleay says ' I have no doubt that the Bellamira part was inserted by Heywood to bombast out Marlowe's short play. This is III, 1 ; IV, iv, v ; V, 1 ' (*op. cit.*, I, 298), while elsewhere he says ' In the scenes with Bellamira and Pilia-Borza there is a good deal not by Marlowe. This is not due to original collaboration, but to alteration by Heywood *c.* 1632 ' (*op. cit.*, II, 61, 62). This opinion has been denied by Fräulein Margaret Thimme who has studied the metrical and stylistic characteristics of the play, and is strongly of the belief that it is all Marlowe's work. A very careful examination of all this evidence leaves me unable to advance matters much further, though one additional factor should be emphasised. What tells most strongly against accepting the view of Fleay, attractive though it is at first sight, is the question of diction. Heywood had a well-known, unusual diction, which was dealt with by Rupert Brooke, in his monograph on Webster, by Professor H. D. Gray in the *Modern Language Review* (XXII, 389), and by Mr. F. L. Lucas in his edition of Webster. A study of the suspect scenes with this in mind has led to very meagre results, and certainly makes it impossible, in my judgment, to speak with anything like the certainty

of Mr. Fleay. These scenes contain a mere handful of
words that are not used elsewhere in Marlowe; and, on
the other hand, do not contain many of the specifically
Heywoodian words and phrases. We must, therefore, I
think, give a verdict of *Not proven* at the very least when
asked to believe these scenes are by Heywood : the more
probable explanation would seem to lie in the gradual
processes of degradation and minor alteration of the text
outlined above, together with more drastic operations from
time to time. Assuming, as we surely may with Professor
Tucker Brooke, that there were at least two revisions, the
suggested interpolations are not of such a character that
any one of half a dozen playwrights could not have produced
them on demand. The Bellamira scenes only suggest situa-
tions which were commonplace in Elizabethan literature ;
and, as we have seen, the Friars' incident is present in its
essentials in a contemporary chap-book.[1]

IV

SOURCES

WE have no certain knowledge of any book or event which
led Marlowe to write *The Jew of Malta*, but two important
theses have been advanced to account for its appearance.

The first of these, by L. Kellner (*Englische Studien*, 1887,
x, 80 ff.), is based on the adventurous history of a Portuguese
Jew who achieved great notoriety in the sixteenth century.
Juan Miques or Michesius is to be heard of in various
countries. ' The illustrious Republic of Venice, the mighty
kingdom of Spain, the conceited government of France, and
even the haughty Papacy, all saw themselves endangered
by him ' (Graetz, *Hist. of the Jews*, iv, 632). Finally he

---

[1] After the above was in type, it came to my knowledge that Mr. A. M.
Clark, in his forthcoming study of Heywood, will confirm the ascription
of additional scenes to him, and owing to Mr. Clark's kindness in com-
municating his views, I am able to realize that there is more to be said in
its favour; for instance, the crowding of Act V as an indication of earlier
expansion.

settled down in Constantinople about 1555, where he became
an ally and friend of the Sultan Selim II over whom he
seems to have acquired great influence. He plotted continuously against the Christians, and was made Duke of
Naxos and the Cyclades, assuming the name of Joseph
Nassi. He was led to believe that he might become King
of Cyprus and hoped to establish a new Jewish state in
Palestine on the sea of Tiberias. We are told that on the
strength of a half-promise given by the Sultan he had prepared a crown and a banner bearing the words ' Josephus
Rex Cypri ' (Foglietta, *De Sacro Foedere in Selimum*,
quoted by Kellner, p. 97). He was undoubtedly a man of
tremendous power, since he had the complete confidence of
Selim II, but he was surrounded by enemies, many of them
of European nationality, for Nassi's schemes offended and
attacked many great states. Kellner argues that this
brilliant figure arrested the attention of Marlowe, and was
the prototype of Barabas.

The difficulty many scholars found in accepting this theory
lay in the inability of either Kellner or A. Wagner (who
accepted this view in his edition of *The Jew of Malta*) to show
that Marlowe had ever heard of Miques. Recently, however,
in a brilliant article (*Review of English Studies*, Oct. 1929,
p. 385 ff.) Miss Ethel Seaton has proved beyond a doubt
that a collection of chronicles on Turkish affairs made by
Philip Lonicerus, published in 1578, and again in 1584, was
well known to Marlowe. Now in this book, on page 3
of Vol. II of the 1584 edition, there is a long reference to
Miques. Further she shows that in Belleforest's *Cosmographie Universelle* there are at least two detailed references
to him : one of which ' by connecting Miques with the great
Jewish banking interests in Lyons, Marseilles and in Italy '
accords well with Marlowe's text (I, 1, 122 f. ; IV, 1, 74 f.),
and ' partly meets Professor Tucker Brooke's objection that
Miques' fame rested upon political rather than commercial
interests ' (*op. cit.*, p. 392).

It was partly the absence of this link which caused Professor Tucker Brooke to throw doubt on this theory, and to argue that the events in the life of Michesius did not square with those Marlowe depicts in his character of Barabas. He wrote (*Times Literary Supplement*, June, 1922), ' I believe that considerably more similarity to Marlowe's Barabas is found in the character of a later Jew of Constantinople, David Passi, whose career reached its culmination, after half-a-dozen years of European notoriety, in March, 1591, some eleven months before the earliest extant reference to *The Jew of Malta*. . . . This David, more distinctly than Joseph Nassi at an earlier period, was involved in the Turkish designs on Malta ; and, . . . instead of [adopting] Joseph's consistently Anti-Christian attitude, he pursued a boggling policy, playing off Turk against Christian after the fashion of Marlowe's Barabas. He was closely connected with English diplomacy in the Mediterrean, and was a person of particular interest to English political observers. What I know of David Passi is derived chiefly from records digested in the Calendar of State Papers. These, of course, cannot have been known to Marlowe ; but the essential facts about Passi are not likely to have been unfamiliar to Marlowe who had the privilege of conversation with such connoisseurs of English foreign policy as Raleigh and the Walsinghams.' Professor Tucker Brooke goes on to outline the career of this man and shows him lording it in Constantinople and then by a series of interesting extracts he describes his duplicity and overthrow in the spring of 1591.

The recent investigations of Dr. Leslie Hotson certainly substantiate Professor Tucker Brooke's belief that Marlowe was in touch with current diplomatic gossip, for he has been able to show that Marlowe was employed as a secret agent for the Privy Council in 1587 ' in matters touching the benefitt of his Countrie '. Further, Miss de Kalb (in an unpublished thesis, and in her letter to the *Times Literary*

Supplement) has brought together considerable new material to show that Marlowe was much in company of agents of the Crown, and it may well be that rumours and scraps concerning this active conspirator came to him. That probably is all it amounts to. Professor Tucker Brooke agrees that it is unlikely that ' the main theme of the tragedy was founded upon printed material ', and I believe that it was from rumours and gossip, emphasised and exaggerated by contemporary feeling about Jews, that Marlowe derived his inspiration. Once given the idea of depicting a Jew, raised to power as well as to affluence, we can leave Marlowe's own gifts to provide the rest. Out of a haze of surmise and unreliable report he saw clearly enough the main lines of his character. His reading and general knowledge of recent and current history gave him the rest.[1]

V

MARLOWE AND MACHIAVELLI

WHATEVER may be our opinion of *The Jew of Malta* as a play, we are forced to give it particular attention because of the great influence it had on the conception subsequent dramatists held of Machiavelli, since Machiavelli is so omnipresent and important a constituent of Elizabethan drama. Dr. Mario Praz writes : ' The two plays which gave birth to the type of the Machiavellian knave on the English stage are *The Jew of Malta* and Kyd's *The Spanish Tragedy*. Indeed, the question of Machiavellian influence on Eliza-

---

[1] The recent researches of Dr. Lucien Wolf (*Transactions*, Jewish Hist. Soc. of Eng., 1924–1927, xi, pp. 1–91) have established the fact that several families of wealthy and influential Jews were resident in Elizabethan London. Among them was the famous Alvaro Mendez, a kinsman of Juan Miques, who settled in Constantinople after the death of Miques in 1579, and soon became an enemy of David Passi, the royal favourite. Since Marlowe was involved in secret politics, was it not possible for information concerning both these men to reach his ears, the more so when we remember that a fierce quarrel between Mendez, the kinsman of Juan Miques, and David Passi was in progress during 1591–92, and that this quarrel was well known in English diplomatic circles ? Indeed Elizabeth upheld the character of Mendez to the Sultan against her own ambassador in Turkey.

bethan drama is complicated by the influence of these two plays, which was still more far-echoing than it is thought. Very seldom the dramatists had a first-hand acquaintance with Machiavelli's writings ; most of the time the villainous traits in the characters of their dramas are borrowed from Kyd's and Marlowe's Machiavellians : at the utmost, fresh illustration was derived from Gentillet.'

Probably Marlowe had learned something of Machiavelli while still at Cambridge. Gabriel Harvey, who was then in residence there, was well read in the Florentine's works, and constantly quotes them in his marginal annotations (see Gabriel Harvey's *Marginalia*, ed. G. C. Moore Smith), as well as in his letters ; and it was Harvey who, only two years before Marlowe came into residence at Benet College, wrote thus to a friend : ' And I warrant you sum good fellowes amongst us begin nowe to be prettely wel acquayntid with a certayne parlous booke callid, as I remember me, *Il Principe* di Niccolo Machiavelli, and I can peradventure name you an odd crewe or tooe that ar as cuninge in his *Discorsi* . . . in his *Historia Fiorentina*, and in his *Dialogues della Arte della Guerra* tooe . . . , as University men were wont to be in their *parva Logicalia* and *Magna Moralia* and *Physicalia* of both sorts : *verbum intelligenti sat.*' (*Letter Book*, ed. E. J. L. Scott, p. 79.)

It is evident from this that Marlowe had an opportunity —indeed knowing his character we may go further and say that Marlowe was bound to learn of the doctrines of Machiavelli while at Cambridge. In his well-known monograph (*Machiavelli and the Elizabethan Drama*) Edward Meyer has said that ' it may be stated as an absolute certainty that had *the Prince* never been written, Marlowe's three great heroes would not have been drawn with such gigantic strokes ' (pp. 33, 34), and an examination of the character of Barabas shows how indebted Marlowe is to the influence of Machiavelli. It is necessary to put it thus, because Marlowe, although probably acquainted with the original writings of the Italian, was certainly acquainted with those of Gentillet. Now Gentillet had written in 1576 a violent attack on Machiavelli (*Discours sur les moyens de bien gouverner et maintenir en bonne paix un royaume . . . Contre N. Machiavel*) in which he denounced him as one of the most infamous of men, and stated the maxims of his two books *The Prince* and *The Discourses* in sentences as pithy and striking as they were misleading and unjust. This book became the 'grand Arsenal' from which hundreds of writers, who never read a word of the original, drew their knowledge of Machiavelli. Indeed, so far as England was concerned, no translation of *The Prince* is known before 1640. Those who knew no Italian were forced to draw their knowledge either from the French translations of *The Prince*, or from the poisoned source of Gentillet's book, which was not only available in French, but had been translated into English in 1577, and probably circulated in manuscript until its publication in 1602. Marlowe, at any rate, seems to have known both the Machiavelli original and the 'Contre-Machiavelli' as it came to be called,—though it is from the latter that he seems to derive most material for *The Jew*.

Meyer (*op. cit.*) gives a careful and detailed analysis of the play, and shows how it is influenced at every point by Gentillet's work, and to this the reader must be referred. One or two examples, however, may be given: Gentillet (as translated by Paterick, 1602) writes, ' (Machiavelli) hath handled how a tyrannie ought to be builded, that is, by crueltie, perfidie, craft, perjurie, impietie, revenges, contempt of counsell and friends, entertainment of flatterers, tromperie, the hatred of vertue, covetousness, inconstancie and other like vices . . . Secondly by maintaining and keeping subjects . . . in poverty and necessity . . . Thirdly he adds another mean, namely to build fortresses against them . . . For poverty is no sufficient mean to contain a people in obedience, for they are never unfurnished of arms ' (p. 348). From this one passage alone we may see the general picture the *Contre-Machiavelli* constantly portrays, and it is evident how many of the traits of a tyrant have been taken over bodily by Marlowe and incorporated into his sketch of Barabas. If we wish to be more particular than this we may note how the reference to fortresses here is caught up in the Prologue :

> Hence comes it that a strong-built citadel
> Commands much more than letters can import.

VI

THEORIES OF COMPOSITION

ALL critics of *The Jew of Malta* have drawn attention to its uneven quality. It begins with some of the finest scenes Marlowe ever penned : the opening scene, for example, shows Barabas at the height of his success, and is handled with great strength and dignity, but towards the end of the second act this controlling power seems to fail and we are fobbed off with two acts of vastly inferior drama. It is true, however, that once again in the last act some signs of great dramatic skill and comprehension are to be noted, but the play as a whole fails lamentably to live out its early promise. Many reasons have been suggested for this. It has been said that Marlowe tired after the first scenes were written and lost interest : or again that he found himself unduly pressed and was forced to deliver his manuscript to the playhouse whatever its condition, and so hurriedly sketched out a popular continuation of his beginning, which practically wrote itself : others think that after he had finished the first two acts he simply plotted out the main lines of the subsequent acts, paying more attention to Act V than to Acts III and IV.

Obviously we are here in speculative regions, and something may be said in support of each of these theories, though it will not be easy to command general support for any one of them, or for the opinions supporting them.

Consider the first : that Marlowe tired after the first acts. It is possible : it is an opinion that can reasonably be held, but there is little tangible evidence to be produced in its support, except the undoubted fact that the last three acts show a very evident loss of control. It seems a little easy to account for this by saying Marlowe tired of his work. When we consider the labours of many of the Elizabethan dramatists, and when we reflect on what we know of Marlowe's own life and personality, it is difficult to believe that, having created his character, the working-out of the plot in detail was too much for him.

The view that Marlowe wrote the work, substantially as we have it, under pressure from the theatrical company, has some attractions. If we may suppose that Marlowe was urged to produce his transcript in advance of what he thought to be his allotted time, then we can easily believe that he fell back on the easiest method, i.e. the ordinary ' blood and thunder ' type of melodrama. To a man of Marlowe's powers much that now remains in Acts III, IV and V would have flowed rapidly from his pen, rising, despite all obstacles, to moments of something near greatness from time to time. Mr. Bullen's modification of this theory assumes that ' the play was required at very short notice, and that Marlowe merely sketched roughly the last three acts, leaving it to another hand to fill in the details ; or it may be that he put the play aside, under stress of more pressing work, with the intention of resuming the half-told story at a later date, an intention frustrated by his sudden death ' (Bullen, *Marlowe's Works*, I, xl).

A modern, and quite different, view has been advanced to explain the play. According to this view, it has been misunderstood, and we are invited to regard it ' not as a tragedy, or as a " tragedy of blood ", but as a farce . . . farce of the old English humour, the terribly serious, even savage comic humour, the humour which spent its last breath on the decadent genius of Dickens . . . It is the humour of that very serious (but very different) play, *Volpone.*' Again a few lines later we are told 'the last words of Barabas complete this prodigious caricature' (T. S. Eliot, *The Sacred Wood*, p. 84). This view seems to postulate considerable powers of detachment from contemporary taste and practice on the part of Marlowe. Around him he saw the work of such writers as Kyd, whose *Spanish Tragedy* set the fashion which long outlasted Marlowe—a fashion which gave to the Elizabethan stage tragedies of blood as innumerable as they were successful. Marlowe himself in *Tamburlaine* had made considerable play with this love of rant and bloodshed, and other works of his are not free from it. What is there to make us believe that suddenly he saw the folly of all this and turned to make it material for caricature ? Even if we do so believe, there still remains unexplained the differences between different parts of the play. Suppose we swallow the theory of farce (as here defined) for the last acts, in what spirit are we to believe Marlowe conceived the first two acts ?

Whatever our conclusions as to the authorship of this play, we are forced, I believe, to agree that, as it now stands, it cannot be dignified with the name of tragedy. Marlowe was still immature : he was reaching forward to what he was to perform in *Edward II* (though even there his gifts were limited), but in *The Jew of Malta* the great possibilities which the initial strokes of his portrait of Barabas prepare us for, are never consummated. Barabas is conceived on the great scale—the poise and mastery of Marlowe are at their best in these first scenes—but it all crumbles away before long, and the Jew becomes the mere plaything of the popular imagination—an imagination that, whetted by such stories and fanned by sedulous rumour, was to lead to the fanatical display of intolerance which attended the execution of Dr. Lopez a few years later. Hence there is no inevitability in the final scenes, no sense of the passing of something great ; and we acquiesce gladly in the destruction of Barabas, and know the world is well rid of him :

> Die, life ! fly, soul ! tongue curse thy fall, and die.

We have only to compare these last moments of Barabas with the final hour of Faustus to see how far Marlowe has failed here in the evocation of any feelings of pity and terror. ' Policy ', which has been the key-note of all the thoughts and actions of Barabas, is here seen to have over-reached itself, and our relief at the removal of an intolerable and swollen monster is tinctured with no dram of pity. And the whole construction of the play leads up to this end : Henslowe's mention of the cauldron in his accounts in 1598 shows that the play concluded then in the same way as it does now, and we may be allowed to assume that the same *finale* delighted the audiences that saw the play first produced some ten years earlier.

To conclude : Marlowe saw the way in which he could utilise this conception of a Jew brought from prosperity into adversity, and rising again by the use of so-called Machiavellian devices. He saw, too, how all this could be conceived of on a gigantic scale, and executed in a *bravura* style. And it suited his temperament, if ever a play did. The little that we know of him suggests a full-blooded enthusiastic man of the world : we need not press the terms too far, but ' Marlowe who dyed swearing ', the 'atheistical ' follower of Machiavelli, was just such a man as would love the full-bodied gusto of *The Jew*. And so he created it for the most part : once he had passed the crucial moment in the Second Act there was no recall.[1] Marlowe might, as we have seen, have wished to write a great tragedy, but he missed his chance, and once the critical speeches in Act II were written all his instincts, and the instincts of his audience, compelled him to follow one path—a path which led to the final attempt of Barabas to deceive both Turks and Christians and to its over-reaching conclusion.

---

[1] The conversation between Barabas and Ithamore, II, iii. 168 ff.

It is left for us to extract what we can from this mis-directed masterpiece, and even its ruins are great. For in *The Jew* Marlowe has poured much of his own tremendous energy : the play is everywhere alive, even at those moments at which it most conflicts with our modern prepossessions. The zest of Ithamore, the controlled fury of Barabas cer-tainly produce scenes we are unaccustomed to : the whole-sale slaughter of nunneries is too much for our modern finicky stomachs. But, in disdaining this rich fare, we have to be on our guard lest we reject much that is worth having, as well as the worthless. *The Jew of Malta* is a challenge to our powers of assimilation. Certainly, if we go to it expecting the modern, restrained, well-made play with its infinite care over details, we shall be disappointed ; but if we try to see in it what its earliest audiences saw—a play about a very terrible and powerful alien, endowed with all the resources of wealth and unencumbered by any Christian scruples—then we shall get from it something of what its creator intended—a vigorous, vital drama written in the vigorous and vital language of which he was so great a master.

THE JEW OF MALTA

DRAMATIS PERSONÆ

FERNEZE, *Governor of Malta.*
LODOWICK, *his son.*
SELIM CALYMATH, *son to the* GRAND SEIGNIOR.
MARTIN DEL BOSCO, *vice-admiral of Spain.*
MATHIAS, *a gentleman.*
JACOMO, } *friars.*
BARNARDINE, }
BARABAS, *a wealthy Jew.*
ITHAMORE[1], *a slave.*
PILIA-BORZA, *a bully, attendant to* BELLAMIRA.
TWO MERCHANTS.
THREE JEWS.
KNIGHTS, BASSOES, OFFICERS, GUARD, SLAVES, MESSENGER, *and*
    CARPENTERS.
KATHERINE, *mother to* MATHIAS.
ABIGAIL, *daughter to* BARABAS.
BELLAMIRA, *a courtesan.*
ABBESS.
NUN.
MACHIAVEL as Prologue-speaker.

Scene, Malta.

This list was (substantially) added by Reed. It does not appear
in the Quarto. On the back of the title-page of the Bodleian copy
of the Quarto (Malone 915), in a hand of about 1750, appears the
following :

THE GHOST OF MACHIVEL.
FARNEZE GOVERNER OF MALTA.
LODOWICK HIS SON } *both in love with* ABIGAL.
MATHIAS }
SELIM CALYMATH, *the Turkish Prince.*
A TURKISH BASHAW.
MARTIN DEL BOSCO, *a spanish Captain.*
BARABAS, *the rich Iew.*
ITHIMER, *his Man.*
PILIO BORZA, *the Curtizans Man.*
3 FRYERS.
2 MARCHANTS.
MATER, *Mother to* MATHIAS.
ABEGAL, *the Jew's daughter.*
THE COURTIZAN.
2 NUNS. [2]

[1] Usually *Ilthimore* in Q.   [2] Noted by Tucker Brooke.

TO MY WORTHY FRIEND, MASTER THOMAS HAMMON, OF GRAY'S INN, ETC.

THIS play, composed by so worthy an author as Master Marlowe, and the part of the Jew presented by so unimitable an actor as Master Alleyn, being in this later age commended to the stage : as I ushered it unto the Court, and presented it to the Cock-pit, with these Prologues and Epilogues here inserted, so now being newly brought to the press, I was loath it should be published without the ornament of an Epistle ; making choice of you unto whom to devote it ; than whom (of all those gentlemen and acquaintance, within the compass of my 10 long knowledge) there is none more able to tax ignorance, or attribute right to merit.   Sir, you have been pleased to grace some of mine own works with your courteous patronage ; I hope this will not be the worse accepted, because commended by me ; over whom, none can claim more power or privilege than yourself.   I had no better a new year's gift to present you with ; receive it therefore as a continuance of that inviolable obligement, by which he rests still engaged ; who, as he ever hath, shall always remain, 20

Tuissimus,

THO. HEYWOOD.

Introduction, Verses, etc.

3. *Master Alleyn*] Perhaps the most celebrated of early actors. He was born in 1566, and is said to have been ' bred a stage player '. He was one of Worcester's Men in 1583 ; later he joined the Admiral's Men (1589–97) and then is said to have ' leafte playing ', although we find him resuming his calling at the opening of the Fortune Theatre in 1600. He became a servant of Prince Henry with his fellows in 1604, but probably retired soon after this.   Certainly by 1605 he was wealthy, and about this time began the negociations which led to the purchase of the manor of Dulwich, and the ultimate foundation of the school and hospital of the College of God's Gift at Dulwich.   He died in 1626. For over twenty years contemporary poets and dramatists lauded his talent.   Nashe classes him with

24

Tarleton, Knell, and Bentley: Weever and Ben Jonson compare him with Roscius, as does Fuller a little later. He played three of Marlowe's most famous parts: Tamburlaine, Faustus and Barabas. (See Greg. *op. cit.*, Vol. II, *passim.*) See also below: *Prol. to the Stage*, line 4.

4–5. *the Court*] The Cockpit in the palace of Whitehall seems first to have been used for plays in the reign of James I, but the auditorium was small and Charles reconstructed the old Cockpit into a new theatre at Whitehall. The first definite reference we have to its use is on 7 April 1634, when Herbert (*Dramatic Records*, ed. J. Q. Adams, p. 55) records a play there. It may of course have existed as early as 1632 or 1633 as Professor Adams suggests (*Shakespearean Playhouses*, p. 394), but we cannot be certain whether *The Jew* was performed in the old or new Theatre. The words on the title-page ' In His Majesties Theatre at Whitehall' show that the Cockpit in Drury Lane (see l. 5) is not intended here. There is, however, the bare possibility that ' at Court ' may only mean in the King's presence at Hampton Court, S. James's or Richmond.

5. *the Cock-pit*] This theatre stood in Drury Lane and was also known as the Phœnix. A full account of it is given by Adams (*op. cit.*, pp. 348–367). The title-page tells us *The Jew* was presented there by her Majesties Servants at the *Cock-pit*, and we know that Queen Henrietta's Men occupied that theatre between 1625 and 1636 (Adams, *op. cit.*, p. 355). It is interesting to note that it was to this company that a licence was granted on 3 September 1624 to perform Heywood's play *The Captives*: For the Cockpit Company; A new Play, called, *The Captive, or The Lost recovered*; written by Hayward (J. Q. Adams, *Dram. Records of Sir Henry Herbert*, p. 29).

6–7. *newly brought to press*] The question whether ' newly ' in such cases means ' anew ' or ' for the first time ' can hardly be decided except by the context. Professor Tucker Brooke compares the phrase ' Newly imprinted, and in conuenient places imperfect matter amended ' on the title-page of the 1592 edn. of the *Faustbook*, and the title-page to the 1590 ed. of *Tamburlaine*, ' Now first and newlie published '. In *The Jew* the presumption would seem to be that it had hitherto been unpublished, despite the fact it had been registered in 1594 (see *Intro.*, p. 4). It is, perhaps, worth noting that *A Knack to Know a Knave*, which was produced on 10 June 1592 and entered in the Stationers' Register on 7 January 1594, bears on the title-page the words ' Newlie set foorth, . . .' See also *Locrine, c.* 1591, *Mucedorus*, 1598, etc.

11. *tax*] censure; the earliest references in the O.E.D. are 1548 in Patten's *Exped. Scotl.* E viij, ' Apertly to tax thir goouernour w^t ye note of dissimulation', and then in 1569 where a letter of Lord Cecil's is quoted : ' To think of us as our evil willers are disposed . . . to tax us.'

12–14. *Sir, . . . patronage*] Heywood dedicates the First Part of *The Iron Age* (printed 1632) ' To my Worthy and much Respected Friend, Mr. Thomas Hammon of Grayes Inne, Esquire ' (Dyce). Also the second part of *The Fair Maid of the West*, 1631, is dedicated to ' Thomas Hammon, Esquire, of Graies Inne '.

17. *new year's gift*] ' Apparently, then, the play had been acted at Court shortly before New Year's Day, 1633 ' (Adams, *Sh. Playhouses*, p. 395). For the custom of giving poems on New Year's Day, see Cartwright, *Comedies*, etc., 1651, pp. 279–286.

22. *Tho. Heywood*] On the nature of Heywood's possible concern with this play, see *Intro.*, p. 6.

THE PROLOGUE SPOKEN AT COURT

GRACIOUS and great, that we so boldly dare
('Mongst other plays that now in fashion are)
To present this, writ many years agone,
And in that age thought second unto none,
We humbly crave your pardon : We pursue
The story of a rich and famous Jew
Who liv'd in Malta : you shall find him still,
In all his projects, a sound Machiavill ;
And that's his character. He that hath past
So many censures, is now come at last   10
To have your princely ears : grace you him ; then
You crown the action, and renown the pen.

Prologue.

Pro. 8. *Machiavill*] *Macheuill* Quarto.

Prologue] Prof. J. Q. Adams, in
his *Shakespearean Playhouses*, p.
395, seems to have been misled by
the editor of the 1874 edition of
Heywood's works into saying that
' A Speech Spoken to Their Two
Excellent Majesties at the First
Play Play'd by the Queen's Servants
in the New Theatre at Whitehall '
was printed *along with* the Prologue
to *The Jew* in 1637. This is not so.
The Speech is from Heywood's
Pleasant Dialogues and Drammas
(1637), 232, and has nothing necessarily to do with the *Jew* prologue,
which is not in that book. The
point is of importance because
Adams (p. 395) suggests that it
helps to determine the date of the
opening of the new Cockpit in
Court. I owe this information to
the kindness of Sir E. K. Chambers.

4. *in that age . . . none*] See
Intro., p. 1, for popularity of this
play on the Elizabethan stage.
8. *sound*] thorough-going. For
other instances of *sound* in this
sense compare *Faustus*, I, i, 47, 90,
etc.
10. *censures*] judgments, opinions. The word was used in this
sense in the Elizabethan period and
throughout the seventeenth century. See for example in *Richard
III*, II. ii. 144 : ' To give your
censures in this weighty business ' ;
Fletcher, *False One*, I, i :
' My opinion
Is, still committing it to graver
censure,
You pay the debt you owe him.'

26

EPILOGUE SPOKEN AT COURT

IT is our fear (dread sovereign) we have bin
Too tedious ; neither can't be less than sin
To wrong your princely patience : if we have,
(Thus low dejected) we your pardon crave :
And, if aught here offend your ear or sight,
We only act, and speak, what others write.

Epilogue.

6. *act, and speak,*] Act, and Speake, Q : *act and speak*, Robinson : *act and speak* Dyce etc.

THE PROLOGUE TO THE STAGE

WE know not how our play may pass this stage,
But by the best of poets in that age
The Malta-Jew had being and was made;
And he, then by the best of actors play'd:
In *Hero and Leander*, one did gain
A lasting memory; in Tamburlaine,
This Jew, with others many, th' other wan
The attribute of peerless, being a man
Whom we may rank with (doing no one wrong)
Proteus for shapes, and Roscius for a tongue,   10
So could he speak, so vary; nor is't hate
To merit in him who doth personate
Our Jew this day; nor is it his ambition
To exceed or equal, being of condition
More modest: this is all that he intends,
(And that too, at the urgence of some friends)
To prove his best, and, if none here gainsay it,
The part he hath studied, and intends to play it.

2. *best of poets*] The Quarto edition stars ' best of ' and in the margin prints *Marlo*. Some exaggeration of the author's high reputation is natural in the circumstances perhaps.

4. *best of actors*] Here again the Quarto has a marginal note *Allin*. See above for life of this actor (*Epis. Ded.*, l. 3).

5–6. *In Hero . . . memory*] Marlowe's personal reputation as a poet seems largely to have depended on the extraordinary popularity of *Hero and Leander*, as is shown by the frequent quotations in the Miscellanies of that age, in the continual allusions thereto, as in *Every Man in his Humour*, IV, 1, and in the eleven or more editions of the poem before 1638.

6–8. *in Tamburlaine . . . peerless*] As Dyce pointed out, despite the ambiguous punctuation, the reference to ' Tamburlaine ', ' this Jew ', etc., can only be understood as applying to ' th'other ', i.e. Alleyn, not Marlowe. For detailed discussion see *Tamburlaine* in this edition, pp. 11 ff. The passage illustrates the difference between dramatic and other kinds of literature in Elizabethan regard : the success of *Hero and Leander* ensured the ' lasting memorie ' of Marlowe as a poet, while the success of his great dramas seems mainly to redound to the credit of the actor who created the title-rôles.

7. *wan*] An Elizabethan form of won, frequently used, for example, by Drayton in his *Polyolbion* (Broughton).

10. *Proteus*] A marine deity, subject to Poseidon, who had the power of assuming any shape at will. Hence a term of praise to the actor who could assume a wide range of parts. His transformation figures in Spenser's *Faerie Queene*, Book III, viii, 40 *et seq.*

10. *Roscius*] A famous Roman comic actor. It was a favourite trick of Elizabethan writers to compare their contemporary actors with Roscius. See note on Alleyn above.

11. *he speak, so vary*] An illustration of ' chiastic ' order. He could speak as Roscius, and assume as many forms as Proteus.

12. *in him*] The Quarto edition has a star after this, and in the margin is printed *Perkins*. Richard Perkins was one of the most famous actors of his day. He belonged to Worcester's Men in 1602 or earlier, then to the Queen's Men from 1603 to 1619 ; to the Revel's Company (1619–23) ; to the King's Men (1623–25) ; then to Queen Henrietta's (1625–37) according to Fleay (*Stage*, p. 374). Webster pays him the compliment of making special reference to him in the Epilogue to the *White Devil* (1612). We know he played Sir John Belfare in *Shirley's Wedding* (1626), Fitzwater in Davenport's *K. John and Matilda* (*c.* 1629), Capt. Goodlack in Heywood's *Fair Maid of the West* (1630), Hanno in Nabbes's *Hannibal and Scipio* (1635), as well as here (before 1633). Wright (*Hist. Histrionica*) tells us he died during the Commonwealth period. His portrait is at Dulwich.

18. *and*] Holthausen (*Eng. Stud.*, lx, 395) needlessly proposes *he*.

EPILOGUE TO THE STAGE

AT THE COCK-PIT

IN graving, with Pygmalion to contend,
Or painting, with Apelles, doubtless the end
Must be disgrace : our actor did not so,
He only aim'd to go, but not out-go.
Nor think that this day any prize was play'd ;
Here were no bets at all, no wagers laid :
All the ambition that his mind doth swell,
Is but to hear from you (by me) 'twas well.

1. *Pygmalion*] The renowned Greek sculptor who is fabled to have fallen in love with his own handiwork—the statue of Galatea. The legend was the subject of a famous poem of Marston : *The Metamorphosis of Pigmalion's Image*, 1598.

2. *Apelles*] The Greek painter who flourished about 332 B.C. He was the most celebrated artist of his time, and so much admired by Alexander that he would allow no one else to paint his portrait.

5. *prize was play'd*] A metaphor from the fencing-school : to engage in a contest or match. Greene in his *Upstart Courtier*, 1592, refers to a man strutting up and down ' like the usher of a Fence-school about *to play his prize* '. How this was done we learn from the following : ' The manner of the proceeding of our fencers in their schools is this ; first, they which desire to be taught at their admission are called scholars, and, as they profit, they take degrees, and proceed to be provosts of defence ; and that must be wonne by public trial of their proficiency and of their skill at certain weapons, which they call prizes, and in the presence and view of many hundreds of people ; and at their next and last prize, well and sufficiently performed, they do proceed to come . . . maisters of fence as we commonly call them ' (quoted by Strutt and taken from *The Third University of England*, 1615).

6. *no wagers laid*] There is an interesting letter preserved in the *Henslowe Papers* (ed. Greg, p. 32) concerning a theatrical wager in which it is asserted that Ed. Alleyn will equal either Bentley or Knell (two other actors) in any of their own parts. Collier says that wagers were not uncommon as to the comparative merits of rival actors, and in the Prologue of *The Knight of the Burning Pestle* the Citizen says that his prentice Ralph ' should have played Jeronimo with a shoemaker for a *wager* '. See also *The Gull's Hornbook*, etc.

THE PROLOGUE

Enter MACHIAVEL

Mach. Albeit the world think Machiavel is dead,
    Yet was his soul but flown beyond the Alps ;
    And, now the Guise is dead, is come from France,
    To view this land, and frolic with his friends.
    To some perhaps my name is odious,

Prologue.

The Prologue : Enter Machiavel] Ellis : *Macheuil.* Quarto, Wagner :
Act I. Enter Machiavel. Reed, Collier : *Enter Machiavel. Prologue.*
Robinson : *Enter Machiavel.* Dyce to Bullen.
    1. *think*] Q, Reed, Collier, Dyce, Bullen, Wagner : *thinks* Robinson,
Cunningham.

Enter Machiavel] This soliloquy
of Machiavel had for its prototype a
well-known Latin poem of Gabriel
Harvey, *Epigramma in effigiem
Machiavelli,* which has for its head-
ing : *Machiavellus ipse loquitur,* and
in many of its lines is so similar to
Marlowe's work as to suggest that
it was actually in his mind when
composing this Prologue. For a
detailed examination see E. Meyer's
*Machiavelli and the Elizabethan
Drama,* pp. 22 ff.
    1–4. *Albeit . . . friends*] Meyer
(*op. cit.*), p. 40, writes : ' These four
lines show Marlowe thought
Machiavelli had come to England
from France ; and such was the
case, through Gentillet as Patericke
had said.' See *Intro.,* p. 12.
    2. *Yet . . . Alps*] i.e. the soul of
Machiavelli had suffered metamorphosis into that of Guise. Cf.
Churchyard's *Charitie* (1595),
Auchinleck reprint, p. 97 :

' Fine Macheuill is now from Flor-
    ence flown
  To England where his welcome is
    too great,

His busie books are heere so red
    and known
That charitie thereby hath lost her
    heat.'
    3. *the Guise is dead*] Henry of
Lorraine, 3rd duke of Guise, the
implacable enemy of the Hugenots,
was assassinated at La Noue, near
Blois, by order of the King of France
on 23 December 1588. He had
been the prime agent in the
massacre of S. Bartholomew's Eve,
1572, and from his earliest days
had plotted against the throne in
underground ways. Hence the references here to his likeness to the
popular Elizabethan impression of
Machiavel. Marlowe deals fully
with the duke of Guise in *The
Massacre at Paris* (q.v.). It seems
characteristic of Marlowe to hark
back near the beginning of one play
to the themes of those previously
written. Compare the opening
lines of *Faustus* and the clearer
echo of *Tamburlaine* in lines 340–
347 of that play. Clearly, this
prologue was not written earlier
than the first months of 1589, and
despite Wagner (see *Intro.,* p. 4)

But such as love me, guard me from their tongues,
And let them know that I am Machiavel,
[And weigh not men, and therefore not men's words.]
Admir'd I am of those that hate me most:
Though some speak openly against my books,   10
Yet will they read me, and thereby attain
To Peter's chair; and, when they cast me off,
Are poison'd by my climbing followers.
I count religion but a childish toy,
And hold there is no sin but ignorance.
Birds of the air will tell of murders past:
I am asham'd to hear such fooleries.
Many will talk of title to a crown:
What right had Cæsar to the empery?
Might first made kings, and laws were then most sure 20

7. *And*] Q, etc: *Now* Holthausen.   19. *empery*] Reed, Coll., Bull. to Wag.: *empire* Q, Rob., Cunn.

the whole play probably dates from the same time.

6. *guard*] ward, protect, i.e. my friends protect me from the tongues of my enemies.

7. *And*] Holthausen (*Eng. Stud.*, XL, 395) curiously finds *And* ' unverständlich', and proposes *Now* instead.

10. *my books*] The most famous work of Machiavelli was *Il Principe* (the Prince), in which he set forth his famous advice to monarchs concerning the art of government. Besides this he wrote his *Discourse on Livy* and a treatise on the art of War, and other works. See *Intro.*, p. 13. Marlowe is here probably referring to the common gossip against Machiavelli, such as is echoed in the phrase ' a very Machiavel ', or in ' pestilent Machiavellian doctrines ', etc.

11–13. *Yet . . . followers*] Compare with III, iv. 92 ff.

14–15. *I . . . ignorance*] Consciously, or otherwise, these lines sum up the spirit of *Faustus*, and in *Twelfth Night*, IV, ii. 46 we have,

' I say there is no darkness but ignorance '.

16. *Birds . . . past*] Compare the story of the cranes of Ibycus. This line seems to be some hearer's objection to his theories, and in lines 17 ff. Machiavelli gives his answer.

19. *empery*] Reed is followed by all the editors except Robinson and Cunningham in amending the Quarto reading of *empire* to *empery* to complete the scansion of the line. *Empery* is a commonly used Elizabethan word, as in ' Ruling in large and ample *empery* O'er France '. *Henry V*, I, ii. 226: ' Nausicaa ! Flower of all this *empery* '. Chapman's *Homer*, *Odyssey*, viii. 623. It is defined in the O.E.D. as ' The territory ruled by an Emperor '; or in a wider sense as ' The territory of an absolute or powerful ruler '. Marlowe is particularly fond of it; see *Tamburlaine*, 126, 228, 841, etc.; *Dido*, 100, 1325; *Edward II*, 1850. Wagner thinks the Quarto compositor set up the more usual form *empire* in error.

When, like the Draco's, they were writ in blood.
Hence comes it that a strong built citadel
Commands much more than letters can import :
Which maxim had [but] Phalaris observ'd,
H'ad never bellow'd, in a brazen bull,
Of great ones' envy : o' the poor petty wights
Let me be envied and not pitied.
But whither am I bound ? I come not, I,
To read a lecture here in Britain,
But to present the tragedy of a Jew,   30

21. *Draco's*] Reed, etc. : *Drancus* Q. 24. *had* [*but*]] Dyce to Bull. conj. : *had* Q to Rob. : *had but* Ellis, Wag. 25. *H'ad*] Dyce : *H'had* Q, Coll. : *He had* Reed, Rob., Cunn., etc. 26. *o' the*] Dyce : *o' th'* Q to Rob., Wag. : *of the* Cunn. to Ellis. 29. *here*] Q, etc. : *to you here* Dyce[2] conj. *Britain*] Q to Cunn., Ellis, Wag. : *Britainy* Bull.

21. *Draco's*] Draco was the Athenian legislator about 624 B.C. whose laws were so rigorous that the orator Demades said of them that ' they were not written with ink but with blood '. These savage laws continued until the more human code of Solon, a generation later. The Quarto compositor misunderstood the word and set it up as *Drancus*.

24. *Phalaris*] Phalaris was the tyrant or ruler of Acragas in Sicily, *c.* 570–554 B.C. His name became legendary for excessive cruelty ; and in especial he is said to have had made for him a brazen bull into which his victims were placed, and a fire lighted beneath, so that they were roasted alive. He was at last overthrown by a popular rising, and burned in his brazen bull. Nashe, in his *Lenten Stuffe* (McKerrow, *Works*, III, 151, line 25), mentions praise of Phalaris as one of the unworthy or ridiculous subjects affected by the learned. Dr. McKerrow instances a dialogue by Ulrich von Hutten, entitled *Phalarismus,* or sometimes *Apologia pro Phalarismo,* published *c.* 1517.

had [*but*]] *but* was added first by Dyce to complete the scansion. Brennan (*Beiblatt zur Anglia*, 1905, p. 208) suggests that *Maxime* of the Quarto is a mistake for *maximae*, remarking that Machiavelli has given more than one. This is more ingenious than convincing.

26. *wights*] This is spelled *wites* in the Quarto, and Brereton thinks our modern word *wits* is a more likely equivalent.

28. *I come not, I*] The reiteration of I is for emphasis, as in *Two Gentlemen of Verona,* v. iv. 132, ' I care not for her, *I* ', and in *Richard III*, III. ii. 76 : ' *I* do not like these several councils, *I.*' See also here below, iv. iii. 41 ; *Dido*, 221, *Sp. Trag.*, III. x, 84, etc.

29. *Britain*] The Quarto reading of *Britaine* is altered by Bullen to Britainy. This alteration, although metrically an improvement, is confusing to the modern reader, who thinks Brittany in the N.W. of France is intended, whereas in Elizabethan English, Britaine in various spellings generally connoted Britain as it undoubtedly does here. E. K., in the gloss to the *Shepheard's Calendar,* says, ' King Edgare . . . reigned here in Britanye ' ; and again in the *Faerie Queene*, III, iii. 52, we read ' All Britany doth burne in armes bright '. Compare also Marlowe's *Edward II*, II. ii. 42, ' Unto the proudest peere of *Britanie* '.

Who smiles to see how full his bags are cramm'd,
Which money was not got without my means.
I crave but this,—grace him as he deserves,
And let him not be entertain'd the worse
Because he favours me.   [*Exit.*

35. *Exit*] Dyce to Ellis : *omit* Q to Rob., Wag.

35. *favours*] resembles, having similar characteristics. The O.E.D. gives no example earlier than 1609 in Jonson's *The Case is Altered*, III, iii. : ' This young lord Chamont *Favours* my mother.'

30–35.] As he said the last words Machiavel probably drew aside the curtains which enclosed the rear-stage, and thus discovered Barabas in his counting-house, represented by a table and bags of gold upon it within the rear-stage. Compare the similar introduction of the hero in *Faustus*, l. 28. Stage direction.

(The main divisions of the Elizabethan stage should be constantly in the mind of the reader—the fore-stage or outer-stage, or ' apron ', jutting into the auditorium ; the rear-stage or inner-stage, or ' study '' which could be enclosed by curtains at will ; and the upper stage or ' balcony '. The play might take place in any one, or two or all of these as were required. Often the fore-stage and rear-stage were in use together, and were treated as one stage—in these notes described as the whole-stage).

ACT I

SCENE I

BARABAS *discovered in his counting-house, with heaps of gold before him.*

Bara. So that of thus much that <u>return</u> was made:
And of the third <u>part</u> of the Persian ships,
There was the venture summ'd and satisfied.
As for those Samnites, and the men of Uz,

Act I. Scene i.

Dyce : *Act the First*, Scene I. Rob., Cunn., Bull., Ellis : *Actus I* Wag. *omit* Q to Coll. Throughout the scenes are not marked in the Quarto *Barabas* discovered] Dyce, Ellis : *Enter Barabas* Q to Rob., Cunn., Bull. Wag.
1. *Bara.*] Reed, etc. *Jew.* Q. 4. *Samnites*] Coll. to Cunn. : *Samintes* Q, Reed : *Samarites* Deighton conj. : *Sabans* Bull., Ellis, Wag. : *Samiotes* Brennan conj.

1 ff.] Gilchrist, as quoted in Collier's ed. of *The Jew*, p. 252, says : ' The time when *The City Madam* was produced corresponding so exactly with the period of *The Jew of Malta's* revival by Heywood, tempts me to believe Massinger indebted to Marlowe for the turn of Luke's soliloquy in Act III, Sc. iii, of his comedy.' The general terms employed are similar, but I think there is no clear evidence of direct imitation.

4. *Samnites*] This was the name originally given to the people inhabiting the mountainous centre of the S. half of Italy. Bullen proposes *Sabans*, the ancient name of the people of Yemen, for he says : ' Between the *Samnites* and the *men of Uz* there can be no possible connexion. My emendation suits the context. We have Saba for Sabæa in *Dr. Faustus*, xii. 25, etc.' Deighton notes on this (*The Old Dramatists*, p. 120) : ' But surely *Sabans* is a very violent change, and there

seems no other justification for it than the fact that the Sabæans are mentioned, Job i. 15, as falling on Job's herds. I would read *Samarites*. The enmity between the Jews and Samaritans would account for the scornful tone of Barabas' words and as *Uz*, so far as its position has been ascertained, lay either East or S. East of Palestine, there would be nothing strange in its being associated by Marlowe with Samaria.' Brennan (*Beiblatt zur Anglia*, 1905, p. 208) says : ' A small forgotten Boer-like people like the *Samnites* is out of place among the Mediterranean trading nations of the 16th century ; the same objection lies against the *Samarites*. The *Sabans* are too far away, not so much from Malta as from the letters [of the Quarto] : the Samiotes are nearer to both, and at the same time Eastern enough to lend colour, classical enough to lend dignity, to the line.' Miss Ethel Seaton (*Rev. Eng. Studies*, v. 398) suggests *Saenites* or

35

That brought my Spanish oils, and wines of Greece,
Here have I purs'd their paltry silverlings.
Fie ; what a trouble 'tis to count this trash !
Well fare the Arabians, who so richly pay
The things they traffic for with wedge of gold,
Whereof a man may easily in a day   10
Tell that which may maintain him all his life.
The needy groom, that never finger'd groat,

6. *purs'd*] Dyce : *purst* the rest.   *silverlings*] Rob., etc. : *siluerbings* Q,
Reed, Coll.

Scænites on the score of minim misprints, and argues that it could be supported by the cosmographers, such as Ziegler, Belleforest and Nicholay. This reading, she suggests, ' would give point to the contrast drawn between the poor nomads and the wealthy Arabians '. I think she is probably right.

4. *men of Uz*] The exact position of the land of Uz is disputed. Some think it to be N. of Palestine, while others would place it to the S.E., in the neighbourhood of Edom. Marlowe is probably using it in a vague sense, as connoting people of wealth, although there may have been in his mind a memory of Job's great wealth and prosperity, which Barabas comments on later. See I, ii. 181 ff.

6. *silverlings*] The Quarto reading *siluerbings* is evidently a *b* for *l* compositor's error, which was easily made, as *b* was in the compartment immediately above *l* in the compositor's ' case '. Skeat and Mayhew (*Glossary of Tudor and Stuart Words*) say that it means a shekel, and Tindale's translation of *Acts*, xix. 19 reads, ' They counted the price of them and founde it fifty thousande *silverlynges* '. A little later . Dyce notes it is used by Coverdale in the same sense (*Isaiah*, vii. 23). It is here used with a tone of contempt.

8 *fare*] Here used as a subjunctive. Barabas invokes a blessing on the Arabians, who pay so lavishly.

the Arabians] As above in line 4 (*men of Uz*) and below in line 19 (*Indian mines*), Marlowe is using

Arabians in a vague way, with the desire of evoking visions of Eastern opulence in the minds of his audience.

9. *traffic*] to bargain or deal for a commodity. Compare Eden's *Decades* 317 : ' They do not gladly permitte the Portugales to *traffic* in theyr kyngedome ', and see also *Macbeth*, III. v. 4, etc.

wedge of gold] Gold was, and is, frequently melted and moulded into ingots or wedges for convenience of transport. R. Eden's translation of Sebastian Munster's *First Bookes on America*, ed. Arber, p. 29, reads, ' They gather it (gold) with great laboure and melte it and caste it, fyrste into masses or *wedges*, and afterwarde into brode plates '. Similarly in *Richard III*, I. iv. 26, we find ' *Wedges* of gold, great anchors, heaps of pearl ', and cf. *Tamburlaine*, I. i, 12.

11. *Tell*] to count, as in *King Lear*, II. iv. 54, ' Thou shalt have as many dolours for thy daughters as thou canst *tell* in a year '. And see below line 16.

12. *groat*] A silver piece worth fourpence, and used here in its colloquial sense of a coin of small value. Needless to say, it was not current coin in Malta at this time, however common in Marlowe's England ! See also ' gray *groat* ' Act IV. iv. 122.

12, 13. *The needy groom . . . much coin*] The impecunious servant, unused to even the smallest wealth, would find such a pile as this miraculous.

Would make a miracle of thus much coin ;
But he whose steel-barr'd coffers are cramm'd full,
And all his life-time hath bin tired,
Wearying his fingers' ends with telling it,
Would in his age be loath to labour so,
And for a pound to sweat himself to death :
Give me the merchants of the Indian mines,
That trade in metal of the purest mould ;   20
The wealthy Moor, that in the eastern rocks
Without control can pick his riches up,

15. *tired*] a trisyllable.

16. *Wearying*] Instead of *Wearying* Brereton proposes *Wearing*, citing Dekker's *Seven Deadly Sins of London* (Arber, p. 15) : ' Those heapes of Siluer, in telling of which thou hast worne out thy fingers ends, will be a passing bell ' ; also the same author's *Pennywise* (Bang's *Materialien*, lines 763 ff.) and *The Honest Whore* (Pearson's ed., p. 56). Brereton adds that these parallels ' are the more significant as Dekker was profoundly influenced by Marlowe and sometimes echoes his very words '.

19–33.] Professor Tucker Brooke suggests (privately) that it is possible that this account of the merchants of the Indian mines and their treasures is based on a work published in London in 1577 : *The History of Trauayle in the West and East Indies . . . Gathered in Parte, and done into Englyshe by Richard Eden. Newly set in order, augmented, and finished by Richard Willes.* Cf. fol. 397 and verso : ' Of the Ilande of Zailon and the precious stones founde there . . . There is also a very long mountayne, at the foote wherof are founde many precious stones, named *Piropi*, commonly called Rubines, or Rubies. The Merchauntes iewelers come by them by this means. Fyrst, going to the kyng, they bye of hyn a certayne measure of that grounde where suche stones are founde. . . . Not far from the sayde mountayne, are founde diuers other sortes of pre-

cious stones, as Jasynthes, Saphires, Topases, and suche lyke.' And on fol. 414 verso : ' For they (i.e. the Portugese in India) had a very fayre Diamond of the weyght of xxxii caractes, esteemed to be worth xxxv thousande crownes. They had also a pearle of the weyght of xxiiii caractes.'

19. *the Indian mines*] See also in *Tamburlaine*, II. v. 41 : ' Then will we march to all those *Indian Mines*,' and *The First Part of Jeronimo*, II. ii. 34 : ' Lorenzo's bounty I do more unfold, Than the greatest mine of Indian's brightest gold ' (Brereton).

21–32.] Miss Ethel Seaton (*Review Eng. Studies*, v. 397) writes of these lines that they suggest ' a combination of the riches of the country of Samarcand : " Les esmeraudes y abondent lesquelles on tire, et recueille des creuaces des rochers . . . certains vents soufflans, on les voit reluire és montaignes " (Belleforest *Cosmographie Universelle* (1575), II, 1444, 1150), with Pliny's account of the amethysts picked up in the desert, and with Ziegler's picturesque description of the Arabs at their work in the Isthmus where smaragds are to be found : " Topazius lapis vicinis locis effoditur, perlucidus, splendore aureo refulgens, ut interdiu uideri non possit, noctu exploratur ab his qui colligunt, et signo imposito sub die effoditur" (Ziegler, *Terræ Sanctæ Descriptio*, 1536, f. lxi).'

4

And in his house heap pearl like pibble stones,
Receive them free, and sell them by the weight !
Bags of fiery opals, sapphires, amethysts,
Jacinths, hard topaz, grass-green emeralds,
Beauteous rubies, sparkling diamonds,
And seld-seen costly stones of so great price,
As one of them, indifferently rated,
And of a caract of this quantity,   30
May serve, in peril of calamity,
To ransom great kings from captivity.
This is the ware wherein consists my wealth ;
And thus methinks should men of judgment frame
Their means of traffic from the vulgar trade,
And, as their wealth increaseth, so inclose
Infinite riches in a little room.

23. *pearl*] Q to Cunn., Wag. : *pearls* Bull., Ellis.   23. *pibble stones*] Q :
pebble-stones, Reed, etc.   25. *amethysts*] Reed, etc. : *Amatists* Q.   30.
caract] Dyce¹ : *carrect* Q, Reed, Coll., Wag. : *carat* Rob., Dyce², to Ellis.

23. *pearl*] There seems no need to write *pearls* as do Cunningham and other editors. Shakespeare constantly uses the singular form in a plural sense, as in *Sonnet* xxxiv. 13 : ' Ah ! but thy tears are *pearl* which thy love sheds', and see below Act I. i. 87 : ' Of Persian silks, of gold, and orient *pearl*', and constantly in *Tamburlaine*, as at v. ii.79.

25. *Bags*] Mr. Brennan writes (*Beiblatt zur Anglia*, 1905, p. 208) : ' Barabas dwells on the word and draws it out, as he lovingly gloats over the bulk of wealth. Gesture would help the effect', and he suggests that *Bags* seems to have the value of a line.

28. *seld-seen*] seldom-seen. See also *The Spanish Tragedie*, III. xii. 3 : ' Why, is not this a strange, and *seld seene* thing.' The word is used in this form as early as the time of King Alfred. And cf. *Coriolanus*, II. i. 229.

29. *indifferently*] impartially. Marlowe makes use of the phrase again in this play, see I. ii. 187, where the full form occurs, viz. ' valued at indifferent rate', and v. iii. 29.

30. *caract*] The Quarto reading *carrect* was emended by Dyce to the now obsolete form *caract* in his first edition, and subsequently to *carat*. It originally connoted a measure of weight used for diamonds and other precious stones, at first ¹⁄₁₄₄ of an ounce. Prof. Case compares with *Comedy of Errors*, IV. i. 28 : ' How much your chain weighs to the utmost *Caract* (*charect* F) ' : Jonson, *Every Man In*, III. ii. 22 : ' No beautie, no ; you are of too good *caract*, To be left so, without a guard, or open.' So in 1616 folio, p. 35, where the scene is number iii.

34–35. *frame . . . trade*] i.e. Guide their business away from the line taken by vulgar (petty) trade.

37. *Infinite . . . room*] Dr. F. S. Boas, in *Shakespeare and his Predecessors*, p. 50, notes : ' As Barabas fingers the glittering coins and hovers with the rapture of a lover over his precious jewels', his " seld-seen costly stones " ; as he follows in fancy the track of his argosies . . . avarice becomes transfigured. It ceases to be a sordid vice, and swells to the proportions of a passion for

But now how stands the wind ? *Back to reality*
Into what corner peers my halcyon's bill ?
Ha ! to the east ? yes.   See how stands the vanes ?   40
East and by south : why, then, I hope my ships
I sent for Egypt and the bordering isles
Are gotten up by Nilus' winding banks :   *Business*
Mine argosy from Alexandria,
Loaden with spice and silks, now under sail,
Are smoothly gliding down by Candy-shore
To Malta, through our Mediterranean sea.
But who comes here ?

40. *stands*] Q, Bull., Ellis, Wag. : *stand* Reed, etc.   48. *Enter . . .*]
Dyce, Ellis : After *How now ?* Q, Reed, Coll., Rob., Cunn., Bull., Wag.

the infinite, though it be only for
" infinite riches in a little room ".'
We have thus in Marlowe's Jew a
vein of idealism which is wanting in
the more miserly Skylock.

38.] It has been suggested to me
by Mr. Attwater that at this point
Barabas comes out from his counting-house, on the rear-stage, and
draws the curtains behind him.
' *But now how stands the wind* ' suggests an exterior, and perhaps
Barabas looks up at the halcyon
hanging in view of the audience
from one of the posts of ' the
heavens '. Further, we may consider the possibility that Barabas
would not wish his merchant callers
to see the huge sums he had near at
hand. The audience would realize
that, the curtains being closed, Barabas had stepped outside—probably
into the street hard by his house.

39. *Into what corner . . . halcyon's bill ?*] Steevens writes : ' The
halcyon is the bird otherwise called
the kingfisher. The ordinary opinion was that [the dead body of] this
bird, if hung up, would vary with
the wind, and by that means show
from what point it blew.' Sir
Thomas Browne, in his *Vulgar
Errors*, Bk. iii. cap. x., puts it more
briefly : ' That a Kingfisher, hanged
by the bill, sheweth in what quarter
the wind is.'

40. *stands*] This has been altered
by most editors to *stand*, but without reason, except that it offends
modern English usage. It was
good Elizabethan English, and
Abbott, § 333, goes into great detail
as to its use by Shakespeare.

41. *East and by south*] Compare
the boxing of the compass in Lyly's
Gallathea, I. iv. 53 ff.

44. *argosy*] A favourite Elizabethan word to describe large
carrying merchant-ships, popularly
supposed to be derived from the
famous mythical ship Argo. The
O.E.D. derives it from the Italian
Ragusea, a vessel of Ragusa. The
earliest English form is ragusye,
which by transposition becomes
argosea, and so Hakluyt speaks of
' *arguzes* of Venice '. It is a favourite
word of Marlowe's, who uses it in
Tamburlaine, Part II, Act I, i. 41, and
in *Dr. Faustus*, I. i. 128. Compare
also *The Merchant of Venice*, I. i. 9,
etc. The text is never very clear
as to whether *argosy* is a singular
or plural. Thus in line 76 ' mine
argosy ' of l. 71 is referred to by the
merchant as *them*, while a few lines
lower (80) Barabas speaks of *her*.

46. *Candy-shore*] Candia, the
Italian name for the island of
Crete.

48, 49. *But who . . .*] Wagner
regards the word *Barabas* as an

Enter a Merchant.

How now !

Merch. Barabas, thy ships are safe,
    Riding in Malta road ; and all the merchants   50
    With other merchandise are safe arriv'd,
    And have sent me to know whether yourself
    Will come and custom them.
Bara. The ships are safe thou say'st, and richly fraught ?
Merch. They are.
Bara.   Why, then, go bid them come ashore
    And bring with them their bills of entry :
    I hope our credit in the custom-house
    Will serve as well as I were present there.
    Go send 'em threescore camels, thirty mules,
    And twenty waggons, to bring up the ware.   60
    But art thou master in a ship of mine,
    And is thy credit not enough for that ?
Merch. The very custom barely comes to more

---

49. *Barabas*] omit Wag., and read *But who . . . safe*, as one line.
59. *'em*] Coll. to Ellis : *vm* Q, Wag. : *them* Reed.

interpolation, and eliminates it so that we may read as one line :
' But who comes here. How now !
    Enter a Merchant.
    Merch. Thy ships are safe.'
There seems no strong reason in favour of this regularising of the line, and I have left it with the Stage Direction coming before the exclamation ' *How now!*' rather than after this, as in the Quarto, etc.
    50. *Malta road*] a roadstead or haven, as in *The Merchant of Venice*, v. i. 288. ' my ships Are safely come to *road*.'
    50–54.] A suspicious passage. Apart from the possible corruption suggested by Wagner of ll. 48–49 above, line 50 has eleven syllables, and the repetition of ' safe ' and ' safe arriv'd ' is unpleasing. Then again ' Merchants ' followed by ' Merchandise ' is cacophonous, and line 52 can only be scanned with

great difficulty, while the last two words of it seem to belong to the next line. The passage, however, must stand, for no tampering with it can render it really satisfactory.
    52, 53. *yourself . . . custom them*] Will you yourself come and pass them through the custom-house ? Here *custom* probably implies the presentation of their bills of entry (l. 56) as well as the actual cash payments necessary (ll. 63–65).
    56. *bills of entry*] Entry here must be pronounced as a trisyllable. See Abbott's *Shakespearean Grammar*, § 477 : ' R, and liquids in dissyllables, are frequently pronounced as though an extra vowel were introduced between them and the preceding consonant.' See farther on in this scene, line 134 : ' I have no charge, nor many children.'
    63. *The very custom barely*] the Customs dues alone.

Than many merchants of the town are worth,
And therefore far exceeds my credit, sir.
Bara. Go tell 'em the Jew of Malta sent thee, man :
Tush ! who amongst 'em knows not Barabas ?
Merch. I go.
Bara.   So, then, there's somewhat come.   Sirrah,
Which of my ships art thou master of ?
Merch. Of the Speranza, sir.
Bara.   And saw'st thou not   70
Mine argosy at Alexandria ?
Thou couldst not come from Egypt, or by Caire,
But at the entry there into the sea,
Where Nilus pays his tribute to the main,
Thou needs must sail by Alexandria.
Merch. I neither saw them, nor inquir'd of them.
But this we heard some of our seamen say,
They wonder'd how you durst with so much wealth
Trust such a crazed vessel, and so far.
Bara. Tush ; they are wise ! I know her and her strength. 80
But go, go thou thy ways, discharge thy ship,
And bid my factor bring his loading in.

                              [*Exit Merchant.*

67. *amongst*] Reed to Wag. : *amougst* Q. 68, 69.] Two lines in Wag.
div. after *come* : others in three lines div. after *go, come.* 69. *master of*]
Reed to Ellis : *master off* Q, Wag. 70, 71. *And saws't . . . Alexandria*]
as one line, Reed to Rob. 81. *But*] Rob. to Wag. : *By* Q : *Bye* Reed,
Coll. 82. *Exit . . .*] Reed, etc. : *omit* Q.

67. *amongst*] The Quarto misprint *amougst* is of the familiar *u* for
n type.
68, 69.] This is usually printed as
three lines. See *text note*. Wagner
attempts to scan as two lines, but
the division would seem to come
after *Sirrah.* The nine syllable
arrangement of the next line is
characteristic of Marlowe. The
first five words of Barabas are to
himself. Then he shouts at the
departing merchant and, by an
effective touch, inquires which of
his numerous ships he commands.
Holthausen (*op. cit.*) would read,

' So then, there's somewhat. Come
    Sirra,
 Which of my ships art thou [now]
    Master of ? '
72. *Thou . . . Caire*] See *2 Tamburlaine,* I. iii. 19 : ' By *Cario*
runs to *Alexandria* Bay, Darotes'
streams, . . .'
76. *them . . . them*] See note on
line 44. Should we read *her . . .
her* to conform with line 80 below ?
82. *factor*] agent. The factor
was often the merchant's agent or
' buyer '. Compare *Richard III,*
IV. iv. 71 : ' Richard yet lives, hell's
black intelligencer, Only reserved

And yet I wonder at this argosy.

Enter a Second Merchant.

Sec. Merch. Thine argosy from Alexandria,
　　　Know, Barabas, doth ride in Malta road,
　　　Laden with riches, and exceeding store
　　　Of Persian silks, of gold, and orient pearl.
Bara. How chance you came not with those other ships
　　　That sail'd by Egypt ?
Sec. Merch.　　　　　　　Sir, we saw 'em not.
Bara. Belike they coasted round by Candy-shore　　　90
　　　About their oils or other businesses.
　　　But 'twas ill done of you to come so far
　　　Without the aid or conduct of their ships.
Sec. Merch. Sir, we were wafted by a Spanish fleet,
　　　That never left us till within a league,
　　　That had the galleys of the Turk in chase.
Bara. O, they were going up to Sicily.　Well, go
　　　And bid the merchants and my men despatch,
　　　And come ashore, and see the fraught discharg'd.
Sec. Merch. I go.　　　　　　　　　[*Exit.* 100
Bara. Thus trowls our fortune in by land and sea,

---

97. *Well, go*] A separate line Rob. to T. Brooke : lines 97, 98 div. after
Well, Holthausen.　99. *fraught*] Q, Dyce, etc. : *freight* Reed, Coll., Rob.
101. *trowls*] Q to Dyce¹, Cunn. to Wag. : *trolls* Dyce².

their *factor*, to buy souls.' See also
below, II. iii. 241.
　88. *How chance*] How chances it ?
an elliptical phrase, as in *Midsummer Night's Dream*, I. i. 129 :
' *How chance* the roses there do fade
so fast ? ' Cf. *Merry Wives of
Windsor*, v. v. 229. See Abbott,
§ 37, for discussion of these phrases
in general.
　96. *That had . . . in chase*] That
were chasing the Turkish galleys.
　99. *fraught*] a cognate of freight,
and frequently used by Shakespeare. See *The Merchant of
Venice*, II. vii. 30 : ' A vessel of our
country *richly fraught*.'

101. *trowls*] to come in abun-
dantly like a flowing stream.
Compare Gascoigne's *Steele Glasse*,
Arber's edn., 68 :

' He that can winke at any foul
　abuse,
　As long as gaines come *trouling* in
　therwith,'

and Dekker's *Shoemaker's Holiday*,
v. ii. 191 : ' Fritters and pancakes
comes *trowling* in in wheele bar-
rowes.'
　fortune . . . sea] Compare the
title of Heywood's play, *Fortune by
Land and Sea*, c. 1607 (?).

And thus are we on every side enrich'd :
These are the blessings promis'd to the Jews,
And herein was old Abraham's happiness :
What more may heaven do for earthly man
Than thus to pour out plenty in their laps,
Ripping the bowels of the earth for them,
Making the sea[s] their servants, and the winds
To drive their substance with successful blasts ?
Who hateth me but for my happiness ?   110
Or who is honour'd now but for his wealth ?
Rather had I, a Jew, be hated thus,
Than pitied in a Christian poverty :
For I can see no fruits in all their faith,
But malice, falsehood, and excessive pride,
Which methinks fits not their profession.
Haply some hapless man hath conscience,
And for his conscience lives in beggary.
They say we are a scatter'd nation :
I cannot tell ; but we have scambled up   120

---

102. *every*] Reed to Wag. : *enery* Q.   108. *sea*[*s*]] Dyce, etc. : *sea* Q to Rob., Wag.   *servants*] Q, etc. : *servant* Wag.

103-4. *These . . . happiness*] See, especially, Genesis xv. 14, 18 ; xvii. 8.

108. *Making the sea*[*s*] *their servants*] The Quarto reading, ' Making the sea their seruants ', has been amended to read as in our text. Wagner proposes ' Making the sea their servant ' on the grounds that *s* is frequently added at end of words incorrectly, but is seldom omitted, as in the Folio version of *Henry VIII*, v. iii. 174, and *Two Gentlemen of Verona*, i. iii. 88. He takes the addition of the *s* in *servants* to have arisen from the influence of *winds* at the end of the line.   Is it possible that we could leave the original reading, and regard *sea* as a collective noun ?

114-116. *For I can see . . . profession*] The thought of Barabas here is singularly like that expressed by Shylock when speaking of Christian example (III. i. 67 ff.), and

we may also see another example of it in this play in v. ii. 115 ff.   Marlowe used it previously in 2 *Tamburlaine*, II. i. 33 ff., where Baldwin refutes the charge of treachery and violence to their profession by stating that
     ' with such Infidels,
In whom no faith nor true religion rests,
We are not bound to those accomplishments,
The holy laws of Christendom enjoin.'
See note there in this edition.

117. *Haply some hapless man*] By luck some luckless man.   An example of the common Elizabethan habit of playing on words.   See above, line 33 : ' This is the ware wherein consists my wealth.'

120. *scambled*] scrambled.   It is used in Shakespeare's *King John*, IV. iii. 146 : ' And England now is

More wealth by far than those that brag of faith:
There's Kirriah Jairim, the great Jew of Greece,
Obed in Bairseth, Nones in Portugal,
Myself in Malta, some in Italy,
Many in France, and wealthy every one:
Ay, wealthier far than any Christian.
I must confess we come not to be kings:
That's not our fault: alas, our number's few,
And crowns come either by succession,
Or urg'd by force; and nothing violent,   130
Oft have I heard tell, can be permanent.
Give us a peaceful rule; make Christians kings,
That thirst so much for principality.
I have no charge, nor many children,
But one sole daughter, whom I hold as dear
As Agamemnon did his Iphigen:

left, To tug and *scamble* and to part by the teeth,' and compare *Henry V*, I. i. 4, and *Much Ado*, v. i. 94. The modern form *scramble* does not occur until some time later.

122. *Kirriah Jairim*] Koeppel notes that I Chronicles ii., thrice mentions the border city of Kiriath Jearim in a connexion which makes it look like a personal name.

123. *Nones in Portugal*] Graetz (*Hist. of Jews*, IV. 706 ff.) tells a romantic story of the beautiful Portuguese Jewess, Maria Nuñes, captured by an English ship while trying to reach Holland. She bewitched the captain, an English duke, and made an impression on Queen Elizabeth, who invited her to an audience, and drove with her in an open carriage through the streets of London. Dr. Wolf, in his *Jews in Elizabethan England*, draws attention to the presence in London of an important Portuguese Jew, Dr. Hector Nunez.

129, 131. *And crowns . . . permanent*] A direct reminiscence of the main idea of Chapter II of *The Prince*: ' If the Prince be a person of competent industry, he will be

sure to keep himself in the throne, unless he be supplanted by some great and more than ordinary force; and even then when so supplanted, fortune can never turn tail, or be adverse to the usurper, but he will stand fair to be restored.'

133. *That . . . principality*] The same idea is vigorously expressed in *Tamburlaine*, II. vii. 12 ff:
' The thirst of reign and sweetness of a crown
That caused the eldest son of heavenly Ops
To thrust his doting father from his chair,' etc.

134. *I have . . . many children*] Children is a trisyllable. Barabas is here emphasising his isolated state; he is not charged with many responsibilities or many children—but one only daughter. But see I. ii. 151.

136. *As Agamemnon did his Iphigen*] Agamemnon, while on his way to the Trojan war, was at Aulis with his fleet and there had the misfortune to offend Artemis. The goddess prevented the fleet from sailing, and Calchas the soothsayer said that Artemis could

And all I have is hers.—But who comes here ?

Enter three Jews.

First Jew. Tush, tell not me ; 'twas done of policy.
Sec. Jew. Come, therefore, let us go to Barabas ;
    For he can counsel best in these affairs :   140
    And here he comes.
Bara.   Why, how now, countrymen !
    Why flock you thus to me in multitudes ?
    What accident's betided to the Jews ?
First Jew. A fleet of warlike galleys, Barabas,

---

137. *Enter*...] Dyce, Bullen and Ellis add : ' A change of scene is supposed here : to a street or to the Exchange.'   143. *accident's*] Q, etc. : *accident* Wag.

---

only be appeased by the sacrifice of Agamemnon's daughter Iphigeneia. This with great reluctance Agamemnon did, and the fleet then set sail. Pliny tells us (*Nat. Hist.* XXXV. 10) that the picture by Timanthes representing Agamemnon hiding his face at her sacrifice was one of the most famous works of antiquity. An early translation of the *Iphigenia in Aulis* was made by Lady Lumley (MS. Reg. 15A. IX), who died in 1577. It was first published in 1909 by the Malone Society. Marlowe refers again to the assemblage of the Greeks at Aulis in *Dido*, v. i. 238.

137. *Enter three Jews*] If the suggestion at line 38 be not adopted this is the obvious place where Barabas will close the curtains on the rear-stage. ' A change of scene is supposed here,—to a street or to the Exchange ', writes Dyce, and this is accepted by Bullen and Ellis. But there is no need for this. Assuming Barabas has not already emerged into the street (see note on line 38), we are to imagine him rising and coming forward at line 141 : *And here he comes.* He does not want his fellow-countrymen in his counting-house, so closes it, and comes forward to meet them. When Dyce wrote, the understanding of the principles of Elizabethan

staging was in its infancy, and both he and Bullen are the victims of this circumstance in their attempts to localise scenes.

138. *Tush . . . not*] Almost the words with which *Othello* opens : ' Tush ! Never tell me ', etc.

138. *policy*] This is one of the most frequently recurring words in the play, and is here meant to suggest a deceitful underhand method of procedure. Dr. Mario Praz (*Machiavelli and the Elizabethans*, pp. 14 ff.) gives a very full and convincing exposition of the gradual differentiation in the use of this word *policy* in the sixteenth century. He there shows how the word came to be associated with the popular conception of Machiavelli and with his disreputable principles. Marlowe uses the word constantly in this sense throughout the play (e.g. in this scene, line 179), but for another use see I. ii. 160.

142. *in multitudes*] There are only three in the deputation. Is Barabas ironically commenting on the way of his compatriots to rush to him in every difficulty ?

143. *accident's*] Wagner reads *accident* and defends it with a learned note, but unfortunately bases it on a mistaken belief that this is the Quarto reading. It is not the reading of either of the two

Are come from Turkey, and lie in our road :
And they this day sit in the council-house
To entertain them and their embassy.

Bara. Why, let 'em come, so they come not to war ;
Or let 'em war, so we be conquerors.—
[*Nay, let 'em combat, conquer, and kill all.*   150
So they spare me, my daughter, and my wealth.] [*Aside.*

First Jew. Were it for confirmation of a league,
They would not come in warlike manner thus.

Sec. Jew. I fear their coming will afflict us all.

Bara. Fond men, what dream you of their multitudes ?
What need they treat of peace that are in league ?
The Turks and those of Malta are in league :
Tut, tut, there is some other matter in't.

First Jew. Why, Barabas, they come for peace or war.

Bara. Haply for neither, but to pass along,   160
Towards Venice, by the Adriatic sea,
With whom they have attempted many times,
But never could effect their stratagem.

Third Jew. And very wisely said ; it may be so.

Sec. Jew. But there's a meeting in the senate-house,
And all the Jews in Malta must be there.

Bara. Hum ; all the Jews in Malta must be there !
Ay, like enough : why, then, let every man
Provide him, and be there for fashion-sake.
If anything shall there concern our state,   170

---

160. *Haply*] Dyce to Ellis : *Happily* Q to Rob., Wag.   167. *Hum*]
Reed to Ellis : *Vmh* Q, Wag.

Quartos Wagner saw, nor of the
copies at Oxford and Cambridge.

146, 147. *And they this day . . .
embassy*] And they (the Maltese
Governor and his friends) sit in the
council-house to entertain them (the
Turks) and their embassy.

152. *Were it . . . league*] were it
only for confirmation of a league.

155. *Fond*] foolish. The univer-
sal Elizabethan usage of this word.
See Shakespeare, etc., *passim.*

157. *those*] Marlowe thus in-
directly refers to the rulers of
Malta as above in line 146.

162, 163. *With whom . . . stratagem*] Against whom they have
frequently attempted a surprise
attack, etc.

169. *for fashion-sake*] as a
formality. See *As You Like It,*
III. ii. 249 : 'For fashion sake I
thank you for your society.'
O.E.D. gives a reference to Calvin
on Psalm xl. 7 : 'Worshipping God
slyghtly *for fashyon sake.*'

Assure yourselves I'll look—*unto myself.*   [*Aside.*

First Jew. I know you will.—Well, brethren, let us go.

Sec. Jew. Let's take our leaves.   Farewell, good Barabas.

Bara. Do so.   Farewell, Zaareth ; farewell, Temainte.

[*Exeunt Jews.*

And, Barabas, now search this secret out.

Summon thy senses, call thy wits together :

These silly men mistake the matter clean.

Long to the Turk did Malta contribute ;

Which tribute all in policy, I fear,

The Turks have let increase to such a sum   180

---

171. *unto myself*] Q, etc.: *unto't myself* Coll. conj.   *Aside*] Q, Reed, Dyce, etc. *omit* Coll., Rob.   174. *Do so.   Farewell* . . .] Q, Reed, Coll., Rob., Wag.   *Farewell,* . . . Dyce to Ellis.   *Exeunt Jews*] Reed, etc. : omit Q.   180. *Turks have*] Q, Reed, Coll., Bull. to Wag.: *Turk has* Rob. to Cunn.

171. *Aside*] This was omitted by Collier, who thought that it applied to the whole line.   Clearly Barabas only says the words *unto myself* as an aside, for he is answered by the 1st Jew, who naturally assumes the conclusion will be *to it myself* or some such words and replies without waiting for the end of the sentence. It will be noticed how frequently Marlowe makes use of the aside, often in a way difficult to justify by modern standards.

174. *Do so.   Farewell* . . .] The Quarto and early editions here read 'Doe so ; Farewell,' etc.   This was emended by Dyce, who remarks that 'Doe so' is 'evidently a stage-direction which has crept into the text, and which was intended to signify that the Jews *do* take their leaves of Barabas : the Quarto has no *Exeunt*'.   Wagner, however, follows the Q and early editors and retains the words ; for, he says, '*Exeunt* is often omitted in early Quartos, while *do so* is an unfamiliar S.D.'.   In this view Collier strongly concurs (MS.).   Moreover, *Do so* is a summary of the directions of Barabas to the Jews.   I think the original text should stand, and that 'Do so' is an ironical aside of Barabas, weary of his lingering co religionists.

Zaareth . . . Temainte]   Marlowe's close knowledge of the book of Job (see below, scene. ii., lines 182 ff.) makes it possible that these names are a reminiscence of his reading of Job xi., ii., which speaks of Job's friends, *Zophar* the Naamathite, and Eliphaz the *Temanite.*

177. *silly*] foolish, simple.   Compare i. ii. 171.

clean] entirely, completely.   Mr. Ivor B. John points out in his note to *Richard II*, iii. i. 10 that ' this idiom is at least as old as Alfred the Great'.   Compare his Preface to his Translation of the *Cura Pastoralis* : ' Swæ clæne hio waes oþfeallenu on Angelcynne ', 'So clean was she (learning) fallen away among the English people'.   And compare iv. iv. 53.

178.   It was customary for even the great Mediterranean powers to make contributions for the sake of buying peace from the Turks.   See *Calendar of State Papers (Venetian)*, passim.

179. *policy*] See note on line 138.

180. *The Turks have*] The reading of the Q and many editors.   It was altered to the singular by Robinson, in order presumably to agree with line 178.   It does not seem worth disturbing the text, however, for such a reason.   There appears to be

As all the wealth of Malta cannot pay ;
And now by that advantage thinks, belike,
To seize upon the town ; ay, that he seeks.
Howe'er- the world go, I'll make sure for one,
And seek in time to intercept the worst,
Warily guarding that which I ha' got.
Ego mihimet sum semper proximus :
Why, let 'em enter, let 'em take the town.   [*Exit.*

SCENE II.—*The Senate House.*

Enter FERNEZE *governor of Malta*, Knights, *and* Officers ;
met by CALYMATH, *and* Bassoes *of the* Turk.

Fern. Now, bassoes, what demand you at our hands ?

187. *proximus*] Reed to Wag : *proximas*, Q.

Act I.   Scene ii.

Rob., Cunn., Bull., Ellis : omit Q and others.   *The Senate House*] Bull.
Enter . . .] Dyce, Cunn., Ellis : *Enter Gouernors of Malta, Knights met
by Bassoes of the Turke ; Calymath.* Q, Reed, Coll. : *Enter Gouernor . . .
Calymath.* Wag. : Rob. adds *and officers.*   1. *Fern*] *Gouer.* Q, and *Gov.*
throughout play. Q. *bassoes*] Q, Dyce, etc. : *Bashaws* Reed, Coll., Rob.

some confusion between the Turks
in general and the Turk their leader.

187. *Ego mihimet sum semper
proximus*] One of Marlowe's many
tags from the Classics.   This is a
misquotation from Terence's *Andria*,
IV. i. 12 : ' Proximus sum egomet
mihi.'   It is correctly quoted in the
contemporary Latin play *Victoria*,
l. 173, and cf. *Two Gentlemen of
Verona*, II. vi. 23.   It will be noticed
how little appropriate Latin and
Latin mythology is in the mouths
of several of his speakers, as here,
and as in *Tamburlaine*, where that
hero swears by Jove, and Zenocrate
knows well the story of Turnus,
Lavinia, and Æneas.   Marlowe, in
short, gives point to the words
spoken by Kempe in *The Return
from Parnassus*, IV. 5 : ' Few of the
university pen plaies well, they
smell too much of that writer Ovid,
and that writer Metamorphosis, and
talke too much of Proserpina and
Jupiter.'

proximus] The Quarto misprints
proximas : a frequent *a* for *u* error

of Elizabethan compositors of play-
books.

Scene ii.

Scene II] This scene takes place
within the Senate-house (see I. i.
165).   Probably the whole stage is
used, and the Governor, surrounded
by his knights, enters from one door
and is ' met by ' the Turks, who enter
from the other door.   The Governor
then assumes his seat in state on the
rear-stage.   At *line* 15 Calymath
and his bassoes stand aside on the
fore-stage while the knights deliber-
ate.   At line 160 the knights depart, and at this point we may
imagine the curtains to be closed
again, leaving Barabas and the
Jews alone in the partially localised
street—which has been the scene of
the action in scene i.

S.D. *governor of Malta*] Wagner
suggests that the erroneous form
Gouernors of the Quarto is due to
the following *s* in *Knights*.   See
below line 10.

1. *bassoes*] This is a variant form
of the word *bashaws*—a military

First Bas. Know, knights of Malta, that we came from
  Rhodes,
    From Cyprus, Candy, and those other isles
    That lie betwixt the Mediterranean seas.
Fern. What's Cyprus, Candy, and those other isles
    To us, or Malta ? what at our hands demand ye ?
Cal. The ten years' tribute that remains unpaid. ▬
Fern. Alas, my lord, the sum is over-great !
    I hope your highness will consider us.
Cal. I wish, grave governor, 'twere in my power   10
    To favour you ; but 'tis my father's cause,
    Wherein I may not, nay, I dare not dally.
Fern. Then give us leave, great Selim Calymath.
Cal. Stand all aside, and let the knights determine,
    And send to keep our galleys under sail,

10. *governor*] Dyce, Bull., Ellis, Wag. : *governors* Q, Reed, Coll., Rob., Cunn. So in lines 17, 27, 32. 13. *Selim Calymath*] Cunn. adds stage-direction, *Consults apart : Consults apart with the Knights.* Bull., Ellis.

title borne by princes and high civic functionaries of the Ottoman or Egyptian empires. It has been re-placed in modern times by the word pasha. *Bassowes* is used by Kyd, *Soliman and Perseda*, I. v. 12 : 'Call home my *Bassowes* and my men of war.' In the later scenes Marlowe uses the form *bashaws.* See III. v. 1 ; v. i. 68 ; v. ii. 18 ; v. v. 51.
  2. *knights of Malta*] The Knights of S. John of Jerusalem had made Rhodes their head-quarters from 1310 onwards till the island was captured by Soliman in 1522. Then in 1530 Charles V gave them Malta, and here they stayed till the island surrendered to Napoleon in 1798. Their heroic struggle against Soliman brought them great fame, and they are frequently mentioned in Elizabethan drama. Compare Massinger's *The Maid of Honour*, I. i. 67 ff. :
        'You are Sir
A Knight of Malta, and as I have
    heard,
Have serv'd against the Turke.'
And see also Beaumont and

Fletcher, *The Knight of Malta* ; Kyd, *Soliman and Perseda* ; Webster, *The White Devil.*
  3. *Candy*] Crete.
  4. *That lie . . . seas*] The Adriatic, Euxine, Ægean, Terrene, Mare Siculum, etc., were all re-garded as parts of the Mediter-ranean.
  10. *grave*] influential, experienced. Used as an epithet of respect. See below, line 313. Compare *Othello*, I. iii. 76 : 'Most potent, *grave* and reverend signiors.'
  governor] The Quarto and many editors print *governors* here and again in lines 17, 27 and 32. There is evidently a confusion which may have arisen from a belief of Mar-lowe's that Malta was governed by a council of knights. The altera-tion to *governor* makes the scene more easily followed I think.
  13. *give us leave*] A polite re-quest for privacy for consultation.
  14. *Stand all aside*] Collier adds a note : 'The Governor and the Maltese knights here consult apart, while Calymath gives these direc-tions'—viz. lines 15, 16.

For happily we shall not tarry here.—
Now, governor, how are you resolv'd ?
Fern. Thus : since your hard conditions are such
That you will needs have ten years' tribute past,
We may have time to make collection   20
Amongst the inhabitants of Malta for't.
First Bas. That's more than is in our commission.
Cal. What, Callapine ! a little courtesy.
Let's know their time, perhaps it is not long ;
And 'tis more kingly to obtain by peace
Than to enforce conditions by constraint.
What respite ask you, governor ?
Fern.   But a month.
Cal. We grant a month ; but see you keep your promise.
Now launch our galleys back again to sea,
Where we'll attend the respite you have ta'en,   30
And for the money send our messenger.
Farewell, great governor, and brave knights of Malta.
Fern. And all good fortune wait on Calymath !
                    [*Exeunt Calymath and Bassoes.*
Go one and call those Jews of Malta hither :

16. *happily*] Q, etc. : *haply* Rob.   17. *how*] Q to Cunn., Wag.   [*say,*] *how* Bull.   *say, how* Ellis.   27. As one line Wag. : As two lines Q, etc.   So lines 55 and 62.   30, *respite*] respit Q.   33. *Exeunt . . .*] Dyce to Ellis: *Exeunt* Q to Rob., Wag., after line 32.

16. *happily*] haply, by luck. See above, I. i. 117.
17. *how*] To complete the scansion of this line Bullen suggested the introduction of the word *say*. This Ellis boldly adopted without any indication in his text.   See textual note.   A slight lengthening of *governor* in saying the line is all that is required.
19. *needs*] of necessity : a frequent Elizabethan construction.
20, 21. *We . . . for't*] In the Third Act of the 1663 version of *Faustus* an account of the siege of Malta is given, and evidently this particular scene was utilised by the adaptors, since we have these two lines almost verbally repeated :

' they desir'd time to make collection
Amongst the inhabitants of the Malta for it.'
23. *Callapine*] Also the name of the son of Bajazeth in the second part of *Tamburlaine*.
27. *What . . . month*] A single metrical line.   Governor pronounced as two syllables.   So also in lines 32 and 83.
30. *attend*] await.   And so later, Act II. i. 34 ; Act v. v. 104.
33. *Exeunt . . .*] The Quarto has *Exeunt* after line 32 ; and we might possibly leave it there on the assumption that Ferneze makes his farewells as the Turkish deputation is slowly leaving the scene.

Were they not summon'd to appear to-day ?
First Off. They were, my lord ; and here they come.

Enter BARABAS *and three* Jews.

First Knight. Have you determin'd what to say to them ?
Fern. Yes ; give me leave :—and, Hebrews, now come near.
From the Emperor of Turkey is arriv'd
Great Selim Calymath, his highness' son,   40
To levy of us ten years' tribute past,
Now, then, here know that it concerneth us.
Bara. Then, good my lord, to keep your quiet still,
Your lordship shall do well to let them have it.
Fern. Soft, Barabas ! there's more 'longs to't than so.
To what this ten years' tribute will amount,
That we have cast, but cannot compass it
By reason of the wars, that robb'd our store ;
And therefore are we to request your aid.
Bara. Alas, my lord, we are no soldiers :   50
And what's our aid against so great a prince ?
First Knight. Tut, Jew, we know thou art no soldier ;
Thou art a merchant and a money'd man,
And 'tis thy money, Barabas, we seek. —
Bara. How, my lord ! my money !
Fern.   Thine and the rest ;
For, to be short, amongst you't must be had.
First Jew. Alas, my lord, the most of us are poor !
Fern. Then let the rich increase your portions.

36. *First Officer*] Dyce : *Officer* Q and others.   38. *Hebrews*] Reed to
Wag. : *Hebrws* Q.   57. *First Jew*] Dyce, etc. :   *Jew* Q, etc.

44. *Your lordship . . . it*] Compare *True Tragedy*, 1:
' Your highness shall do well to
  grant it them.'
45. *'longs*] belongs.   Compare
Henry V, II. iv. 80 : ' The glories
that *long* to him.'
47. *cast*] computed.   Compare
Antony and Cleopatra, III. ii. 17 :
' Think, speak, *cast*, write, sing,
number.'
  compass] get possession of, obtain. See lower, line 128, and
compare *Two Gentlemen of Verona*,
II. iv. 214 :
' If not, *to compass* her I'll use my
  skill.'
  57. *First Jew*] The speaker is
apparently not Barabas, but one of
the other Jews.   Dyce and subsequent editors label him 1*st Jew*.
  58. *let the rich . . . portions*] let
the richer among you increase the
portions due from the poorer.

Bara. Are strangers with your tribute to be tax'd ?

Sec. Knight. Have strangers leave with us to get their
    wealth ?   60
    Then let them with us contribute.

Bara. How ! equally ?

Fern.   No, Jew, like infidels ;
For through our sufferance of your hateful lives,
Who stand accursed in the sight of heaven,
These taxes and afflictions are befall'n,
And therefore thus we are determined ;
Read there the articles of our decrees.

Officer. [reads] *First, the tribute-money of the Turks shall all
be levied amongst the Jews, and each of them to pay one-
half of his estate.*   70

Bara. How, half his estate ! I hope you mean not mine.
                                      [*Aside.*

Fern. Read on.

Officer. [reads] *Secondly, he that denies to pay, shall straight
become a Christian.*

Bara. How! a Christian? Hum, what's here to do ? [*Aside.*

Officer. [reads] *Lastly, he that denies this, shall absolutely lose
all he has.*

Three Jews. O my lord, we will give half !

68. *Officer* [*reads*]] Dyce, Ellis : *Reader* Q to Rob., Cunn., Bull., Wag. And so lines 73, 76. 71. *Aside*] Dyce to Bull. : omit Q to Rob., Wag. And so line 75.

62. *How . . . infidels*] One metrical line. Brereton calls ' How equally ? ' an amphibious section. That is to say, these words form the latter part of one verse, and the former part of the verse following. He quotes *Lear,* IV. vi. 212, and Abbot, § 513.

64. *Who stand . . . heaven*] For the Crucifixion of Christ as was commonly believed. See ll. 108 ff., *post.*

62-65.] With this hypocritical justification of Christian injustice, compare above I. i. 114-116 and note thereon.

71. *How . . . mine*] Wagner scans ' How, half's /estate ?/I hope/you mean/not mine.

73, 74. *Secondly . . . Christian*] Compare *The Merchant of Venice,* IV. i. 386 : ' Two things provided more, that, for this favour, He presently become a Christian.' Halliwell quotes from Coryat's *Crudities,* 1611, p. 234 : ' All their (i.e. Italian Jews) goods are confiscated as soone as they embrace Christianity.'

73. *denies*] refuses, withholds. Compare *Macbeth,* III. iv. 128 : ' Sayest thou that Macbeth *denies* his person.'

Bara. O earth-mettled villains, and no Hebrews born!

And will you basely thus submit yourselves   80

To leave your goods to their arbitrement?

Fern. Why, Barabas, wilt thou be christened?

Bara. No, governor, I will be no convertite.

Fern. Then pay thy half.

Bara. Why, know you what you did by this device?

Half of my substance is a city's wealth.

Governor, it was not got so easily;

Nor will I part so slightly therewithal.

Fern. Sir, half is the penalty of our decree;

Either pay that, or we will seize on all.   90

         [Exeunt Officers, on a sign from Ferneze.

Bara.   *Corpo di Dio!* stay: you shall have half;

Let me be us'd but as my brethren are.

Fern. No, Jew, thou hast denied the articles,

And now it cannot be recall'd.

---

79. *mettled*] *mettall'd* Q.   90. *Exeunt* . . .] Ed. : Dyce, Ellis, after line 94 : *omit* all others.   91. *Dio*] *deo* Q.   *half*] Q to Cunn., Wag. : *the half* Bull., Ellis.   94. *And now*] *omit* Wag. and read *It cannot be recall'd.* Bar. *Will you then steal My goods? Is theft,* etc.

79. *O*] An extra-metrical word, possibly dropping in inadvertently from the previous line. See on I. i. 48, 49.

earth-mettled] ignominious, endued with earthly mettle or spirit. See farther on, lines 215 ff. Contrast the frequent use of *metal* with various adjectives by Shakespeare, as in *Julius Caesar*, I. ii. 313 : 'Thy *honourable metal* may be wrought from that it is disposed', or *op. cit.*, I. i. 66 : ' See whether their *basest metal* be not moved.' The Quarto spelling *mettall'd* and the more modern *mettled* appear to have been used indiscriminately in Shakespeare's time.

83. *convertite*] convert, as in *King John*, v. i. 19 ; *Lucrece*, 743, etc. It is also used by Heywood in *The Captives*, v. iii. 183.

91. *Corpo di Dio!*] Body of God. Scarcely the words we should have expected from a Jew ! I have modified a suggestion of Mr. Brereton and moved Dyce's S.D. up four lines. The Governor does not want to give Barabas too much time, and his dismissal of his officers calls forth a hasty curse from Barabas, followed by a calculated *Stay !* as his quick mind foresees the increased loss he is incurring by his obstinacy.

half] Bullen and Ellis have ' the half ', but this is unnecessary, as half by itself is a common Elizabethan usage.

93–96. *No, Jew . . . religion*] Wagner reads this as three lines, for metrical reasons, and omits the words ' *And now* ' in his text. His reasons, however, do not seem very convincing and utterly distort the rhythm. Lines 93 and 96 are metrically correct, and 94 and 95 suggest the abrupt and violent action of the Governor.

5

Bara. Will you, then, steal my goods ?

Is theft the ground of your religion ?

Fern. No, Jew ; we take particularly thine,

To save the ruin of a multitude :

And better one want for a common good,

Than many perish for a private man :   100

Yet, Barabas, we will not banish thee,

But here in Malta, where thou gott'st thy wealth,

Live still ; and, if thou canst, get more.

Bara. Christians, what, or how can I multiply ?

Of naught is nothing made.

First Knight. From naught at first thou cam'st to little wealth,

From little unto more, from more to most :

If your first curse fall heavy on thy head,

And make thee poor and scorn'd of all the world,

'Tis not our fault, but thy inherent sin.   110

Bara. What, bring you Scripture to confirm your wrongs ?

Preach me not out of my possessions.

Some Jews are wicked, as all Christians are ;

But say the tribe that I descended of

Were all in general cast away for sin,

Shall I be tried by their transgression ?

The man that dealeth righteously shall live :

99–100. *And better . . . man*] Cf. S. John xi. 50, 'it is expedient for us that one man should die for the people, and the whole nation perish not.'

105. *Of naught . . . made*] Compare *King Lear*, I. i. 90 : 'Nothing will come of nothing', and later, I. iv. 144. All these probably may be referred back to the Latin tag, 'ex nihilo nihil fit'.

108. *If . . . curse*] Refers, no doubt, to the belief that the Jews lay under a curse in consequence of the Crucifixion. In answer to Pilate, all the people said, 'His blood be on us and on our children'. Matthew xxvii. 25. Compare ll. 63 ff., *ante* :

'For through our sufferance of your hateful lives,
Who stand accursed in the sight of heaven,
These taxes', etc.

111. *What, . . . wrongs ?*] Compare *The Merchant of Venice*, I. iii. 98 : 'The devil can cite Scripture for his purpose.' Mr. C. K. Pooler (Arden edn.) cites also Riche, *Honestie of this Age* (Percy Society), p. 60 : 'The usurer . . . have (sic) learnd of the devill to allege the holy Scriptures.'

117. *The man . . . live*] An idea that is continuously expressed in the Old Testament, e.g. Proverbs x. 2 : 'righteousness delivereth

And which of you can charge me otherwise ?

Fern. Out, wretched Barabas !

   Sham'st thou not thus to justify thyself,   120

   As if we knew not thy profession ?

   If thou rely upon thy righteousness,

   Be patient, and thy riches will increase.

   Excess of wealth is cause of covetousness :

   And covetousness, O, 'tis a <u>monstrous</u> sin !

Bara. Ay, but theft is worse : tush ! take not from me then,

   For that is theft ; and, if you rob me thus,

   I must be forc'd to steal, and compass more.

First Knight. Grave governor, list not to his exclaims :

   Convert his mansion to a nunnery ;   130

   His house will harbour many holy nuns.

Fern. It shall be so.

Re-enter Officers.

        Now, officers, have you done ?

First Off. Ay, my lord, we have seiz'd upon the goods

   And wares of Barabas, which, being valu'd,

   Amount to more than all the wealth in Malta :

   And of the other we have seized half.

Fern. Then we'll take order for the residue.

119–122. *Out . . . righteousness*] Dyce, etc. : three lines in Q to Rob., divided after *thus* and *not.* 126. *Ay, . . . then*] Q, etc.: Wag. divides into two lines *Ay, But theft, etc.* 129. *governor*] Dyce, etc. : *governors* Q to Rob. *list*] Q to Dyce, Wag. : *listen* Cunn., Bull., Ellis. 132. *Re-enter Officers*] Dyce, Ellis : *Enter officers* Q to Rob., Cunn., Bull. ; after line 130 ; Wag. after line 131. 133. *First Off.*] Dyce : *Off* Q, Rob., Cunn., Bull., Wag. : *Officers* Reed, Coll. 137. *Fern.*] Rob., etc. : *omit* prefix Q to Coll. and assign to Officer.

---

from death ', and xii. 28 : ' In the way of righteousness is life.' Job iv. 7 ; Ezekiel xviii. 8, 9, etc.

121. *thy profession*] Perhaps here a reflection on the religious profession of Barabas, as contrasted with his temporal profession as usurer. ' Profession ', as in line 146 below, however, is usually employed to denote a religious creed.

126. *tush !*] an exclamation expressing annoyance or surprise. As in I. i. 80.

Ay, . . . then,] Wagner would make two separate lines of this, treating it as an irregularity caused by the interjection. See Abbot, § 512.

129. *list*] Cunningham and others alter to *listen* for metrical reasons. But a pause after *governor* is easily made, and the balance of the line restored without this change.

136. *of the other*] from the other merchants.

137. *Fern. Then . . .*] In the

Bara. Well, then, my lord, say, are you satisfied ?
    You have my goods, my money, and my wealth,
    My ships, my store, and all that I enjoy'd ;   140
    And, having all, you can request no more ;
    Unless your unrelenting flinty hearts
    Suppress all pity in your stony breasts,
    And now shall move you to bereave my life.
Fern. No, Barabas ; to stain our hands with blood
    Is far from us and our profession.
Bara. Why, I esteem the injury far less,
    To take the lives of miserable men
    Than be the causers of their misery.
    You have my wealth, the labour of my life,   150
    The comfort of mine age, my children's hope ;
    And therefore ne'er distinguish of the wrong.
Fern. Content thee, Barabas ; thou hast naught but right.
Bara. Your extreme right does me exceeding wrong :
    But take it to you, i' the devil's name !
Fern. Come, let us in, and gather of these goods
    The money for this tribute of the Turk.

Quarto this speech was wrongly included in that of the officer, but it is clearly right, as Robinson and subsequent editors have seen, to assign it to the Governor Ferneze.

take . . . residue] make the necessary dispositions. ' To take order ' is frequently employed in Shakespeare. See *2 Henry IV*, III. ii. 18: ' I will take such order '.

residue] here *residue* must mean the parts confiscated by Ferneze.

139–144.] The whole of this passage is re-echoed by Shakespeare in *The Merchant of Venice*, IV. i. 373 ff. : ' Nay, take my life and all ', etc.

142, 143. *flinty hearts . . . breasts*] Compare *The Merchant of Venice*, IV. i. 31 : ' From brassy bosoms and rough hearts of flint.'

150, 151. *my wealth . . . children's hope*] Note here how Barabas mentions his daughter and his

ducats in the same breath as in the more famous scene later, II. i. 47.

my children's hope] This, and the preceding reference of Barabas to his children, I. i. 134 (' nor many children '), is curious. Had he more than Abigail previously, or does he merely use the plural in the general sense of progeny, whatever the number ?

152. *distinguish of*] to perceive or note the difference between things. The O.E.D. quotes from H. Smith's *Works* (1866), I. 97 : ' To defend usury, they distinguish upon it, as they *distinguish of* lying.' Also used by Shakespeare in *2 Henry VI*, II. i. 129 : ' Sight may *distinguish of* colours ', and in *Hamlet*, III. ii. 69 : ' Since my dear soul was mistress of her choice, And could *of* men *distinguish*.'

156. *gat er*] obtain (probably by sale). See also II. iii. 27 for another use.

First Knight. 'Tis necessary that be look'd unto :
    For, if we break our day, we break the league,
    And that will prove but simple policy.   160
            (Exeunt all except Barabas and the three Jews.
Bara. Ay, policy ! that's their profession,
    And not simplicity, as they suggest.
    The plagues of Egypt, and the curse of heaven,
    Earth's barrenness, and all men's hatred,
    Inflict upon them, thou great *Primus Motor !*
    And here upon my knees, striking the earth,
    I ban their souls to everlasting pains,
    And extreme tortures of the fiery deep,
    That thus have dealt with me in my distress !
First Jew. O yet be patient, gentle Barabas !   170
Bara. O silly brethren, born to see this day ;
    Why stand you thus unmov'd with my laments ?
    Why weep you not to think upon my wrongs ?
    Why pine not I, and die in this distress ?
First Jew. Why, Barabas, as hardly can we brook

160. *Exeunt . . .*] Dyce, Bull. to Wag. : *Exeunt* Q to Rob. : *Exeunt, except the Jews.* Cunn.   165. *Primus*] Reed to Wag. : *Primas* Q.

160. *policy*] prudent or statesman-like management. Hence, here *simple policy* is the negation of this. In the next line Barabas plays on another Elizabethan usage of this word where ' policy ' denotes ' state-craft ', and he gives the word ' policy ' a deceitful, crafty, under-hand implication, as it is used in the *Faerie Queene*, I. iv. 12 :
'Ne ruld her Realmes with lawes,
    but *pollicie*.'
For this use, see lower, line 273.

160. *Exeunt . . .*] Dyce writes : ' On their departure, the scene is supposed to be changed to a street near the house of Barabas.' But see note on staging at beginning of this scene (p. 48).

161–2.] Barabas seizes on the word *policy* and contrasts it with *simple* and *simplicity*. These, in-deed, are other terms for the *right* of line 153, which is part of *our pro-*

fession (line 146) to which Barabas here refers.

164. *hatred*] a trisyllable. So *hundred* below, line 185.

165. *Primus Motor*] the original source of motion. A periphrasis of Barabas for God.

167. *ban*] *curse.* Compare *William of Palerne*, line 1644 : ' I may *banne* that I was born ', and for the substantive use, see *King Lear*, II. iii. 19 : ' Sometime with lunatic *bans*, sometime with prayers.'

172–174. *Why . . . distress*] Note the repetition of the form into which the line is cast, and how it limits the idea to be expressed to a single line. This is not unfrequent in the early dramatists, and indeed is frequently found in Shakespeare's earlier plays. See, for example, *Richard III*, I. iii. 228 ff., and IV. iv. 92 ff.

The cruel handling of ourselves in this :
Thou seest they have taken half our goods.

Bara. Why did you yield to their extortion ?
You were a multitude, and I but one ;
And of me only have they taken all.   180

First Jew. Yet, brother Barabas, remember Job.

Bara. What tell you me of Job ? I wot his wealth
Was written thus : he had seven thousand sheep,
Three thousand camels, and two hundred yoke
Of labouring oxen, and five hundred
She asses : but for every one of those,
Had they been valu'd at indifferent rate,
I had at home, and in mine argosy,
And other ships that came from Egypt last,
As much as would have bought his beasts and him, 190
And yet have kept enough to live upon ;
So that not he, but I, may curse the day,
Thy fatal birthday, forlorn Barabas ;
And henceforth wish for an eternal night,
That clouds of darkness may inclose my flesh,
And hide these extreme sorrows from mine eyes :
For only I have toil'd to inherit here
The months of vanity, and loss of time,
And painful nights, have bin appointed me.

181. *remember Job.*] Marlowe is evidently writing directly with the Bible before him, and quoting almost textually from Job i. 3 : ' His substance also was seven thousand sheep, and three thousand camels, and five hundred yoke of oxen, and five hundred she asses.' The divergence is perhaps due to Marlowe's desire to avoid repetition. Cf. Shakespeare's use of the O.T. in *The Merchant of Venice,* where Shylock ' quotes Scripture for his purpose ' (i. iii. 78 ff.)

187. *indifferent*] see above, I. i. 29.

192–3. *So that not he . . . Barabas*] ' After this opened Job his mouth, and cursed his day . . .

and said, " Let the day perish wherein I was born ",' etc. (Job iii. 1 ff.).

194. *wish . . . eternal night*] This image is typical of Marlowe : a gloomy and spacious idea, such as he frequently expresses. Possibly derived from Senecan reading, where *Noctis æternæ chaos* recurs. He uses much the same image later, see Act II. i. 16. It should be noted, however, that the ideas of Job iii. 4 ff. may have given him inspiration here.

198–9. *months of vanity . . . appointed me.*] See Job vii. 3 : ' So I am made to possess *months of vanity*, and wearisome *nights* are *appointed* to me.'

Sec. Jew. Good Barabas, be patient.   200

Bara. Ay, ay : Pray, leave me in my patience.   You, that

    Were ne'er possess'd of wealth, are pleas'd with want ;

    But give him liberty at least to mourn,

    That in a field, amidst his enemies,

    Doth see his soldiers slain, himself disarm'd,

    And knows no means of his recovery :

    Ay, let me sorrow for this sudden chance ;

    'Tis in the trouble of my spirit I speak :

    Great injuries are not so soon forgot.

First Jew. Come, let us leave him ; in his ireful mood   210

    Our words will but increase his ecstasy.

Sec. Jew. On, then : but, trust me, 'tis a misery

    To see a man in such affliction :

    Farewell, Barabas.

Bara.   Ay, fare you well.   [*Exeunt.*

  See the simplicity of these base slaves.

---

201. *Ay, ay*] Brennan conj. ; but as part of line 200.   *Ay, I* Reed
to Cunn., Ellis : *I, I* Q, Bull., Wag.   *in my*] Q to Wag. : *my* Brennan
conj.   201–2. *You, that . . . want ;*] Dyce² :   Q to Dyce¹, Cunn. read as
one line : *that were* omit Bull. conj. : *that* omit Ellis.   214. *Exeunt . . .*]
Dyce, Wag. : *Exeunt* after Barabas, Q to Rob., Cunn. to Ellis.

201–2. *Ay . . . want*] Of the
many proposed alterations to these
lines, Mr. Brennan (*op. cit.*) would
rearrange them to read :

'*Sec. Jew.* Good Barabas, be patient.
  Bara.   Ay, ay :
    Pray, leave me my patience.
    You that were
    Never possesst of wealth are
    pleas'd with want,'

and adds : 'The pauses of Barabas' meditative irony fill out the
Ay and *Pray* into feet. By omitting
the *in*, which is just *in* and could
easily creep in between *me* and *my*,
I seem to gain some point : don't
drive me out of the only possession
left to me.'   I have partly accepted
his suggestion, but there seems
no need to drop *in*. The word
patience is a trisyllable here, as is
patient in line 200. The Quarto
'I, I' makes it impossible to say

whether 'Ay, I' or 'Ay, ay' is
intended here, but the rearrangement suggested above necessitates
the understanding of the words as
'Ay, ay'.

211. *ecstasy*] 'In the usage of
Shakespeare and some others, it
stands for every species of alien-
ation of mind, whether temporary
or permanent, proceeding from joy,
sorrow, wonder, or any other
exciting cause ' (Nares' *Glossary*).
Marlowe uses it again in *Tamburlaine*, v. ii. 175 : ' And have no hope
to end our *ecstasies* ', and it is
frequent in Shakespeare, see *Hamlet*,
passim.

215. *simplicity*] folly. Compare
I. ii. 162.

base slaves] A term of contempt. Compare Pistol's ' *Base* is
the *slave* that pays ', *Henry V*, II.
i. *Base* combines the ideas of
lowness and contempt.

Who, for the villains have no wit themselves,
Think me to be a senseless lump of clay,
That will with every water wash to dirt!
No, Barabas is born to better chance,
And fram'd of finer mould than common men,   220
That measure naught but by the present time.
A reaching thought will search his deepest wits,
And cast with cunning for the time to come:
For evils are apt to happen every day.
But whither wends my beauteous Abigail?

                (Enter ABIGAIL, *the Jew's daughter.*

O, what has made my lovely daughter sad?
What, woman! moan not for a little loss:
Thy father has enough in store for thee.

Abig. Not for myself, but aged Barabas:
Father, for thee lamenteth Abigail: 230
But I will learn to leave these fruitless tears;
And, urg'd thereto with my afflictions,
With fierce exclaims run to the senate-house,
And in the senate reprehend them all,
And rent their hearts with tearing of my hair,

---

225. *Enter Abigail . . . daughter*] Q to Rob., Cunn., Bull., Wag. : Enter *Abigail*, Dyce, Ellis, after line 224. 229. *Not*] Q to Dyce[1], Cunn., Ellis, Wag. : *Nor* Dyce [2], Bull. conj. 235. *rent*] Q, Dyce, Cunn., Wag. : *rend* Reed to Rob., Bull., Ellis.

216. *for*] because.
villains . . . themselves]
Marlowe is here playing on the words ' base slaves ' and ' villains'. The *villanus* in medieval times was often little better than a slave, and regarded as a senseless clodhopper.
222–3. *A reaching . . . come*]
A far-seeing intelligence (or mind) will explore its utmost resources, and with shrewd reckoning prepare for future happenings. Brereton, however, suggests that ' a reaching thought ' is metonymy for ' an ambitious thinker ', and quotes from *The Tragedy of Woodstock*, IV. iii. 58 : ' Th'art a rare statesman, Nimble ; th'hast a *reaching* head.'

225. *Enter Abigail*] The name Abigail Marlowe would have found as one of David's wives in I Samuel xxv.
233. *exclaims*] outcries. Used before in this sense in line 129. Compare *I Henry VI*, IV. iv. 30: ' And York as fast upon your grace *exclaims*.' Kyd's *Spanish Tragedy*, III. vii. 3 : ' mine *exclaims*, that have surcharged the air With ceaseless plaints.'
235. *rent*] This is a common Elizabethan spelling, which modern editors have altered to *rend*. Thus we have Coverdale translating Joel ii. 12 : ' *Rente* your herts, and not youre clothes.' This pun is found elsewhere in Marlowe. Cf. *Edward*

Till they reduce the wrongs done to my father.

Bara. No, Abigail ; things past recovery

Are hardly cur'd with exclamations.

Be silent, daughter ; sufferance breeds ease,

And time may yield us an occasion,   240

Which on the sudden cannot serve the turn.

Besides, my girl, think me not all so fond

As negligently to forego so much

Without provision for thyself and me :

Ten thousand portagues, besides great pearls,

Rich costly jewels, and stones infinite,

Fearing the worst of this before it fell,

I closely hid.

Abig.   Where, father ?

Bara. In my house, my girl.

Abig. Then shall they ne'er be seen of Barabas ;   250

For they have seiz'd upon thy house and wares.

Bara. But they will give me leave once more, I trow,

To go into my house.

Abig.   That may they not ;

236, *reduce*] Q to Dyce¹, Cunn. to Wag. : *redress* Dyce² conj. 245.
portagues] Reed to Wag. : *portagnes* Q.   248. *Where, father ?*] Q, etc. :
Where ? Wag. and prints ' I closely hid. *Abig.* Where ? *Bar.* In my
house, my girl ', as one line.

II, line 2127 : ' Well may I rent
his name, that rends my heart.'
And also l. 2287.
   236. *reduce*] diminish. The
O.E.D. gives under the year 1560
Daus, tr. *Sleidane's* Comm. 341b :
' When thys . . . semed over long,
Clement the sixt *reduced* [L. redegit]
the same unto fifty years.' There
seems no reason therefore to adopt
Dyce's conjectural *redress*.
   239. *sufferance*] patience, endur-
ance. So in *The Merchant of Venice*,
I. iii. 110 : ' For *sufferance* is the
badge of all our tribe.' It is also
found in Heywood's *Proverbs* :
' Best is to suffer : for of *suffrance*
cometh ease.'
   240–1. *And time . . . serve the
turn*] Time, which cannot sud-

denly serve our turn, may in due
course offer us an opportunity.
   242. *fond*] foolish.
   245. *portagues*] Nares' *Glossary*,
' Portague, Portegue, Portigue, s.
A Portugese gold coin worth
between £3 10s. and £4 10s.'
Compare Lyly, *Midas*, II. ii. 41 :
' An egg is eaten at one sup, and
a *portague* lost at one cast ', and
Jonson, *The Alchemist*, I. i. 461 :
Drugger : ' Yes, I've a *portague* ', etc.
The Quarto misprints *Portagnes*—
an *n* for *u* error (compare I. i.
67).
   248–9. *I closely . . . girl*] Here
as before Wagner omits a word
father so as to secure a five-foot
line. And so again with less certainty at line 281.

For there I left the governor placing nuns,
Displacing me ; and of thy house they mean
To make a nunnery, where none but their own sect
Must enter in ; men generally barr'd.

Bara. My gold, my gold, and all my wealth is gone !
You partial heavens, have I deserv'd this plague ?
What, will you thus oppose me, luckless stars,   260
To make me desperate in my poverty ?
And, knowing me impatient in distress,
Think me so mad as I will hang myself,
That I may vanish o'er the earth in air,
And leave no memory that e'er I was ?
No, I will live ; nor loathe I this my life :
And, since you leave me in the ocean thus
To sink or swim, and put me to my shifts,
I'll rouse my senses, and awake myself.
Daughter, I have it : thou perceiv'st the plight   270
Wherein these Christians have oppressed me :
Be rul'd by me, for in extremity
We ought to make bar of no policy.

Abig. Father, whate'er it be, to injure them
That have so manifestly wronged us,
What will not Abigail attempt ?

Bara.   Why, so.
Then thus : thou told'st me they have turn'd my house
Into a nunnery, and some nuns are there ?

---

256. *sect*] sex, as frequently in Elizabethan usage : See *2 Henry IV*, II. iv. 41 : ' So is all her *sect* ; an they be once in a calm, they are sick ', etc. *They* in l. 255 refers to the nuns, and *men generally barr'd* in l. 257 rounds off the statement.

257. *generally*] in general. Men were usually not allowed to enter within the nunnery precincts except they were priests, confessors or the like.

263. *so . . . as*] We should expect to read *that* here. The use of these two conjunctions having the force of ' As the result of which '

was a frequent Elizabethan construction. See Abbott, § 109, and compare *Love's Labour's Lost*, II. i. 174 :

  ' You shall be *so* received
As you shall deem yourself lodged
  in my heart.'

268. *put me . . . shifts*] to bring to an extremity. Compare Moryson's *Itinerary*, I, p. 195 : ' These knights were much *driven to their shifts*, to get money for that journey.'

276. *Why, so.*] An exclamation of satisfaction, and agreement.

Abig. I did.

Bara.   Then, Abigail, there must my girl
  Entreat the abbess to be entertain'd.   280

Abig. How! as a nun?

Bara.   Ay, daughter; for religion
  Hides many mischiefs from suspicion.

Abig. Ay, but, father, they will suspect me there.

Bara. Let 'em suspect; but be thou so precise
  As they may think it done of holiness.
  Entreat 'em fair, and give them friendly speech,
  And seem to them as if thy sins were great,
  Till thou hast gotten to be entertain'd.

Abig. Thus, father, shall I much dissemble.

Bara.   Tush!
  As good dissemble that thou never mean'st   290
  As first mean truth and then dissemble it:
  A counterfeit profession is better
  Than unseen hypocrisy.

---

281. *daughter*] Q, etc.: *omit* Wag. conj.   290. *mean'st*] Q, etc.:
meant'st, Cunn.   293. *unseen*] Q, etc.: *unforeseen* Cunn.: *unseeing* Brere-
on conj.

280. *entertain'd*] Usually employed in the sense of ' being taken
into service ', rather than in our
modern connotation. See *Julius
Cæsar*, v. v. 60: ' All that serv'd
Brutus, I will *entertain* them.'
Abigail's service, the next line shows
us, is to be that of a religious.
  281, 2. *for   religion . . . suspicion*] The first of innumerable
passages in this play betraying
Marlowe's views on institutional
religion. Note his whole treatment
of the Friars in particular. Meyer
(*op. cit.*) notes, ' This, of course, is
Gentillet II. i. and *Principe*, Cap.
18 '.
  284. *precise*] well behaved, perfect, puritanical. Cf. *Edward II*,
II. i. 46: ' Mine old lord while he
liv'd was so *precise*, That he would
take exceptions at my buttons.'
  288. *Till . . . entertain'd*] Till
you have got yourself received.

289. *dissemble*] conceal, put on
false appearances.
  290–1. *As   good . . . dissemble
it*] A good example of the current belief concerning Machiavelli's
teaching.
  291. *As first . . . it*] Barabas
here insinuates that nuns entering
the convent, at first sincerely, but
afterwards only by feigning, assert
their vocation.
  292. *counterfeit*] spurious, deceitful.
  profession] a technical term
applied to religious who were professed, or solemnly bound to their
order. Here it may possibly only
refer to Abigail's promises without
any more specific intention.
  293. *unseen*] J. le Gay Brereton
(*Beiblatt zur Anglia*, 1905, p. 205)
notes: ' Cunningham reads *unforeseen*, and conceives Marlowe's
meaning to be " that a steady con-

Abig. Well, father, say I be entertain'd,
    What then shall follow ?

Bara.   This shall follow then ;
    There have I hid, close underneath the plank
    That runs along the upper-chamber floor,
    The gold and jewels which I kept for thee.
    But here they come ; be cunning, Abigail.

Abig. Then, father, go with me.

Bara.   No, Abigail, in this   300
    It is not necessary I be seen :
    For I will seem offended with thee for't :
    Be close, my girl, for this must fetch my gold.
                  [*They retire.*

Enter FRIAR JACOMO, FRIAR BARNARDINE, Abbess, *and
a* Nun.

294. *say*] Q, etc. : *say* [*that*] Bull. : *say that* Ellis.   300. *father,*] Q,
etc. : *omit* Wag. conj. *in this*] Q, etc. : *omit* Elze conj.   303. *They
retire*] Dyce, Ellis : *They draw back* Cunn., Bull. : *omit* Q to Rob., Wag.
303. *Enter* . . .] Dyce, Ellis, Bull. : *Enter three Fryars and two Nuns.* Q
to Rob., Wag. : *Enter two Friars and two Nuns.* Cunn.

sistent piece of acting is better than
to have to put on the hypocrite
at a moment's warning ''. Perhaps
we should read '' *unseeing* hypocrisy ''—i.e. an habitual aimless
hypocrisy such as Barabas might
attribute to the Nuns. But most
likely some words have dropped
out.' But why should not *unseen*
be taken plainly as meaning *un-
detected* ? This is a logical continuation of the idea expressed in
line 291. The passage is another
of Marlowe's attacks upon the
' precisians ' (cf. l. 284) ; and it
develops the idea in the preceding
lines : It is as good to pretend
something you never mean (as
when Abigail pretends to believe
in Christianity) as to begin sincerely and end (as the precisians
do) by dissembling practices.

294. *say*] In this line also Bullen
thinks a word is missing and conjectures *say* [*that*]. Ellis (as usual)
boldly prints it so without comment.

299. *cunning*] From the O.E.
cunnan, M.E. *cunnen* ; to know.
Here used in the sense of skill or
craft as in *King John*, IV. i. 54 :
' Nay, you may think my love was
    crafty love,
And call it *cunning*.'

301. *It* . . . *seen*] i.e. It is necessary that I be not seen.

303. *Be close*] Be secret. Cf.
Nashe, *Summer's Last Will*, etc.
(Hazlitt, *Dodsley*, viii. 64), ' Because that sex keep nothing *close*
they hear '.

303. *Enter* . . .] The Quarto mis-
takenly reads ' *Enter three friars* ',
but only two have any part in the
play as it now stands. Have we
here one clue to a revision or
revisions ? The whole passage is
suspicious ; see the different appel-
lations of the Abbess in lines 306,
312, 315, where in the Q she is
called 1. Nun, Nun and Abb.
respectively, and the verse lining of
lines 326–30, etc. It will be

Friar Jac. Sisters,
 We now are almost at the new-made nunnery.
Abb. The better ; for we love not to be seen :
 'Tis thirty winters long since some of us
 Did stray so far amongst the multitude.
Friar Jac. But, madam, this house
 And waters of this new-made nunnery   310
 Will much delight you.
Abb. It may be so : But who comes here ?

        [Abigail comes forward.

Abig. Grave abbess, and you, happy virgins' guide,
 Pity the state of a distressed maid !
Abb. What art thou, daughter ?
Abig. The hopeless daughter of a hapless Jew,
 The Jew of Malta, wretched Barabas ;

---

304. *Friar Jac.*] Dyce, Ellis, Bull. :   1 *Fri.* others.   304, 5. *Sisters, . . .
nunnery*] Dyce, Wag. : others as one line.   306. *Abb.*] Dyce, Ellis, Bull:
1 *Nun* others.   310. *waters*] Q   to Cunn., Ellis : *cloisters* Bull. conj. :
quarters Wag., T. Brooke.   312.   *Abb.*] Dyce, Ellis, Bull. : *Nun* others.
Abigail . . .] Dyce to Bull. :   *omit* Q to Rob., Wag.

noticed also, that we cannot still be in the Senate-house, and that at some point (probably at entry of Abigail, line 225) we must, therefore, imagine that Barabas comes forward on to the front stage which is presumably the street before the Senate-house.

306, 312. *Abb.*] Substituted by Dyce in place of *1. Nun* and *Nun* of the Quarto, etc. He adds, ' that both speeches belong to the Abbess is evident'. I think the Quarto S.D. *Enter . . . two Nuns* shows that no effort was made to distinguish between the two. The Abbess was necessarily a Nun : her rank is only important when the dialogue commences, and she is called ' madam ' or ' abbess ' almost indifferently—as indeed would have been the medieval practice.

310. *waters*] There is no reason for the alteration to *quarters* proposed by Wagner and Tucker Brooke, still less to *cloisters* as conjectured by Bullen.   The near proximity of water was an absolute necessity to the medieval nunnery, and indeed there are few monastic sites on which we cannot till trace the existence of the stew-ponds, etc.
 new-made nunnery] An unnecessary repetition of l. 305, and probably an interpolation, due to copyist or printer. Lines 309–11 are very irregular and further evidence of the suspicious nature of some of this scene (see note on l. 303).

313. *Grave abbess, and you, happy virgins' guide,*] Here Abigail appeals to the Abbess and to the two Friars, I imagine. The Friars, as we shall see, are the Confessors to the Nuns, and therefore may well be looked on and addressed as their guides and directors.

316. *hopeless . . . hapless*] Marlowe was always subject to this vice of punning (despite Mr. Bullen's remarks), though not so given to it in this play as in *Tamburlaine.*

Sometimes the owner of a goodly house,
Which they have now turn'd to a nunnery.
Abb. Well, daughter, say, what is thy suit with us ?   320
Abig. Fearing the afflictions which my father feels
    Proceed from sin, or want of faith in us,
    I'd pass away my life in penitence,
    And be a novice in your nunnery,
    To make atonement for my labouring soul.
Friar Jac. No doubt, brother, but this proceedeth of the
    spirit.
Friar Barn. Ay, and of a moving spirit too, brother : but
    come,
    Let us entreat she may be entertain'd.   330
Abb. Well, daughter, we admit you for a nun.
Abig. First let me as a novice learn to frame
    My solitary life to your strait laws,
    And let me lodge where I was wont to lie :
    I do not doubt, by your divine precepts
    And mine own industry, but to profit much.
Bara. As much, I hope, as all I hid is worth.   [*Aside.*
Abb. Come, daughter, follow us.
Bara. [*coming forward*] Why, how now, Abigail !

318. *Sometimes*] Q, etc. : *Sometime* Cunn., Ellis.   326, 328. *brother*]
Q, etc. : *omit* Wag.   339. *Prefix* Bara.] Bara. [coming forward] Dyce, Ellis :
omit others.

318. *Sometimes*] An Elizabethan form of the modern *sometime*. It is unnecessary to amend it as Cunningham and Ellis have done.

325. *labouring soul*] labouring here used in the sense of striving or struggling against the wickedness of the world. Analogous to the passage in *Hamlet*, III. iv. 113 : ' Oh, step between her and her *fighting* soul.'

326, 328. *brother*] Wagner omits these words, and he is probably right. They seem to be there merely for comic emphasis, and ruin what small chance the lines have of any metrical form.

332. *a novice*] Before entering on the final and irrevocable vows the candidate was required to serve for some considerable time in the noviciate, so that she might test the strength of her longing for the religious life. If after due time she felt convinced of her vocation, she took the veil and was professed, and henceforth dead to the secular world.

333. *strait*] strict, rigorous. Compare *1 Henry IV*, IV. iii. 79 : ' Some certain edicts and some *strait* decrees.'

336. *but*] There is a great temptation to remove this word. As it is, ' industry ' must be reduced to two syllables—' ind'stry '.

What mak'st thou 'mongst these hateful Christians? 340
Friar Jac. Hinder her not, thou man of little faith,
  For she has mortified herself.
Bara.   How! mortified!
Friar Jac. And is admitted to the sisterhood.
Bara. Child of perdition, and thy father's shame!
  What wilt thou do among these hateful fiends?
  I charge thee on my blessing that thou leave
  These devils and their damned heresy!
Abig. Father, forgive me—
Bara.   Nay, back, Abigail.
  And think upon the jewels and the gold,
  The board is marked thus that covers it.   350
                                   [*Whispers to her.*
  Away, accursed, from thy father's sight!
Friar Jac. Barabas, although thou art in misbelief,
  And wilt not see thine own afflictions,
  Yet let thy daughter be no longer blind.
Bara. Blind friar, I reck not thy persuasions,
  The board is marked thus that covers it. [*Aside to her.*
  For I had rather die than see her thus.
  Wilt thou forsake me too in my distress,

---

347. *devils*] *diuels* Q. 348. *forgive*] Dyce, Ellis, Wag. : *give* Q and others.
She goes to him] S.D. added by Cunn., Bull., Ellis after *forgive me*— 350.
Whispers to her] Q to Coll., Wag. : Before 348 Rob. : After 348 Cunn : *Aside
to Abigail in a whisper* Dyce, Ellis, and so in 356. 356. *thus*] Dyce, etc. :
thus † Q, Rob. *Aside* . . .] *omit* Q, Reed, Cunn., Bull., Wag. : *Aside
to his daughter* Rob.

340. *What mak'st thou*] what are
you doing : a very frequent construction. Compare *Richard III*,
I. iii. 124 : ' *What mak'st thou* in my
sight '.
  342. *mortified*] become dead to
the world in becoming a nun. The
ceremony of admission to the final
vows of the religious orders emphasised this ' death unto life '.
Cf. *Love's Labour's Lost*, I. i. 28 : ' My
loving lord, Dumain is *mortified* :
. . . To love, to wealth, to pomp,
I pine and die ', etc.
  348. *forgive me*—] Dyce's emen-

dation of *give* to *forgive* seems to
meet the sense of this passage.
  355. *I reck . . . persuasions*] I
am unconcerned by your arguments. See *King John*, v. v. 11 :
' The English Lords, By his *per-
suasion*, are again fallen off.'
  356.] The Quarto reads *thus* † to
signify the mark that Barabas is to
make with his hand while he is
speaking. This mark Bullen suggests indicates the notch in the
plank under which the treasure is
concealed.

Seduced daughter ? *Go, forget not.* [*Aside to her.*
Becomes it Jews to be so credulous ?   360
To-morrow early I'll be at the door. [*Aside to her.*
No, come not at me ; if thou wilt be damn'd,
Forget me, see me not, and so, be gone !
Farewell ; remember to-morrow morning.

[*Aside to her.*

Out, out, thou wretch !
    [*Exit, on one side, Barabas.   Exeunt, on the other side,
       Friars, Abbess, Nun, and Abigail : and, as they are
       going out,*

Enter MATHIAS.

Math. Who's this ? fair Abigail, the rich Jew's daughter,
Become a nun ! her father's sudden fall
Has humbled her, and brought her down to this :
Tut, she were fitter for a tale of love,
Than to be tired out with orisons :   370
And better would she far become a bed,
Embraced in a friendly lover's arms,
Than rise at midnight to a solemn mass.

Enter LODOWICK.

Lod. Why, how now, Don Mathias ! in a dump ?

359. *forget not.*] Reed to Cunn., Ellis : *forget not, go.* Bull. : *forget it not.* Wag., Dyce² conj. : *forget net* Q.   359. 361. 364. *Aside . . . her*] Q to Rob., Wag. : *Aside to her in a whisper* Dyce, Ellis : *omit* Cunn. 365. *Out . . . wretch !*] Q and others : *omit* Cunn.   *Exit . . .*] Dyce, Bull., Ellis : *omit* Q Rob., Cunn. : *Exeunt.* Reed, Coll., Wag.

373. *Than rise . . . mass*] The religious orders varied somewhat in their practices, but in general the 24 hours were divided into twelve equal parts. The night was divided into two equal portions, between which came the night-office of matins, followed by lauds. The general practice was to rise in the middle of the night for matins and to return to the dorter afterwards. (See *English Monasteries*, A. H. Thompson, p. 137.) Mass, of course, was not celebrated until during the day-offices—generally between terce and sext, i.e. 9–12 a.m. Abigail, in II. i. 55, again refers to the night-offices about midnight.

374. *dump*] a fit of abstraction or musing. Palsgrave has ' I fall into a *dumpe* or musyng upon thynges '. A contemporary notice on Ford, the dramatist, reads : ' Deep in a *dump* John Ford was alone got
    With folded arms and melancholy hat.'

Math. Believe me, noble Lodowick, I have seen
   The strangest sight, in my opinion,
   That ever I beheld.

Lod.   What was't, I prithee ?

Math. A fair young maid, scarce fourteen years of age,
   The sweetest flower in Cytherea's field,
   Cropt from the pleasures of the fruitful earth,   380
   And strangely metamorphis'd [to a] nun.

Lod. But say, what was she ?

Math.   Why, the rich Jew's daughter.

Lod. What, Barabas, whose goods were lately seiz'd ?
   Is she so fair ?

Math.   And matchless beautiful ;
   As, had you seen her, 'twould have mov'd your heart,
   Though countermur'd with walls of brass, to love,

381. *metamorphis'd*] Q : *metamorphos'd* Reed to Dyce, Bull., Wag. : *metamorphosed*, Cunn., Ellis. *nun*] Q to Rob., Ellis : *to a nun* Dyce, Bull., Wag. : *a nun* Cunn. 384. *Is . . . fair*] Q, etc. : *She is so fair and matchless*, etc., Wag. who assigns all to *Math.* 386. *countermur'd*] Coll. (MS.) conj., Deighton conj. *countermin'd* Q, etc.

('So quotes Gifford from the "Times' Poets".' *Introduction* to Hartley Coleridge, Massinger and Ford's *Dramatic Works*, p. xlix.)

378. *fourteen years*] This is just Juliet's age, and cf. close parallel later in *Romeo and Juliet*, iv. v. 28 : 'Death lies on her like an untimely frost, Upon the *sweetest flower* of all the *field*.' The women's parts on the Elizabethan stage, being sustained by boys, it was essential that the heroines should be as young as possible. It may well be that both Marlowe and Shakespeare allowed to the fullest degree for the early age at which Jewesses and Italian women come to womanhood.

379. *Cytherea*] a form of the surname of Aphrodite, derived from the town of Cythera in Crete, or from the island of Cythera, where the goddess was said to have first landed. Hence here used to denote a girl of surpassing beauty.

381. *metamorphis'd*] I have retained this spelling as it was evidently common in Marlowe's day, e.g. Beaumont and Fletcher, *Spanish Curate*, iv. vii. 14. *Merry Wives of Windsor* (1602 ed., W. W. Greg), l. 323 : 'Now Ieshu blesse me, am I *methomorphised ?* ' See also O.E.D.

386. *countermur'd*] This conjecture of Collier (MS.) and Deighton (*The Old Dramatists*, p. 120) seems to me to have considerable substance. *Countermin'd* does not make very good sense, and the O.E.D. states that it is used erroneously for *countermur'd*, and gives a further example of the same mistake. Countermur'd, i.e. protected by one wall behind another as a reserve defence, is exactly the meaning here, and we may compare a very similar passage of Kyd's in *The Spanish Tragedy* (ed. Boas), iii. vii. 16 :

'Where, *countermurde* with walls of diamond
   I find the place impregnable.'

6

Or, at the least, to pity.

Lod. And if she be so fair as you report,
'Twere time well spent to go and visit her :
How say you ? shall we ?   390

Math. I must and will, sir ; there's no remedy.

Lod. And so will I too, or it shall go hard.
Farewell, Mathias.

Math.   Farewell, Lodowick. [*Exeunt severally.*

388. *And*] Q to Dyce[1], Cunn. to Wag.: *An* Dyce[2]. 393. *Exeunt . . .*]
Dyce, Bull., Ellis: *Exeunt* others.

The error arises from a misreading by the compositor of his MS. It would not be difficult for a man ignorant of the precise meaning of the two words to read *ur* as *in*.

ACT II

SCENE I.—*Outside the house of Barabas.*

Enter BARABAS, *with a light.*

Bara. Thus, like the sad presaging raven, that tolls
The sick man's passport in her hollow beak,
And in the shadow of the silent night
Doth shake contagion from her sable wings,
Vex'd and tormented runs poor Barabas
With fatal curses towards these Christians.
The incertain pleasures of swift-footed time
Have ta'en their flight, and left me in despair;
And of my former riches rests no more

Act II. Scene i.
Reed, Coll., Dyce: *Act the Second, Scene i.* Rob., Cunn. to Ellis: *Actus Secundus* Q, Wag.
7. *incertain*] Q, Reed, Coll., Dyce, Wag.: *uncertain* Rob., Cunn., Bull., Ellis.

Scene I] Outer-stage and balcony. As Barabas is on the outer-stage the scene remains unlocalised until the entry of Abigail at line 20 on the balcony indicates he is before the nunnery—his former home. From I. ii. 361 and II. i. 34 we know they are to meet at dawn, but Barabas is unable to sleep, and so is waiting impatiently before the house. The purpose of the light he carries is to emphasise to the Elizabethan audience that it is night, since it was impossible to darken the Elizabethan stage appreciably. Abigail, also, does not yet expect her father, but finds the time opportune to make her search. Thus both soliloquise unconscious of the other's presence at first, until line 43.
1–4. *the sad presaging raven . . . wings*] Marlowe here combines the two common superstitions prevalent concerning the raven. Shakespeare has several references to them, as in *Othello*, IV. i. 21, and *King John*, IV. iii. 153. Collier (quoted by Dyce) notes that Guilpin's *Skialetheia*, 1598, echoes Marlowe's lines very closely : ' Like to the fatall ominous raven, which tolls the sick man's dirge within his hollow beak.' Bullen compares with Peele's *David and Bethsabe*:

' Like as the fatal raven, that in his voice
Carries the dreadful summons of our death',

which, as Dyce notes, is imitated from Du Bartas' *L'Arche* (Peele's *Works*, ed. Bullen, vol. II, p. 29). See also Furness's note in his Variorum edition of *Much Ado About Nothing*, II. iii. 86.

But bare remembrance ; like a soldier's scar,   10
That has no further comfort for his maim.
O Thou, that with a fiery pillar ledd'st
The sons of Israel through the dismal shades,
Light Abraham's offspring ; and direct the hand
Of Abigail this night ; or let the day
Turn to eternal darkness after this :
No sleep can fasten on my watchful eyes,
Nor quiet enter my distemper'd thoughts,
Till I have answer of my Abigail.

Enter ABIGAIL *above.*

Abig. Now have I happily espied a time   20
    To search the plank my father did appoint ;
    And here, behold, unseen, where I have found
    The gold, the pearls, and jewels which he hid.
Bara. Now I remember those old women's words,
    Who in my wealth would tell me winter's tales,

---

22. *unseen*] Reed, etc.: *(unseen)* Q. 25. *wealth*] Q to Cunn., Ellis, Wag. : *youth* Bull. conj.

11. *maim*] a disabling hurt or wound.   Compare *1 Henry IV*, IV. i. 42 : ' Your father's sickness is a *maim* to us ', and Nashe, *Lenten Stuffe* (*Works*, ed. McKerrow, III. 153), ' as great a *maime* to any man's happinesse as can be feared from the hands of miseries '. The passage means, ' Like the scar of a soldier who has no further consolation for his wound '.

20–41.] Both Barabas and Abigail carry on their monologues, unconscious of the presence of the other, until, in line 43, Barabas sees Abigail on the balcony above. (See note at head of scene.)   The Elizabethan stage lent itself to such a piece of stage-craft rather more successfully than would the modern stage.

25. *in my wealth*] Bullen writes : ' These words have little meaning ; I suspect that we should read " in my *youth* ".' But is not Marlowe here using the word in the sense of *weal, prosperity*, etc., as in Malory, Book IX, cap. 37 : ' But whanne sekenes toucheth a prysoners body thenne may a prysoner say al *wealthe* is hym berafte.' The old women naturally retailed their fancies to Barabas, since no one in Malta provided better pasturage for spirits and ghosts than did this master-hoarder.

winter's tales] M. Jusserand writes : ' A winter's tale meant a fairy story, an old woman's tale, its very unlikelihood being one of its charms ', and in support of this quotes this passage, and one from Peele's *Old Wives' Tale*, l. 75 (Gayley's edn.) : ' This sport does well ; but methinks, gamner, *a merry winter's tale* would drive away the time trimly.'
And see *Macbeth*, III. iv. 64 :
' A woman's story at a winter's fire
  Authoriz'd by her grandam.'

And speak of spirits and ghosts that glide by night
About the place where treasure hath bin hid :
And now methinks that I am one of those :
For, whilst I live, here lives my soul's sole hope,
And, when I die, here shall my spirit walk.   30

Abig. Now that my father's fortune were so good
As but to be about this happy place ;
'Tis not so happy : yet, when we parted last,
He said he would attend me in the morn.
Then, gentle Sleep, where'er his body rests,
Give charge to Morpheus that he may dream
A golden dream, and of the sudden walk,
Come and receive the treasure I have found.

Bara. Bueno para todos mi ganado no era :
As good go on, as sit so sadly thus.   40
But stay : what star shines yonder in the east ?
The loadstar of my life, if Abigail.
Who's there ?

Abig.   Who's that ?

37. *walk*] Q to Rob., Wag. : *wake* Dyce to Ellis.   39. *Bueno* . . .] Rob.,
etc. : *Birn para todos, my ganada no er* Q, Reed : *Buen* etc., Coll.

29. *my soul's sole hope*] An
inevitable pun to almost all Elizabethan writers. Compare its use
more effectively than here in *The
Merchant of Venice*, IV. i. 123 :

'Not on thy *sole*, but on thy *soul*,
   harsh Jew,
Thou mak'st thy knife keen.'

35-6. *Then . . . dream*] Here
Marlowe seems to have in mind
Ovid's *Met.*, XI. 623 ff., where
Sleep (Somnus) on receiving from
Ino the command of Juno, bids his
son Morpheus to appear in the form
of a dream before Halcyone.
Morpheus is here pronounced as a
trisyllable.

37. *walk*] *walke* is the reading of
the Quarto, and as it makes quite
good sense I have not ventured to
amend it to *wake* as do Dyce and all
later editors except Robinson and
Wagner. Walk is an old Scotch

form = awake, as in G. Douglas,
King Hart, Canto 2, 42 : ' The King
began to *walk*, and harde the beir
(= cry).'

39. *Bueno* . . . *era*.] This is
Dyce's emendation of a very corrupt version of this Spanish proverb. It may be freely rendered
' My flock (i.e. wealth) is not good
for all '.

41. *But stay . . . east*] There
seems, as Dyce first suggested, an
obvious echo of this in *Romeo and
Juliet*, II. ii. 2 :

'But soft ! what light through yonder window breaks,
It is the East and Juliet is the sun.'

42. *loadstar*] The pole-star, the
leading (lode) or guiding star. Compare Hawes' *Pastime of Pleasure*
(E.E.T.S. edn., 1928), xviii. 2136 :

' The bryght *lodes sterre*
   Of my true herte.'

Bara.   Peace, Abigail! 'tis I.
Abig. Then, father, here receive thy happiness.
Bara. Hast thou't?
Abig. Here. [*Throws down bags.*] Hast thou't?
    There's more, and more, and more.
Bara.   O my girl,
⎫ My gold, my fortune, my felicity;
⎮ Strength to my soul, death to mine enemy;
⎮ Welcome the first beginner of my bliss: 50
    O Abigail, Abigail, that I had thee here too,
    Then my desires were fully satisfied:
    But I will practise thy enlargement thence:
    O girl! O gold! O beauty! O my bliss!
                              [*Hugs his bags.*
Abig. Father, it draweth towards midnight now,
    And 'bout this time the nuns begin to wake;
    To shun suspicion, therefore, let us part.
Bara. Farewell, my joy, and by my fingers take
    A kiss from him that sends it from his soul.
                              [*Exit Abigail above.*
    Now, Phœbus, ope the eye-lids of the day,   60

45. *Hast thou't*] *Add to Abigail's speech below* Deighton conj. 46, 47. *Here
. . . more*] Three lines in Q div. after *Here, thou't, more.* 46. *Throws down
bags*] Dyce to Ellis: Q and others insert after line 45. 51. *Abigail, Abigail*]
Reed, etc.: *Aigal, Abigal* Q, Wag. 59. *Exit . . . above*] Dyce, etc.:
omit Q to Rob., Wag.

45. *Hast thou't*] Deighton (*The
Old Dramatists*, p. 121) says that
these words seem to be quite out of
place in the mouth of Barabas.
They belong to Abigail only, and
are said by her in inquiry whether
Barabas has caught the bags which
in the dim light of the coming dawn
she has thrown down. He would
read therefore:

' Then, father, here receive thy
    happiness [throws down bags]:
    hast thou't?
There's more, and more, and more.
    [Throws down MORE bags].'

But Deighton is beside the mark.
It is natural for Barabas to say in

answer to ' receive thy happiness
(i.e. treasure), ' Have you really got
it?'
47–50. *O my girl . . . my bliss*]
The whole of this passage seems to
have been in Shakespeare's mind
while writing the famous scene in
The Merchant of Venice, II. viii. 15,
where Shylock bewails confusedly
the loss of his daughter and his
ducats. And cf. earlier in *The Jew*,
I. ii. 150.
55. *it draweth . . . midnight*]
See I. ii. 373 and note at beginning
of this scene.
60. *eye-lids . . . day*] This
phrase has been much used by
poets. Bullen aptly quotes Job

And, for the raven, wake the morning lark,
That I may hover with her in the air ;
Singing o'er these, as she does o'er her young.
Hermoso placer de los dineros.   [*Exit.*

SCENE II.—*An open place.*

Enter FERNEZE, MARTIN DEL BOSCO, Knights, *and* Officers.

Fern. Now, captain, tell us whither thou art bound ?
Whence is thy ship that anchors in our road ?
And why thou cam'st ashore without our leave ?
Bosco. Governor of Malta, hither am I bound ;
My ship, the Flying Dragon, is of Spain,
And so am I ; Del Bosco is my name, \
Vice-admiral unto the Catholic King.
First Knight. 'Tis true, my lord ; therefore entreat him well.
Bosco. Our fraught is Grecians, Turks, and Afric Moors.

64. *Hermoso . . .*] Dyce, Cunn., Ellis : *Hermoso Piarer, de les Denirch* Q,
Reed, Coll., Bull.   *de los*] Dyce, Cunn., Ellis : *el del* Rob.

Act II.   Scene ii.

Added by Rob., Cunn. to Ellis.   *Enter . . .*] *Enter Governor . . . the
Knights* Q. 9. *fraught*] Q, Dyce : *freight* Reed, Coll.

xli. 18, ' His eyes are like the *eyelids
of the morning*', and cf. Milton's well-
known ' Under the opening *eyelids
of the Morn*'. It is, of course, not
altogether in place on the lips of
Barabas.

61. *the raven,*] alluding to lines
1 ff. of this scene. See for this
coupling of raven and lark, *Titus
Andronicus*, III. i. 158 : ' Did ever
raven sing so like a *lark.*'

64. *Hermoso . . . dineros*] Collier
writes : ' We have before seen
Barabas using an unintelligible
jargon between Italian and Spanish,
such as possibly may have been
spoken by the Jews of Malta. Perhaps what is meant here is an
exclamation on the beautiful
appearance of money, *Hermoso
parecer de los dineros*, but it is

questionable whether this would be
good Spanish.' Dyce finally put
the matter straight.

Scene II.

Scene II] Dyce and Bullen
localise this as the Senate-house.
It may be (to conform with I. ii.),
but there seems no need to make
use of the inner-stage here. Ferneze
meets Del Bosco in the open place
or street—on the outer-stage.

8. *entreat*] deal with, as frequently in Elizabethan authors ;
see *post*, v. ii. 17. Compare *Richard
II*, III. i. 37 : ' For God's sake,
fairly let her be *entreated*', and
Troilus and Cressida, IV. iv. 115,
' *Entreat* her fair', etc.

9. *fraught*] freight, as in I. i. 99.
Here used to designate the human

For late upon the coast of Corsica,   10
Because we vail'd not to the Turkish fleet,
Their creeping galleys had us in the chase :
But suddenly the wind began to rise,
And then we luff'd and tack'd, and fought at ease :
Some have we fir'd, and many have we sunk ;
But one amongst the rest became our prize :
The captain's slain ; the rest remain our slaves,
Of whom we would make sale in Malta here.

Fern. Martin del Bosco, I have heard of thee :
Welcome to Malta, and to all of us ;   20
But to admit a sale of these thy Turks,
We may not, nay, we dare not give consent,
By reason of a tributary league.

First Knight. Del Bosco, as thou lov'st and honour'st us,
Persuade our governor against the Turk :
This truce we have is but in hope of gold,
And with that sum he craves might we wage war.

Bosco. Will knights of Malta be in league with Turks,
And buy it basely too for sums of gold ?
My lord, remember that, to Europe's shame,   30

---

11. *Turkish*] Gilchrist conj., Dyce, etc. : *Spanish* Q to Coll.   14. *luff'd and tack'd*] Dyce, etc. : *left and tooke* Q to Rob.

cargo that has been captured and is now brought for sale to Malta.

11. *vail'd*] lowered our topsails in salutation and in respect. So in *Tamburlaine*, I. ii. 195 :

' And Christian merchants, that with Russian stems
Plow up huge furrows in the Caspian Sea,
Shall *vail* to us, as Lords of all the lake,'

and also see Nashe's *Lenten Stuffe*, 1599, p. 14 : ' They (the batteries at Yarmouth) have their thundering tooles to compell Deigo Spanyards to ducke, and strike the winde and collicke in his paunch, if he praunce too neere them, and will not *vaile* to the Queene of England.'

Turkish] The Quarto reading of Spanish is evidently an error, and was first corrected by Gilchrist.

14. *luff'd and tack'd*] The Quarto reads ' left and tooke ', but this makes no sense, and the correction as proposed by Dyce has been adopted by all subsequent editors. *Luff'd*, a nautical term, signifying the turning of the ship's head towards the wind, in order to make off. Compare *Antony and Cleopatra*, III. x. 18, and Prof. Case's note thereon (Arden edn.).

23. *a tributary league*] an alliance on terms of money payments. See lines 28, 29. Compare Lambarde's *Perambulation of Kent* (1826), p. xii : ' These therefore were by Julius Caesar subdued to the Romane Empire, and their countrie made a *tributarie* Province.'

The Christian Isle of Rhodes, from whence you came,
Was lately lost, and you were stated here
To be at deadly enmity with Turks.

Fern. Captain, we know it ; but our force is small.

Bosco. What is the sum that Calymath requires ?

Fern. A hundred thousand crowns.

Bosco. My lord and king hath title to this isle,
And he means quickly to expel you hence ;
Therefore be rul'd by me, and keep the gold :
I'll write unto his majesty for aid,   40
And not depart until I see you free.

Fern. On this condition shall thy Turks be sold.
Go, officers, and set them straight in show.—

[Exeunt Officers.

Bosco, thou shalt be Malta's general ;
We and our warlike knights will follow thee
Against these barbarous misbelieving Turks.

Bosco. So shall you imitate those you succeed ;
For, when their hideous force environ'd Rhodes,
Small though the number was that kept the town,

32. *stated*] Q, etc. :   *stationed* Wag.   44. *Exeunt . . .*] Dyce, Bull., Ellis :   *omit* Q, and others.

31. *The Christian Isle of Rhodes*] so called because it was the head-quarters of the Knights of the Order of the Hospital of S. John of Jerusalem from about 1309 until their expulsion in 1522 by the Turks under Solyman II. After this expulsion they settled in Malta in 1529 ; hence the reference by Del Bosco to the Knights of their former home.

32. *stated*] placed, stationed or established. This is a rare use of the word, but it does not seem necessary to alter to *stationed* as proposed by Wagner. The O.E.D. gives no example after this until 1734.

37–8. *My lord . . . hence*] As a fief of Sicily, Malta fell to the crown of Aragon in 1282 when Peter of Aragon became master of Sicily.   By the marriage of Ferdinand II of Aragon in 1469 with Isabella of Castile, and the union of the two Peninsular king-doms in 1474, Sicily (and Malta) became part of the dominions of Castile.   In 1529 Charles V granted Malta to the Knights of S. John, retaining, however, the suzerainty of the Spanish crown over the Island.

48–51.] The siege of Rhodes and the surrender of the Knights upon terms was one of the greatest events of the century.   Marlowe exagger-ates in this passage ; for, though it is true that the numbers within the city were infinitesimal compared with the ' hideous force ' brought to the siege by the Turks, at the same time it must be remembered that the capitulation of December 28th, 1522, allowed the Knights to evacuate the city with their arms

They fought it out, and not a man surviv'd   50
   To bring the hapless news to Christendom.
Fern. So will we fight it out ; come, let's away :
   Proud daring Calymath, instead of gold,
   We'll send thee bullets wrapt in smoke and fire :
   Claim tribute where thou wilt, we are resolv'd—
   Honour is bought with blood, and not with gold.
                                   [*Exeunt.*

SCENE III.—*The Market Place.*

Enter Officers, *with* ITHAMORE *and other* Slaves.

First Off. This is the market place ; here let 'em stand :
   Fear not their sale, for they'll be quickly bought.
Sec. Off. Every one's price is written on his back,
   And so much must they yield, or not be sold.
First Off. Here comes the Jew : had not his goods bin
      seiz'd,
   He'd give us present money for them all.

54. *thee*] Reed, etc. : *the* Q.

Act II. Scene iii.

Added by Bull., Ellis. *Enter . . . with Ithamore . . .*] Dyce, etc.,
with slaues Q to Rob., Wag.
   4. After *sold* Q has *Ent. Bar.*   5, 12. *bin*] Q : *been*, Reed, etc.   6. *give*]
Q to Dyce, Wag. : *given* Cunn. to Ellis.

and property, and also allowed the
people to leave Rhodes at any time
within the next three years, etc.
For a full account of the siege and
the treaty, see C. Torr's *Rhodes in
Modern Times*, 1887, p. 24 ff.
   54. *bullets . . . fire*] Bullen compares *King John*, II. i. 227 : 'And
now, instead of *bullets wrapt in fire* ',
but it is a reminiscence perhaps of
Tamburlaine, II. iii. 19 : ' And
bullets like Jove's dreadful thunder-
bolts, *Enrol'd in flames* and fiery
s mouldering mists.'

Scene III.

Scene III] This scene localises
i tself : ' *This is the market place* ', and
is on the outer-stage throughout.

Dyce and Bullen suggest a change
of scene at line 222, but this is
clearly impossible, since line 221 is
indissolubly linked to both what
precedes and what follows it.   The
scene remains as before, but we are
to suppose one of the side doors (or
less possibly the curtains of the
inner-stage) to represent Barabas'
house.
   6. *present money*] cash payment,
ready money.   The O.E.D. gives
no example before 1600, when it
quotes Blount's translation of
Conestaggio, p. 249 : ' To whom
they granted many things, as
titles, rents for life, offices, and to
some, *present money*.'

Enter BARABAS.

Bara. In spite of these swine-eating Christians,
    Unchosen nation, never circumcis'd ;
    Such as (poor villains) were ne'er thought upon
    Till Titus and Vespasian conquer'd us,   10
    Am I become as wealthy as I was :
    They hop'd my daughter would ha' bin a nun ;
    But she's at home, and I have bought a house
    As great and fair as is the governor's : ⎫
                                              ⎬
    And there, in spite of Malta, will I dwell,
    Having Ferneze's hand ; whose heart I'll have ;
    Ay, and his son's too, or it shall go hard.
    I am not of the tribe of Levi, I,
    That can so soon forget an injury.
    We Jews can fawn like spaniels when we please ; 20
    And when we grin we bite ; yet are our looks
    As innocent and harmless as a lamb's.
    I learn'd in Florence how to kiss my hand,
    Heave up my shoulders when they call me dog,

8–10. *Unchosen . . . us*] All in brackets in Q.   9. *as* (*poor villains*)]
Q, Rob. (without brackets), Bull., Ellis, Wag.: *poor villains as* Reed,
Coll.: *Poor villains such as* Dyce, Cunn.   12. *ha'*] Q, Dyce, Bull., Ellis,
Wag.: *have* Reed, Coll., Rob., Cunn.

9. *villains*] serfs (*villani*), men of
no consequence. Much used by
Elizabethan writers.
    10. *Titus . . . us*] The campaign
against Judea in the years 66–70
was conducted first by Vespasian,
and after his recall to Rome as
emperor in 69 by his son Titus, who
finally took the city of Jerusalem on
the 8th of September, 70.
    16. *Having Ferneze's hand*] with
the assent of Ferneze, or perhaps
with a written guarantee of safety
from him. The name Ferneze probably due to the fame of Alexander
Farnese, Duke of Parma. Used by
Jonson in *Volpone* and *The Case is
Altered*.
    18. *tribe of Levi*] There seems to
be nothing to show that the priestly
caste were so forgiving. The injury

to the Levite in Judges xix., etc.,
was terribly avenged. Meyer (*op.
cit.*) suggests that ' this idea of an
injury never forgot probably came
from Gentillet, iii. 6 '.
    23–5. *I learned in Florence . . .
friar*] Florence, the home of
Machiavelli. A good example of
the popular Elizabethan conception
of Machiavelli's policy and teaching. The whole of the passage
reminds us of Shylock's famous out-
burst, i. iii. 110 ff., in a later play.
Compare also Shakespeare's picture
of the Florentine ceremonious kiss-
ing of hands in *Othello*, ii. i. 168 ff.
Meyer (*op. cit.*) takes the reference
to Florence as meant to suggest
discipleship to Machiavelli, but
adds that not a word of this speech
really comes from the Italian.

And duck as low as any bare-foot friar ;
Hoping to see them starve upon a stall,
Or else be gather'd for in our synagogue,
That, when the offering-basin comes to me,
Even for charity I may spit into't.
Here comes Don Lodowick, the governor's son,   30
One that I love for his good father's sake.

Enter LODOWICK.

Lod. I hear the wealthy Jew walked this way :
I'll seek him out, and so insinuate,
That I may have a sight of Abigail ;
For Don Mathias tells me she is fair.
*Bara. Now will I show myself to have more of the serpent
than the dove ; that is, more knave than fool.   [Aside.*
Lod. Yond' walks the Jew : now for fair Abigail.
Bara. Ay, ay, no doubt but she's at your command.   [Aside.
Lod. Barabas, thou know'st I am the governor's son.   40

36-7. *Now . . . fool*] Q to Dyce, Wag. Three lines div. after *myself,
dove* ; Cunn. to Ellis. *than*] Reed, etc. : *then* Q. 37. *Aside*] Dyce,
Bull., Ellis : *omit* others.   39. *Aside*] Dyce, Cunn. to Ellis : *omit*
others.

25. *duck . . . friar*] See again
for the use of ' duck ' as a term of
derision for the behaviour of Friars
below in Act III. iii. 55. It is also
used in Heywood's *The Captives*,
I. ii. 122 : ' When we *duck* or
congee', and in *Lust's Dominion*
(Hazlitt's *Dodsley*, XIV., p. 125) :
' Come, hands off, leave your *duck-
ing.*' Cf. McKerrow's note in his
edition of Nashe, III. 78.

26. *starve . . . stall*] A stall was
' a bench or form where anything
was set for sale ' (Johnson). Did
Barabas hope to see the Christians
exposed for sale, and starving for
lack of purchasers ?

27. *gather'd for*] a collection made
for. An indirect passive form now
obsolete. The O.E.D. gives also a
quotation from Dr. King's *Sermons*,
57 : ' Few Sundays come over our
head, but decayed householders, or

shipwrackt merchants are *gathered
for*'.

28-9. *offering-basin . . . spit
into't*] Cf. Jonson's *Magnetic Lady*,
v. vi. : ' if my sister Will bid an
offering for her maid and him, As
a benevolence to them, after supper,
I'll *spit* into the *bason.*'

31. *One . . . sake*] With the
irony here, compare *Edward II*,
I. i. 128.

33. *insinuate*] to bring oneself
into   favour,   ingratiate.   Cf.
Richard III, I. iv. 146 : ' He would
insinuate with thee but to make thee
sigh.'

36. *serpent . . . dove*] A reminiscence of Matthew x. 16 : ' Be ye
therefore wise as serpents, and
harmless as doves.' Barabas has
withdrawn somewhat at the entry
of Lodowick, and is only seen by
him after this, at line 38.

Bara. I would you were his father too, sir ! that's all the
harm I wish you : *The slave looks like a hog's cheek new
singed.*   [*Aside.*

Lod. Whither walk'st thou, Barabas ?

Bara. No further : 'tis a custom held with us,
That when we speak with Gentiles like to you,
We turn into the air to purge ourselves ;
For unto us the promise doth belong.

Lod. Well, Barabas, canst help me to a diamond ?

Bara. O, sir, your father had my diamonds.   50
Yet I have one left that will serve your turn:
*I mean my daughter ; but, ere he shall have her,
I'll sacrifice her on a pile of wood :
I ha' the poison of the city for him,
And the white leprosy.*   [*Aside.*

Lod. What sparkle does it give without a foil ?

41–3. *I . . . singed*] Two lines prose in Q, Reed, Coll., Dyce, Wag.
As verse in two lines div. after *harm* Rob. : as verse in three lines div.
after *sir, looks* Cunn., Bull., Ellis.   43. *Aside*] Rob., Dyce, Cunn. to Ellis:
omit Q to Coll., Wag.   47. *into*] Q to Rob., Dyce² to Wag. : *unto* Dyce¹.
55. *Aside*] Rob. to Ellis : *after line* 53 Q to Coll., Wag.

42, 43. *The slave ... singed*] Alluding to Lodowick's ostentatiously
well-shaven face—a sign of the
well-groomed man.   Cf.   Eno-
barbus's picture of Antony when
he first visited Cleopatra, ' Being
barber'd ten times o'er ', II. iii.
232. Holthausen (*op. cit.*) reads :
' I would you were his father too,
[good] Sir ;
That's all the harm I wish you—
The slave looks like a hog's cheek
new[ly] singed.'

47. *We turn . . . ourselves.*] Is
this merely an excuse on the part of
Barabas to explain his action in his
previous speech when he has turned
aside to address the audience ?
Or is it, perchance, Marlowe's
personal experience or prejudice ?

54. *poison of the city*] A difficult
passage.   Dyce conjectures that
' City ' is a misprint, but gives no
reasons.   Koeppel would read
' cicuta ', and Holthausen proposes
' Styx '.   Koeppel further proposed

to alter ' I ' at the beginning of the
line to ' And '.   Perhaps what
Barabas refers to is III. iv. 64 : ' It
is a precious powder that I bought,
Of an Italian, in Ancona ', etc.

55. *white leprosy*] certain stages
of this disease are characterised by
a white flaky series of scales which
were considered to be highly con-
tagious.   The leper was thus often
thought of in this most repulsive
and terrifying state.

56. *foil*] A thin leaf of metal
placed under a gem to set off its
brilliancy.   This passage from
Marlowe is the first use in this sense
quoted in the O.E.D.   Barabas in
his reply to Lodowick means that
Abigail is as yet secluded from the
world and has not been presented
to adult company in all the magni-
ficence of a rich man's only child.
The opulent setting he could afford
her would be a foil to her own
beauty.   In the next line he plays
on another use of the word *foiled*

Bara. The diamond that I talk of ne'er was foil'd :
    But, when he touches it, it will be foil'd :   [*Aside.*
    Lord Lodowick, it sparkles bright and fair.

Lod. Is it square or pointed ? pray, let me know.   60

Bara. Pointed it is, good sir,—*but not for you.*   [*Aside.*

Lod. I like it much the better.

Bara.   So do I too.

Lod. How shows it by night ?

Bara.   Outshines Cynthia's rays :—
    You'll like it better far a nights than days.   [*Aside.*

Lod. And what's the price ?

Bara. Your life, and if you have it [*Aside*].—O my lord,
    We will not jar about the price ; come to my house,
    And I will give't your honour—*with a vengeance.* [*Aside.*

Lod. No, Barabas, I will deserve it first.

Bara.   Good sir,
    Your father has deserv'd it at my hands,   70
    Who, of mere charity and Christian ruth,
    To bring me to religious purity,

---

58. *Aside*] Coll., Dyce to Ellis : *omit* Q, Reed, Rob., Wag. *it will*] Q to
Dyce : *he will* Cunn., Bull.   64. *a*] Q to Dyce¹, Wag. : *o'* Dyce ² to Ellis.
66. *and*] Q to Dyce¹, Wag.: *an* Dyce² to Ellis.   *Aside*] Coll. to Wag.:
omit Q, Reed. 69, 70. *Good . . . hands*] Dyce to Wag. : one line in Q to
Rob.   71. *ruth*] Q to Coll., Dyce, Wag. : *truth* Rob., Cunn., Bull., Ellis.

in the sense of *defiled.* Compare
Gascoigne's *Works* (1587), p. 300:
' Rather chose to die . . . than
filthie men should *foile* their
chastitie ', and McKerrow's *Nashe*,
II. 226 and note there.

    60. *square or pointed*] Cf.
Harrison, *Desc. of Eng.*, III. ix (ed.
Furnivall, II., p. 65): ' Sometime
also they find pretious stones
(though seldome) and some of them
perfectlie squared by nature, and
much like the diamond, found of
late in a quarrie of marble at Naples,
which was so perfectlie pointed, as if
all the workemen in the world had
consulted about the performance of
that workmanship.'

    61. *Pointed*] Note the play on
pointed and appointed implied here.

For a comparison of the lines 56–60
see Harington's *Epigrams*, Bk. I,
No. 4.   Of a pointed Diamond,
given by the Author to his wife. . . .
' The Gem is cleare, and hath nor
    needs no foile,
Thy face, nay more, thy fame is
    free from soile.'

    67. *jar*] quarrel or dispute. The
O.E.D. quotes Latimer's *Last
Sermon before Ed. VI* : ' They will
jer now a dayes one with an other,
excepte they have all.'

    71. *ruth*] There is no need to alter
to truth as do Robinson and others.
W. Wagner (*Shakespear Jahrb.*, XI.
73), using Cunningham's text,
actually proposes *ruth* as a conjectural emendation !

And, as it were, in catechising sort,
To make me mindful of my mortal sins,
Against my will, and whether I would or no,
Seiz'd all I had, and thrust me out a doors,
And made my house a place for nuns most chaste.

Lod. No doubt your soul shall reap the fruit of it.

Bara. Ay, but, my lord, the harvest is far off:
And yet I know the prayers of those nuns   80
And holy friars, having money for their pains,
Are wondrous ;—*and indeed do no man good ;* [*Aside.*
And, seeing they are not idle, but still doing,
'Tis likely they in time may reap some fruit,
I mean, in fullness of perfection.

Lod. Good Barabas, glance not at our holy nuns.

Bara. No, but I do it through a burning zeal,
Hoping ere long to set the house a-fire ;
For, though they do a while increase and multiply,
I'll have a saying to that nunnery.   [*Aside.*
As for the diamond, sir, I told you of,   91
Come home, and there's no price shall make us part,
Even for your honourable father's sake.
It shall go hard but I will see your death.   [*Aside.*
But now I must be gone to buy a slave.

Lod. And, Barabas, I'll bear thee company.

Bara. Come, then ; here's the market place.

---

76. *a*] Q to Dyce[1], Wag. : *o'* Dyce[2] to Ellis.   90. *saying*] Q, etc. : *savin* Dyce[1].

73. *in catechising sort*] in the manner of a catechist.

81. *holy friars*] Both W. Wagner and A. Wagner independently suggest the omission of ' holy '. The latter realises, however, that with some slurring of the words ' friars, having ' the line can be left.

90. *I'll have a saying to that nunnery*] I shall have something to say to that nunnery. Dyce quotes from Barnabe Barnes' *Divils Charter,* 1607 : ' For I must *have a saying to* those bottels.' *He drinketh.* His original emendation was *a savin,* which he supported by a quotation from Gerarde's *Herball,* p. 1378, ed. 1633 : ' The leaues of *Savin* boyled in wine and drunke . . . expell the dead childe, and kille the quick.' This has nothing but its ingenuity to commend it ! Cf. Dekker, *Shoemaker's Holiday,* II. v. 15 : ' They'll *have a saying to* you for this deed.'

What's the price of this slave ? two hundred crowns !
  do the Turks weigh so much ?
First Off. Sir, that's his price.   100
Bara. What, can he steal, that you demand so much ?
  Belike he has some new trick for a purse ;
  And if he has, he is worth three hundred plates,
  So that, being bought, the town seal might be got
  To keep him for his life-time from the gallows :
  The sessions-day is critical to thieves,
  And few or none 'scape but by being purg'd.
Lod. Rat'st thou this Moor but at two hundred plates ?
First Off. No more, my lord.
Bara. Why should this Turk be dearer than that Moor ? 110
First Off. Because he is young, and has more qualities.

97–99. *Come . . . much*] prose in Q, as verse div. after *place, crowns*
Cunn. 98. *What's . . . of*] Q, etc. : *What price is on* Cunn. 99. *Turks*]
Reed, etc. : *Turke* Q. 103. *And*] Q, etc. : *An* Dyce². 103, 108. *plates*]
plats Q.

102. *new trick . . . purse*] new
way of stealing a purse. Elizabethan literature has many references to this art, and that it had
reached a high state of development
may be inferred from a letter
written by Fleetwood to Lord
Burghley in 1585 describing an
academy of thieves : ' There were
hung up two devices—the one was
a pocket and the other a purse.
The pocket had in it certain
counters, and was hung about with
hawk's bells, and over the top did
hang a little scaring bell ; . . . and
he that could take a piece of silver
out of the purse without the noise
of any of the bells, he was adjudged
a judicial nipper, i.e. a pickpurse or
cutpurse.'

103. *And if*] if indeed—a common Elizabethan use, as in *Richard
II*, IV. i. 49 : ' *And if* I do not, may
my hands rot off ! ' In modern
editions this is often printed as *an if*,
just as and = if is printed as *an*.
See textual note to line 112.

plates] pieces of silver money,
especially used of the Spanish
coin *real de plata*, the eighth

part of a piastre or Spanish
dollar. See Tyndale's version of
Matthew xxvii. 3 : ' xxx plattes
of silver ', and *Antony and Cleopatra*, V. ii. 92 :
  ' realms and islands were,
As *plates* drop'd from his pocket,'
and also *Faerie Queene*, II. 7. v.

103–7. *And if . . . purg'd*]
This passage is a little difficult but
seems to mean : ' If he has a new
way of purse-stealing, he is worth
three hundred plates, provided that
a perpetual pardon or charter with
the town-seal upon it can be got to
keep him from the gallows, since the
Sessions-days are crucial to thieves,
and few or none escape except they
are purged of their offences.' Here
purgation seems to imply clearing by trial as in *Winter's Tale*,
III. ii. 7 : ' This session . . . Let
us . . . Proceed to justice . . .
Even to the guilt or the *purgation* ',
and see *As You Like It*, V. iv. 105 :
' Let him put me to my *purgation*.'
There may possibly be some reference to the clearing by sworn testimony as to character, as in the
Anglo-Saxon compurgation.

Bara. What, hast the philosopher's stone ? and thou hast,
  break my head with it, I'll forgive thee.

Slave. No, sir ; I can cut and shave.

Bara. Let me see, sirrah ; are you not an old shaver ?

Slave. Alas, sir, I am a very youth !

Bara. A youth ! I'll buy you, and marry you to Lady
  Vanity, if you do well.

Slave. I will serve you, sir.

Bara. Some wicked trick or other. It may be, under
  colour of shaving, thou'lt cut my throat for my goods.
  Tell me, hast thou thy health well ?   123

Slave. Ay, passing well.

Bara. So much the worse : I must have one that's sickly,
  and't be but for sparing victuals : 'tis not a stone of
  beef a day will maintain you in these chops. Let me
  see one that's somewhat leaner.

---

112. *and*] Q to Rob., Bull., Wag. : *an* Dyce, Cunn., Ellis, 114.
Slave] Reed, etc. : *Itha* Q. And so in lines 116, 119, 123. 125.
and't] Reed, Coll. : *and* Q, Rob., Cunn., Bull. : *an't* Coll., Dyce, Ellis, Wag.

112. *philosopher's stone*] A solid
substance supposed by alchemists
to possess the property of changing
other metals into gold or silver.
According to some it had the power
of curing all wounds and diseases.
Hence in part the assurance of
Barabas. Cf. *The Alchemist*, I. i.
454.
  and] if. In common use among
our early writers. See Abbott,
§ 101.
  114. *Slave.*] The Quarto mis-
printed Ithamore's name here,
confusing the two slaves.
  115. *old shaver*] Originally a term
of contempt applied to clerics with
their shaven crowns. Dekker,
*Belman of London (Lanthorne and
Candlelight)* 1608, Dent, p. 262,
speaking of certain money cheats,
has : ' Oh Fleete-Streete ! Fleete-
streete ! how hast thou bene trimd,
washed, *Shaven* and Polde by these
deere and damnable Barbers ? '
  117. *Lady Vanity,*] A well-known
allegorical character in the old
Moralities. In Jonson's *The Devil
is an Ass*, I. i., we have : ' *Sat.* What
Vice ? What kind would'st thou
have it of ? *Pug.* Why any.
Fraud, or Covetousness, or *Lady
Vanity*, or Old Iniquity '. *Lady
Vanity* is also a character in the
interlude called *The Marriage of
Witt and Wisedome* in the play of
Sir Thomas More. Jonson, *Volpone*,
II. iii. 21 : ' Get you a cittern, *Lady
Vanity,*' etc.
  124. *So much the worse . . .*]
Compare with Shylock's grudging
testimony, *Merchant of Venice*,
II. v. 46 : ' The patch is kind enough,
but a huge feeder ', and see also earlier
in the same scene his complaint of
Lancelot as one who ' gormandises '.
  126. *chops*] Used contemptuously
or humorously of the jaws, and of
the mouth. Another form of *chaps.*
Here used to signify a bloated or
fat face, as in 2 *Henry IV*, II. iv .214,
or Middleton's *Blurt, Master-Constable,* I. ii, ' You *chops* ! '

7

First Off. Here's a leaner ; how like you him ?

Bara. Where wast thou born ?

Itha. In Thrace ; brought up in Arabia.   130

Bara. So much the better ; thou art for my turn.
      An hundred crowns ?   I'll have him ; there's the coin.
            [*Gives money.*

First Off. Then mark him, sir, and take him hence.

Bara. *Ay, mark him, you were best ; for this is he*
      That by my help shall do much villany.   [*Aside.*
      My lord, farewell : Come, sirrah, you are mine.
      As for the diamond, it shall be yours :
      I pray, sir, be no stranger at my house ;
      All that I have shall be at your command.

            Enter MATHIAS *and* KATHERINE.

Math. *What makes the Jew and Lodowick so private ?* 140
      I fear me 'tis about fair Abigail.   [*Aside.*

Bara. Yonder comes Don Mathias : let us stay ;
      He loves my daughter, and she holds him dear :
      But I have sworn to frustrate both their hopes,
      And be reveng'd upon the—*governor.*   [*Aside.*
            [*Exit Lodowick.*

Kath. This Moor is comeliest, is he not ?   speak, son.

---

129. *wast*] Reed, etc. : *was* Q, Dyce[1]. 132. *Gives money*] Dyce, Ellis ; *omit* others. 133, *sir*] Q, etc. : *Barabas*, Wag. 135. *Aside*] Dyce to Ellis : *omit* others. 139. *Enter* . . .] Dyce : *Enter Mathias, Mater*, Q, Wag. : *Enter Mathias and his Mother*, Reed to Rob., Cunn. to Ellis. 140. *makes*] Q, etc. : *make* Dyce[2]. 141. *Aside*] Dyce, Ellis : *omit* others. 145. *Exit Lodowick*] Dyce : Bull., Ellis, after line 142 : *omit* others. *governor*] Add *Aside* Dyce.

133. *mark him*] put your mark on him. Barabas quibbles on this in the following line.

142-5.] Barabas says this confidentially to Lodowick, as part of his design to inflame Mathias. As Lodowick is going the Jew says in an aside the word *governor*—which was not what Lodowick, perhaps, would have expected ! He returns again at line 218.

142. *stay*] stop, cease our con-

versation. See T. Wilson's *Logic*, II. K. ij : ' Aesope coulde not utter his minde at large, but dyd stammer, and *staye* muche in his speche ' (O.E.D.).

145. *Exit Lodowick*.] Bullen and Ellis make Lodowick go out after line 142, but it seems probable that he heard all of Barabas's speech—except the last word. See note above, 142-5.

Math. No, this is the better, mother, view this well.

Bara. Seem not to know me here before your mother,
    Lest she mistrust the match that is in hand:
    When you have brought her home, come to my house;
    Think of me as thy father; son, farewell.   151

Math. But wherefore talk'd Don Lodowick with you?

Bara. Tush, man! we talk'd of diamonds, not of Abigail.

Kath. Tell me, Mathias, is not that the Jew?

Bara. As for the comment on the Maccabees,
    I have it, sir, and 'tis at your command.

Math. Yes, madam, and my talk with him was [but]
    About the borrowing of a book or two.

Kath. Converse not with him; he is cast off from heaven.
    Thou hast thy crowns, fellow. Come, let's away. 160

Math. Sirrah Jew, remember the book.

Bara.   Marry, will I, sir.
            [*Exeunt Katherine and Mathias.*

First Off. Come, I have made a reasonable market; let's
    away.   [*Exeunt Officers with Slaves.*

Bara. Now let me know thy name, and therewithal
    Thy birth, condition, and profession.

Itha. Faith, sir, my birth is but mean; my name's
    Ithamore; my profession what you please.

Bara. Hast thou no trade? then listen to my words,
    And I will teach [thee] that shall stick by thee:
    First, be thou void of these affections,   170
    Compassion, love, vain hope, and heartless fear,
    Be mov'd at nothing, see thou pity none,
    But to thyself smile when the Christians moan.

157. [*but*]] Dyce, Bull., Ellis, Wag.: *omit* others. 161. *book*] Q, etc.:
books Reed, Coll. 162. *Exeunt . . .*] Dyce, etc.: *After line* 160 Q, Rob.:
After book, line 161, Reed, Coll. 162. *a*] Q, etc.: *omit* Ellis. 163. *Exeunt . . .*]
Dyce, Bull., Ellis: *omit* Q, Rob., Cunn., Wag.: *Exit* Reed, Coll. 169.
[*thee*]] Reed, etc.: *omit* Q.

155. *comment . . . Maccabees,*] a   167. *Ithamore*] Ithamar was one
disquisition or commentary on the   of the sons of Aaron, see Numbers
Book of Maccabees, naturally of   xxvi. 60.
great interest to the Jews.

Itha. O, brave, master ! I worship your nose for this.
Bara. As for myself, I walk abroad a nights
    And kill sick people groaning under walls :
    Sometimes I go about and poison wells ;
    And now and then, to cherish Christian thieves,
    I am content to lose some of my crowns,
    That I may, walking in my gallery,   180
    See 'em go pinion'd along by my door.
    Being young, I studied physick, and began
    To practise first upon the Italian ;
    There I enrich'd the priests with burials,
    And always kept the sexton's arms in ure
    With digging graves and ringing dead men's knells :

175. *a*] Q to Dyce[1], Wag. : *o'* Dyce[2] to Ellis.   181. *pinion'd along*] Q.
etc. : *along pinion'd* Elze conj.   184. *enrich'd*] Reed, etc. : *enric'd* Q.
185. *ure*] Q, etc. : *use* Rob.

174. *worship your nose*] It was evidently an important part of the make-up of Barabas that he should wear a huge false nose, for we find W. Rowley in *A Search for Money* (1609 : Percy Soc. reprint, 1840, p. 19) describes Monsieur Money with ' his visage (or vizard) like the artificial Jewe of Maltaes nose . . . upon which nose, two casements were built, through which his eyes had a little ken of us ' (Reed). See also Chapman's *The Blind Beggar of Alexandria* (Parrott's edn., p. 16), Sc. iii. 28 ff. Cleanthes, disguised as the usurer, has a big nose, and Samathis (l. 141) exclaims 'Oh ! he hath a great nose', to which her maid answers, ' 'Tis no matter for his nose, for he is rich'. See also Creizenach, *Geschichte des neueren Dramas*, IV. 514, for other examples of this convention.

175. *As for myself . . .*] This passage from *The Jew* is quoted by Mr. T. S. Eliot in his short study of Marlowe's blank verse (*The Sacred Wood*, p. 84) as an example of the new tone which the dramatist develops in his versification to suit 'this farce . . . of the old English humour, the terribly serious, even savage comic humour, the humour which spent its last breath on the decadent genius of Dickens.' Barabas, in Mr. Eliot's view, is nothing less than ' a prodigious caricature '. For comment on this see *Intro.*, p. 16, and compare the passage in *Titus Andronicus*, v. i. 98 ff., where Aaron discourses in much the same fashion concerning his wholesale villanies, as noted by Bullen.

180. *in my gallery*] The platform or balcony constructed on the outside of a house, at some distance from the ground. See note at beginning of Act III.

181. *See 'em go pinion'd . . .*] Elze writes (*op. cit.*, 2nd Series, iii.), ' The second line hardly admits of scansion. Perhaps the words should be transposed : " See 'em go | along | pini | on'd by | my door ".' Brereton suggests omitting ' by ', and cites *Arden of Feversham*, l. 128 : ' Come this morning but *along my door.*'

185. *kept . . . in ure*] in regular use or exercise. *Ure* was frequently used in conjunction with *keep* about 1580 and for a century afterwards. The O.E.D. gives from Latimer's *Sermons* (Parker Soc.), p. 416 : ' I pray you, *keep* your hand *in ure.*'

And, after that, was I an engineer,
And in the wars 'twixt France and Germany,
Under pretence of helping Charles the Fifth,
Slew friend and enemy with my stratagems :   190
Then, after that, was I an usurer,
And with extorting, cozening, forfeiting,
And tricks belonging unto brokery,
I fill'd the gaols with bankrouts in a year,
And with young orphans planted hospitals ;
And every moon made some or other mad.
And now and then one hang himself for grief,
Pinning upon his breast a long great scroll
How I with interest tormented him.
But mark how I am blest for plaguing them ;   200
I have as much coin as will buy the town.
But tell me now, how hast thou spent thy time ?
Itha. Faith, master,
In setting Christian villages on fire,
Chaining of eunuchs, binding galley slaves.
One time I was an hostler in an inn,
And in the night time secretly would I steal

---

194. *bankrouts*] Q : *bankrupts* Reed, etc.   207. *I*] Q, etc.: *omit* Coll.
(MS.) conj., Cunn.

189. *Charles the Fifth*] Charles V
(1500–1558), Roman emperor and
(as Charles I) king of Spain, was
engaged in war with Francis I (Italy
being the stake) on two occasions, a
final peace being made at Crépy in
1544. It is important to note,
in connection with the theory of
Kellner identifying Juan Migues
as the prototype of Barabas (see
Intro., p. 9), that M. A. Levy in
his monograph on Migues tells us
that he was connected with the
great banking family of Mendez
which financed Charles V and
Francis I, and that he himself was
involved in these interests.

192. *cozening*] cheating, fraudu-
lent dealing. The O.E.D. gives a
quotation from 1576—Fleming,
Caius' Eng. Dogges (1880), p. 27 :

'With colourable shifts and cloudy
cossening.'

193. *brokery*] The business of a
broker. In Barabas' case it refers,
no doubt, to the various methods,
more or less dishonest, by which he
acted as middleman in transactions.
Bishop Hall in his *Satires*, written
soon after *The Jew*, speaks of those
who ' busie their braines with
deeper *brokerie*' (1753 edn., p. 28).

206–8.   *hostler . . . throats*]
Medieval inns, innkeepers and their
servants were favourite subjects for
satire and condemnation. See, for
example, *Statutes of the Realm*, I.
102 : ' Such offenders . . . going
about by night, do commonly
resort and have their meetings and
hold their evil talk in taverns more
than elsewhere, and there do seek

To travellers' chambers, and there cut their throats:
Once at Jerusalem, where the pilgrims kneel'd,
I strewed powder on the marble stones,   210
And therewithal their knees would rankle, so
That I have laugh'd a-good to see the cripples
Go limping home to Christendom on stilts.

Bara. Why, this is something : make account of me
As of thy fellow ; we are villains both :
Both circumcised ; we hate Christians both :
Be true and secret ; thou shalt want no gold.
But stand aside, here comes Don Lodowick.

Enter LODOWICK.

Lod. O Barabas, well met ;
Where is the diamond you told me of ?   220
Bara. I have it for you, sir ; please you walk in with me :
What, ho, Abigail ! open the door, I say !

Enter ABIGAIL.

Abig. In good time, father ; here are letters come
From Ormus, and the post stays here within.

---

221. *please you*] Q, etc.: *please* Wag.   222. *Enter* . . .] Q, etc.:
Enter . . . *with letters* Dyce, Ellis.

shelter, lying in wait and watching
their time to do mischief' (1285).
And all readers of *The Cloister
and the Hearth* will remember the
tavern-scenes depicted there.

211. *rankle*] Here used in its strict
sense, it means ' to fester '.

212. *a-good*] heartily. See *Two
Gentlemen of Verona*, IV. 4, 170:

' And at that time I made her weep
    a good,
For I did play a lamentable part,'

and Collier quotes from Turber-
ville's *Songes and Sonets*, p. 37 :

' It makes me *laugh a good* to see thee
    lowre
And long to looken sad.'

213. *stilts*] crutches. Compare
The Tale of Beryn, 2380 :

' A crepill he saw comyng
Oppon a *stilt* vnder his kne.'

215. *villains both*] This frank
avowal of villainy is . utterly at
variance with the self-justification
of Barabas in his earlier speeches,
and is part of the whole change of
attitude suggested in the speech
above, ll. 175 ff.

222. *What, ho, . . .*] Dyce and
Bullen note here that the scene
shifts to the front of Barabas'
house.   More probably his house
was meant to be represented by one
of the side-doors, as abutting on to
the market place.   It is only this
that is necessary—a door was sufficient to localise the whole thing
for the Elizabethans. (See note on
p. 78.)

224. *Ormus*] The famous city on

Bara. Give me the letters.   Daughter, do you hear ?
   Entertain Lodowick, the governor's son,
   With all the courtesy you can afford,
   Provided that you keep your maidenhead :
   Use him as if he were a—*Philistine ;*
   Dissemble, swear, protest, vow to love him,   230
   He is not of the seed of Abraham.   *[Aside.*
   I am a little busy, sir ; pray, pardon me.
   Abigail, bid him welcome for my sake.

Abig. For your sake and his own he's welcome hither.

Bara. Daughter, a word more ; *kiss him, speak him fair,*
   And like a cunning Jew so cast about,
   That ye be both made sure ere you come out.

Abig. O father, Don Mathias is my love !

Bara. I know it : yet, I say, make love to him ;
   Do, it is requisite it should be so.   *[Aside to her.*
   Nay, on my life, it is my factor's hand ;   241
   But go you in, I'll think upon the account.
       [Exeunt Abigail and Lodowick.

230. *to love*] Q, etc. : *love to* Dyce conj., Bull., Ellis, Wag.   231. *Aside*] Coll. to Cunn., Ellis : *After line* 229 Q, Wag. : *After line* 233 Bull. 237. Dyce, Bull., Ellis here add *Aside to her* : *omit* the rest : *After line* 235 Cunn. 240. *Aside* . . .] Dyce, Bull., Ellis : *omit* the rest. 242. *Exeunt* . . .] Reed, etc. : *Exeunt . . . into the house* Dyce, Ellis : *omit* Q, Wag.

the shores of the Persian Gulf.   It was renowned for its trade in spices, drugs, silks, pearls, etc.   It recalls to us the traffic Barabas had with the Arabians and their wedges of gold (I. i. 8 ff.).

224. *post*] a messenger or letter-carrier.   Compare *Edward II*, v. i. 128 : ' Another *post* !   What news brings he ', and 2 *Henry IV*, Induct. 37 :

   ' the *Postes* come tyring on,
 And not a man of them brings
   other newes.'

230. *to love him*] Dyce conjectured, and subsequent editors adopted his conjecture, that this should read, *love to him*, on the

grounds that it is so printed in lines 239 and 248.   This is very uncertain, and the original had better stand. Wagner's statement that the B.M. copies read *tol oue* is inaccurate.

237. *made sure*] betrothed.   Bullen quotes Cotgrave's definition, ' Accordailles, the betrothing or *making sure* of a man and woman together '.   Compare Middleton's *The Roaring Girl*, III. ii. 122 : ' To him was I *made sure* 'ith' sight of heaven.'   See also below line 336, and again *contract* in III. vi. 22.

242. *Exeunt* . . .] A necessary S.D., as is seen by l. 276, where the Quarto reads, ' Enter Lodowicke and Abigall '.

The account is made, for Lodowick dies.
My factor sends me word a merchant's fled
That owes me for a hundred tun of wine :
I weigh it thus much [*snapping his fingers*] ! I have
    wealth enough.
For now by this has he kiss'd Abigail ;
And she vows love to him, and he to her.
As sure as heaven rain'd manna for the Jews,
So sure shall he and Don Mathias die :   250
His father was my chiefest enemy.

Enter MATHIAS.

Whither goes Don Mathias ? stay a while.
Math. Whither, but to my fair love Abigail ?
Bara. Thou know'st, and heaven can witness it is true,
    That I intend my daughter shall be thine.
Math. Ay, Barabas, or else thou wrong'st me much.
Bara. O, heaven forbid I should have such a thought.
    Pardon me though I weep ; the governor's son
    Will, whether I will or no, have Abigail ;
    He sends her letters, bracelets, jewels, rings.   260
Math. Does she receive them ?
Bara. She ? no, Mathias, no, but sends them back ;
    And, when he comes, she locks herself up fast ;
    Yet through the key-hole will he talk to her,
    While she runs to the window looking out

243. *Lodowick*] Q, Reed to Rob., Wag. : *Lodovico*, Dyce : *Lodowick he* Cunn., Bull., Ellis. 246. *snapping . . . fingers*] Dyce to Ellis : *omit* Q, Reed to Rob., Wag. 251. *Enter . . .*] Dyce to Ellis : *After line* 252 Q, Reed to Rob., Wag. 254. *it*] Q, etc. : *this* Rob., Cunn., Bull., Ellis.

243. *Lodowick dies*] Here, and again later (see III. ii. 6, 10), the metre calls for a word of four syllables, and Dyce, on the strength of *Lodovico* in III. iv. 8 so alters it throughout. This seems rash in face of the recurrence of the form Lodowick, though as Bullen points out in his note on III. ii. 6, an abbreviated form of ' Lodovico ', such as ' Lod ' or ' Lodo ', might have been wrongly interpreted by the printer. In this particular passage there seems to be a definite dramatic gain in allowing a slight pause before Barabas pronounces the final word *dies*, and therefore I have not adopted Dyce's conjecture or still less that of Cunningham.

251. *was*] This seems strange. We should rather expect *is*.

When you should come and hale him from the door.
Math. O treacherous Lodowick !
Bara. Even now, as I came home, he slipt me in,
    And I am sure he is with Abigail.
Math. I'll rouse him thence.   270
Bara. Not for all Malta ; therefore sheathe your sword ;
    If you love me, no quarrels in my house ;
    But steal you in, and seem to see him not :
    I'll give him such a warning ere he goes,
    As he shall have small hopes of Abigail.
    Away, for here they come.

       Enter LODOWICK *and* ABIGAIL.

Math. What, hand in hand ! I cannot suffer this.
Bara. Mathias, as thou lov'st me, not a word.
Math. Well, let it pass ; another time shall serve. [*Exit.*
Lod. Barabas, is not that the widow's son ?   280
Bara. Ay, and take heed, for he hath sworn your death.
Lod. My death ! what, is the base-born peasant mad ?
Bara. No, no ; but happily he stands in fear
    Of that which you, I think, ne'er dream upon,
    My daughter here, a paltry silly girl.
Lod. Why, loves she Don Mathias ?
Bara. Doth she not with her smiling answer you ?
Abig. *He has my heart ; I smile against my will.* [*Aside.*
Lod. Barabas, thou know'st I have lov'd thy daughter long.
Bara. And so has she done you, even from a child. 290
Lod. And now I can no longer hold my mind.
Bara. Nor I the affection that I bear to you.
Lod. This is thy diamond ; tell me, shall I have it ?

---

270. *rouse*] Reed, etc. : *rouze*, Q, Rob., Wag.   278. *lov'st*] Q to Dyce,
Wag. : *lovest* Cunn. to Ellis.   279. *Exit*] Q to Rob., Cunn., Bull., Wag. :
Exit into the house Dyce, Ellis.   282. *My . . . mad*] Q, etc. : *omit* Reed,
Coll.   288. *Aside*] Dyce, etc. : *omit* Q to Rob.

270. *rouse*] a metaphor from
hunting : strictly to drive a beast
from his lair. Hence used figuratively by Mathias to show his
disdain for his rival. Compare

Richard II, ii. iii. 128 : ' To *rouse*
his wrongs and chase them to the
bay.'
  283. *happily*] haply—by chance.

Bara. Win it, and wear it ; it is yet unsoil'd.
      O, but I know your lordship would disdain
      To marry with the daughter of a Jew :
      And yet I'll give her many a golden cross,
      With Christian posies round about the ring.
Lod. 'Tis not thy wealth, but her that I esteem ;
      Yet crave I thy consent.   300
Bara. And mine you have ; yet let me talk to her.—
      This offspring of Cain, this Jebusite,
      That never tasted of the Passover,
      Nor e'er shall see the land of Canaan,
      Nor our Messias that is yet to come ;
      This gentle maggot, Lodowick, I mean,

294. *unsoil'd*] Q, Reed, Rob., Dyce, etc. : *unfoil'd* Coll. conj., Wag.   297.
yet] Reed to Wag. : *yer* Q.   *After line* 308 *Aside* Reed to Ellis : *After line*
305 Q, Rob., Wag.   310. *It's*] Q, Rob., to Wag. : *It is* Reed, Coll.

294. *unsoil'd*] It is tempting to
read with Collier and Wagner
unfoil'd—a very simple compositor's
error. Earlier in this scene (line 58)
we have heard Barabas say, ' But
when he touches it (i.e. Abigail), it
will be foil'd (i.e. defiled) '. The two
words, however, bear so similar a
meaning that it seems best to leave
the Quarto reading undisturbed.
    297. *golden cross*] A piece of
money having a representation of
a cross marked on one side of it.
For example, the Portuguese coins
called ' crusadoes ' current in
Shakespeare's time were stamped
with a cross. They were of gold
and valued at three shillings of
English money. This was one of the
hoary jokes of Elizabethan writers ;
see e.g. *As You Like It,* II. iv. 10 :
' I should bear no *cross* if I did bear
you, for I think you have no money
in your purse ', and cf. *2 Henry IV*,
I. ii. 223 ff., *Every Man in his
Humour*, v. i. etc.
    298. *posies*] mottoes : see *The
Art of English Poesie* (Arber, p. 72) :
' Of short Epigrames called Posies
. . . we . . . do paint them now a
dayes upon the backe sides of our
fruite trenchers of wood, or use them

as devices in rings and armes.'
Compare also *The Merchant of
Venice*, v. i. 147 :

' A hoop of gold, a paltry ring,
That she did give me, whose *poesy*
          was
. . . ' Love me, and leave me not.'

Here *posies* refers to the superscrip-
tion round the edge of the coins.
    302. *Jebusites*]   A   tribe   of
Canaanites who were dispossessed
of Jerusalem by King David. The
passage perhaps was suggested by
a reminiscence of Judges xix. 11 ff. :
' and the servant said unto his
master, Come I pray thee, and let
us turn in into this city of the
Jebusites, and lodge in it. And
his master said to him, We will not
turn aside hither into the city of a
stranger, that is *not of the children
of Israel.*'
    306. *gentle maggot*] The usual
play on the two words, *gentle* and
Gentile is here intended by Marlowe. See, for a good example,
Kyd's *Jeronimo*, Part I (ed. F. S.
Boas, p. 337) : ' So good night,
kind *gentles*, For I hope thers nevere
a jew among you all.' And compare
Shakespeare's ' We all expect a

Must be deluded : let him have thy hand,
But keep thy heart till Don Mathias comes. |
Abig. *What, shall I be betroth'd to Lodowick ?*
Bara. *It's no sin to deceive a Christian ;*   310
For they themselves hold it a principle,
Faith is not to be held with heretics :
But all are heretics that are not Jews ; \
This follows well, and therefore, daughter, fear not. \ *[Aside.*
I have entreated her, and she will grant.
Lod. Then, gentle Abigail, plight thy faith to me.
Abig. I cannot choose, seeing my father bids :
Nothing but death shall part my love and me.
Lod. Now have I that for which my soul hath long'd. 319
Bara. *So have not I ; but yet I hope I shall.*   *[Aside.*
Abig. *O wretched Abigail, what hast thou done ?*   *[Aside.*
Lod. Why on the sudden is your colour chang'd ?
Abig. I know not : but farewell ; I must be gone.
Bara. Stay her, but let her not speak one word more.

314. *Aside*] Dyce to Ellis : *omit* Q to Rob., Wag.   315. S.D. *To Lodowick*
in Rob., Cunn.: *omit* the rest.   321. *thou*] Coll. to Ellis : *thee* Q, Reed,
Wag.   *Aside*] Dyce to Ellis : *omit* Q to Rob., Wag.

gentle answer, Jew' (*Merchant of
Venice*, IV. i. 34). There is also a
play on *gentle* = ' maggot, or
bait '. *Maggot* at a later date than
this came to mean a capricious
or whimsical person, but here
Barabas is using the term in its most
offensive light—and speaks of Lodowick as a mere grub—a crawling,
insignificant worm.
   310. *It's no sin . . .*] Despite two
abominably weak lines this passage
echoes the same idea Marlowe states
in more characteristic vein in
2 *Tamburlaine*, II. i. 32 ff. :
   'for with such infidels,
In whom no faith nor true religion
   rests,
We are not bound to those accomplishments,
The holy laws of Christendom
   enjoin.'
See note in Miss Fermor's ed.
(*ad loc.*).

   314. *This follows well*] The
technical language of the logic
school, see Wagner in *Faustus*, 202 :
' Yes I know, but that follows not ',
and 212, etc.
   316. *plight thy faith*] The plighting
of faith, or betrothal, was a most
solemn act in medieval times, and
once two people had said the few
necessary words (generally in the
presence of a witness) they were
' contracted together ' and almost
indissolubly bound to each other.
Hence Barabas can say after this
with real truth, ' She is thy wife '.
   324. *Stay her*] *Stay* seems to be
used here, as usually, to mean
' Arrest ' or ' Stop '. Is it possible
it may be used in the sense of ' support ' or ' hold up ' ? Compare
Faerie Queene, I. vi. 35 :

' And in his hand a Iacob's staffe,
To *staye* his wearie limbes upon.'

Lod. Mute o' the sudden ! here's a sudden change.

Bara. O, muse not at it ; 'tis the Hebrews' guise,
　　That maidens new-betrothed should weep a while :
　　Trouble her not ; sweet Lodowick, depart :
　　She is thy wife, and thou shalt be mine heir.

Lod. O, is't the custom ? then I am resolv'd :　　　　330
　　But rather let the brightsome heavens be dim,
　　And nature's beauty choke with stifling clouds,
　　Than my fair Abigail should frown on me.—
　　There comes the villain ; now I'll be reveng'd.

Enter MATHIAS.

Bara. Be quiet, Lodowick ; it is enough
　　That I have made thee sure to Abigail.

Lod. Well, let him go.　　　　　　　　　　[*Exit.*

Bara. Well, but for me, as you went in at doors
　　You had bin stabb'd : but not a word on't now ;
　　Here must no speeches pass, nor swords be drawn. 340

Math. Suffer me, Barabas, but to follow him.

Bara. No ; so shall I, if any hurt be done,
　　Be made an accessary of your deeds :
　　Revenge it on him when you meet him next.

Math. For this I'll have his heart.

Bara. Do so. Lo, here I give thee Abigail !

325. *o' the*] Reed to Ellis : *a the* Q, Wag.　331. *rather*] Reed, etc : *rathe* Q.
343. *accessary*] Q to Coll., Dyce, Bull., Wag. : *accessory* Rob., Cunn., Ellis.

326. *guise*] custom or habit. The word was commonly used in this sense in the Elizabethan period. For the idea see Judges xi. 37 ff. : ' Let me alone two months, that I may go up and down upon the mountains, and bewail my virginity, I and my fellows.'

330. *resolv'd*] satisfied, freed from doubt. Compare Fletcher's *Faithful Shepherdess*, ii. 184 : ' I am re-solved my Chloe yet is true ', and *Julius Caesar*, III. i. 131, etc.

331. *rather*] The Quarto reading *rathe* is a misprint found in all the copies I have examined.

brightsome] The O.E.D. says ' it is a vaguer word than *bright*, leaving more to the imagination '.

338. *as . . . at doors*] This must refer to Mathias' exit at line 279, when he passes Lodowick and Abigail who have just emerged. Barabas takes the opportunity of exacerbating the rancour between the two.

343. *accessary*] The correct spelling, so that the modernisation of Robinson and others may be ignored. See Shakespeare, *Richard III*, I. ii. 192 : ' To both their deaths shalt thou be *accessary* ', etc.

Math. What greater gift can poor Mathias have ?
    Shall Lodowick rob me of so fair a love ?
    My life is not so dear as Abigail.
Bara. My heart misgives me, that, to cross your love/ 350
    He's with your mother, therefore after him.
Math. What, is he gone unto my mother ?
Bara. Nay, if you will, stay till she comes herself.
Math. I cannot stay ; for, if my mother come,
    She'll die with grief.   [*Exit.*
Abig. I cannot take my leave of him for tears :
    Father, why have you thus incens't them both ?
Bara. What's that to thee ?
Abig.   I'll make 'em friends again.
Bara. You'll make 'em friends ! are there not Jews enow
    in Malta,
    But thou must dote upon a Christian ?   360
Abig. I will have Don Mathias ; he is my love.
Bara. Yes, you shall have him : Go, put her in.
Itha. Ay, I'll put her in.   [*Puts in Abigail.*
Bara. Now tell me, Ithamore, how lik'st thou this ?
Itha. Faith, master, I think by this
    You purchase both their lives ; is it not so ?
Bara. True ; and it shall be cunningly perform'd.
Itha. O, master, that I might have a hand in this !
Bara. Ay, so thou shalt ; 'tis thou must do the deed :
    Take this, and bear it to Mathias straight.   370
                         [*Gives a letter.*

---

357. *incens't*] Q, Wag. : *incensed* Reed to Ellis.   359. *enow*] Q, Dyce,
Ellis, Wag. : *enough* Reed, Coll, Rob., Cunn., Bull.   363. *Puts in Abigail*]
Dyce to Ellis : *Exit Abigail* Reed, Coll. : *omit* Q, Rob., Wag.   370. *Gives a
letter*] Dyce to Ellis : *omit* Q, Reed to Rob., Wag.

350. *My heart misgives me*] I have
a presentiment of evil. As in *3
Henry VI*, iv. vi. 94 :

' So doth *my heart misgive me*,
In these conflicts what may befall
him.'

366. *purchase*] Here used with
no sense of monetary considerations

being necessary—it simply con-
notes to obtain, or get possession
of. Compare *Titus Andronicus*,
ii. iii. 275 : ' Do this and *purchase*
us thy lasting friends.'
    370. *Take this . . .*] There seems
to have been no time for Barabas
to prepare this feigned challenge,
unless we may assume it to have

And tell him that it comes from Lodowick.

Itha. 'Tis poison'd, is it not ?

Bara. No, no ; and yet it might be done that way :
    It is a challenge feign'd from Lodowick.

Itha. Fear not ; I will so set his heart a-fire,
    That he shall verily think it comes from him.

Bara. I cannot choose but like thy readiness :
    Yet be not rash, but do it cunningly.

Itha. As I behave myself in this, employ me hereafter.

Bara. Away, then !   [*Exit Ithamore.*
    So, now will I go in to Lodowick,   381
    And, like a cunning spirit, feign some lie,
    Till I have set 'em both at enmity.   [*Exit.*

---

380. *Exit Ithamore*] Dyce, Ellis : *Exit* Reed to Rob., Cunn., Bull. : *After line* 379 Q.   381. *in to*] etc. : *unto* Q, Dyce[1], Cunn.

been written prior to his entry at the beginning of the scene. His purchase of Ithamore may have been, in part, with this message in mind.

ACT III

Scene I.—*A street: Outside* Bellamira's *house.*

Enter Bellamira.

Bell. Since this town was besieg'd, my gain grows cold :
The time has bin, that but for one bare night
A hundred ducats have bin freely given :
But now against my will I must be chaste.
And yet I know my beauty doth not fail.
From Venice merchants, and from Padua
Were wont to come rare-witted gentlemen,

Act III. Scene i.

Act III. Reed, Coll., Dyce : *Act the Third, Scene i.* Rob., Cunn. to Ellis.
Actus Tertius Q, Wag. *Enter Bellamira*] Dyce : *Enter a Curtezane,* Q to
Rob., Wag. : *Enter Bellamira, a courtesan* Cunn. to Ellis.
1. *Bell.*] No prefix Q.

Scene I] The scene is a street—perhaps near Bellamira's house. (See lines 10–11.) Dyce writes, ' Bellamira appears, we may suppose, in a veranda or open portico of her house (that the scene is not the interior of the house is proved by what follows) '; Bullen says, ' Bellamira displays herself on a balcony ', and refers to a stage-direction in R. Brome's *Covent Garden Weeded* : ' Enter Dorcas above on a Bellconie. Gabriel gazes at her. Dorcas is habited like a curtizan of Venice.' But there is nothing to support either of these opinions that Bellamira's house is the scene of the action. The audience knew who she was by her opening soliloquy, and nothing more was needed at this point. The fact that it was on the outer-stage suggested an open place or street to the audience.

1. *Since . . . besieg'd*] There is some confusion here. The siege does not actually begin until Scene v of this Act. Is it possible that Bellamira's speech originally followed that scene ?

my gain grows cold] I gain but little. Compare *Merchant of Venice,* II. vii. 73 : ' Your suit is cold '.

6. *Venice*] The greatest trading centre of the Mediterranean of the Middle Ages. ' Once did she hold the gorgeous East in fee ; And was the safeguard of the West ' (Wordsworth, *On the Extinction of the Venetian Republic*).

Padua] Padua was one of the oldest of the Italian universities and was founded by Frederick II in 1228. Galileo held the chair of mathematics there for six years from 1593. It seems to have been a favourite with Elizabethan writers. Compare Greene's *Mamillia* : ' The Citie of Padua renowned . . . for the antiquitie of the famous Universitie,' or Chapman's *All Fools,* I. i. 316, *The Gentleman Usher,* I. i. 199.

Scholars I mean, learned and liberal ;
And now, save Pilia-Borza, comes there none,
And he is very seldom from my house ;   10
And here he comes.

Enter PILIA-BORZA.

Pilia. Hold thee, wench, there's something for thee to spend.
[*Showing a bag of silver.*
Bell. 'Tis silver ; I disdain it.
Pilia. Ay, but the Jew has gold,
And I will have it, or it shall go hard.
Bell. Tell me, how cam'st thou by this ?
Pilia. Faith, walking the back-lanes, through the gardens,
I chanced to cast mine eye up to the Jew's counting-
house, where I saw some bags of money, and in the night
I clambered up with my hooks ; and, as I was taking
my choice, I heard a rumbling in the house ; so I took
only this, and run my way. But here's the Jew's man.
Bell. Hide the bag.   23

Enter ITHAMORE.

Pilia. Look not towards him, let's away. Zoon's, what a
looking thou keep'st, thou'lt betray's anon.
[*Exeunt Bellamira and Pilia-Borza.*
Itha. O, the sweetest face that ever I beheld ! I know she is

---

12. *Showing* . . .] Dyce, Ellis : *omit* Q and others.   13. etc. *Bell.*] Curt. Q.
23. *Enter Ithamore*] Dyce to Ellis : *After line* 22 Q and others.   25. *betray's*]
Q, Dyce, Bull., Ellis, Wag. : *betray us* Reed to Rob., Cunn.   *Exeunt* . . .]
Rob., Dyce to Ellis : *omit* Q to Coll., Wag.

11. *Pilia-Borza.*] A descriptive
name analogous to the Italian
Tagliaborse, a pickpocket. Collier
(MS.) proposes Piglia Borza.

20. *my hooks*] Broughton (*op.
cit.*) refers to Reed's notes on
2 Henry IV, v. iv. 8, as well as
Fletcher's *Women Pleased*, III. ii. :
'The thief that undertakes that,
Must have a *hook* will pose all hell
to hammer', and *Albumazar*, III.
iii. :

' Is not this braver than sneak all
    night in danger,
Picking of locks, or *hooking*
    clothes at windows.'

But Pilia Borza apparently used
his hooks to help climb up to the
counting-house.

24. *Zoon's*] A variant of Zounds,
an oath contracted from God's
wounds, and very frequently found
in Elizabethan literature.

a courtesan by her attire : now would I give a hundred
of the Jew's crowns that I had such a concubine.　Well,
I have deliver'd the challenge in such sort,
As meet they will, and fighting die ; brave sport.　30
[*Exit.*

SCENE II.—A Street.

Enter MATHIAS.

Math. This is the place : now Abigail shall see
Whether Mathias holds her dear or no.

Enter LODOWICK.

What, dares the villain write in such base terms ?
[*Looking at a letter.*
Lod. I did it ; and revenge it, if thou dar'st !　[*They fight.*

Act III.　Scene ii.

Rob., Cunn., Bull., Ellis : *omit* Q and rest.
　2. *Enter Lodowick*] Dyce, Bull., Ellis, Wag. : *Enter Lodowick reading* Q,
Reed to Rob., Cunn.　3. *Looking at a letter*] Dyce : *Reading a letter*, Cunn.
to Ellis : *Reading* Wag. : *omit* Q to Rob.　*Math.*] Q to Coll'., Dyce, Bull.
to Wag. : *Lod.* Rob., Cunn.　4. *Lod.*] Q to Dyce, Bull. to Wag. : *Math.* Cunn.
I . . . dar'st] As a quotation in Rob., who inverts lines 3 and 4 and gives
both to *Lod.*

27. *a courtesan . . . attire*] The
Elizabethan courtesan was known
by the loose-bodied flowing gown.
See Middleton's, *The Black Book*
(*Works*, ed. Bullen, VIII. 24) : ' a
gallant bawd indeed below her
loose-bodied satin '.　And compare
Vol. I. 233, *Michaelmas Term*,
I. ii. 14 :
' dost dream of virginity now ?
remember a loose-bodied gown,
wench, and let it go.'

Scene II.

Scene II] There was no break
here, I believe, and the play ran on
with the scene in the open street,
Barabas appearing ' above ' on the
balcony.
　1–4.] The opening lines of the
scene present great difficulty owing
to the Quarto S.D. in line 3, ' *Enter
Lodow. reading* '.　' The challenge
was from Lodowick to Mathias ',
writes Collier, and Cunningham

accepts this statement, but it is not
at all certain that it is true.　All
we know is that Ithamore was sent
with ' a challenge *feigned* from
Lodowick ', and he was ordered to
say that it came from Lodowick
(see II. iii. 371, 374).　Barabas then
went to find Lodowick with the
intent ' to feign some lie, Till I have
set 'em both at enmity '.　In a later
scene, however (III. iii. 20 ff.), Ithamore says that he carried the challenge writ by his master ' first to
Lodowick, and *inprimis* to Mathias '.
The whole situation is not helped by
the unsatisfactory nature of lines
3–4 of this scene, which do not
seem to follow one another naturally.　Perhaps here in the forty
years' interval which elapsed before
the play was printed, something has
fallen out.
　4. *Enter Barabas above*] The fight
takes place near to Barabas' house,
and he appears on his balcony (the

Enter BARABAS *above.*

Bara. O, bravely fought! and yet they thrust not home.
Now, Lodowick! now, Mathias! So;   [*Both fall.*
So, now they have show'd themselves to be tall fellows.
[*Cries within*] Part 'em, part 'em!
Bara. Ay, part 'em now they are dead. Farewell, farewell.
[*Exit.*

Enter FERNEZE, KATHERINE, *and* Attendants.

Fern. What sight is this? my Lodowick slain!   10
These arms of mine shall be thy sepulchre.
Kath. Who is this? my son Mathias slain!
Fern. O Lodowick, hadst thou perish'd by the Turk,
Wretched Ferneze might have veng'd thy death.
Kath. Thy son slew mine, and I'll revenge his death.
Fern. Look, Katherine, look! thy son gave mine these wounds.
Kath. O, leave to grieve me, I am griev'd enough.
Fern. O, that my sighs could turn to lively breath;
And these my tears to blood, that he might live.

6. *Lodowick*] Q to Rob., Cunn., Bull., Wag.: *Lodovico* Dyce, Ellis.
And so in line 10.   *Both fall*] Dyce to Ellis: *omit* Q and others.   9. *Exit*]
Q to Rob., Cunn. to Wag.: *Exit above* Dyce.   *Enter Ferneze . . .*]
Dyce, Ellis: *Enter Governor, Mater* Q, Wag.: *Enter Governor, Mother,* Reed,
Coll.: *Enter Governor and Mathias's Mother,* Rob., Cunn., Bull.   17.
grieve] Reed to Wag.: *griue* Q.

upper-stage of the Elizabethan theatre), whence he can look down on the struggle.

6. *Lodowick*] Bullen notes 'here and elsewhere, for the sake of metre, Dyce prints *Lodovico*. Perhaps he is right, for the name may have been contracted into "Lod" or "Lodo" in the MS. from which the play was printed'.

7. *tall fellows*] lusty, strong, valiant. Often used, as here, tinged with irony. Compare *Twelfth Night*, I. iii. 20: 'He's as *tall* a man as any in Illyria', or *Romeo and Juliet*, II. iv. 31: 'A very good blade! a very *tall* man.' Also Dekker's *Seuen Deadly Sinnes of London* (Arber, 21): 'Though a Lye haue but short legs (like a Dwarfes) yet it goes farre in a little

time, *Et crescit eundo*, and at last prooues a *tall fellow*.'

11. *These arms . . . sepulchre*] Dyce very aptly here compares *3 Henry VI*, II. v. 115:
'*These arms of mine* shall be thy winding sheet
My heart, sweet boy, *shall be thy sepulchre*.'
It should be noted that these lines do not occur in the *True Tragedy*.

17. *leave to grieve me*] cease to grieve me. This usage is common in Shakespeare, as in *Hamlet*, III. iv. 66:
'Could you on this fair mountain *leave* to feed,
To batten on this moor.'

18. *lively*] of or pertaining to life (and so re-vitalising). The O.E.D. gives examples of this use from the

Kath. Who made them enemies ? 20
Fern. I know not ; and that grieves me most of all. |
Kath. My son lov'd thine. \
Fern.   And so did Lodowick him.
Kath. Lend me that weapon that did kill my son,
      And it shall murder me.
Fern. Nay, madam, stay ; that weapon was my son's,
      And on that rather should Ferneze die.
Kath. Hold ; let's inquire the causers of their deaths, |
      That we may venge their blood upon their heads.)
Fern. Then take them up, and let them be interr'd
      Within one sacred monument of stone ; 30
      Upon which altar I will offer up
      My daily sacrifice of sighs and tears,
      And with my prayers pierce impartial heavens,
      Till they [reveal] the causers of our smarts,

34. *they [reveal]*] Dyce to Wag. : *they* Q, Reed, Rob. : *they disclose* Coll. conj.

eleventh century downwards, e.g. Usk's *Testament of Love*, line 121 : ' Utterly these thinges be no dremes ne japes, to throw to hogges, it is *lyfelych* meate for children of trouth ', and Grafton's *Chronicle*, II. 755 : ' With a maladie . . . so grievously taken, that his *lively* spirites began to faile.'

29. *Then . . . up*] Ferneze's order reminds us of the necessity of leaving no dead bodies on the outer-stage. All movements there were bound to take place in full sight of the audience, and dramatists took care to make their characters die on the inner-stage, where the curtains could be closed over them, or else, as here, they have them carried off by friends, soldiers, etc. Concerning this Mr. W. Archer (*Quarterly Review*, ccviii. 454) writes : ' In over a hundred plays which we have minutely examined (including all Shakespeare's tragedies) there is only a small minority of cases in which explicit provision is not made, either by stage direction or by a line in the text, for the removal of bodies.'

31–2. *altar . . . tears*] Bullen cites in connection with this *Two Gentlemen of Verona*, III. ii. 73 :
' Say that upon the *altar* of her beauty
You *sacrifice* your *tears*.'

33. *prayers pierce . . . heavens*] A very early variant of this occurs in Langland's famous line (B. x. 461) : ' Percen with a *pater-noster*, the paleys of heuene.'

impartial] For the use of ' impartial' erroneously for ' partial' compare the quarto edition of *Romeo and Juliet*, l. 1856 : ' Cruel, unjust, impartiall destinies', and see Onions, *Sh. Gloss.* Bullen cites the use of ' unpartial' in the sense of ' unkindly' in Peele's *Arraignment of Paris* :
Pro. ' Th' unpartial daughters of Necessity
      Bin aiders to her suit',
and see III. i. 115 : ' For Paris' fault y-*pierced* the *unpartial* skies.'

34–5. *Till . . . hearts*] The sense requires something here to complete it, and Dyce's emendation satisfies the needs of line 34. The whole passage is awkward, but

Which forc'd their hands divide united hearts:
Come, Katherine; our losses equal are,
Then of true grief let us take equal share.

[*Exeunt with the bodies.*

SCENE III.—*The same.*

Enter ITHAMORE.

Itha. Why, was there ever seen such villany.
So neatly plotted, and so well perform'd?
Both held in hand, and flatly both beguil'd?

Enter ABIGAIL.

Abig. Why, how now, Ithamore! why laugh'st thou so?
Itha. O mistress! ha, ha, ha!
Abig. Why, what ail'st thou?
Itha. O, my master!
Abig. Ha!
Itha. O mistress! I have the bravest, gravest, secret, subtle,
     bottle-nosed knave to my master, that ever gentleman
     had!   11
Abig. Say, knave, why rail'st upon my father thus?
Itha. O, my master has the bravest policy.
Abig. Wherein?
Itha. Why, know you not?

36. *Katherine*] Reed to Wag.: *Katherina* Q.   37. *Exeunt . . .*] Dyce,
Bull., Ellis: *Exeunt* Q to Rob., Cunn., Wag.

Act III.   Scene iii.

Rob., Cunn. to Ellis: *omit the rest.*

appears to mean: (I will pray daily)
till the heavens which forced their
hands to divide united hearts, reveal those who have caused our
griefs.

Scene III.

Scene III] Again there seems no
need here to localise the scene as
'A room in Barabas' house', as do
Dyce and Bullen. Ithamore enters,
and the locality recalls to him what

had happened there a short while
previously, and his words follow
naturally.

3. *held in hand*] Dyce says this
means 'kept in expectation, having
their hopes flattered'. It occurs
as early as Chaucer's *Troilus and
Criseyde*, II. 477: 'But that I wyl
not *holden hym in honde.*'

10. *bottle-nosed*] Another reference to the conventional Jewish
make-up. Compare II. iii. 174.

Abig. Why, no.

Itha. Know you not of Mathia[s'] and Don Lodowick['s]
    disaster ?

Abig. No : what was it ? 19

Itha. Why, the devil invented a challenge, my master writ
    it, and I carried it, first to Lodowick, and *imprimis* to
    Mathia[s] ;
    And then they met, [and,] as the story says,
    In doleful wise they ended both their days.

Abig. And was my father furtherer of their deaths ?

Itha. Am I Ithamore ?

Abig. Yes.

Itha. So sure did your father write, and I carry the challenge.

Abig. Well, Ithamore, let me request thee this :
    Go to the new-made nunnery, and inquire 30
    For any of the friars of St. Jaques,
    And say, I pray them come and speak with me.

Itha. I pray, mistress, will you answer me to one question ?

Abig. Well, sirrah, what is't ?

Itha. A very feeling one ; have not the nuns fine sport with
    the friars now and then ?

Abig. Go to, Sirrah Sauce ! is this your question ? get ye gone.

Itha. I will, forsooth, mistress. [*Exit.*

17. *Mathia[s']*] Reed, etc. : *Mathia* Q : *Lodowick['s]* Reed, etc. :
Lodowick Q. 22. *Mathia[s]*] Reed, etc. : *Mathia* Q. 23. *[and,]*] Rob.,
Dyce to Wag. : *omit* Q to Coll. 31. *Jaques*] Coll. to Wag. : *Jaynes* Q,
Reed : *James* Coll. conj. 33. *to*] Q, Dyce, Wag. : *but* Rob., Cunn., Bull.,
Ellis : *omit* Reed, Coll.

17. *Mathia[s']* . . . *Lodowick[s']*]
The Quarto *Mathia* and *Lodowick*
reading is probably due to the compositor's dislike of running over the
line here, especially as it is the last
line of a page (Sig. F. 2 *recto*), and
consequently would have meant an
ugly beginning of the page with a
line of one word on F. 2 *verso*.
Similarly *Mathia* in line 22 is
squeezed in at the end of the line in
the Quarto.
21. *imprimis*] Ithamore does not
know the meaning of the word, but

it is a necessity of his newly-won
position. Note that his statement
that he carried the challenge ' first
to Lodowick ' appears to contradict
II. iii. 370.
31. *St. Jaques*] The Dominicans
or Black Friars were commonly
referred to as Jacobins, from their
church of S. Jaques in Paris. (See
note, p. 124.) The Quarto misprints Jaynes—a compositor's misreading of the MS. perhaps.
33–8.] An interpolated piece of
clowning ?

Abig. Hard-hearted father, unkind Barabas,
    Was this the pursuit of thy policy,   40
    To make me show them favour severally,
    That by my favour they should both be slain ?
    Admit thou lov'dst not Lodowick for his sire,
    Yet Don Mathias ne'er offended thee :
    But thou wert set upon extreme revenge,
    Because the Governor dispossess'd thee once,
    And couldst not venge it, but upon his son ;
    Nor on his son, but by Mathias' means ;
    Nor on Mathias', but by murdering me.
    But I perceive there is no love on earth,   50
    Pity in Jews, nor piety in Turks.
    But here comes cursed Ithamore with the friar.

Enter ITHAMORE *with* FRIAR JACOMO.

Friar Jac. Virgo, salve.
Itha. When duck you ?

40. *pursuit*] Q, etc. : *purpose* Coll. (MS.) conj.   43. *sire*] Dyce to Wag. : *sinne* Q to Rob.   46. *Governor*] Cunn., Ellis, Wag. : *Prior* Q to Dyce, Bull. : *Sire* T. Brooke.   51. *nor*] Q, etc. : *or* Rob., Cunn., Bull.   52. *Enter . . .*] Dyce to Ellis : *Enter Ithamore, Fryar,* Q, Wag. : *Enter Ithamore and Friar* Reed to Rob.

41. *severally*] separately, individually. The O.E.D. quotes Hooker's *Eccl. Pol.* v. lxviii., § 2 : ' In speaking unto every communicant *severally*.'

43. *sire*] Dyce's emendation of *sire* for *sinne* of the Quarto is almost certainly right.

45. *extreme*] utmost, most violent, as in *Coriolanus*, IV. v. 74 : ' the painful service, The *extreme* dangers . . . are requited, But with that surname.'

46. *Governor*] Cunningham's emendation to *Governor* is the most satisfactory. Certainly there seems to be little reason for *Prior*, whereas the next line almost demands *Governor* in the preceding one. Professor Tucker Brooke proposes *sire*, which deserves consideration, as *Prior* might then be a mistake arising from imperfect hearing.

51. *Pity in Jews*] Again we are reminded of the trial scene in *The Merchant of Venice*, IV. i. 78 ff., where Antonio says :

' You may as well do any thing most hard,
As seek to soften that—than which what's harder ?—
His Jewish heart.'

nor] Robinson, Cunningham and Bullen silently emend this to *or*.

54. *When duck you*] *When* is an exclamation of impatience born of excessive zeal on the part of Ithamore. *Duck you* to curtsy or make reverence. Compare, for this practice of friars, Heywood's *Captives*, I. ii. 122 : ' And when we *duck* or congee . . .', Fletcher's *Woman's Prize*, I. iii : 'had I not *duck'd* quickly like a Fryer', and II. iii. 25 *ante*.

Abig. Welcome, grave friar : Ithamore begone.

[*Exit Ithamore.*

Know, holy sir, I am bold to solicit thee.

Friar Jac. Wherein ?

Abig. To get me be admitted for a nun.

Friar Jac. Why, Abigail, it is not yet long since

That I did labour thy admission,   60

And then thou didst not like that holy life.

Abig. Then were my thoughts so frail and unconfirm'd,

And I was chain'd to follies of the world :

But now experience, purchased with grief,

Has made me see the difference of things.

My sinful soul, alas, hath pac'd too long

The fatal labyrinth of misbelief,

Far from the sun that gives eternal life !

Friar Jac. Who taught thee this ?

Abig.   The Abbess of the house,

Whose zealous admonition I embrace :   70

O, therefore, Jacomo, let me be one,

Although unworthy, of that sisterhood.

Friar Jac. Abigail, I will : but see thou change no more,

For that will be most heavy to thy soul.

Abig. That was my father's fault.

55. *Exit Ithamore*] Coll. to Ellis : *Exit* Q, Reed, Wag.   63. *And*] Q to
Rob., Wag.: *As* Dyce.   68. *sun*] Dyce² to Ellis : *Sonne* (Son) Q, Rob.,
Dyce¹, Wag. : *son* Reed.   71. *Jacomo*] Reed to Wag. : *Iacomi* Q.

60. *labour thy admission*] exert
myself to procure thy admission.

Compare Kyd, *Spanish Tragedie*, III.:
'My lord, I write as my extremes
  require
That you would *labour my delivery*',
and similarly in *Richard III*, I. iv.
246.

62. *unconfirm'd*] Not yet made
firm or sure. This is the earliest use
of the word quoted by the O.E.D.

68. *sun*] The Q spelling *Sonne*
here makes it difficult to know
whether Sun or the Son [of Man]
is intended.   In III. iii. 47 the
Quarto spelling *sonne* cannot

possibly be anything but *son*, but
we cannot argue much from that
unfortunately. Here either reading
seems possible, and I have kept
to Dyce's suggestion as the one best
filling the general sense of the
passage.

70. *zealous admonition*] Admonition is here used to imply ' counsel ',
without any very strong sense of
reproof or censure being attached
to it, as in I Corinthians x. 11 :
' These things . . . are written for
our *admonition*.'

embrace] A specialised use of the
word connoting joyful acceptance.
See O.E.D. *embrace*, 2. h.

Friar Jac.   Thy father's ! how ?

Abig. Nay, you shall pardon me. *O Barabas,*
　Though thou deservest hardly at my hands,
　Yet never shall these lips bewray thy life.   [*Aside.*

Friar Jac. Come, shall we go ?

Abig.   My duty waits on you.   [*Exeunt.*

SCENE IV.—*A room in the house of* BARABAS.

Enter BARABAS, *reading a letter.*

Bara. What, Abigail become a nun again !
　False and unkind ! what, hast thou lost thy father ?
　And, all unknown, and unconstrain'd of me,
　Art thou again got to the nunnery ?
　Now here she writes, and wills me to repent :
　Repentance ! *Spurca !* what pretendeth this ?
　I fear she knows ('tis so) of my device
　In Don Mathias' and Lodovico's deaths :
　If so, 'tis time that it be seen into ;
　For she that varies from me in belief,   10

---

78. *Aside*] Dyce to Ellis: *omit* the rest.

Act III. Scene iv.

Rob., Cunn. to Ellis: *omit* the rest. 6. *pretendeth*] Q, Rob. to Wag. :
portendeth Reed, Coll. 8. *Mathias' and Lodovico's*] Reed to Dyce, Bull,
Ellis : *Mathias and Lodovicoes* Q and Wag. : *Mathias's and Lodowick's*
Coll., Cunn.

78. *bewray*] to reveal or expose the true character of a person or thing, as in Coverdale's version of Matt. xxvi. 73 : ' Thy speach *bewrayeth* thee ', and Greene's *Pandosto* (Hazlitt, p. 31), ' Seeing Franion had *bewrayed* his secrets '.

Scene IV.

Scene IV . . .] Probably in this scene use was made of the inner-stage, and the scene represented a room within the house of Barabas, for at line 46, he sends Ithamore for the pot of rice, and proceeds to doctor it—a proceeding even Barabas would prefer to do within doors !

6. *Spurca*] This apparently is from the Latin *spurcus*, through the Italian *sporcus*, and is the comment of Barabas on repentance—base, dirty.

pretendeth] intends, means. Compare *Macbeth* II. iv. 24 : ' What good could they *pretend ?* ' *Portendeth*, of the early editors, is clearly an unwarrantable alteration.

8. *Mathias' and Lodovico's*] As this is (substantially) the Quarto reading I have left it, although, as has been said (II. iii. 243), it is an unusual form of Lodowick's name.

Gives great presumption that she loves me not;
Or, loving, doth dislike of something done.
But who comes here?

Enter ITHAMORE.

                      O Ithamore, come near;
Come near, my love; come near, thy master's life,
My trusty servant, nay, my second self;
For I have now no hope but even in thee;
And on that hope my happiness is built:
When saw'st thou Abigail?
Itha.   To-day.
Bara.   With whom?
Itha. A friar.
Bara. A friar! false villain, he hath done the deed.   20
Itha. How, sir!
Bara.   Why, made mine Abigail a nun.
Itha. That's no lie; for she sent me for him.
Bara. O unhappy day!
    False, credulous, inconstant Abigail!
    But let 'em go: and, Ithamore, from hence
    Ne'er shall she grieve me more with her disgrace;
    Ne'er shall she live to inherit aught of mine,
    Be bless'd of me, nor come within my gates,
    But perish underneath my bitter curse,
    Like Cain by Adam, for his brother's death.   30
Itha. O master!
Bara. Ithamore, entreat not for her: I am mov'd,
    And she is hateful to my soul and me:
    And, 'less thou yield to this that I entreat,

---

13. *Enter Ithamore*] Dyce to Ellis: *After line* 12, Reed, Coll.: *omit*
Q, Rob., Wag. 15. *self*] Dyce² to Wag., Dyce¹ conj. *life* Q to Dyce¹.
34. *'less*] Coll. conj.: Dyce to Wag.: *least* Q, Reed, Rob.

11. *presumption*] grounds for be- | 28. *come . . . gates*] Note the
lief, supposition. | scriptural reminiscence, as often
15. *self*] The Quarto here had *life*, | with Barabas.
probably a compositor's error, his | 30. '*Like . . . Adam*] Not strictly
eye being caught by the word *life* | true: see Genesis iv. 9 ff.
which ends the preceding line. | 34. *'less*] This was first proposed

I cannot think but that thou hat'st my life.

Itha. Who, I, master ? why, I'll run to some rock,
  And throw myself headlong into the sea ;
  Why, I'll do anything for your sweet sake.

Bara. O trusty Ithamore ! no servant, but my friend !
  I here adopt thee for mine only heir :   40
  All that I have is thine when I am dead ;
  And, whilst I live, use half ; spend as myself ;
  Here, take my keys,—I'll give 'em thee anon ;
  Go buy thee garments ; but thou shalt not want :
  Only know this, that thus thou art to do :
  But first go fetch me in the pot of rice
  That for our supper stands upon the fire.

Itha. I hold my head, my master's hungry
  I go, sir.   [*Exit.*

Bara. Thus every villain ambles after wealth,   50
  Although he ne'er be richer than in hope :
  But, husht !

    Enter ITHAMORE *with the pot.*

Itha.   Here 'tis, master.

Bara.   Well said, Ithamore !
  What, hast thou brought the ladle with thee too ?

36. *rock*] Q, etc. : [*huge*] *rock* Cunn.   42. *half*] Reed, etc. : *helfe* Q.
48. After *hungry* Dyce adds *Aside.*

by Collier in place of the *least* of the
Quarto and the early editors which
is clearly out of place. '*Less* is not
altogether convincing, but is reasonably possible.

36. *Who . . . master ?*] Holthausen (*op. cit.*) would improve the
scansion by transposing ' Who,
master ? I ? '

39-44.] Note here the way in
which Barabas mischievously de-
lights in deceiving Ithamore by
making promises, and then quali-
fying them. ' All that I have is
thine—when I am dead ', etc.'
Hence in lines 50, 51 Barabas can
congratulate himself on winning
an adherent who is richer only in
hope.

48. *I hold*] I wager, as in *The
Taming of the Shrew*, III. ii. 85 :
' I hold you a penny.'   Prof.
Warwick Bond in the Arden edn.
of this play also quotes from Florio's
Second Frutes, 1591 : ' I holde a
shilling that I winne this game.'
See also *Merchant of Venice*, II. iv.
62.

52. *But, . . . Ithamore*] This is
three lines in the Quarto and other
editors, but can better be treated
as one line, especially if we could
omit *husht*, for which a mere dash
could be substituted.

Well said,] Compare 2 *Tambur-
laine*, v. i. 176 :
  Cas.   Here they are my Lord.
  Tam.   Well said. . . .

Itha. Yes, sir ; the proverb says, he that eats with the devil
  had need of a long spoon ; I have brought you a ladle.
Bara. Very well, Ithamore then now be secret ;
  And, for thy sake, whom I so dearly love,
  Now shalt thou see the death of Abigail,
  That thou mayst freely live to be my heir.   59
Itha. Why, master, will you poison her with a mess of rice-
  porridge ? that will preserve life, make her round and
  plump, and batten more than you are aware.
Bara. Ay, but, Ithamore, seest thou this ?
  It is a precious powder that I bought
  Of an Italian, in Ancona, once,
  Whose operation is to bind, infect,
  And poison deeply, yet not appear
  In forty hours after it is ta'en.
Itha. How, master ?
Bara. Thus, Ithamore :   70
  This even they use in Malta here, ('tis call'd
  Saint Jaques' Even,) and then I say they use

72. *Jaques'*] Coll., etc : *Jaques* Q, Reed, Wag.

54–55. *he that eats . . . spoon*]
This proverb has been in use since
Chaucer's time at least. See *The
Squire's Tale*, 594 :

' Therfore bihoveth hire a ful long
    spoon
  That shal ete with a feend.'

It would be useless to multiply
references to it throughout Elizabethan literature.
  62. *batten*] to grow fat, to feed
voraciously. Compare *Coriolanus*,
IV. v. 34, ' Go, and *batten* on cold
bits ', and Jonson's *Bartholomew
Fair*, 1614, II. i. (Cunningham's,
Gifford's ed., II. 163a) : ' it makes
her fat you see ; she *battens* with
it.'
  64–8. *It is . . . ta'en*] Mario
Praz (*op. cit.*, p. 35) says : ' These
Machiavellian poisons, punctual
like clock-work, became no less of
a regular property of the Eliza-

bethan stage than the Senecan
bloody blades ', and adds references
to *Edward II*, 2363 ff., and *Alphon-
sus Emperor of Germany* (where the
powder of Barabas has grown to a
whole box of poisons).
  65. *an Italian, in Ancona*] The
Marranos or Portuguese Jews found
an asylum in Ancona. They were
subjected to the Inquisition by
Paul IV in 1555, and some of them
were released in 1556 in consequence of a peremptory note from
the Sultan Solyman to the Pope.
Graetz, *Hist. Jews*, ed. 1892, IV.
604 ff., 615. This ' Italian ' may
have been a co-religionist, and only
an Italian perforce.
  72. *they use*] they, i.e. the inhabitants of the island, are accustomed to . . . Compare Spenser's
Faerie Queene, v. viii. 17 : ' Her
name Mercilla most men *use* to
call.'

To send their alms unto the nunneries :
Amongst the rest bear this, and set it there ;
There's a dark entry where they take it in,
Where they must neither see the messenger,
Nor make inquiry who hath sent it them.

Itha. How so ?

Bara. Belike there is some ceremony in't.

    There, Ithamore, must thou go place this pot :   80

    Stay ; let me spice it first.

Itha. Pray, do, and let me help you, master.

    Pray, let me taste first.

Bara. Prithee, do. What say'st thou now ?

Itha. Troth, master, I'm loath such a pot of pottage should

    be spoiled.

Bara. Peace, Ithamore ! 'tis better so than spar'd.

    Assure thyself thou shalt have broth by the eye :

    My purse, my coffer, and myself is thine.

Itha. Well, master, I go.   90

Bara. Stay ; first let me stir it, Ithamore.

    As fatal be it to her as the draught

    Of which great Alexander drunk, and died :

    And with her let it work like Borgia's wine,

---

80. *pot*] Reed to Wag. : *plot* Q. 82. *master*] Reed, etc. : *Mr.* Q, and so in line 85. 84. After *do* Dyce and Ellis add *Ithamore tastes.* 87. After *spar'd* Dyce and Ellis add *Puts the powder into the pot.*

88. *by the eye*] i.e. in abundance. The O.E.D. quotes *Piers Plowman's Crede*, 84 : ' Grete-hedede quenes wiþ gold *by the eiȝen*', and Beaumont and Fletcher, *Knight of the Burning Pestle*, II. ii. 23 : ' Here's money and gold *by th' eye*, my boy.'

93. *Alexander drunk, and died*] Alexander the Great (B.C. 356–323) is said to have died of a fever, aggravated by the quantity of wine he had drunk at a banquet. Plutarch says (North, 1612 ed., p. 710) : ' For he did sumptuously feast Nearchus, and one day when he came out of his bath according to his manner, being readie to go to bed, *Medius* one of his Captaines

besought him to come to a banquet to him to his lodging. *Alexander* went thither, and dranke there all that night and the next day, so that he got an ague by it.'

94–5. *And with . . . poisoned*] The name of the Borgias was and still is connected in men's minds with every kind of poisoning and treachery. It was long believed that Pope Alexander VI (Rodrigo Borgia) died of poison, although recent historians do not think this to be true. Cæsar Borgia, his son, was frequently suspected of getting rid of his enemies by poisoned wine, gems, books, etc. The reference is made, Meyer thinks (*op. cit.*),

Whereof his sire, the Pope, was poisoned !
In few, the blood of Hydra, Lerna's bane,
The juice of hebon, and Cocytus' breath,
And all the poisons of the Stygian pool
Break from the fiery kingdom ; and in this
Vomit your venom, and envenom her   100
That like a fiend hath left her father thus !

Itha. What a blessing has he given't ! was ever pot of rice-
porridge so sauced ?   What shall I do with it ?

Bara. O my sweet Ithamore, go set it down ;
And come again as soon as thou hast done,
For I have other business for thee.

Itha. Here's a drench to poison a whole stable of Flanders
mares : I'll carry't to the nuns with a powder.

103. After *sauced* Dyce and Ellis add *Aside.*

' with the intent to call up in the audience's imagination Machiavelli, popularly supposed to have been Cæsar's councillor'.

96. *In few*] in short. Compare *2 Henry IV*, I. i. 112 : ' *In few* ; his death . . . tooke fire and heate away ', and Beaumont and Fletcher, *A King and No King*, IV. iii : ' the cause . . . which, *in few*, is my honour '.

Hydra . . . bane] The hydra, a monstrous serpent with nine heads, was the terror of the countryside of Lerna. It was one of the labours of Hercules to subjugate this monster. Compare *Tamburlaine*, IV. iv. 21 : ' Or, winged snakes of Lerna, cast your stings, And leave your venoms in this tyrant's dish.'

97. *juice of hebon*] There is much dispute as to what species of plant is here referred to (see Furness, *Hamlet*, Variorum edn., p. 101). It probably means henbane (*Hyoscyamus*), which is a strong narcotic poison, although ' Nicholson (*N. Sh. Soc. Transactions*, 1880–2) shows that the yew was considered a most deadly poison ; that Ebenus was medievally applied to different trees, including the yew ; that Marlowe, Spenser, and Reynolds use Heben for the yew, and he maintains that in *Hamlet* Shakespeare was adopting the description of the yew found in Holland's *Pliny*, 1600 ' (Arden edn. *Hamlet*).

Cocytus' breath] Cocytus was a tributary of the Acheron or of the Styx, a river in Hades. Virgil describes it as the river which surrounds the underworld.

98. *poisons . . . pool*] The Styx was the river supposed to flow round the world of the dead. In later times it was identified with a lofty waterfall near Nonacris in Arcadia. The ancients regarded the water as poisonous ; it is still called the Black Water by the natives.

107. *drench*] A draught, or dose of medicine (usually administered to an animal). Here used by Ithamore to express his contempt of his victims. Cf. *The Two Angry Women of Abingdon* (Hazlitt's *Dodsley*, VII. 303) : ' Nay, faith, sir, we must have some smith to give the butler a *drench*, or cut him in the forehead, for he hath got a horse's disease, namely the staggers.'

108. *with a powder*] Prof. Case notes : ' There is not much sense in this *with a powder* as the powder

Bara. And the horse-pestilence to boot; away!

Itha. I am gone: 110
        Pay me my wages, for my work is done.   [*Exit.*

Bara. I'll pay thee with a vengeance, Ithamore!   [*Exit.*

SCENE V.—*An open place in the City.*

Enter FERNEZE, MARTIN DEL BOSCO, Knights, *and* Basso.

Fern. Welcome, great basso: how fares Calymath?
        What wind drives you thus into Malta road?

Bas. The wind that bloweth all the world besides,
        Desire of gold.

Fern.   Desire of gold, great sir?
        That's to be gotten in the Western Inde:
        In Malta are no golden minerals.

Bas. To you of Malta thus saith Calymath:
        The time you took for respite is at hand

---

111. *Exit*] Q to Rob., Cunn. to Wag.: *Exit with the pot* Dyce.

Act III. Scene v.

Bull., Ellis: *omit* others.   *Enter . . .*] Dyce, Ellis: *Enter Governor, Bosco, Knights, Bashaw* Q and rest.
   1. *basso*] Dyce to Ellis: *Bashaws* Q: *Bashaw* Reed to Rob., Wag.   And so throughout the scene.   2. *drives you thus*] Q to Dyce, Ellis, Wag.: *thus drives you* Cunn., Bull.

has already spiced the drench. Did Ithamore really say "with a pox"—a common addendum at the time? That would explain Barabas's supplementary remark (l. 109) suggested by "a whole stable"," etc.

109. *to boot*] as well, into the bargain. Compare *Macbeth*, IV. iii. 35:

'I would not be the villain that thou think'st
For the whole space that's in the tyrant's grasp,
And the rich East *to boot*.'

Scene V.

Scene V.] An unlocalised open place or street, and played on the outer-stage.

1. *great basso*] I have adopted Dyce's emendation here for the sake of uniformity. We have the form *bassoes* in Act I, Sc. ii, and it is also used by Marlowe in *Tamburlaine*. There seems no need for the plural form, and the final *s* may well be a printer's gift to us. Professor Tucker Brooke points out (privately) that the plural form may be due to the fact that sometimes one, sometimes several emissaries from the Turk appeared, according to the elaborateness of the production, and draws attention to the S.D. of *Common Conditions* (l. 1750): 'Here entreth *Leostines* with a lorde or two more.'
   2. *drives you thus*] For the sake of the rhythm Cunningham and Bullen prefer to read *thus drives you*.

For the performance of your promise pass'd ;
And for the tribute money I am sent.   10

Fern. Basso, in brief, shalt have no tribute here,
Nor shall the heathens live upon our spoil :
First will we race the city-walls ourselves,
Lay waste the island, hew the temples down,
And, shipping off our goods to Sicily,
Open an entrance for the wasteful sea,
Whose billows, beating the resistless banks,
Shall overflow it with their refluence.

Bas. Well, governor, since thou hast broke the league
By flat denial of the promis'd tribute,   20
Talk not of racing down your city-walls ;
You shall not need trouble yourselves so far,
For Selim Calymath shall come himself,
And with brass bullets batter down your towers,
And turn proud Malta to a wilderness,
For these intolerable wrongs of yours ;
And so farewell.

Fern. Farewell :   [*Exit Basso.*
And now, you men of Malta, look about,
And let's provide to welcome Calymath :   30
Close your port-cullis, charge your basilisks,
And, as you profitably take up arms,

---

15. *off*] Reed to Bull. : *of* Q, Wag. 28. *Exit Basso*] Reed, etc. : *omit*
Q, Cunn. 29. *you*] Q to Cunn., Wag. : *ye* Bull., Ellis.

---

9. *promise pass'd*] The Quarto
reads *promise past*, which may
mean, as here, ' your promise duly
given ', or else ' your promise of the
past'.

13. *race*] raze. A variant form
frequently used at the time. And
see line 21.

17. *resistless*] i.e. unresisting, as
in *Tamburlaine*, v. ii. 334 : ' Must
Tamburlaine by their *resistless*
powers . . . Conclude a league of
honour.'

18. *refluence*] a flowing back.

This is the earliest usage of the word
given by the O.E.D.

31. *basilisks*] A large cannon of
brass, so named from a supposed
resemblance to the serpent called
the basilisk. It threw a shot
weighing about 200 pounds, and
was the largest kind of ordnance.
Compare Harrison's *Description of
England*, II. xvi : ' Basiliske
[weigheth] 9000 pounds, eight
inches and three quarters within the
mouth.' Cf. *Tamburlaine*, I. iv. 2.

32. *profitably*] i.e. in your own
interests, to your own profit.

So now courageously encounter them ;
For by this answer, broken is the league,
And naught is to be look'd for now but wars,
And naught to us more welcome is than wars. [*Exeunt.*

SCENE VI.—*Courtyard of the Nunnery.*

Enter FRIAR JACOMO *and* FRIAR BARNARDINE.

Friar Jac. O brother, brother, all the nuns are sick,
    And physic will not help them ; they must die.
Friar Barn. The abbess sent for me to be confess'd :
    O, what a sad confession will there be !
Friar Jac. And so did fair Maria send for me :
    I'll to her lodging ; hereabouts she lies.   [*Exit.*

Enter ABIGAIL.

Friar Barn. What, all dead, save only Abigail ?
Abig. And I shall die too, for I feel death coming.
    Where is the friar that convers'd with me ?
Friar Barn. O, he is gone to see the other nuns.   10
Abig. I sent for him ; but, seeing you are come,
    Be you my ghostly father : and first know,
    That in this house I liv'd religiously,
    Chaste, and devout, much sorrowing for my sins ;
    But, ere I came—

36. *than*] Reed to Ellis : *then* Q, Wag.

Act III.   Scene vi.

Bull., Ellis : *Scene V* Rob., Cunn. : *omit* the rest.   *Enter Friar . . .*]
Dyce to Ellis : *Enter two Friars* Reed to Rob., Wag. : *Enter two Fryars
and Abigall* Q.
    1. *Friar Jac.*] Dyce to Ellis : *1 Fry.* Q, Rob., Wag. : *1st Friar.* Reed,
Coll.   3. *Friar Barn.*] Dyce to Ellis : *2 Fry.* Q, Rob., Wag. : *2nd Friar,*
Reed, Coll.

35–6.] This mannerism by which
one line echoes the other seems most
common in *Tamburlaine.*

Scene VI.
Scene VI] Acted on the outer-
stage, the place being the courtyard of the nunnery.   The Friars
are about to enter to the several
chambers of the nuns (see lines
3–6).

Friar Barn. What then ?

Abig. I did offend high heaven so grievously
    As I am almost desperate for my sins :
    And one offence torments me more than all.
    You knew Mathias and Don Lodowick ?   20

Friar Barn. Yes ; what of them ?

Abig. My father did contract me to 'em both ;
    First to Don Lodowick ; him I never lov'd ;
    Mathias was the man that I held dear,
    And for his sake did I become a nun.

Friar Barn. So : say how was their end ?

Abig. Both, jealous of my love, envied each other ;
    And by my father's practice, which is there
                                            [*Gives writing.*
    Set down at large, the gallants were both slain.

Friar Barn. O, monstrous villany !   30

Abig. To work my peace, this I confess to thee :
    Reveal it not ; for then my father dies.

Friar Barn. Know that confession must not be reveal'd ;
    The canon law forbids it, and the priest
    That makes it known, being degraded first,
    Shall be condemn'd, and then sent to the fire.

Abig. So I have heard ; pray, therefore, keep it close.
    Death seizeth on my heart : ah, gentle friar,
    Convert my father that he may be sav'd,   39
    And witness that I die a Christian !   [*Dies.*

Friar Barn. Ay, and a virgin too ; that grieves me most.

---

28. *Gives writing*] Dyce : *Gives a paper* Cunn., Bull. : *omit* Q, Reed
to Rob., Wag.   40. *Dies*] Reed, etc. : *omit* Q.

---

22. *My father . . . both*] See
above II. iii. 237 and rest of scene.
It will be noticed that Abigail
realises the impiety of her double
betrothal in the eyes of the Church.
This, of course, follows from what
has been said above (p. 95) as to
the binding nature of the plighting
of troth or contract.

28. *practice*] scheming, treachery.
Compare *Othello*, v. ii. 291 :

' O thou Othello, that wert once so
    good,
Fall'n in the *practice* of a damned
    slave.'

34–6. *The canon law . . . fire*]
See 4th Lateran Council, § 21,
Caveat autem . . .

9

But I must to the Jew, and exclaim on him,
And make him stand in fear of me.

Enter FRIAR JACOMO.

Friar Jac. O brother, all the nuns are dead ! let's bury
    them.
Friar Barn. First help to bury this ; then go with me,
    And help me to exclaim against the Jew.
Friar Jac. Why, what has he done ?
Friar Barn. A thing that makes me tremble to unfold.
Friar Jac. What, has he crucified a child ?   50
Friar Barn. No, but a worse thing : 'twas told me in shrift,
    Thou know'st 'tis death, and if it be reveal'd.
    Come, let's away.   [*Exeunt.*

50. *has*] Reed, etc.: *haa* Q.   52. *and*] Q, Reed to Rob., Wag. : *an* Dyce
to Ellis.

42. *exclaim on*] accuse. Compare
Kyd's *Spanish Tragedy*, III. xiv. 70 :
' What a scandale went among the
kings
To heare Hieronymo *exclaim on*
thee.'
47. *exclaim against*] Generally
used as being less emphatic than
exclaim on, and as meaning ' to rail
at, to complain of '. Compare
Hamlet, II. ii. 370 : ' Their writers
do them wrong to make them
exclaim against their own succession ' ; *Othello*, II. iii. 314, etc.
50. *crucified a child*] Dyce notes
here, ' A crime with which the Jews
were often charged ', and adds a
note of Isaac Reed to the effect that
Tovey in his *Anglia Judaica* has
given several instances which are
upon record of these charges
against the Jews, which he observes
were never made but at such times
as the King was manifestly in great
need of money. The alleged
crucifixion of Hugh of Lincoln
(dated 1255, by Matthew Paris)
gave a great impetus to the popular
belief in this practice. The first
recorded case was that of S.
William of Norwich in 1144, and
Mr. Walter Rye gives a list of seven
others recorded between then and
1279.

ACT IV

SCENE I.—*A street outside the house of* BARABAS.

Enter BARABAS *and* ITHAMORE. *Bells within.*

Bara. There is no music to a Christian's knell:
How sweet the bells ring, now the nuns are dead,
That sound at other times like tinkers' pans!
I was afraid the poison had not wrought;
Or, though it wrought, it would have done no good,
For every year they swell, and yet they live;
Now all are dead, not one remains alive.

Itha. That's brave, master: but think you it will not be
known?

Bara. How can it, if we two be secret?   10

Itha. For my part, fear you not.

Bara. I'd cut thy throat if I did.

Itha.   And reason too.
But here's a royal monastery hard by;
Good master, let me poison all the monks.

Act IV. Scene i.

Act IV] Reed, Coll., Dyce, *Actus Quartus* Q, Wag.: *Act the Fourth, Scene
I* Rob., Cunn. to Ellis.
    1. *to*] Q to Coll., Dyce to Wag.: *like* Rob.   8. *master*] Reed, etc.: *Mr.* Q.
And so in lines 21, etc.

Scene I] The scene is a street, probably outside the house of Barabas. It is possible that Barabas and Ithamore come out through the curtains of the rear-stage, and it is with a gesture towards them in line 94 that Barabas says, 'Come to my house . . . this night', and it is through them, Ithamore and Barnardine go after line 105.
    1. *to*] compared with, equal to.

There is no need for Robinson's alteration to *like*. See *The Tempest,* II. i. 178: 'Who in this kind of merry fooling am nothing *to* you.' A good example is the proverb: 'There is no fishing *to* the sea nor service *to* the King.'
    8. *master*:] a possible interpolation, as the word is much used by Ithamore. The line scans perfectly without it.

119

Bara. Thou shalt not need, for now the nuns are dead,
    They'll die with grief.

Itha. Do you not sorrow for your daughter's death ?

Bara. No, but I grieve because she liv'd so long,
    An Hebrew born, and would become a Christian.
    Cazzo, diabolo !   20

Itha. Look, look, master ; here comes two religious cater-
    pillars.

        Enter FRIAR JACOMO *and* FRIAR BARNARDINE.

Bara. I smelt 'em ere they came.

Itha. God-a-mercy, nose ! Come, let's begone.

Friar Barn. Stay, wicked Jew ; repent, I say, and stay.

Friar Jac. Thou hast offended, therefore must be damn'd.

Bara. I fear they know we sent the poison'd broth.

Itha. And so do I, master, therefore speak 'em fair.

Friar Barn. Barabas, thou hast——

Friar Jac. Ay, that thou hast——   30

Bara. True, I have money ; what though I have ?

Friar Barn. Thou art a——

Friar Jac. Ay, that thou art, a——

Bara. What needs all this ? I know I am a Jew.

    20. *Cazzo, diabolo*] Dyce to Wag. : *Catho diabola*, Q to Rob.   22. *Enter*
. . .] Dyce, Ellis : *Enter the two Fryars* the rest.

20. *Cazzo, diabolo.*] Dyce quotes
from Gifford's *Jonson*, II. 48 : ' A
petty oath, a cant exclamation,
generally expressive, among the
Italian populace, who have it constantly in their mouth, of defiance
or contempt.' For another explanation see *Dict. of Anglicised
Words*, ed. C. A. M. Fennell.
Compare Marston's *Malcontent*,
v. ii. 220 : ' Yet when he married
her, tales off, and *Catso*, for
England!' See also *ib.* I. i. 147 and
Middleton's *Blurt, Master-Constable*,
v. i. 41, etc.

21. *caterpillars*] A term of contempt. Compare 2 *Henry VI.* 2440 :
' Courtiers, gentlemen, they call
false *caterpillars* ', and Heywood's

Captives, II. ii. 97 : ' But that
caterpillar, that old . . . worm ! '

24. *God-a-mercy, nose !*] A further
jest at Barabas' nose. Cf. II. iii. 174
and III. iii. 10. A possible actor's
interpolation ? See Onions (*Sh.
Gloss.*), where *God-a-mercy* is defined
as equivalent to ' God reward you '.

29. *Barabas, thou hast*——] The
whole of this passage reflects the
dramatist's consistent ' guying ' of
the Friars, whom he here makes
more ridiculous than ever—and
each the echo of the other. Like
Rosencrantz and Guildenstern, or
Dogberry and Verges, they ' hunt in
pairs ', and are at their quintess-
ential best (or worst) when together. See also above, lines 6 and 15.

Friar Barn. Thy daughter——

Friar Jac. Ay, thy daughter——

Bara. O, speak not of her, then I die with grief.

Friar Barn. Remember that——

Friar Jac. Ay, remember that——

Bara. I must needs say that I have been a great usurer. 40

Friar Barn. Thou hast committed——

Bara. Fornication : but that was in another country ;
    and besides, the wench is dead.

Friar Barn. Ay, but, Barabas,
    Remember Mathias and Don Lodowick.

Bara. Why, what of them ?

Friar Barn. I will not say that by a forged challenge they
    met.

*Bara. She has confess'd, and we are both undone;
    My bosom inmate! but I must dissemble.—*   50
                        [*Aside to Ithamore.*

O holy friars, the burden of my sins
Lie heavy on my soul! then, pray you, tell me,
Is't not too late now to turn Christian ?
I have been zealous in the Jewish faith,
Hard-hearted to the poor, a covetous wretch,
That would for lucre's sake have sold my soul.
A hundred for a hundred I have ta'en ;
And now for store of wealth may I compare
With all the Jews in Malta ; but what is wealth ?

---

50. *inmate*] Dyce to Wag. :   *inmates* Q to Rob. :   *intimates* T. Brooke.
52. *Lie*] Q to Coll., Dyce to Wag. :   *Lies* Rob.

50. *inmate*] Here seems to mean 'bosom friend, or intimate', i.e. Abigail. Prof. Tucker Brooke proposes to read *intimates*, suggesting something has been dropped from the Quarto *inmates*.

52. *Lie*] Robinson reads *Lies*, but this is unnecessary : ' The nominative singular is frequently followed by a plural verb when a plural genitive intervenes ' (Dyce).

57. *A hundred . . . hundred*] i.e. Usury at the rate of one hundred per cent. Bacon in his essay ' On Usury ' recommends that ' Usury, in general shall be reduced to Five in the Hundred ', while an Elizabethan writer in 1561 expresses his horror that Venetian Jews are allowed ' to take gaiges of ordinarie for xv. in the hundred by the yere, and if at the yeres end the gaige be not redemed, it is forfeite, or at the least dooen away at a great disadvauntage '. Thomas, *Historye of Italye.*

I am a Jew, and therefore am I lost.   60
Would penance serve for this my sin,
I could afford to whip myself to death.

Itha. And so could I ; but penance will not serve.

Bara. To fast, to pray, and wear a shirt of hair,
And on my knees creep to Jerusalem.
Cellars of wine, and sollars full of wheat,
Warehouses stuff'd with spices and with drugs,
Whole chests of gold, in bullion, and in coin,
Besides, I know not how much weight in pearl,
Orient and round, have I within my house ;   70
At Alexandria merchandise unsold ;
But yesterday two ships went from this town,
Their voyage will be worth ten thousand crowns ;
In Florence, Venice, Antwerp, London, Seville,
Frankfort, Lubeck, Moscow, and where not,
Have I debts owing ; and, in most of these,
Great sums of money lying in the banco ;
All this I'll give to some religious house,
So I may be baptiz'd, and live therein.

Friar Jac. O good Barabas, come to our house !   80

Friar Barn. O no, good Barabas, come to our house !

61. *penance*] Q to Dyce, Bull. to Wag. : *any penance,* Cunn.   *serve*] Q to Rob., Cunn., Bull. : *serve [to atone]* Dyce, Ellis, Wag.   68. *bullion*] Reed to Ellis : *Bulloine* Q : *Bullione* Wag.   71. *unsold*] Q to Rob., Cunn. to Wag. : *untold* Dyce.

61.] See textual note for various suggestions as to the right completion of this line. There are so many short lines in the play that we may well leave it as it stands.

65. *And . . . creep*] A promise, perhaps founded upon a remembrance by Marlowe of the medieval custom of creeping to the Cross on Good Friday. See *Piers Plowman*, XXI. 475 : ' *And creop on kneos to the croys*, and cusse hit for a Iuwel.'

66. *sollars*] lofts or upper rooms commonly used in medieval times as granaries or store rooms. See Tusser's *Husbandry*, 129 : ' Then dresse it and laie it *in soller* vp

sweete ', and also Mayhew and Skeat's *Glossary*.

68. *bullion*] Misread by the Quarto compositor as Boulogne, as is evident from the fact that he gives it italics (*Bulloine*), as was usually the case with place-names.

70. *Orient and round*] See note on *orient*, v. iii. 28. *Round* here may refer to lesser or ' seed ' pearls, or may be merely a vague poetic epithet with *orient* attaching to pearl.

71. *unsold*] Dyce proposed to read *untold* here, and it is certainly the word we might have expected. *Unsold*, however, should remain, as it is a perfectly sound reading.

And Barabas, you know——

Bara. I know that I have highly sinn'd :

You shall convert me, you shall have all my wealth.

Friar Jac. O Barabas, their laws are strict !

Bara. I know they are, and I will be with you.

Friar Barn. They wear no shirts, and they go barefoot too.

Bara. Then 'tis not for me ; and I am resolv'd

You shall confess me, and have all my goods.

Friar Jac. Good Barabas, come to me.   90

Bara. You see I answer him, and yet he stays ;

Rid him away, and go you home with me.

Friar Jac. I'll be with you to-night.

Bara. Come to my house at one o'clock this night.

Friar Jac. You hear your answer, and you may be gone.

Friar Barn. Why, go, get you away.

Friar Jac. I will not go for thee.

Friar Barn. Not ! then I'll make thee, rogue.

86. Cunn. and Bull. add S.D. *To F. Jac.*, and so after line 94.   88.
Cunn. and Bull. add S.D. *To F. Barn*, and so after line 91.   89. Ellis adds
S.D. *To Friar Barnardine*.   92. *Rid*] Q. Rob to Wag : *Bid* Reed, Coll.   93.
Friar Jac.] Dyce, etc. :   2. Q : 2d *Friar* Reed to Rob.   98. *rogue*] Coll.,
conj., T. Brooke : *goe* Q : *go* the rest.

85. *their laws are strict*] This is
the first intimation that we have
that the two friars are not both
members of the same order.   Perhaps, however, we should not press
Jacomo's words too far, and should
only take them to mean that the
administration of the laws were
strict in Barnardine's house.   Certainly, from III. iii. 30 we are
entitled to infer that the nunnery
was served by the friars of St.
Jaques.   But there seems much
ground for believing that Marlowe
was very hazy about all this, for
he makes Abigail send to the
nunnery for the friars, and not to
their friaries at all (III. iii. 30).
And it must always be borne in
mind that these scenes are suspect,
and may have been interpolated
with imperfect assimilation.

92. *Rid*] Remove (with violence).

Compare Peele's *Edward I* (Dyce's
edn., p. 408), ' I *rid* her not; I made
her not away ', and see note on III.
i. 233 in the Arden edn. of *2 Henry
VI*.

93. *Friar Jac.*] Friar Jacomo is
the First Friar, and the speech
evidently belongs to him.   It was
so attributed first by Dyce who
altered the Quarto 2, without note
and has been followed by later
editors.

98. *rogue*] I have adopted the
reading first suggested by Collier
(MS.) and given by Professor
Tucker Brooke.   The Quarto has
goe, but from the following line it
seems clear that *rogue* is the word
required, while from the preceding
lines the compositor may have
expected the word *go*, and set it
up in defiance of his MS.

Friar Jac. How! dost call me rogue? [*They fight.*
Itha. Part 'em, master, part 'em.   100
Bara. This is mere frailty : brethren, be content.—
    Friar Barnardine, go you with Ithamore :
    You know my mind ; let me alone with him.
Friar Jac. Why does he go to thy house? let him be gone.
Bara. I'll give him something, and so stop his mouth.
          [*Exit Ithamore with Friar Barnardine.*
    I never heard of any man but he
    Malign'd the order of the Jacobins ;
    But do you think that I believe his words?
    Why, brother, you converted Abigail ;
    And I am bound in charity to requite it,   110
    And so I will. O Jacomo, fail not, but come.
Friar Jac. But, Barabas, who shall be your godfathers?
    For presently you shall be shriv'd.
Bara. Marry, the Turk shall be one of my godfathers,
    But not a word to any of your covent.
Friar Jac. I warrant thee, Barabas.   [*Exit.*
Bara. So, now the fear is past, and I am safe ;

99. *They fight*] Rob. to Ellis : *Fight* Q, Wag.   103. Prefix *Ith.* before
this line in Q to Rob.   103. Cunn. to Ellis add S.D. Aside *to F. Barn.*
after *with him.*   104. *Friar Jac.*] Dyce to Ellis : Prefix omitted Q to
Rob., Wag.   105. *Exit . . .*] Dyce to Ellis : *Exit* Q : *Exeunt* Wag. :
Exeunt Ithamore and Friar Reed to Rob.   111. *Jacomo*] Reed to Ellis :
Iocome Q, Wag.   115. *covent*] Q, Dyce to Wag. : *convent* Reed to Rob., Cunn.

103, 104] In the Quarto and
early editions these lines were
given to Ithamore in error. It is
fairly clear that line 103 is spoken
to Friar Barnardine as an aside
(see Text note). If we adopted the
Quarto reading it would be necessary to consider line 103 as an aside
to Barabas and would give Ithamore credit for more resource and
initiative than seems warranted.
   107. *order of the Jacobins*] The
Dominican Order, originally applied to the French members of the
order, from the church of St.
Jacques, in Paris, near which they
built their first convent. Compare
above, and *Massacre at Paris,*

111. *Jacomo*] The Quarto compositor evidently found it difficult
to read this word, or rather in all
probability it was so contracted he
did not know how to expand it :
here he makes it *Jocome,* and in line
119 it becomes *Jocoma.* See also
Jacomi (III. iii. 71) ; *Jocoma* (IV.
iii. 1, 14).
   114. *the Turk*] Barabas needs the
presence of Ithamore, for his in-
tentions in part were dependent on
the aid of the Turk (see line 130).
   115. *covent*] convent. The Latin-
ised spelling *convent* was not introduced into England before about
1550.   Compare the surviving
spelling of *Covent* Garden still.

For he that shriv'd her is within my house :
What, if I murder'd him ere Jacomo comes ?
Now I have such a plot for both their lives,   120
As never Jew nor Christian knew the like :
One turn'd my daughter, therefore he shall die ;
The other knows enough to have my life,
Therefore 'tis not requisite he should live.
But are not both these wise men to suppose
That I will leave my house, my goods, and all,
To fast and be well whipt ?   I'll none of that.
Now, Friar Barnardine, I come to you :
I'll feast you, lodge you, give you fair words,
And, after that, I and my trusty Turk—   130
No more, but so : it must and shall be done.   [*Exit.*

SCENE II.—*The same.*

Enter BARABAS.

Bara. Ithamore, tell me, is the friar asleep ?

Enter ITHAMORE.

Itha. Yes ; and I know not what the reason is :
Do what I can, he will not strip himself,

119. *Jacomo*] Reed to Ellis : *Jocoma* Q, Wag.   124. *'tis . . . live* Q,
etc. : *tis requisite he should not live,* Deighton conj.   131. *Exit*] Rob.,
Cunn. to Ellis : *omit* the rest.

Act IV.   Scene ii.

Rob., Cunn. to Ellis : *omit* the rest.   *Enter Barabas*] *Enter Barabas and
Ithamore* Rob., Cunn. to Ellis.   *Enter Ithamore* Q, Reed, Dyce, Wag.:
omit the rest.

124. *'tis . . . live*] Deighton (*op.
cit.*) proposes to rearrange here for
better flow of the verse, as ' *tis
requisite he should not live* '.   This
was anticipated by Dyce and con-
demned, for, as he says, ' lest the
reader should suspect that the
author wrote, " Therefore 'tis requisite he should not live ".   I may
observe that we have had before
a similar form of expression, " It
is not necessary I be seen " ' (I. ii.

301).   The confusion may, however,
have arisen from the *not* falling
early in the next line having caught
the compositor's eye.

131. *No more, but so*] A frequently used Elizabethan expression.   See again below, IV. iv.
83.

Scene II.

Scene II] Although the scene is
the same as the last, it is necessary to

Nor go to bed, but sleeps in his own clothes;
I fear me he mistrusts what we intend.

Bara. No; 'tis an order which the friars use:
Yet, if he knew our meanings, could he 'scape?

Itha. No, none can hear him, cry he ne'er so loud.

Bara. Why, true; therefore did I place him there:
The other chambers open towards the street.   10

Itha. You loiter, master; wherefore stay we thus?
O, how I long to see him shake his heels!

Bara. Come on, sirrah:
Off with your girdle; make a handsome noose.—

                [Ithamore makes a noose in his girdle.
     Friar, awake! *[They put it round the Friar's neck.*

Friar Barn. What, do you mean to strangle me?

Itha. Yes, 'cause you use to confess.

Bara. Blame not us, but the proverb, Confess and be
     hanged. Pull hard.

---

11. *we*] Q, etc.: *me* Rob.   14. *Ithamore* . . .] Cunn., Bull.: *omit* Q to Rob.: Dyce and Ellis as printed here with slight verbal change.   15. *They put* . . .] As in line 14.

indicate a slight'pause in the action, to give Barabas time to 'feed and lodge' Barnardine. Jacomo has also been told to come 'at one o'clock' (IV. i. 94). Ithamore in response to Barabas's question comes out through the curtains, so that the audience can at once localise the scene. See also below, notes on line 15 and line 25.

6. *'tis an order . . . use*] The Friars were not allowed by the rules of their Orders to undress completely at night, but lay down in their robes.

use] to pursue or follow as a custom. Compare *The Winter's Tale*, III. ii. 243 : 'So long I daily vow to *use* it.'

12. *shake his heels.*] A euphemism for hanging. The O.E.D. gives a quotation dated 1595 from A. B.'s *Noblen. Asse. D.*33 : 'Whereupon, he caused him with the rest, to be hanged by the neckes, and (as the common proverbe is) sent them

to *shake their heeles* against the winde.' And cf. Chapman's *May-Day*, I. 10.

15. *Friar, awake*] As Dyce suggests, it is probable that at this point Barabas drew aside the curtains of the alcove, or inner-stage, and discovered the Friar asleep.

17. *'cause . . . confess*] because you are accustomed to confess, i.e. to hear confessions.

18. *Confess . . . hanged*] A proverb of the time. See Ray's *Proverbs*, and compare Dekker's *Honest Whore*, Part II, Act v. ii. 100 :

'*Duke.* 'Tis well done to confess.
Matheo : Confess and be hanged . . .
    is't not so ? '

Shakespeare plays upon this in *The Merchant of Venice*, III. ii. 35 :

'*Bass.* Promise me life, and I'll
    confess the truth.
Por. Well then *confess and live.*'

Friar Barn. What, will you have my life ?   20
Bara. Pull hard, I say.   You would have had my goods.
Itha. Ay, and our lives too : therefore pull amain.

                              [*They strangle him.*

'Tis neatly done, sir, here's no print at all.
Bara. Then is it as it should be.   Take him up.
Itha. Nay, master, be ruled by me a little.   So, let him
     lean upon his staff ; excellent ! he stands as if he
     were begging of bacon.
Bara. Who would not think but that this friar liv'd ?
What time a night is't now, sweet Ithamore ?
Itha. Towards one.   30
Bara. Then will not Jacomo be long from hence.   [*Exeunt.*

20. *have*] Rob. to Wag., Coll. conj.: *save* Q to Coll. 22. *They strangle
. . .*] Dyce to Ellis: *omit* the rest. 25. *master*] Reed to Wag.:
Mr. Q. 25. Dyce adds a S.D. *Takes the body, sets it upright against the
wall, and puts a staff in its hand.* 30. *one*] Q inserts after this Enter
Iocoma. Others rightly put it in line 1 next scene. 31. *Jacomo*] Reed
to Ellis: *Iocoma.* Q, Wag. *Exeunt*] Reed to Ellis : *omit* Q, Wag.

20. *have*] The Q. and early
editors read *save*, but this is not
easily made sense unless we adopt
Bullen's conjectural reading :
' What will you ?   Save my life.'
The mistake of *s* for *h*, however, is
much more likely to have caused
the difficulty; and, as Ellis notes,
the retort of Barabas, ' You would
have *had* my goods ', justifies the
emendation.

21 ff.] The rest of this scene and
the next should be compared with
Heywood's *The Captives* (III. 3,
and IV. 1), ed. Judson, for very
close similarities of situation (see
Intro., p. 7).

23. *here's no print*] no mark
remaining of the cord on his neck.
Compare *Venus and Adonis*, 353 :
' His tender cheek receives her soft
hand's *print.*'

25.] Dyce's S.D. reads : ' Takes
the body, sets it upright against

the wall, and puts a staff in its
hand.'   At this point I think
Ithamore brought the Friar's body
out from the inner-stage and stood
it up against one of the posts of the
' heavens ' or of the upper-stage
and propped it up by the staff,
after which he and Barabas retired
and drew the curtains behind them.
Compare *Titus Andronicus*, v. i.
135 :

' Oft have I digg'd up dead men
     from their graves,
And set them upright at their dear
     friends' door.'

27. *begging of bacon*] Abbott,
§ 178, explains this apparent par-
ticiple as a verbal noun, before
which a prepositional ' a ', ' in ',
etc., should be inserted.   These
words remind us of the story of
Dan Hugh of Leicester (see *Intro.*,
p. 7).

SCENE III.—*The same.*

Enter FRIAR JACOMO.

Friar Jac. This is the hour wherein I shall proceed ;
O happy hour, wherein I shall convert
An infidel, and bring his gold into our treasury !
But soft ! is not this Barnardine ? it is ;
And, understanding I should come this way,
Stands here a purpose, meaning me some wrong,
And intercept my going to the Jew.
Barnardine !
Wilt thou not speak ? thou think'st I see thee not ;
Away, I'd wish thee, and let me go by :   10
No, wilt thou not ? nay, then, I'll force my way ;
And, see, a staff stands ready for the purpose :
As thou lik'st that, stop me another time !

[*Strikes him, and he falls.*

Act IV. Scene iii.

Rob, Cunn. to Ellis : *omit* the rest. *Enter . . .*] Reed to Wag :
Enter Iocoma, after ii. 30 *ante* Q.
2. *O happy hour*] Q to Ellis : *omit* Wag., line ending at *Infidel.* 6.
a] Q to Dyce[1], Cunn., Wag. : *o'* Dyce[2]. 13. *Strikes . . .*] Rob., Cunn.,
Bull. : *Strike him, he fals.* Q, Reed, Coll., Wag. : *Takes the staff, and strikes
down the body.* Dyce : *Takes . . . and strikes the body, which falls down.*
Ellis. *Enter . . .*] Reed to Wag. : *omit Ithamore* Q.

Scene III.

Scene III.] There is no break
between this and the previous
scene : Barabas knows Jacomo is
to come in a few minutes, and he
and Ithamore withdraw (see note
above). Jacomo enters and at
once sees Barnardine before him
against the post.
1. *proceed*] Used here in an
emphatic sense to denote making
progress, or prospering. This is
the earliest example cited by the
O.E.D., which adds Jonson's
Catiline, III. i : ' These things,
when they *proceed* not, they go
backward.'
2-3. *O happy . . . treasury*]
Wagner boldly proposed omitting
the words *O happy hour*, and then
arranging the remainder as two
lines. Bullen retains the words, but

is tempted to arrange them as a
separate line. The repetition certainly has little point, and the
second ' wherein ', like the first,
refers to ' hour ' in line 1. Wagner's
emendation has much to commend
it, but we are here dealing with one
of the most suspicious parts of the
play textually, and I have not
felt justified in removing any evi-
dences.
4. *But soft . . .*] Note the very
close parallel of the situation here
with that in *The Captives*, IV. ii. 23,
' But soft, there's one before me ',
etc.
6. *a purpose*] Elizabethan speech
permitted the use of *a* for *on*.
Compare *Romeo and Juliet*, III. i. 93 :
' A plague *a* both your houses.'
7. *intercept*] to intercept. Per-

Enter BARABAS *and* ITHAMORE.

Bara. Why, how now, Jacomo ! what has thou done ?

Friar Jac. Why, stricken him that would have struck at
    me.

Bara. Who is it ?   Barnardine ! now, out, alas, he is slain.

Itha. Ay, master, he's slain ; look how his brains drop out
    on's nose.

Friar Jac. Good sirs, I have done't : but nobody knows
    it but you two ; I may escape.   20

Bara. So might my man and I hang with you for company.

Itha. No ; let us bear him to the magistrates.

Friar Jac. Good Barabas, let me go.

Bara. No, pardon me ; the law must have his course :
    I must be forc'd to give in evidence,
    That, being importun'd by this Barnardine
    To be a Christian, I shut him out,
    And there he sate : now I, to keep my word,
    And give my goods and substance to your house,
    Was up thus early, with intent to go   30
    Unto your friary, because you stay'd.

Itha. Fie upon 'em ! master ; will you turn Christian, when
    holy friars turn devils and murder one another ?

Bara. No ; for this example I'll remain a Jew :
    Heaven bless me ! what, a friar a murderer ?
    When shall you see a Jew commit the like ?

Itha. Why, a Turk could ha' done no more.

Bara. To-morrow is the Sessions ; you shall to it.
    Come, Ithamore, let's help to take him hence.

Friar Jac. Villains, I am a sacred person, touch me not. 40

14. *Jacomo*] *Iocoma* Q. 17. *master*] Reed to Wag. : *Mr.* Q.   *And so in
line* 32.

haps Marlowe wrote ' And t' intercept ', and the sign of the infinitive
was omitted by the compositor,
who tended to absorb the *t*' in the
preceding *d* of *And.* Cf. McKerrow,
Notes on Bibliographical Evidence,
p. 27.

18. *on's nose.*] *On* was frequently
used for *of* before a contracted
pronoun, as here. Compare *Lear*,
IV. v. 20: 'The middle *on's* face',
etc. See Abbott, § 182.

Bara. The law shall touch you ; we'll but lead you, we :
'Las I could weep at your calamity !—
Take in the staff too, for that must be shown :
Law wills that each particular be known. [*Exeunt.*

SCENE IV.—*Outside* BELLAMIRA'S *house.*

Enter BELLAMIRA *and* PILIA-BORZA.

Bell. Pilia-Borza, didst thou meet with Ithamore ?
Pilia. I did.
Bell. And didst thou deliver my letter ?
Pilia. I did.
Bell. And what thinkest thou ? will he come ?
Pilia. I think so : and yet I cannot tell ; for, at the reading of the letter, he looked like a man of another world.
Bell. Why so ?
Pilia. That such a base slave as he should be saluted by such a tall man as I am, from such a beautiful dame as you.   II

Act IV. Scene iv.

Rob., Cunn. to Ellis : *omit* the rest. *Enter Bellamira*] Dyce to Ellis : *Enter Curtezant* Q, Wag. : *Enter Courtezan* Reed to Rob. I. etc. *Bell.*] Curt. Q.

6. *and*] Q, Reed to Cunn., Wag. : *but* Bull., Ellis.

41. *we'll . . . we*] See note on Prologue, 28.

43, 44. *Take in . . . known.*] It was necessary to produce the instrument which was the cause of any misadventure ' whereby (as Cowell, *The Interpreter,* 1637, says) any Christian soule commeth to a violent end, without the fault of any reasonable Creature. For example, if a horse should strike his keeper, and so kill him ', etc., etc. The horse, or tree, or whatever it might be, was forfeited to God, ' that is, to be sold and distributed to the Poore ', the King being the agent for that purpose.

44. *particular*] each individual thing. Cf. *The Winter's Tale,* IV. iv. 144 :
' Your doing,
So singular in each *particular*.'

Scene IV.

Scene IV.] Outer-stage. The scene is before the house of Bellamira, and may be taken as an example of the ' threshold scenes ' described by Sir E. K. Chambers (*Eliz. Stage,* III. 60). Bellamira summons her maids to bring a ' running-banquet ' to them (line 92), just as Mistress Arden (*Arden of Feversham*) prepares and serves her husband with breakfast in front of his house (I. 360 ff.). At line 140 they rise to go in to sleep, and pass in through the middle curtains. W. Wagner (*Sh. Jahrb.* XI. 74 f.) thinks that Heywood's hand is particularly visible in this scene.

9. *base slave*] See above I. ii. 215.
10. *tall man*] See above, III. ii. 7.

Bell. And what said he ?

Pilia. Not a wise word ; only gave me a nod, as who should
say, ' Is it even so ? ' ; and so I left him, being driven
to a non-plus at the critical aspect of my terrible
countenance.

Bell. And where didst meet him ?   17

Pilia. Upon mine own free-hold, within forty foot of the
gallows, conning his neck-verse, I take it, looking of
a friar's execution ; whom I saluted with an old hempen proverb, *Hodie tibi, cras mihi*, and so I left him to
the mercy of the hangman : but, the exercise being
done, see where he comes.

Enter ITHAMORE.

18. *foot*] Q to Cunn., Wag. : *feet* Bull., Ellis.   21. *Hodie*] Reed, etc. :
Hidie Q.

15. *non-plus*] A common phrase
in Elizabethan English to denote
a state of perplexity. Compare
Chapman's *Widows Tears*, v. iii.
370 : ' For my part I am at a *non-
plus* ', etc.
   critical] censorious, fault finding. Compare *Othello*, II. i. 120 :
' I am nothing, if not *critical*.'
   18. *foot*] Silently corrected to
feet by Bullen and Ellis !
   19. *neck-verse*] A Latin verse,
usually the beginning of the 51st
Psalm, which was given to male-
factors to read when they claimed
' benefit of clergy '. It is frequently
referred to by the Elizabethan
writers, see Middleton's *No wit
. . . like a Woman's*, v. i. 351 :
' You can but put me to my book,
      sweet brother,
And I've my *neck-verse* perfect
      here and here ',
and Harrison's *England*, II. xi., and
Cowell's *The Interpreter* (*ad loc.*].
   of] Frequently used in Elizabethan times for *on*. See Schmidt's
Shakespeare Lexicon, 799, or
Abbott, § 175.
   20, 21. *hempen proverb*] Perhaps a
proverb said at the foot of the
gallows, since *hempen* is frequently
used in phrases and locutions,

referring to the hangman's halter.
See below, line 27.
   21. *Hodie . . . mihi.*] Professor
Tucker Brooke cites a possible
source of the phrase in the Vulgate
Liber Ecclesiastici, XXXVIII. 23 :
' mihi heri, et tibi hodie.' The
Quarto misprints *Hidie*, for the
compositor evidently found his copy
difficult to read, and all foreign
words were liable to suffer at his
hands.   See the two Spanish
proverbs in II. i. 39 and 64, the
Latin *proximus* (I. i. 187), *Primus*
(I. ii. 165), or the Italian *Cazzo,
diabolo* (IV. i. 20).
   22. *exercise*] Generally used to
indicate some kind of religious
ceremony or devotion. The
Puritans at this time were used to
have week-day preachings which
they called exercises. Marlowe
humorously uses the word to
describe the ceremonial of an
execution. For examples of its
proper use see *Richard III*, III. ii.
109 :
' I thank thee, good Sir John, with
      all my heart
I am in debt for your last *exercise* ',
and also Middleton's *The Mayor of
Queenborough*, v. i. 244, ' I was
never better pleased at an *exercise* '.

Itha. I never knew a man take his death so patiently as
this friar; he was ready to leap off ere the halter was
about his neck; and when the hangman had put on
his hempen tippet, he made such haste to his prayers,
as if he had had another cure to serve; well, go whither
he will, I'll be none of his followers in haste: and, now
I think on't, going to the execution, a fellow met me
with a muschatoes like a raven's wing, and a dagger
with a hilt like a warming pan, and he gave me a
letter from one Madam Bellamira, saluting me in such
sort as if he had meant to make clean my boots with
his lips; the effect was, that I should come to her
house: I wonder what the reason is; it may be she
sees more in me than I can find in myself: for she
writes further, that she loves me ever since she saw
me, and who would not requite such love? Here's
her house, and here she comes, and now would I were
gone; I am not worthy to look upon her.   41
Pilia. This is the gentleman you writ to.
*Itha. Gentleman! he flouts me; what gentry can be in a
poor Turk of tenpence? I'll be gone.*   [*Aside.*

31. *muschatoes*] Q, Dyce, Bull., Ellis, Wag.: *mustachios* Reed, Coll.,
Rob., Cunn.   44. *Aside*] Dyce to Ellis: *omit* the rest.   And so in line 46.

27. *hempen tippet*] the noose of
the rope, the hangman's halter.
Compare Nashe, *The Unfortunate
Traveller*, 67: 'I scapde dauncing
in a *hempen* circle.'
28. *cure to serve*] A parish to
minister to, as in the Act 13 Eliz.,
c. 20, § 2: 'His Curat . . . that
shall there *serve the Cure* for hym'
(O.E.D.).
31. *with a muschatoes*] Innumerable spellings are to be found of our
word moustache, and Marlowe here
uses the plural form with a singular
construction. The O.E.D. gives
another instance from Field's
Woman is a Weathercock, v. 1:

'Abra . . . And a huge *mus-
    tachios ?*
Neu. A verie Turkes.'

See also Middleton's *The Black Book*
(*Works*, ed. Bullen), VIII. 14: 'His
crow-black *muchatoes* were almost
half an ell from one end to the other.'
44. *Turk of tenpence*] A derog-
atory phrase meant to indicate the
contempt felt by a Christian for an
infidel Turk. The 'tenpenny infidel' is a term applied to the Turk
in the play of *Westward Hoe*, 1607,
iv. 1. Dyce quotes John Taylor,
'in some verses on Coriat,' *Workes*,
1630, p. 82:
'That if he had a *Turke of ten
    pence* bin', etc.
Also see Middleton's *A Fair Quarrel*,
III. i. 73, we get 'A valiant *Turk*,
though not worth *tenpence*'. A
similar phrase, *Eightpenny soldier*,
occurs in *1 Henry IV*, III. iii. 119,

Bell. Is't not a sweet-faced youth, Pilia ?

Itha. Again, sweet youth ; [*Aside*]—Did not you, sir, bring
the sweet youth a letter ?

Pilia. I did, sir, and from this gentlewoman, who, as myself and the rest of the family, stand or fall at your
service.   50

Bell. Though woman's modesty should hale me back,
I can withhold no longer ; welcome, sweet love.

Itha. Now am I clean, or rather foully, out of the way.
                                                      [*Aside.*

Bell. Whither so soon ?

*Itha. I'll go steal some money from my master to make me
handsome* [*Aside*] : Pray, pardon me ; I must go see
a ship discharged.

Bell. Canst thou be so unkind to leave me thus ?

Pilia. And ye did but know how she loves you, sir !

Itha. Nay, I care not how much she loves me.   60
Sweet Bellamira, would I had my master's wealth for
thy sake !

Pilia. And you can have it, sir, and if you please.

Itha. If 'twere above ground I could, and would have it ;
but he hides and buries it up, as partridges do their
eggs, under the earth.

Pilia. And is't not possible to find it out ?

Itha. By no means possible.

Bell. What shall we do with this base villain, then ?
                                       [*Aside to Pilia-Borza.*

53. *Aside*] Dyce, Bull., Ellis : *omit* the rest.   56. *Aside*] Dyce to
Ellis : *omit* the rest.   59. *And*] Q to Rob., Bull., Wag. : *An* Dyce, Cunn.,
Ellis.   *ye*] Q to Rob., Cunn. to Wag. : *you* Dyce.   61. *Bellamira*] Reed,
etc. : *Allamira* Q.   63. *and if*] Q to Rob., Wag. : *an if* Dyce, Cunn. to
Ellis.   69. *Aside* . . .] Rob to Ellis : *omit* Q to Coll., Wag.

and Chapman's *Widow's Tears,*
v. i. 45.

45. *sweet-faced youth*] Compare *A
Midsummer Night's Dream,* I. ii. 87 :
'Pyramus is a *sweet-faced* man ', or
Shirley's *A Grateful Servant,* i. ii. :
'Is't not *a sweet-faced* boy.'

53. *clean . . . the   way*] com-
10

pletely bewildered.   *Clean* here
means 'entirely ', 'altogether ', as
in I. i. 177, and Marlowe plays on
its more ordinary use to contrast
it with foul.   The same association
of ideas is in his mind in *Dr.
Faustus* : 'Go and make *clean* our
boots which lie *foul* on our hands.'

Pilia. Let me alone ; do but you speak him fair ;   70
    [*Aside to her.*

But you know some secrets of the Jew,
Which, if they were reveal'd, would do him harm.
Itha. Ay, and such as—Go to, no more ! I'll make him
    send me half he has, and glad he scapes so too. Pen
    and ink : I'll write unto him ; we'll have money straight.
Pilia. Send for a hundred crowns at least.
Itha. Ten hundred thousand crowns.—[*writing*] *Master*
    Barabas,—
Pilia. Write not so submissively, but threatening him.
Itha. Sirrah Barabas, send me a hundred crowns.   80
Pilia. Put in two hundred at least.
Itha. I charge thee send me three hundred by this bearer, and
    this shall be your warrant : if you do not—no more, but so.
Pilia. Tell him you will confess.

70. *Aside* . . .] Dyce to Ellis :   after l. 71.   Rob. : *omit* the rest.
71. *But you know*] Q to Rob., Wag. : *But you know, sir* Dyce, conj. : *But*
[*sir,*] *you know,* Cunn., Bull., Ellis.   74. *Pen and ink*] Q to Rob., Wag. :
omitted in text and treated as a S.D. Cunn., Bull. : *omit* Dyce[1], Ellis.   76.
After *least* Q to Rob., Cunn., Wag. have S.D. *He writes :* others *omit.*
77. *writing*] Dyce to Ellis : *omit* the rest. *Master*] Reed, etc. : *Mr.* Q.
79. *threatening*] Q, Rob. to Wag. : *threaten* Reed, Coll. After prefix to 80,
82, 85, Dyce and Ellis add S.D. *Writing.*

71. *But you know* . . . *Jew.*] A nine-syllable line, and several emendations have been proposed—rather unnecessarily. Besides those in *Text Note* Brennan suggests, ' But you ⟨must⟩ know ', and Brereton ⟨I⟩ (i.e. ' Ay) but you know '.

74, 75. *Pen and ink*] Considerable discussion has taken place over this phrase. Dyce omits it, as he regards it as a Stage Direction for the property man's convenience, similar to those noted by Mr. A. W. Pollard in his *Shakespeare Folios and Quartos.* Bullen and Cunningham boldly print it as a Stage Direction. It does not seem certain to me that the words were not meant to be said by Ithamore, and therefore I leave them. There seems to be no

reason why he should not demand pen and ink ; and, in the original Quarto two lines later, there is a S.D. ' He writes ', suggesting that the two lines have given time for him to get his materials together. As Wagner notes, if this is a S.D., ought we not also to regard lines 90 and 123 as of the same nature ? In Heywood's ' *If you know not me* ', etc. (Pearson's ed. I, p. 314), there occurs ' *Pen and Ink !* I'll set it down in black and white ', and in Dekker's *Honest Whore*, Part I, Act v. i. 87, we read, ' Get *pen and ink,* get *pen and ink* ' ; and, a few lines later, as *He writes* in *The Jew*, the S.D. has : ' Re-enter *George* with *pen and ink.*' The command occurs also in *The Massacre at Paris,* Sc. XII, l. 1, and *The Captives,* III. i. 93.

Itha. Otherwise I'll confess all.—Vanish, and return in a
twinkle.

Pilia. Let me alone ; I'll use him in his kind. [*Exit Pilia-*
Borza.

Itha. Hang him, Jew!

Bell. Now, gentle Ithamore, lie in my lap.
Where are my maids ? provide a running banquet ; 90
Send to the merchant, bid him bring me silks,
Shall Ithamore, my love, go in such rags ?

Itha. And bid the jeweller come hither too.

Bell. I have no husband, sweet, I'll marry thee.

Itha. Content, but we will leave this paltry land,
And sail from hence to Greece, to lovely Greece.
I'll be thy Jason, thou my golden fleece ;
Where painted carpets o'er the meads are hurl'd,
And Bacchus' vineyards overspread the world :
Where woods and forests go in goodly green,   100
I'll be Adonis, thou shalt be Love's Queen.
The meads, the orchards, and the primrose-lanes,
Instead of sedge and reed, bear sugar-canes :
Thou in those groves, by Dis above,
Shalt live with me, and be my love.

Bell. Whither will I not go with gentle Ithamore ?

Enter PILIA-BORZA.

87. *Exit . . .*] Cunn. to Wag.: *after* 88 Dyce: *omit* the rest.   90. *run-*
ning] Q to Dyce[1], Bull. to Wag.: *cunning* Dyce[2], Cunn.   99. *over-*
spread] Reed to Ellis : *ore-spread* Q, Wag.

85, 86. *return . . . twinkle*] A
conjuring phrase.

87. *in his kind*] according to his
kind (i.e. kin).

90. *a running banquet*] Dyce in
his second edition emends this to
' a cunning banquet'.   But there is
no need, and it spoils the sense,
which implies a hastily prepared
meal, such as Bellamira's maids
could have compassed in a few
minutes when their mistress commanded them to serve it quickly.
The expression occurs in *Henry*
VIII, i. iv. 12 :

' Some of these
Should find a *running banquet* ere
they rested.'

104–5. ' *Thou in . . . my love* ']
The resemblance of these lines
to Marlowe's famous poem ' *The*
Passionate Shepherd ' will be
noticed.   The dramatic impropriety
of this passage in the mouth of
Ithamore is obvious.

Dis above] contracted from Dives,
a name sometimes given to Pluto,
the god of riches—and of the *lower*
world.   Another of Ithamore's
ludicrous blunders.

Itha. How now ! hast thou the gold ?

Pilia. Yes.

Itha. But came it freely ? did the cow give down her milk
     freely ?   110

Pilia. At reading of the letter, he star'd and stamp'd, and
     turn'd aside : I took him by the beard, and looked
     upon him thus ; told him he were best to send it :
     then he hugged and embraced me.

Itha. Rather for fear than love.

Pilia. Then, like a Jew, he laugh'd and jeer'd, and told
     me he lov'd me for your sake, and said what a
     faithful servant you had bin.

Itha. The more villain he to keep me thus : here's goodly
     'parel, is there not ?   120

Pilia. To conclude, he gave me ten crowns.

Itha. But ten ? I'll not leave him worth a gray groat.
     Give me a ream of paper : we'll have a kingdom of
     gold for't.

112. *beard*] Reed, etc. : *sterd* Q.   115. *than*] Reed, etc. : *then* Q.   121.
After *crowns* Dyce and Ellis add S.D. *Delivers the money to Ithamore.*

109. *give down her milk*] A
technical term borrowed from
farming, signifying ' to let flow '.
The O.E.D. has no example before
Dryden's translation of Ovid's
Fables, 1699.

112. *beard*] The Quarto misprint
sterd is probably due to the compositor's eye catching the word
star'd which stands immediately
above it in line 111.

120. *'parel*] Here used for
apparel. This shortening of words
was common, often for metrical
reasons. See *Romeo and Juliet*,
v. iii. 289 : *'pothecary* for *apothecary*, or *Antony and Cleopatra*, III.
xi. 54 : *'stroyed* for *destroyed*.

121. *he gave . . . crowns.*] Evidently as a gratuity or bribe of
some sort. Dyce and others print
as a S.D. ' Delivers the money to
Ithamore', but this is doubtful.
Ithamore got the 300 crowns he
asked for, as may be seen from lines

107 ff., IV. v. 1 ff. and 20 ff.
and Pilia - Borza got *ten*, but
Ithamore is so exasperated by the
Jew's meanness that he asks for
another 500 crowns and *a hundred*
for Pilia-Borza, IV. iv. 125 ff., and
see IV. v. 18–22.

122. *gray groat*] The O.E.D. says,
' an emphatic equivalent of groat,
and inferentially something of little
value '. Perhaps ' gray ' because
of silver rather than gold. Compare
Harrison's *Description of England*,
II. ii., p. 63 : ' Of thise portion poore
Saint Peter did neuer heare, of so
much as *one graie grote*.' The
phrase seems to have been proverbial. See Heywood's *Proverbs*,
I. xi., ' And I knew him not worth
a gray groat'.

123. *ream . . . kingdom*]   ' A
quibble. *Realm* was often written
ream in the 16th century, and frequently, even if the former spelling
was given, the *l* was not sounded.'

Pilia. Write for five hundred crowns.

Itha. Sirrah Jew, as you love your life, send me five hundred crowns, and give the bearer a hundred.—Tell him I must have't.

Pilia. I warrant, your worship shall have't.

Itha. And if he ask why I demand so much, tell   130 him I scorn to write a line under a hundred crowns.

Pilia. You'd make a rich poet, sir. I am gone. [*Exit.*

Itha. Take thou the money ; spend it for my sake.

Bell. 'Tis not thy money, but thyself I weigh :

Thus Bellamira esteems of gold ;   [*Throws it aside.*

But thus of thee.   [*Kisses him.*

Itha. That kiss again ; She runs division of my lips.

What an eye she casts on me ! it twinkles like a star.

---

126. After prefix S.D. [*writing*] Dyce to Ellis : *omit* the rest. 132. *You'd*] Reed, etc.: *Yon'd* Q. 135. *Thus Bellamira*] Q to Dyce, Bull. to Wag. : [*See*] *thus Bellamira* Cunn. 135. *Throws it aside*] Dyce, Ellis : *Throws it on the floor* Cunn., Bull., Wag. : *omit* Q and the rest. 136. *Kisses him*] Reed, etc. : *Kisse him* Q. 137–38. *She runs . . . star*] Aside in Dyce only.

See Nares, 725, and compare *Pappe with an Hatchet* : ' Let them but chafe my penne, and it shall sweat out a whole *realm* of paper, or make them odious to the whole *Realme.*' Cf. also *Dido*, iv. iii. 18, and *Faerie Queene*, III. v. 53, and v. vii. 23.

127. *the bearer a hundred*] See note on line 121.

135. *Thus . . . gold*] Cunningham's suggested reading, ' See, thus Bellamira ', etc., would not seem to be necessary, as Bellamira is easily pronounced as five syllables (Bellamíra). This is also suggested by Le Gay Brereton (*Beiblatt zur Anglia*, 1905, p. 205).

137. *runs . . . lips*] to run division is ' to execute a rapid melodic passage, originally conceived as the dividing of each of a long succession of long notes into several short ones', O.E.D. Hence here it signifies that Bellamira lavished kisses on him with passionate iteration and variation. The word is also used by Heywood in *A Woman Kild with Kindnes*, Act v. ii. 13 :

' Her lute : Oh God, upon this instrument
Her fingers have run quick division,
Sweeter than that which now divides our hearts,'

and compare Middleton's *Blurt, Master Constable*, Act I. i. 60 : ' If all the wit in this company have nothing to set itself about but to *run division* upon me,' Marston's *Antonio and Mellida*, III. i. 108, and v. i. 114, etc. Further we must note that Ithamore calls for ' That kiss again ' as Orsino calls for ' That strain again ' (*Twelfth Night*, I. i. 4), as though the kiss had were so exquisite he would repeat the sensation caused by Bellamira's lips running upon his, as fingers on the keys of a virginal.

138. *What an eye . . . star*] To *twinkle* is to open and close the eye quickly—to wink. In Chaucer's *Boethius*, II, Prose III, we have :

Bell. Come, my dear love, let's in and sleep together.
Itha. O, that ten thousand nights were put in one,   140
    That we might sleep seven years together afore we wake.
Bell. Come, amorous wag, first banquet, and then sleep.

                            [Exeunt.

SCENE V.—*Outside the house of* BARABAS.

Enter BARABAS, *reading a letter.*

Bara. Barabas, send me three hundred crowns.
    Plain Barabas.   O, that wicked courtesan!
    He was not wont to call me Barabas.
    Or else I will confess : ay, there it goes :
    But, if I get him, *coupe de gorge* for that.
    He sent a shaggy, totter'd, staring slave,
    That, when he speaks, draws out his grisly beard,
    And winds it twice or thrice about his ear ;

140–1.] *O . . . wake.* As prose Dyce : omit *together* Wag. : three lines div. after *one, together, wake* Q.   142. *Exeunt*] Reed, etc. : *omit* Q.

Act IV.   Scene v.

Rob., Cunn. to Ellis : *omit* the rest.
    6. *totter'd*] Q to Dyce[1], Cunn. to Wag. : *tatter'd* Dyce[2].

'She hath now *twinkled* first upon thee with a wikkede *eye.*' Compare Beaumont and Fletcher's *Women Pleased,* IV. i. : 'I saw the wench that twired and *twinkled* at thee.'

140–1] I have ventured to add to line 141 the words 'we wake' (which end a separate line in the Quarto), thus making it an alexandrine, which well suits the drawn-out expectations of Ithamore. Wagner's omission of *together* deprives the line of some of its effect.

142. *wag*] A favourite word of Marlowe's.   See e.g. *Dido,* I. i. 23, III. i. 31, IV. v. 19.

Scene V.

Scene V.] This takes place on the outer-stage and is not very precisely located—perhaps outside Barabas's house. 'When shall I see you *at* my house' he asks in line 57, which would seem to be against those editors who say the scene takes place in his house. On the other hand he pleads he has lost his keys and therefore cannot open his coffers—an unnecessary plea unless he is at home (l. 34).

5. *coupe de gorge*] said, possibly, with an expressive gesture towards his throat.   There was apparently a sinister familiarity about the French phrase for throat-cutting. Compare Pistol's 'Couple a gorge' in answer to Nym's 'I will cut thy throat' (*Henry V,* II. i. 75).

6. *totter'd*] an old form of tattered.   Compare *1 Henry IV,* IV. ii. 37, 'A hundred and fifty *tottered* prodigals', and Lyly, *Endimion,* v. i. : 'whose garment, was so *totterd* that it was easy to number every thread.'   Bullen notes that there is a somewhat similar description of a ruffian in *Arden of Feversham,* II. i. 52 :

Whose face has been a grind-stone for men's swords ;
His hands are hack'd, some fingers cut quite off ; 10
Who, when he speaks, grunts like a hog, and looks
Like one that is employ'd in catzerie
And cross-biting ; such a rogue
As is the husband to a hundred whores :
And I by him must send three hundred crowns.
Well, my hope is, he will not stay there still ;
And when he comes : O, that he were but here !

Enter PILIA-BORZA.

Pilia. Jew, I must ha' more gold.
Bara. Why, want'st thou any of thy tale ?
Pilia. No ; but three hundred will not serve his turn. 20
Bara. Not serve his turn, sir ?
Pilia. No, sir ; and therefore I must have five hundred more.
Bara. I'll rather——
Pilia. O, good words, sir, and send it you were best ; see,
there's his letter.   [*Gives letter.*
Bara. Might he not as well come as send ? pray, bid him
come and fetch it : what he writes for you, ye shall
have straight.
Pilia. Ay, and the rest too, or else——

12. *catzerie*] Q to Coll., Dyce¹, Cunn. to Wag. : *catzery* Dyce² : *cotzerie*
Rob.   13. *such a*] Q to Dyce, Bull. to Wag. : *such a [sort of]* Cunn.   25.
Gives letter] Dyce to Ellis : *omit* the rest.

'A lean-faced writhen knave,
Hawk-nosed and very hollow-eyed,
With mighty furrows in his stormy
brow,
Long hair down his shoulders curled,
His chin was bare, but on his upper
lip
A mutchado which he *wound about
his ear.*'

12. *catzerie*] The O.E.D. ventures
no definition. Nares says (p. 144)
that it is formed from *catso*, ' a low-
lived term of reproach borrowed
from the Italians by ignorant
travellers, who probably knew not
its real meaning. Used to signify
a rogue, cheat or base fellow.' See

above, p. 120, s.v. *cazzo*, and below,
line 14, for a clue to the sense of
the word.
    13. *cross-biting*] cheating, swind-
ling. See *Selimus*, 1950 : ' This is
some cousening coni-catching *cros-
biter* ', and Marston's *What you
will*, III. ii. 279 : ' Perfect state
pollecy, Can *crosse-bite* even sence ;'
and see III. iii. 130, and Middleton's *Your Five Gallants*, II. iii. 334.
    19. *tale*] reckoning. See Exodus
v. 8 : ' And the *tale* of the bricks,
which they did make heretofore
. . . ye shall not diminish ought
thereof.' Barabas refers to the
three hundred crowns he has already
given to Pilia-Borza.

Bara. I must make this villain away [*Aside.*] Please you
  dine with me, sir ;—*and you shall be most heartily*
  poisoned. [*Aside.*
Pilia. No, God-a-mercy. Shall I have these crowns ? 33
Bara. I cannot do it ; I have lost my keys.
Pilia. O, if that be all, I can pick ope your locks.
Bara. Or climb up to my counting-house window : you
  know my meaning.
Pilia. I know enough, and therefore talk not to me of your
  counting-house. The gold ! or know, Jew, it is in my
  power to hang thee. 40
Bara. I am betray'd. [*Aside.*
  'Tis not five hundred crowns that I esteem ;
  I am not mov'd at that : this angers me,
  That he, who knows I love him as myself,
  Should write in this imperious vein. Why, sir,
  You know I have no child, and unto whom
  Should I leave all, but unto Ithamore ?
Pilia. Here's many words, but no crowns : the crowns !
Bara. Commend me to him, sir, most humbly,
  And unto your good mistress as unknown. 50
Pilia. Speak, shall I have 'em, sir ?
Bara. Sir, here they are.
  O, that I should part with so much gold ! [*Aside.*
  Here, take 'em, fellow, with as good a will——
  As I would see thee hang'd [*Aside*] *;* O, love stops my
  breath !

30. *Aside*] Dyce to Wag. : *omit* the rest. 41. *Aside*] Dyce, Bull. to
Wag. : *omit* the rest. 51. *'em*] Reed to Ellis : *'vm* Q, Wag. 51. Dyce and
Ellis add *Gives money* after *are.* 52. *I should*] Q to Rob., Cunn. to Wag. :
I e'er should Dyce, conj. 54. *hang'd*] Q to Wag. : *omit* Brereton conj.
Aside] Dyce to Wag. : *omit* the rest. *O,*] Q to Ellis : *omit* Wag.

36. *Or climb up . . . window*]
Barabas is evidently referring to
the incident mentioned in III. i. 20,
where Pilia-Borza describes his
visit to the Jew's counting-house.
  48. *words*] Pilia-Borza sardonically
draws this word out into two syllables.
  49. *humbly*] a trisyllable. Per-

haps the answer of Barabas to the
above insult of Pilia-Borza.
  50. *as unknown*] i.e. as yet unknown to me.
  54. *As . . . breath*] Mr. Le Gay
Brereton (*op. cit.* 205) says : ' To
mend the measure and to give sense
to the last four words, I would

Never lov'd man servant as I do Ithamore.

Pilia. I know it, sir.

Bara. Pray, when, sir, shall I see you at my house ?

Pilia. Soon enough to your cost, sir. Fare you well. [*Exit.*

Bara. Nay, to thine own cost, villain, if thou com'st !

Was ever Jew tormented as I am ?   60

To have a shag-rag knave to come ⟨convey⟩

Three hundred crowns,—and then five hundred crowns !

Well, I must seek a means to rid 'em all,

And presently ; for in his villany

He will tell all he knows, and I shall die for't.

I have it :

I will in some disguise go see the slave,

And how the villain revels with my gold.'   [*Exit.*

SCENE VI.—*Outside* BELLAMIRA'S *house.*

Enter BELLAMIRA, ITHAMORE, *and* PILIA-BORZA.

Bell. I'll pledge thee, love, and therefore drink it off.

Itha. Say'st thou me so ? have at it ! and do you hear ?

[*Whispers.*

55. *lov'd man servant*] Q to Bull. : *man servant lov'd* Ellis, Wag. 59. *to thine*] Q, Rob. to Wag. : *thine* Reed, Coll. 61. ⟨*convey*⟩] Brereton, conj. : Dyce¹ adds [*and force from me*] : Dyce², Ellis read [*force from me*].

Act IV. Scene vi.

Bull., Ellis : *omit* the rest. *Enter Bellamira . . .*] Dyce to Ellis : *Enter Curtezane . . .* Q, Wag. : *Enter Courtezan . . .* Reed to Rob. 1. etc. *Bell.*] *Curt.* Q. 2. *Whispers . . .*] Dyce to Ellis, Wag. : *omit* the rest.

read : " As I would see thee— ; O, love stops my breath." The snarling tone and vindictive expression of the Jew suddenly give way to fawning before the bully's threatening scowl.' This is probably correct and represents how the line was spoken on the stage.

55. *Never . . . Ithamore.*] Ellis and Wagner print ' Never man servant lov'd ', etc. Brennan remarks that this emendation is ' one of the worst ever made '.

61. *shag-rag*] rascally, ragged. Compare Chapman's *May Day*, ' Ide hire some *shag-ragge* or other

for half a chicken to cut's throat.'

⟨*convey*⟩]   Something   has dropped out here. The emendations of Dyce and Ellis are not very happy. Brereton ingeniously proposes altering ' come ' to ' conie ' and adding catch, i.e. to conycatch. Another suggestion of his I have adopted.

64. *presently*] immediately. See Matthew xxvi. 53, and *Two Gentlemen of Verona*, IV. iv. 76 : ' Go *presently* and take this ring with thee.'

Scene VI.

Scene VI.] As for Scene IV.

Bell. Go to, it shall be so.

Itha. Of that condition I will drink it up :

Here's to thee.

Bell.   Nay, I'll have all or none.

Itha. There, if thou lov'st me, do not leave a drop.

Bell. Love thee ! fill me three glasses.

Itha. Three and fifty dozen : I'll pledge thee.

Pilia. Knavely spoke, and like a knight-at-arms.

Itha. Hey, *Rivo Castiliano !* a man's a man.   10

Bell. Now to the Jew.

Itha. Ha ! to the Jew ; and send me money he were best.

Pilia. What wouldst thou do, if he should send thee none ?

Itha. Do nothing ; but I know what I know ; he's a

murderer.

Bell. I had not thought he had been so brave a man.

Itha. You knew Mathias and the governor's son ; he and

I killed 'em both, and yet never touched 'em.

Pilia. O, bravely done !

Itha. I carried the broth that poisoned the nuns ; and 20

he and I, snicle hand too fast, strangled a friar.

5. *Bell.*] Dyce, etc. : *Pil.* Q to Coll.   12. *he*] Dyce² to Wag. : *you* Q to Dyce¹.   21. *snicle . . . strangled*] Q to Wag. : *snicle hand to fist* Steevens conj. : *snicling too fast* Rob. : *snicle hard and fast*, Cunn. conj. : *Pilia, Two hands snickle-fast—Itha. Strangled* Mitford conj.

4. *Of . . . condition*] *Of* here stands for *on*. Compare *2 Henry IV*, II. iv. 127 : ' God's blessing *of* your good heart.'

5. *Bell.*] Despite Brereton's defence of the ascription of this line to Pilia-Borza in the Quarto it seems to belong to Bellamira.

10. *Rivo Castiliano*] The Arden editors of *1 Henry IV*, referring to a passage in that play in Act II. iv. 111, write a long note on the word *Rivo*, quoting *inter alia* from *Look about You* (Hazlitt's *Dodsley*, VII. 505) : ' And *Rivo* will he cry, and *Castile* too.' Gifford suggested that *Rivo* is ' corrupted perhaps from the Spanish *rio*, which is figuratively used for a large quantity of liquor '.   Perhaps our

expression, they add, ' = the Castilian stream or liquor, i.e. wine (perhaps with a play on *fons Castalius*)'.   See also Middleton's *Blurt, Master Constable*, I. ii. 203 : ' Cry *rivo* hoh ! laugh and be fat.' *Rivo* is a favourite word of Marston's : see for examples Marston's *Works*, ed. Halliwell, I., 239, 244, 274, 284, etc.

12. *he*] This emendation seems necessary, otherwise we are forced to imagine Ithamore is addressing the Jew as if he were present.

21. *snicle hand too fast,*] This corrupt phrase has never been clearly elucidated.   The textual notes show the various emendations that have been proposed.   *Snicle* is a dialect word, belonging to the

Bell. You two alone?

Itha. We two; and 'twas never known, nor never shall be
    for me.

Pilia. This shall with me unto the governor.
[Aside to Bellamira.

Bell. And fit it should: but first let's ha' more gold.
[Aside to Pilia-Borza.

Come, gentle Ithamore, lie in my lap.

Itha. ' Love me little, love me long ' : let music rumble,
    Whilst I in thy incony lap do tumble.

Enter BARABAS, *with a lute, disguised.*

Bell. A French musician!—Come, let's hear your skill. 30

Bara. Must tuna my lute for sound, twang, twang, first.

Itha. Wilt drink, Frenchman? here's to thee with a——
    Pox on this drunken hiccup!

Bara. Gramercy, monsieur.

Bell. Prithee, Pilia-Borza, bid the fiddler give me the posy
    in his hat there.

Pilia. Sirrah, you must give my mistress your posy.

Bara. A votre commandement, madame.

---

25. *Aside* . . .] Dyce to Wag.: *omit* the rest, and so in next line.
29. *incony*] Reed to Wag.: *incoomy* Q. *Enter* . . .] Q to Rob., Cunn.,
Bull., Wag.: *Enter Barabas, disguised as a French musician, with a lute,
and a nosegay in his hat* Dyce, Ellis. 38. *A* . . . *madame*] *A voustre
commandemente Madam.* Q. After *madame* Dyce adds *Giving nosegay.*

N. of England, generally meaning
to snare, to catch in a noose.

  27. *lie in my lap.*] As in *1 Henry
IV*, III. i. 229 : ' Come quick, that
I may *lay* my head *in thy lap* ', and
Hamlet's query to Ophelia, ' Lady,
shall I *lie in your lap* ? ' See also
this expression used earlier, IV. iv.
89, and below, note on lines 28, 29.

  28. *'Love me* . . . *long'*] A proverbial expression, see Ray's *Proverbs* (1678), p. 54, and Heywood's
Proverbs (Farmer's edn.), p. 57 :
' Old wise folk say : love me little,
love me long.'

  28–29. *let music* . . . *tumble*]
Compare *Fedele and Fortunio*, l.
1735, ' that can *tumble* in a Gentle
woman's lap, and *rumble* in her
ears.'

  29. *incony*] sweet, delicate,
pretty. ' A cant word prevalent
about 1600, of doubtful meaning
and of unascertained origin,'
O.E.D. Compare Middleton's
Blurt, Master Constable, II. ii. 24 :
' It makes you have, O, a most
incony body.' Shakespeare uses it
twice in *Love's Labour's Lost*, III. i.
134, and IV. i. 141.

Bell. How sweet, my Ithamore, the flowers smell !

Itha. Like thy breath, sweetheart ; no violet like 'em. 40

Pilia. Foh ! methinks they stink like a hollyhock.

Bara. So now, I am reveng'd upon 'em all :
    The scent thereof was death : I poison'd it.   [*Aside.*

Itha. Play, fiddler, or I'll cut your cat's guts into chitterlings.

Bara. Pardonnez moi, be no in tune yet ; so, now, now all
    be in.

Itha. Give him a crown, and fill me out more wine.

Pilia. There's two crowns for thee : play.

Bara. How liberally the villain gives me mine own gold !
                                           [*Aside.*

Pilia. Methinks he fingers very well.   50

Bara. So did you when you stole my gold.   [*Aside.*

Pilia. How swift he runs !

Bara. You run swifter when you threw my gold out of my
    window.   [*Aside.*

Bell. Musician, hast been in Malta long ?

Bara. Two, three, four month, madam.

Itha. Dost not know a Jew, one Barabas ?

Bara. Very mush : monsieur, you no be his man ?

Pilia. His man !

Itha. I scorn the peasant : tell him so.   60

---

43. *Aside*] Rob. to Wag.: *omit* the rest.   45. Prefix omitted in Q.
Pardonnez moi Coll. to Ellis : *Pardona moy* Q, Reed, Wag.   And so in
l. 71.   48. After *play* Dyce adds S.D. *Giving money.*   49. *Aside*] Q to Rob.,
Cunn., Bull., Wag. : *Aside, and then plays,* Dyce : *Aside.   Barabas then
plays.* Ellis.   58. *monsieur*] Reed to Ellis : *Mounsier* Q, Wag.

---

43. *The scent . . . it.*] Cf. *The
Massacre at Paris,* Scene III, where
the Queen Mother of Navarre is
poisoned by a pair of scented
gloves.   Also see *Edward II,* line
2363, 'I learned in Naples how to
poison flowers', and Alabaster's
Roxana, where the catastrophe is
caused by poisoned flowers.

44. *chitterlings*] The smaller in-
testines of the pig or calf prepared
for eating, and sometimes for use
in sausage-making.   See Dekker,
1 The Honest Whore, III. i. 19 :

' How fare I ? for sixpence a meal,
wench, as well as heart can wish,
with calve's chaldrons, and *chitterlings* ', and also *The Maid of Honour,*
III. i. 92.

47. *fill   me   out . . . wine*] i.e.
pour out.   Cf. Marston's *Antonio
and Mellida* (ed. Halliwell), I, p.
28 : ' *Fill out* Greek wine.'

50. *fingers*] plays on his lute.
Compare Barclay's *Eclogues,* IV.
27 : ' Yet could he pipe and *finger*
well a drone (bag-pipe).'

52. *runs*] See in IV. iv. 137, *ante.*

Bara. He knows it already. [*Aside.*

Itha. 'Tis a strange thing of that Jew, he lives upon pickled
grasshoppers and sauced mushrumbs.

Bara. What a slave's this! the governor feeds not as I do. [*Aside.*

Itha. He never put on clean shirt since he was circumcised.

Bara. O rascal! I change myself twice a-day. [*Aside.*

Itha. The hat he wears, Judas left under the elder when
he hanged himself.

Bara. 'Twas sent me for a present from the Great Cham.

[*Aside.*

Pilia. A masty slave he is; whither now, fiddler? 70

Bara. Pardonnez moi, monsieur; me be no well. [*Exit.*

Pilia. Farewell, fiddler. One letter more to the Jew.

Bell. Prithee, sweet love, one more, and write it sharp.

Itha. No, I'll send by word of mouth now. Bid him deliver
thee a thousand crowns, by the same token that the
nuns loved rice, that Friar Barnardine slept in his own
clothes; any of 'em will do it.

Pilia. Let me alone to urge it, now I know the meaning.

Itha. The meaning has a meaning. Come, let's in:

To undo a Jew is charity, and not sin. [*Exeunt.* 80

61. *Aside*] Dyce to Wag.: *omit* the rest. 70. *masty*] Q: *nasty* Reed
to Cunn.: *musty* Bull. to Wag. 71. *me be*] Reed to Wag.: *we be* Q.
Exit] Q to Rob., Cunn., Bull., Wag.: after *fiddler* in line 72 Dyce, Ellis.

63. *mushrumbs*] One of the many
variant spellings for *mushroom*. It
is all a part with Ithamore's other
burlesque charges, and we have no
reason to doubt the outraged cry
of Barabas in the next line.

67, 68. *Judas . . . himself*] It was
an old belief that Judas hanged
himself upon an elder-tree. Mandeville (ed. Halliwell, p. 93) says
that he saw it near by Jerusalem.
'And faste by, is yit *the Tre of
Eldre*, that *Judas henge him selfe*
upon.' See also *Love's Labour's Lost*,
v. ii. 610, and Sir T. Browne,
Vulgar Errors.

69. *the Great Cham*] One of
the chief figures of medieval times.
The Great Cham was the 7th Emperor
of the Mongols, and Marco Polo

relates much about him and his
wealth, and Mandeville spends
several chapters discussing his
kingdom and its splendours.
(*Travels*, E.E.T.S., caps. XXIV–
XXVII). Compare Dekker's *Old
Fortunatus*, I. ii. :
'I'll travel to the Turkish Emperor ;
And then I'll revel it with *Prester
   John* ;
Or banquet that great *Cham of
   Tartary.*'

70. *masty*] Allied to mastiff, and
meaning 'burly' or 'big-bodied'.
I have ventured to leave this
reading as it is expressive of Pilia-
Borza's view of Barabas—despite
his boasting. The references given
in the O.E.D. are all considerably
later.

ACT V

SCENE I.—*An open place near the walls of the city.*

Enter FERNEZE, Knights, MARTIN DEL BOSCO, *and* Officers.

Fern. Now, gentlemen, betake you to your arms,
And see that Malta be well fortified;
And it behoves you to be resolute;
For Calymath, having hover'd here so long,
Will win the town, or die before the walls.
First Knight. And die he shall: for we will never yield.

Enter BELLAMIRA *and* PILIA-BORZA.

Act V. Scene i.

Reed, Coll., Dyce: *Actus Quintus* Q, Wag.: *Act the Fifth, Scene I*
Rob., Cunn. to Ellis. *Enter* . . .] Dyce, Ellis: *Enter Governor, Knights,
Martin Del Bosco* Q to Rob., Cunn., Bull., Wag.

6. *Enter Bellamira*] Dyce to Ellis: *Enter Curtezane* Q to Rob., Wag.

Scene I] The main action of this Act takes place in an open space in the city. What the exact arrangement was whereby the walls were represented for the play is difficult to understand. They could hardly have been the balcony since Barabas has to be flung from them! Sir E. K. Chambers (*op. cit.*, III. 97) suggests, in connection with *I Henry VI*, that 'the Orleans scenes with the leaping over the walls, and the rapid succession of action in the market place within the town and in the field without seem clearly to point to walls standing across the main stage from back to front'. But there is nothing to suggest this was the method adopted here too. Dyce and others merely add to our difficulties by making the first sixty lines of the scene take place in the Senate-house, so that at line 60 they are forced to remark: ' Here the audience were to suppose that Barabas had been thrown over the walls, and that the stage now represented the outside of the city.' ·Ellis, on the other hand, cuts the knot by ending the scene at line 60, and beginning afresh ' outside the city '. The facts on which we must base our inquiries are these: At line 43 Barabas is led off and swallows the ' sleepy drink ' off the stage. He is carried back unconscious (l. 54). After directions have been given for throwing his body over the walls (l. 58) we find simply an *Exeunt* in the Quarto stage direction, and at line 61 Barabas awakes alone outside the town. Perhaps the body is simply carried off the stage after line 60 and then, by the drawing of the curtains, is discovered lying on the floor of the inner-stage.

Bell. O, bring us to the governor !

Fern. Away with her ! she is a courtesan.

Bell. Whate'er I am, yet, governor, hear me speak :

    I bring thee news by whom thy son was slain :   10

    Mathias did it not ; it was the Jew.

Pilia. Who, besides the slaughter of these gentlemen,

    Poison'd his own daughter and the nuns,

    Strangled a friar, and I know not what

    Mischief beside.

Fern.   Had we but proof of this——

Bell. Strong proof, my lord ; his man's now at my lodging,

    That was his agent ; he'll confess it all.

Fern. Go fetch him straight [*Exeunt Officers*]. I always

    fear'd that Jew.

         Enter Officers *with* BARABAS *and* ITHAMORE.

Bara. I'll go alone ; dogs, do not hale me thus.

Itha. Nor me neither ; I cannot out-run you, constable. 20

    O, my belly !

Bara. One dram of powder more had made all sure :

    What a damn'd slave was I !   [*Aside.*

Fern. Make fires, heat irons, let the rack be fetched.

First Knight. Nay, stay, my lord ; 't may be he will

    confess.

Bara. Confess ! what mean you, lords ? who should

    confess ?

Fern. Thou and thy Turk ; 'twas you that slew my son.

Itha. Guilty, my lord, I confess. Your son and Mathias

---

7. etc. *Bell.*] *Curt.* Q. 12. *Who*] Q to Wag. : *omit* Holthausen. 13. *Poison'd*] Q to Rob., Wag. : *Poisonéd* Dyce : *Poisoned* Cunn. to Ellis : *He poison'd* Holthausen. 18. *him*] Q to Wag. : *'em* Dyce² conj. *Exeunt* . . .] Dyce to Ellis : *omit* the rest. *Enter* . . .] Dyce to Ellis : *Enter, Jew, Ithamore* Q to Coll., Wag. : *Enter Barabas and Ithamore* Rob. 19. *alone*] Q to Ellis : *along* Wag. 23. *Aside*] Dyce, Bull., Ellis : *omit* the rest.

---

20. *out-run . . . constable*] A common phrase at the time : compare Kemp's *Nine Daies Wonder*, 15 : ' I far'd like one that had escaped the stockes, and tride the use of his legs to *out-run* the *constable*.'

148 **THE JEW OF MALTA** [ACT V

were both contracted unto Abigail; [he] forged a
counterfeit challenge. 30

Bara. Who carried that challenge?

Itha. I carried it, I confess; but who writ it? Marry,
even he that strangled Barnardine, poisoned the nuns,
and his own daughter.

Fern. Away with him! his sight is death to me.

Bara. For what, you men of Malta? hear me speak;
She is a courtesan, and he a thief.
And he my bondman: let me have law;
For none of this can prejudice my life.

Fern. Once more, away with him; You shall have law. 40

Bara. Devils, do your worst; *I live in spite of you.* [*Aside.*
As these have spoke, so be it to their souls!—
I hope the poison'd flowers will work anon. [*Aside.*
[*Exeunt Officers with Barabas and Ithamore;
Bellamira, and Pilia-Borza.*

Enter KATHERINE.

Kath. Was my Mathias murder'd by the Jew?

---

29. [*he*]] Reed, etc.: *omit* Q. 41. *I*] Q to Rob., Cunn., Bull., Wag.:
I['ll] Dyce: *I'll* Ellis. 41. *Aside*] Dyce to Wag.: *omit* the rest. 43.
Aside] Dyce to Wag.: *omit* the rest. *Exeunt . . .*] Dyce, Ellis: *Exit* Q to
Rob., Wag.: *Exeunt* Cunn., Bull. *Enter . . .*] Dyce, Ellis: *Enter Mater*
Q, Wag.: *Enter Mother of Mathias.* Reed to Rob., Cunn., Bull.

---

29. *both contracted unto Abigail*]
See III. vi. 22 and note.

[*he*]] Brereton suggests that the
original had *a* i.e. '*a* = he, which
explains better the omission of the
word, since the same letter follows
' forged '.

37–8. *he . . . he*] i.e. Pilia-Borza
. . . Ithamore.

38. *he my bondman*] In medieval
England a master had great power
over his serfs or bondmen, and
could stay many accusations by
refusing to plead in answer to his
own bondman. See for examples
Bracton's Note Book, ed. F. W.
Maitland, *passim*.

let . . . law] C. K. Pooler in the
Arden edition of *The Merchant of*

Venice, IV. i. 314, compares this
passage with the action of Shylock
who demands the law (line 205),
and is told he shall ' have all
justice ' (line 320) and who later
loses his temper like Barabas and
cries, ' Why, then the devil give her
good of it ', etc. (line 343).

41. *I*] Dyce's emendation, followed by Ellis, is tempting, but not
absolutely necessary. The mis-
print ' I ' for ' I'll ' before ' live ' is
easily explainable by absorption,
see note to IV. iii. 7.

43. *poison'd flowers*] The posy
given to Bellamira: see IV. vi. 35 ff.
A method of poisoning much beloved in Italy according to popular Elizabethan belief.

Ferneze, 'twas thy son that murder'd him.

Fern. Be patient, gentle madam ; it was he ;

He forged the daring challenge made them fight.

Kath. Where is the Jew? where is that murderer?

Fern. In prison, till the law has pass'd on him.

Enter Officer.

Off. My lord, the courtesan and her man are dead ;   50

So is the Turk, and Barabas the Jew.

Fern. Dead ?

Off. Dead, my lord, and here they bring his body.

Bosco. This sudden death of his is very strange.

Re-enter Officers, *carrying* BARABAS *as dead.*

Fern. Wonder not at it, sir ; the heavens are just ;

Their deaths were like their lives, then think not
  of 'em.

Since they are dead, let them be buried :

For the Jew's body, throw that o'er the walls,

To be a prey for vultures and wild beasts.

So, now away and fortify the town.   60

　　　　[*Exeunt all, leaving Barabas on the floor.*

Bara. [*rising*] What, all alone ! well fare, sleepy drink !

I'll be reveng'd on this accursed town ;

For by my means Calymath shall enter in :

I'll help to slay their children and their wives,

---

49. *Enter* . . .] Q to Rob., Cunn., Bull., Wag.: *Re-enter First Officer*
Dyce, Ellis. 54. *Re-enter* . . .] Dyce to Ellis: *omit* the rest. 60. *Exeunt*
. . .] Dyce, Bull., Ellis: *Exeunt, bearing body of Barabas, which is to be
supposed flung outside the fortress* Cunn.: *Exeunt* the rest. *Scene II*]
Ellis: *omit* the rest. 61. *Bara.* [*rising*]] Dyce to Bull.: *Bar.* Q to Rob.,
Wag.: *Barabas discovered rising* Ellis.

60. *Exeunt* . . .] See note at
beginning of scene.
　63. *Calymath*] Pronounce ' Cal'-
math '.
　64, 65. *I'll help* . . . *down*,]
Passages very similar to this are
frequent in Marlowe. Cf. *Edward
II*, ll. 396 ff. :
　　11

' I'll fire thy crazed buildings, and
　enforce
The papal towers to kiss the lowly
　ground ',

and see *Faustus*, ll. 710 ff., and *The
Massacre at Paris*, Sc. xxi., l. 64,
and note there.

To fire the churches, pull their houses down,
Take my goods too, and seize upon my lands.
I hope to see the governor a slave,
And, rowing in a galley, whipt to death.

Enter CALYMATH, Bassoes, *and* Turks.

Caly. Whom have we there ? a spy ?

Bara. Yes, my good lord, one that can spy a place   70
Where you may enter, and surprise the town :
My name is Barabas ; I am a Jew.

Caly. Art thou that Jew whose goods we heard were sold
For tribute money ?

Bara.   The very same, my lord :
And since that time they have hir'd a slave, my man,
To accuse me of a thousand villanies :
I was imprisoned, but scap'd their hands.

Caly. Didst break prison ?

Bara. No, no :
I drank of poppy and cold mandrake juice ;   80
And being asleep, belike they thought me dead,
And threw me o'er the walls ; so, or how else,
The Jew is here, and rests at your command.

---

68. *Bassoes*] Dyce to Ellis : *Bashaws* the rest. 69. *there*] Q to Cunn.,
Wag. : *here* Bull., Ellis. 77. *imprisoned*] Cunn., Bull., Wag. : *imprison'd*
Q to Rob. : *imprisonéd* Dyce, Ellis. *scap'd*] Q, Reed, Dyce, Ellis :
(*e*)*scap'd* Rob., Coll., Cunn., Bull., Wag.

67, 68. *I hope . . . death*] Cf.
Tamburlaine, III. iii. 50 ff. :

' And, when they chance to breath
    and rest a space,
Are punished with bastones so
    grievously
That they lie panting on the
    galley's side,
And strive for life at every stroke
    they give.'

69. *there*] Bullen and Ellis both
print *here*—but give no explanation
of the change.

80. *poppy*] Well known for the
soporific qualities of its juice.
Iago knows of its virtues, and those
of the mandrake or mandragora :

'Not *poppy* nor *mandragora,*
Nor all the powerful syrups of the
    world,
Shall ever medicine thee to that
    sweet sleep
Which thou ow'dst yesterday.'

mandrake] Another plant with
narcotic qualities. It is frequently
mentioned in Elizabethan literature, see Prof. R. H. Case's note in
the Arden edition of *Antony and
Cleopatra,* I. v. 4 ; and the very full
and learned disquisition on the
mandrake and its alleged powers by
F. L. Lucas in his edition of *The
Works of John Webster,* Vol. I,
226 ff.

Caly. 'Twas bravely done : but tell me, Barabas,
    Canst thou, as thou report'st, make Malta ours ?
Bara. Fear not, my lord ; for here, against the sluice,
    The rock is hollow, and of purpose digg'd,
    To make a passage for the running streams
    And common channels of the city.
    Now, whilst you give assault unto the walls,   90
    I'll lead five hundred soldiers through the vault,
    And rise with them i' the middle of the town,
    Open the gates for you to enter in ;
    And by this means the city is your own.
Caly. If this be true, I'll make thee governor.
Bara. And, if it be not true, then let me die.
Caly. Thou'st doom'd thyself. Assault it presently.

                                   [Exeunt.

85. *report'st*] Reed to Ellis : *reportest* Q, Wag. 86. *sluice*] Cunn., Bull.,
Ellis, Wag. : Coll. conj. : *Truce* Q, Reed : *trench* Dyce : *turret* or *tower*,
Mitford conj. 89. *City*] Q to Ellis : *Citadel* Wag.

85. *Canst thou . . . ours*] Mr.
Lucas (*op. cit.*, II, 339) points out
that in writing Act III, Scene ii. of
The Devil's Law-Case, it seems clear
that Webster had here in mind *The
Jew of Malta* and its Machiavellian
villain Barabas (cf. '*Betray a Towne
to the Turke*' and '*Italianated Jew*').
  86. *sluice*] The textual note
shows how many attempts have
been made to solve this very difficult line. The Quarto *truce* is
clearly wrong. Dyce's emendation
to *trench* is tempting, but on the
whole I think Collier's suggestion of
sluice best fits what is required.
' The spot intended is plainly that
at which the drainage of the town
passed from the ditch of the fort
into the sea, which would of course
be at a water-gate or sluice '
(Cunningham).
  89. *common channels*] gutters,
drains. Compare *Edward II*, I. i.
186 : ' And in the *channel* christen
him anew.'
  city] Wagner, in keeping with his
love of the five-foot line, reads
Citadel.
  97. *doom'd*] sentenced, given
judgment. Compare *Richard II*,
v. i. 4 :

      ' Caesar's . . . tower
To whose flint bosom my con-
  demned lord
Is *doom'd* a prisoner by proud
  Bolingbroke.'

Scene II.—*The same.*

Alarums within.   Enter CALYMATH, Bassoes, Turks, *and*
BARABAS ; *with* FERNEZE *and* Knights *prisoners.*

Caly. Now vail your pride, you captive Christians,
　　And kneel for mercy to your conquering foe :
　　Now where's the hope you had of haughty Spain ?
　　Ferneze, speak ; had it not been much better
　　To ['ve] kept thy promise than be thus surpris'd ?
Fern. What should I say ? we are captives, and must yield.
Caly. Ay, villains, you must yield, and under Turkish yokes
　　Shall groaning bear the burden of our ire :
　　And, Barabas, as erst we promis'd thee,
　　For thy desert we make thee governor ;　　　　　10
　　Use them at thy discretion.
Bara.　　　　　　　　　　Thanks, my lord.
Fern. O fatal day, to fall into the hands
　　Of such a traitor and unhallow'd Jew !
　　What greater misery could heaven inflict ?
Caly. 'Tis our command : and, Barabas, we give
　　To guard thy person, these our Janizaries :
　　Entreat them well, as we have used thee,
　　And now, brave bassoes, come, we'll walk about
　　The ruin'd town, and see the wrack we made :

Act V.   Scene ii.

Rob., Cunn., Bull. : *Scene III* Ellis : *omit* the rest.   *Alarums . . .*
Dyce, Ellis : omit *Calymath, Bassoes* Rob., Cunn., Bull. : *Alarmes.*
Enter Turkes, Barabas, Gouernour, and Knights prisoners. Q, Reed, Coll.,
Wag.
　　5. *To['ve] kept*] Cunn. : *To kept* Q to Dyce : *To keepe* Wag. : *T'have kept*
Bull., Ellis : *To have kept* T. Brooke.   *than*] Reed to Ellis : *then* Q, Wag.
　　7. *villains*] Q to Ellis : *omit* Wag.   17. *Entreat*] Dyce, Bull., Ellis : *Intreat*
the rest.   18. *bassoes*] Dyce to Ellis : *Bashaws* Q to Rob., Wag.

Scene II.

　　1. *vail*] See note to II. ii. 11.
　　9. *erst*] in the first place, formerly.
See *Faerie Queene*, I. v. 9 : ' The
armes that *earst* so bright did
show ', etc.
　　16. *Janizaries*] Turkish infantry
originally forming the Sultan's

guard and the main part of the
standing army.
　　17. *Entreat*] Deal with, or act
towards. Compare Genesis xii. 16,
' He *entreated* Adam *well* ', and
Faerie Queene, I. x. 7 : ' He them
with speeches meet, does faire
entreat.' See *ante*, II. ii. 8.

Farewell, brave Jew, farewell, great Barabas !   20
>   [*Exeunt Calymath and Bassoes.*

Bara. May all good fortune follow Calymath.
  And now, as entrance to our safety,
  To prison with the governor and these
  Captains, his consorts and confederates.
Fern. O villain, heaven will be reveng'd on thee.
>   [*Exeunt.*

Bara. Away ! no more, let him not trouble me.
  Thus hast thou gotten, by thy policy,
  No simple place, no small authority ;
  I now am governor of Malta ; true,
  But Malta hates me, and, in hating me,   30
  My life's in danger ; and what boots it thee,
  Poor Barabas, to be the governor,
  Whenas thy life shall be at their command ?
  No, Barabas, this must be look'd into ;
  And, since by wrong thou gott'st authority,
  Maintain it bravely by firm policy ;
  At least, unprofitably lose it not :
  For he that liveth in authority,
  And neither gets him friends, nor fills his bags,
  Lives like the ass that Æsop speaketh of,   40

20. *Exeunt* . . .] Bull., Ellis, Dyce after line 21 : *Exeunt* Q to Rob., Cunn., Wag. 25. *Exeunt*] Q to Rob., Cunn., Bull. : *Exeunt Turks with Ferneze and Knights* Ellis ; Dyce after line 26.

22. *as entrance . . . safety*] A figurative use, meaning 'as a beginning to our safety'. The O.E.D. quotes Coverdale's *Ecclus.* I. 5 : 'The everlastinge commaundements are the intraunce of her [wyszdome],' cf. also *Massacre at Paris*, Sc. v. 13.
27.] Dyce notes : 'A change of scene is supposed here—to the Citadel, the residence of Barabas as governor.' Bullen and Ellis agree. There seems to be no need for this change, unless it is thought to be consequent upon 'Within here' (line 47). But these are only

'general words', and cannot be pressed very far.
27. *Thus* . . .] Meyer (*op. cit.*) remarks that the whole of this passage should be compared with the famous seventeenth chapter of *The Prince*, wherein Machiavelli discusses whether it is best for a prince to be beloved or feared. He adds, 'but lines 39–41 [35–37 below] show plainly the influence of Gentillet '.
31. *boots*] avails, profits. Compare Spenser's *Teares of the Muses*, 445 : 'What *bootes* it then to come from glorious Forefathers ? '

That labours with a load of bread and wine,
And leaves it off to snap on thistle tops :
But Barabas will be more circumspect.
Begin betimes ; Occasion's bald behind :
Slip not thine opportunity, for fear too late
Thou seek'st for much, but canst not compass it.
Within here !

Enter FERNEZE, *with a* Guard.

Fern. My lord ?
Bara. Ay, *lord* ; thus slaves will learn.
    Now, governor,—stand by there, wait within,—   50
                                  [Exeunt Guard.
This is the reason that I sent for thee ;
Thou seest thy life and Malta's happiness
Are at my arbitrement ; and Barabas
At his discretion may dispose of both :
Now tell me, governor, and plainly too,
What think'st thou shall become of it and thee ?
Fern. This, Barabas ; since things are in thy power,
I see no reason but of Malta's wrack,
Nor hope of thee but extreme cruelty,
Nor fear I death, nor will I flatter thee.   60
Bara. Governor, good words ; be not so furious ;
'Tis not thy life which can avail me aught ;
Yet you do live, and live for me you shall :
And as for Malta's ruin, think you not
'Twere slender policy for Barabas

47. *Enter Ferneze . . .*] Dyce, Ellis : *Enter Governor . . .* the rest. 50. *Exeunt Guard*] Dyce, Ellis, Wag. : *Exit Guard* Cunn., Bull. : *To the Guard* Reed, Coll. : *omit* Q, Rob. 57. *This, Barabas ;*] Reed to Coll., Dyce to Wag. : *This ; Barabas,* Q, Rob. 58. *wrack*] Q : *wreck* Reed, etc.

44. *Occasion's bald behind*] Compare Chapman's *May-Day*, III. iii. 118 : ' Aurelio, *Occasion is bald*, take her by the forelock', and Marston's *What you will*, IV. i. : ' Would I were Time, then. I thought twas for some thing that the old fornicator was *bald behinde*.' See also *Faerie Queene*, II. iv. 4.

47. *Within here !*] More usually *Within there !* Dyce quotes from *The Hogge hath lost his Pearle,* R. Tailor, 1614 : ' What, ho ! *within here !*' (Sig. E. 2).

To dispossess himself of such a place?
For sith, as once you said, within this isle,
In Malta here, that I have got my goods,
And in this city still have had success,
And now at length am grown your governor,   70
Yourselves shall see it shall not be forgot;
For, as a friend not known but in distress,
I'll rear up Malta, now remediless.

Fern. Will Barabas recover Malta's loss?
 Will Barabas be good to Christians?

Bara. What wilt thou give me, governor, to procure
 A dissolution of the slavish bands
 Wherein the Turk hath yok'd your land and you?
 What will you give me if I render you
 The life of Calymath, surprise his men,   80
 And in an out-house of the city shut
 His soldiers, till I have consum'd 'em all with fire?
 What will you give him that procureth this?

Fern. Do but bring this to pass which thou pretendest,
 Deal truly with us as thou intimatest,
 And I will send amongst the citizens,
 And by my letters privately procure
 Great sums of money for thy recompense:
 Nay, more, do this, and live thou governor still.

Bara. Nay, do thou this, Ferneze, and be free;   90
 Governor, I enlarge thee; live with me;

67. *within*] Q to Dyce, Wag.: *'tis in* Cunn. to Ellis.   82. *His soldiers,
till*] Q to Ellis: *Until* Wag.

67. *sith*] since. As in Middleton's *Father Hubburd's Tales* (ed. Bullen), VIII. 61: ' *Sith* man thou sayest thou wert, I prithee, tell while thou wert man, what mischiefs thee befell.'
 as . . . said] See I. ii. 60 and 102 ff.
 within] Altered to *'tis in* by Cunningham, Bullen and Ellis. Cunningham says he does so ' to complete the sense ', but the alteration is unnecessary.

69. *still . . . success*] Barabas here refers to his success, since he was dispoiled by the Governor's orders in I. ii. 133 ff.
 81. *out-house . . . city*] See line 37 in the next scene as to this outhouse.
 84. *pretendest*] settest forth, holdest out. Compare Middleton's *Changeling*, IV. ii. 91: ' To that wench I *pretend* honest love, and she deserves it.'

Go walk about the city, see thy friends :
Tush, send not letters to 'em ; go thyself,
And let me see what money thou canst make ;
Here is my hand that I'll set Malta free ;
And thus we cast it : to a solemn feast
I will invite young Selim Calymath,
Where be thou present, only to perform
One stratagem that I'll impart to thee,
Wherein no danger shall betide thy life,   100
And I will warrant Malta free for ever.
Fern. Here is my hand ; believe me, Barabas,
I will be there, and do as thou desirest.
When is the time ?
Bara.   Governor, presently.
For Calymath, when he hath view'd the town,
Will take his leave, and sail toward Ottoman.
Fern. Then will I, Barabas, about this coin,
And bring it with me to thee in the evening.
Bara. Do so ; but fail not ; now farewell, Ferneze :
                                    [*Exit Ferneze.*

And thus far roundly goes the business :   110
Thus, loving neither, will I live with both,
Making a profit of my policy ;
And he from whom my most advantage comes,
Shall be my friend.

109. *Exit . . .*] Dyce, Ellis : *Exit Governor* Reed, Coll., Cunn., Bull. :
Exit after line 110, Wag. : *omit* Q, Rob.

96. *cast*] contrive or devise.
Compare Beaumont and Fletcher's
The Captain, II. ii. :
                    ' To *cast*
A cheap way how they may be all
    destroyed,'
and compare Middleton's *Mayor of
Queenborough,* III. i. 24, and *Blurt,
Master Constable,* IV. iii. 6.
96, 97. *a solemn feast . . . Calymath*] Meyer (*op. cit.*) says : ' His
scheme of killing all the Turks at a
banquet is that described in the
Principe as used by Oliverotto da
Fermo.'
110. *roundly*] successfully, in a
thorough-going manner. Compare
Gabriel Harvey's *Letter Book*
(Camden Soc.), p. 46 : ' He never
made ani bones at it, but trudgd up
roundely to work the feat.'
111, 112. *Thus . . . policy*] Note
the alliterative jingle. The lines
are characteristic of Marlowe's
conception of Machiavellian policy.

This is the life we Jews are us'd to lead ;
And reason too, for Christians do the like :
Well, now about effecting this device ;
First, to surprise great Selim's soldiers,
And then to make provision for the feast,
That at one instant all things may be done :   120
My policy detests prevention :
To what event my secret purpose drives,
I know ; and they shall witness with their lives.

[Exeunt.

SCENE III.—The same.

Enter CALYMATH and Bassoes.

Caly. Thus have we view'd the city, seen the sack,
And caus'd the ruins to be new-repair'd,
Which with our bombards' shot and basilisk[s]
We rent in sunder at our entry :
And, now I see the situation,
And how secure this conquer'd island stands,
Environ'd with the Mediterranean sea,

Act V.   Scene iii.

Rob., Cunn., Bull. : *Scene IV.* Ellis : *omit* the rest.   *Enter . . .*] Dyce,
Cunn. to Ellis :   *and Bashaws* Q to Rob., Wag.
    3. *basilisk*[s]] Dyce to Wag. :   *basilisk* Q to Rob.

115, 116. *This is the life . . . like*]
Another example of the attitude
Barabas adopts towards Christian
teaching. Compare Shylock : ' If a
Christian wrong a Jew what should
his sufferance be by Christian
example ? Why, revenge ' (III. i.
69, 70).
    115. *us'd*] accustomed. A fre-
quent Elizabethan use of the word.
Compare *The Merchant of Venice*,
III. i. 48 : ' a beggar that was *used*
to come so smug upon the mart.'
    116. *And reason*] And with reason,
reasonably.
    118. *soldiers*] a trisyllable.
    121. *prevention*] forestalling. Com-
pare *Julius Cæsar*, III. i. 19 : ' Casca
be sudden, for we fear *prevention*.'

Scene III.

Scene III] The same open place ;
Dyce, etc., describe it as ' outside
the walls of the city ', in flat
defiance of what Calymath says at
v. ii. 18, 19: ' We'll walk *about* The
ruined town ', etc.
    3. *bombards*] The earliest kind of
cannon, usually throwing a stone
ball or a very large shot. Cotgrave,
A French and English Dictionary, has
bombarde, a bumbard, or murther-
ing piece, and compare Berners'
Froissart, I. cxliv. 172 : ' Fortyfied
with springalles, *bombardes*, bowes,
and other artillery.'
    basilisk] See Act III. v. 31.

Strong countermur'd with other petty isles ;
And, toward Calabria, back'd by Sicily,
(Where Syracusian Dionysius reign'd),   10
Two lofty turrets that command the town ;
I wonder how it could be conquered thus.

Enter a Messenger.

Mess. From Barabas, Malta's governor, I bring
A message unto mighty Calymath ;
Hearing his sovereign was bound for sea,
To sail to Turkey, to great Ottoman,
He humbly would entreat your majesty
To come and see his homely citadel,
And banquet with him ere thou leav'st the isle.
Caly. To banquet with him in his citadel !   20
I fear me, messenger, to feast my train
Within a town of war so lately pillag'd
Will be too costly and too troublesome :
Yet would I gladly visit Barabas,
For well has Barabas deserv'd of us.
Mess. Selim, for that, thus saith the governor,
That he hath in [his] store a pearl so big,

8. *countermur'd*] Deighton conj.: *countermin'd* Q to Wag. 10. *Where*] Rob.
to Wag.: *When* Q, Reed, Coll.: *Lines* 10 *and* 11 *were transposed in* Q to Coll.
27. *in* [*his*]] Dyce², Bull. to Wag.: *in* Q to Dyce¹, Cunn.

8. *countermur'd*] This conjecture
of Deighton's seems to be the reading required by the sense. And
compare with the former passage,
where the same alteration has been
proposed (Act I. ii. 386).
9–11. *And,* . . . *town*] Robinson's transposition of lines 10 and
11, and emendation in line 10 (see
Text note) have been adopted by
all subsequent editors, but the
situation is still not clear since l. 11
does not seem to belong immediately with what precedes. As Sicily
lies directly between Malta and
Calabria, it is proper to speak of
Malta as ' toward Calabria, back'd
by Sicily ' ; but to speak of ' Two

lofty turrets that command the
town ' (of Malta) looks like a geo-
graphical perversion. Malta, with
reference to Calabria, is backed by
Sicily, but Calabria, with reference
to Malta, is not.
10. *Syracusian Dionysius*] Dionysius the Elder (430–367 B.C.) was
tyrant of Syracuse from the year
405 B.C. to his death. He is said
to have enjoyed greater power and
influence than any other Greek
before Alexander.
17. *your majesty*] This is something of an exaggeration, for Calymath is but the son of the Grand
Seignior.
27. *in* [*his*]] Dyce's emendation

So precious, and withal so orient,
As, be it valu'd but indifferently,
The price thereof will serve to entertain   30
Selim and all his soldiers for a month :
Therefore he humbly would entreat your highness
Not to depart till he has feasted you.

Caly. I cannot feast my men in Malta-walls,
Except he place his tables in the streets.

Mess. Know, Selim, that there is a monastery
Which standeth as an out-house to the town ;
There will he banquet them, but thee at home,
With all thy bassoes and brave followers.

Caly. Well, tell the governor we grant his suit ;   40
We'll in this summer evening feast with him.

Mess. I shall, my lord.   [*Exit.*

Caly. And now, bold bassoes, let us to our tents,
And meditate how we may grace us best
To solemnise our governor's great feast.   [*Exeunt.*

SCENE IV.—*The same.*

Enter FERNEZE, Knights, *and* MARTIN DEL BOSCO.

Fern. In this, my countrymen, be rul'd by me :

---

39. *bassoes*] Dyce, Cunn. to Ellis : *bashawes* Q to Rob., Wag.   And so in line 43.

Act V.   Scene iv.
Rob., Cunn., Bull. : *Scene V* Ellis : *omit* the rest.   *Enter . . .*] Dyce, Ellis : *Enter Gouernor, Knights, Del-bosco,* Q to Rob., Cunn., Bull., Wag.

seems necessary.   The mistake sounds as if it were due to dictation, *his* being contracted in speech to *'s*, which, followed by another *s*, would easily be lost.

28. *orient*] An adjective frequently applied to pearls and precious stones coming from the East—often as a vague poetic epithet. Here used with the sense of preciousness, brilliancy, etc.   Compare *Maundeville's Travels* (Roxburgh Club edition), XXI. 97 : ' ccc. pre-

cious stanes, grete and *orient* '; and compare *Doctor Faustus*, i. 81 : ' Ransack the ocean for *orient pearl.*'   See Prof. Case's note on *Antony and Cleopatra*, I. v. 41, for a very full explanation, with numerous examples.

29. *indifferently*] See I. i. 29.

Scene IV
Scene IV] The scene remains unchanged.

Have special care that no man sally forth
Till you shall hear a culverin discharg'd
By him that bears the linstock, kindled thus;
Then issue out and come to rescue me,
For happily I shall be in distress,
Or you released of this servitude.

First Knight. Rather than thus to live as Turkish thralls,
What will we not adventure?

Fern. On, then; be gone.

Knights.   Farewell, grave governor. 10

                                             [*Exeunt.*

Scene V.—*A hall in the Citadel.*

Enter above, BARABAS, *with a hammer, very busy;
and* Carpenters.

Bara. How stand the cords? how hang these hinges? fast?
Are all the cranes and pulleys sure?

First Carp.   All fast.

Bara. Leave nothing loose, all levell'd to my mind.

10. *Exeunt*] Cunn., Bull.: *Exeunt, on one side, Knights and Martin Del Bosco; on the other, Ferneze* Dyce, Ellis: *omit* Q to Rob., Wag.

Act V. Scene v.
Rob., Cunn., Bull.: *Scene VI* Ellis: *omit* the rest. *Enter . . .*] Coll., Dyce to Ellis substantially: *Enter Barabas with a hammer above, very busy* Reed, Rob.: *Enter with a Hammar aboue, very busie.* Q, Wag.
3. *First Carp.*] Dyce, etc.: *Serv.* Q to Rob.

3. *culverin*] A long cannon firing a shot of 17 to 20 pounds. The word is derived from the Italian *colubro*, a snake, and is another example of the name of a reptile being applied to a cannon. Compare *basilisk*, III. v. 31 and v. iii. 3, and see *I Henry IV*, II. iii. 58.
4. *linstock*] 'A staff about three feet long, having a pointed foot to stick in the ground and a forked head to hold the match.' Compare *Every Man in his Humour*, III. i.: 'Their master-gunner . . . confronts me with his *linstock* ready to give fire', or Middleton's *Roaring Girl*, v. i. 17: 'I spied what *linstock* gave fire to shoot'; Chapman's *All Fools*, v. ii. 44, etc.

6. *happily*] haply, perchance.

Scene V.
Scene V] The whole stage is here used. The S.D. shows that Barabas is seen on the balcony which overhung the inner-stage, superintending the arrangements for the trapdoor which was to precipitate all those who were on it into the cauldron which stood hidden behind the curtains and on the inner-stage below.
3. *First Carp.*] Altered by Dyce and other editors to agree with the prefix for line 8 (*Carp.* in Q).
3. *levell'd to my mind*] here used with the sense of 'arranged', 'comfortable to'.

Why, now I see that you have art, indeed :
There, carpenters, divide that gold amongst you ;
Go, swill in bowls of sack and muscadine ;
Down to the cellar, taste of all my wines.

First Carp. We shall, my lord, and thank you.   [*Exeunt.*

Bara. And, if you like them, drink your fill and die ;
For, so I live, perish may all the world !   10
Now, Selim Calymath, return me word
That thou wilt come, and I am satisfied.
Now, sirrah ; what, will he come ?

Enter Messenger.

Mess. He will ; and has commanded all his men
To come ashore, and march through Malta streets,
That thou may'st feast them in thy citadel.

Bara. Then now are all things as my wish would have 'em ;
There wanteth nothing but the governor's pelf ;
And see, he brings it.

Enter FERNEZE.

5. After *you* Dyce and Ellis add S.D. *Giving Money.* 13. *Enter . . .*]
Q to Rob., Cunn., Bull., Wag. : *after line* 12 Dyce, Ellis. 19. *Enter . . .*]
Dyce to Wag. : after *sum* in same line Q to Rob.   *Ferneze*] Dyce, Ellis :
Governor the rest.

6. *sack*] A general name for
white wines formerly imported
from Spain and the Canaries.
(Sp. *seco* ; Fr. *sec* ; cf. *vin sec.*)
Compare Markham's *English House-
wife*, ii. 149 : ' Your best *sacks* are
of Seres in Spaine, your smaller of
Galicia and Portugall ; your strong
sacks are of the Ilands of the
Canaries.'

muscadine] The Elizabethan
form of muscatel—a strong sweet
wine, with a musk-like perfume,
made from the muscat grape.
Sometimes called muscadel, as in
Taming of the Shrew, III. ii. 174, or
hippocras, as in Beaumont and
Fletcher's *Scornful Ladies*, I. i.
See *The Hog hath lost his Pearl*, IV.
(Hazlitt's *Dodsley*, XI. 491) : ' I'll

undertake to sleep sixteen [hours]
upon the receipt of two cups of
muskadine ', and Armin's *Two
Maids of Moreclacke*, 1609 : ' The
muscadine stays for the bride at
church ' (R. W. Bond).

9. *drink . . . die*] Barabas has
poisoned the wine to remove the
witnesses of his crimes.

10. *For . . . world*] ' This is the
very gist of Machiavelli's treachery '
(Meyer).

18. *pelf*] money, riches. The
word was gradually acquiring a
depreciatory significance in the
16th century, as in Spenser's
Faerie Queene, III. ix. 4 : ' But
all his minde is set on mucky
pelfe.'

Now, governor, the sum ?

Fern. With free consent, a hundred thousand pounds. 20

Bara. Pounds say'st thou, governor ? well, since it is no
more,
 I'll satisfy myself with that ; nay, keep it still,
 For, if I keep not promise, trust not me :
 And, governor, now partake my policy :
 First, for his army, they are sent before,
 Enter'd the monastery, and underneath
 In several places are field-pieces pitch'd,
 Bombards, whole barrels full of gunpowder,
 That on the sudden shall dissever it,
 And batter all the stones about their ears,   30
 Whence none can possibly escape alive :
 Now as for Calymath and his consorts,
 Here have I made a dainty gallery,
 The floor whereof, this cable being cut,
 Doth fall asunder ; so that it doth sink
 Into a deep pit past recovery.
 Here, hold that knife ; and when thou seest he comes,
 And with his bassoes shall be blithely set,
 A warning-piece shall be shot off from the tower,
 To give thee knowledge when to cut the cord,   40
 And fire the house ; Say, will not this be brave ?

Fern. O, excellent ! here, hold thee, Barabas ;
 I trust thy word ; take what I promis'd thee.

Bara. No, governor ; I'll satisfy thee first ;
 Thou shalt not live in doubt of anything.

---

22. *keep it still*] Q to Ellis : *keep it* Wag.   24. *partake*] Q to Dyce, Ellis,
Wag. : *take* Cunn., Bull.   33 *a dainty*] Q, etc. : *dainty* Rob.   37. After
comes Dyce and Ellis add S.D. *Throws down a knife.*   38. *bassoes*] Dyce,
Cunn. to Ellis : *bashaws* Q to Rob., Wag.   And so in lines 50, 51, 59, 67.

24–31. *And, governor, . . . alive*]
This idea Marlowe may have got
from the account in *The Prince* of
the murder of the Turks at a
banquet by Oliverotto da Fermo.
 27. *field-pieces*] light cannon.
 28 *Bombards*] See v. iii. 3.

39. *warning-piece*] A signal gun.
This is the first instance of its use
recorded in the O.E.D. Compare
Chapman's *Bussy d'Ambois*, I. i. 25 :
' As great Seamen (comming neere
their Hauen) are glad to giue a
warning peece.'

Stand close, for here they come.　　[*Ferneze retires.*

　　　　　　　　　　　　　　Why, is not this

A kingly kind of trade, to purchase towns

By treachery, and sell 'em by deceit?

Now tell me, worldlings, underneath the sun

If greater falsehood ever has bin done?　　　　50

Enter CALYMATH *and* Bassoes.

Caly. Come, my companion-bassoes : see, I pray,

　　How busy Barabas is there above

　　To entertain us in his gallery :

　　Let us salute him.　Save thee, Barabas!

Bara. Welcome, great Calymath!

Fern. How the slave jeers at him!　　　　[*Aside.*

Bara. Will't please thee, mighty Selim Calymath,

　　To ascend our homely stairs?

Caly.　　　　　　　　　　　Ay, Barabas.

　　Come, bassoes, attend.

Fern. [*coming forward*] Stay, Calymath ;　　　　60

　　For I will show thee greater courtesy

　　Than Barabas would have afforded thee.

Knight. [*within*] Sound a charge there!

　　　　[*A charge sounded within : Ferneze cuts the cord ;*
　　　　the floor of the gallery gives way, and Barabas
　　　　falls into a cauldron placed in a pit.

---

46. *Ferneze retires*] Dyce to Ellis : *omit* the rest.　49. *sun*] Reed to
Wag. : *summe* Q.　56. *Aside*] Dyce to Wag. : *omit* others.　59. *attend*]
Q to Rob., Cunn., Bull. : *ascend* Dyce, Ellis, Wag.　60. *Fern.* [*coming
forward*] Dyce, Ellis : *Fern.* the rest.　63. *Knight* [*within*] Dyce to Ellis :
Knight the rest.　63. *A charge* . . .] Dyce, Ellis : *A charge, the cable cut,
A Cauldron discovered* Q to Rob., Wag.　*Enter* . . .] Dyce to Ellis : *omit*
the rest.

---

49. *worldlings*] Those devoted to
the interests and gains of the world
—the fellow spirits of Barabas.
The O.E.D. quotes J. Melvill's
Autob. and Diary (Wodrow Soc.),
271 : ' The godlie, for his . . . doc-
trine, lovit him ; the *warldlings*, for
his parentage, and place, reverenced
him.'

63. *A charge* . . .] The Quarto
direction ' A charge, the cable cut,
A Cauldron discovered ', gives us the
essentials of this grand climax of the
play. We read in *Henslowe Papers*
(ed. W. W. Greg), p. 116, that ' j
cauderm for the Jewe ' was among
the theatrical properties of the
Admiral's Men in March, 1598, so

Enter Knights *and* MARTIN DEL BOSCO.

Caly. How now! what means this?

Bara. Help, help me, Christians, help!

Fern. See, Calymath! this was devis'd for thee.

Caly. Treason, treason! bassoes, fly!

Fern. No, Selim, do not fly:
　　See his end first, and fly then if thou canst.

Bara. O, help me, Selim! help me, Christians!   70
　　Governor, why stand you all so pitiless?

Fern. Should I in pity of thy plaints or thee,
　　Accursed Barabas, base Jew, relent?
　　No, thus I'll see thy treachery repaid,
　　But wish thou hadst behav'd thee otherwise.

Bara. You will not help me, then?

Fern.　　　　　　　　　No, villain, no.

Bara. And, villains, know you cannot help me now.
　　Then, Barabas, breathe forth thy latest fate,

---

78. *fate*] Q to Dyce, Wag.: *hate* Cunn. to Ellis.

---

that this scene was evidently part of the original plan of the play, and has not been greatly altered by any subsequent revisions. Professor Perry, in the Introduction to the Williams College acting version, says: ' The effectiveness of the final scene is dependent upon its absolute simplicity. Barabas stands upon the balcony and welcomes Calymath. The balcony is supposed to give way . . . and to precipitate Barabas into a cauldron. . . . As Barabas gives the invitation he moves backward through the curtain as though he were going to meet Selim. Ferneze cuts the cord prematurely; the crash of falling timbers is heard; the crowd rushes on the stage, and then Ferneze draws aside the lower curtain beneath the balcony and Barabas is seen in the cauldron.' Schelling (*Eng. Drama*, p. 115) points out that Cole in Day and Haughton's lost *Six Yeomen of the West* comes to his death similarly in a cauldron; and H. De W. Fuller

(*Sources of Titus Andronicus*, Pub. Mod. Lang. Assocn., 1901, p. 53) suggests that the trap-door arrangement used here was utilised again to represent the burning of Aaron on the stage in the old play from which Vos's *Aran en Titus* is taken. He cites two illustrations of the scene in the first edition of Vos's play (1641).

　charge] A trumpet call—the signal for the attack or for some action. Compare *Henry V*, III. i. 33:
　　' and upon this *charge*
　Cry God for England, Harry, and
　　S. George.'

　Enter . . .] It will be remembered that the Governor had ordered Del Bosco and the Knights to come out from their hiding-place when they heard the discharge of the guns (see v. iv. 3). The ' charge ' had served therefore a double purpose: to destroy the feasting Turks in the ' out-house ' monastery, and to assemble the Maltese Knights at the Citadel.

　78. *fate*] Cunningham alters this

And in the fury of thy torments, strive
To end thy life with resolution :   80
Know, governor, 'twas I that slew thy son,
I fram'd the challenge that did make them meet :
Know, Calymath, I aim'd thy overthrow :
And, had I but escap'd this stratagem,
I would have brought confusion on you all,
Damn'd Christians, dogs, and Turkish infidels !
But now begins the extremity of heat
To pinch me with intolerable pangs :
Die, life ! fly, soul ! tongue, curse thy fill, and die !
                                             [*Dies.*

Caly. Tell me, you Christians, what doth this portend ? 90
Fern. This train he laid to have entrapp'd thy life ;
  Now, Selim, note the unhallow'd deeds of Jews ;
  Thus he determin'd to have handled thee, ⎤
  But I have rather chose to save thy life.   ⎟
Caly. Was this the banquet he prepar'd for us ? ⎦
  Let's hence, lest further mischief be pretended.
Fern. Nay, Selim, stay ; for, since we have thee here,
  We will not let thee part so suddenly :
  Besides, if we should let thee go, all's one,
  For with thy galleys couldst thou not get hence, 100
  Without fresh men to rig and furnish them.
Caly. Tush, governor, take thou no care for that ;
  My men are all aboard,
  And do attend my coming there by this.

86. *Christians*] Q to Rob., Bull. : *Christian* Dyce, Cunn., Ellis, Wag.
89. *Dies*] Reed to Ellis : omit Q, Wag.

to *hate*, for, he says, ' hate was the actuating principle of Barabas, and was hissed out with his latest breath '.
  83. *aim'd*] designed, plotted.
  86. *Christians, dogs*] So the Quarto. Dyce and others print *Christian dogs* apparently to balance the epithet *Turkish infidels.*
  96. *pretended*] intended, pur-
12

posed. Compare Hakluyt's *Voyages* (1810), III, 86 : ' Two small barks . . . wherein he intended to complete his *pretended* voyage.'
  99. *all's one*] it comes to the same result.
  104. *attend*] await. Compare Sonnet XLIV, 12 : ' I must *attend* time's leisure.' This is an oversight on the part of Calymath (or

Fern. Why, heard'st thou not the trumpet sound a charge ?

Caly. Yes, what of that ?

Fern.   Why, then the house was fir'd,
  Blown up, and all thy soldiers massacred.

Caly. O, monstrous treason !

Fern.   A Jew's courtesy ;
  For he that did by treason work our fall,
  By treason hath deliver'd thee to us :   110
  Know, therefore, till thy father hath made good
  The ruins done to Malta and to us,
    Thou canst not part ; for Malta shall be freed,
    Or Selim ne'er return to Ottoman.

Caly. Nay, rather, Christians, let me go to Turkey,
  In person there to mediate your peace ;
  To keep me here will naught advantage you.

Fern. Content thee, Calymath, here thou must stay,
  And live in Malta prisoner ; for come all the world
  To rescue thee, so will we guard us now,   120
  As sooner shall they drink the ocean dry,
  Than conquer Malta, or endanger us.
  So, march away ; and let due praise be given
  Neither to Fate nor Fortune, but to Heaven.

                                        [*Exeunt.*

FINIS.

116. *mediate*] Rob. to Bull., Wag. ; Coll. conj. : *meditate* Q, Reed, Ellis. 119. *in Malta*] Q to Ellis : *here* Wag.   *all*] Reed to Wag. : *call* Q.   124. *Fortune*] Reed to Wag. : *Fottune* Q.   *Exeunt*] Rob. to Ellis : *omit* Q to Coll., Wag.

Marlowe), for he had agreed that the men should feast in the ' out-house ', while he and his bassoes were entertained in the Citadel (see v. ii. 81 and v. iii. 37, etc.).

116. *mediate*] I have accepted the emendation of Robinson with some hesitation. It is adopted by the O.E.D., but at the same time the word *meditate*, having the meaning ' to plan by revolving in the mind ', was in use when Marlowe wrote. See *1 Henry VI*, ii. iv. 60 :

‘ *York.*   Now Somerset, where is your argument ?

  Som.   Here in my scabbard, *meditating* that

Shall dye your white Rose in a bloody red.'

119. *all*] This is the reading of all the Editors, but at the same time *call* is not absolutely impossible.

THE MASSACRE AT PARIS

THE DUKE OF GUISE

THE MASSACRE AT PARIS

INTRODUCTION

I

EARLY HISTORY OF THE PLAY

O UR first certain knowledge of *The Massacre at Paris* is derived from an entry in Henslowe's Diary. There we read ' R[eceived] at the tragedey of the gvyes 30 . . . iij^{ll}xiiij^s.' [1] (Greg. *Henslowe's Diary*, I, 15). From the place of this entry in the diary it is clear that it was produced as one of a series of plays acted by Lord Strange's men at the Rose Theatre in the January-February of 1592/3. Dr. Greg fixes the date as Jan. 26th, although by error Henslowe enters it as being performed on the 30th. It is marked as a new play, and the £3 14s. taken at its first performance was the highest of the season, and compares well with the average takings of £1 14s. per performance during the season. The theatres were closed a few days later, because of the plague ; and it is not until June 1594 that we have any record of its being performed again. Then it was staged by the Admiral's men at the Rose on June 19th, and between that date and the 25th September (both inclusive), ten performances were given, the average takings being a little more than £1 7s. 6d. After these performances, we know nothing of it until an entry in the *Diary* which reads, ' Lent vnto w^m Bor[ne] the 19 of novemb₃, 1598 vpon a longe taney clocke of clothe the some

[1] It should be noted that it is strictly an assumption—though an assumption with little doubt in it—that the ' Gyves ', or ' Gwies ', or ' Guesse ' tragedy are the same as *The Massacre*. Henslowe uses these various titles indifferently, sometimes calling it *The Massacre of France* (see Greg, *op. cit.*).

of xii[s] w[ch] he sayd yt was to Jmbrader his hatte for the gwisse . . . xii[s]' (Greg, *op. cit.*, I, 78). This almost certainly refers to a revival of the play, for Henslowe often speaks of it as the 'gvyes', or 'Gwies', or 'guesse' tragedy. Again, on the 27th of November, the same actor was lent twenty shillings to buy stockings so that he could play this part (*op. cit.*, I, 72). Three years later, either a revival or the wearing out of properties caused renewed expenditure, and £7 14s. 6d. had to be expended (*op. cit.*, I, 149–151). Finally on the 18th Jan 1602 the Admiral's men bought the play with two others from Edward Alleyn for £6 (*op. cit.*, I, 153). Dr. Greg says that 'it is clear therefore that Alleyn brought the play with him when he re-formed the Admiral's company in the spring of 1594. Probably he then acquired it at a division of the stock, when most of the late Lord Strange's men passed under the patronage of the Lord Chamberlain, and Alleyn resumed his independence.' (*Greg*, Malone Soc. reprint of *The Massacre*, vi.)

II
DATE OF THE PLAY

Since the play deals with the death of Henry III, which occurred on 2nd August 1589, and since we know it was acted on the 26th January 1593, it is evident that it must have been written between these dates. But it is difficult to be more precise, although we may probably limit matters further by noting that the reference in Sc. xxi, l. 101 to 'Sixtus' bones' suggests that it was written after the death of Pope Sixtus V on 17th August 1590, and further that since it was entered as *new* in Henslowe's repertoire when performed in January 1593, it may be argued that it was composed during the preceding year, for it was not the practice of Elizabethan dramatists to leave their plays lying about unacted. Between the summer of 1590 and some time in 1592 (probably late that year) seems as close as we can get to an exact date.

III

THE OCTAVO

An early octavo of the play exists, but this is undated, and unfortunately there is no entry of the play in the Stationers' Register. The octavo has the following title page : THE | MASSACRE | AT PARIS : | With the Death of the Duke | of Guife.| As it was plaide by the right honourable the | Lord high *Admirall* his Seruants.| Written by *Chriftopher Marlow*.| [Device (McKerrow No. 290)] | AT LONDON | Printed by E. A. for *Edward White*, dwelling neere | the little North doore of S. Paules | Church, at the figne of | the Gun.[1]   The printer E. A. was Edward Allde, and both he and Edward White were printing and publishing actively till long after Marlowe's death, and are therefore of little use in dating the octavo.[2]   Again Dr. McKerrow in his *Printer's Devices*, etc., p. 113, has demonstrated that Allde was using the device found on the title page of *The Massacre* as early as 1592, and as late as 1626.   These are very wide limits and not helpful.   Our best clue seems to be the information that it was ' played by the Lord High Admiral's Servants '.   The Admiral became Earl of Nottingham in 1596, and after this his company was known as Nottingham's men, and only one play published at a later date fails to give him his new title.   On balance, therefore, we may conclude that the play was published some time after it came into the repertory of the Admiral's men in June 1594 (see above, p. 169).   How long after is a matter for discussion.   Professor Tucker Brooke would like to date it as late as possible, and thinks it follows rather than precedes the revival of 1601.   His evidence, however, as he himself admits, ' is of no great weight ', and an earlier date nearer the plague of 1592–3 seems preferable.[3]

We know that as a result of the plague of 1592–3 the companies were unable to act for some time, and it has been sug-

---

[1] For full collation see Appendix B.
[2] For a detailed study of E. Allde's activities, see R. B. McKerrow's article in *The Library*, New Series, X, 2, 1929.
[3] Tucker Brooke, *The Works of C. M.*, p. 441.

gested it was at such a moment that they were most easily pre-
vailed upon to part with their property for the sake of a little
ready money.   Generally, no doubt, such an exchange was
conducted by ordinary business methods, but occasionally
a play got on to the market without the sanction of its
owners.[1] This may be what happened with *The Massacre*,
and would help to account for its shocking textual condition.

There are two difficulties against a complete acceptance
of the view that the play was parted with for printing soon
after 1592–3.   The first is concerned with the full nature of
the Stage directions, and it is argued that they postulate
a theatre copy which would more probably have been
released after the revival of 1601 than before.   But if, as
I believe, the text we have is a ' stolne and surreptitious '
one, such an argument falls to the ground.   Furthermore,
as we shall see, there are reasons against accepting the present
text as a playhouse manuscript at all.   (See below, p. 173.)
The second objection is much more serious, and is based
on the presence in the text of lines *verbatim*, or almost
so, from other plays.   The most important of these occurs
in Scene XVIII, line 66 : ' Yet Caesar shall go forth.'—a
striking reminiscence of Shakespeare's *Julius Caesar*, II. ii.
28 : ' Yet Caesar shall go forth.'   Now *Julius Caesar* was
not published, so far as we know, before 1623, so that the
words, if borrowed, must come from a stage-performance.
Modern critical opinion inclines to the belief that *Julius
Caesar* was not performed earlier than 1600, which would
necessitate a date for *The Massacre* nearer to that desired
by Professor Tucker Brooke, i.e. after the revival of 1601.
It must be remembered, however, that several critics have
seen the hand of Marlowe in *Julius Caesar* as it now stands,
and the phrase may have been in the earlier draft upon
which Shakespeare worked.   Alternatively may not the
phrase have been a good line which both Marlowe and

---

[1] See, for example, Dr. Greg's Introduction to his edition of *The Merry
Wives of Windsor*.

Shakespeare found in use in the theatre, and adopted without much ado.[1]   Dr. Greg, prefacing the Malone Society reprint of *The Massacre*, p. ix, admits the supposition ' That the echoes were introduced either by actors in performance or by a reporter in his reconstruction of the play '.

While there is much room for dispute as to the date, there is little about the value of this text.   It is certainly one of the worst examples of garbled and mangled texts, and Dr. Pollard's general adjective of ' bad ' for such works seems all too weak to describe this confused and often-times barely intelligible play in its present form.   It has all the marks of its dubious origins : it was never entered at Stationers' Hall—a circumstance in itself arousing suspicion against its printer and publisher.   Then again, its comparative brevity compels our attention.   There are only some 1200 lines in the play, as compared with about double that number in *The Jew* and in each part of *Tamburlaine*, and rather more than double in *Edward II*.   Allde the printer was hard put to it to make a reasonable volume of it ; for, although he printed on the smaller octavo size, instead of using the more usual quarto, he found it necessary to waste much space in order to get his last few pages to cover a fourth sheet.[2]   Thirdly the nature of the stage directions suggests that we have the elaborated explanations of what the writer had seen created before him, rather than as Professor Tucker Brooke believes the result of a ' text . . . based on a theatre-copy '.   If it were the latter, it is not likely that the prompter would have bothered to write in the elaborate directions we have here : he would have contented himself with the briefest words which would remind him of what was necessary.   Thus at the beginning of Scene III, as it reads in the octavo, we find : ' *Enter the King of* Nauar *and* Queen, *and his Mother Queen, the Prince of* Condy, *the*

---

[1] There are also two other passages which have similarities to lines in *The True Tragedy of Richard*, etc., and *3 Henry VI* (see pp. 227, 245).
[2] Thus Sig. C 8^v has several lines wasted, and on D2^v at least five lines could be closed up.   So on D3 at least eight; on D3^v, three; on D4, five, etc.

Admirall, *and the* Pothecary *with the gloues, and giues them to the olde Queene.*' The last words of this stage-direction would probably have figured in a genuine (or ' good ') text printed from a prompt copy, as a marginal note, *Give gloves.* Nothing further was necessary to men who knew their job.

Our doubts, thus aroused by these external features, are increased as soon as the text is examined. Everywhere the hand of some clumsy and insensitive agent is upon it. Scenes have been truncated in such a way that it is difficult to follow them easily or perfectly.[1]   Only with difficulty can many passages be made to yield a meaning, while the versification is even more evil.   A great deal of verse is treated as prose, and at times the rhythmical structure is destroyed by the gross way in which the verse has been chopped up into various lengths.   Dr. Greg goes so far as to say that ' except in a few speeches, it retains little of the character of any piece that Marlowe can be supposed to have written ', and he concludes : ' Even among admittedly garbled versions it has an evil distinction, and must for shortness and fatuity be classed with such pieces as *The Famous Victories of Henry V* and *Orlando Furioso* ' (Malone Soc. reprint, p. x.).[2]

Bad as the state of the text undoubtedly is, there is nothing about it that leads us to believe that, had we the perfect text, we should have a great play. *The Massacre at Paris* is one of the weakest plays of its day.   Its very title is but barely descriptive of it, and Henslowe's alternative *The Guise* much more fitly describes its general purport. It deals in a shambling pedestrian way with events spread over many years, and certainly does not escape a familiar weakness of the historical drama—considerable structural incoherence.   Events are roughly strung together, and whatever interest there is, has to be sought for in Marlowe's power to create moments of dramatic tension and signifi-

---

[1] If we may accept the authenticity of *The Collier leaf* (for which see below, p. 253) we have there a vivid example of what might befall a play between the time of its writing and its ultimate issue from the printing-house.

[2] The evil state of the text has made it seem unnecessary to regularise the large number of irregular lines to a normal pentameter rule.

cance. But even here it is weak, for a mechanical reliance
on poisons and sudden violent death-scenes becomes absurd
in the end. There follow in rapid succession, the poisoning
of the Queen of Navarre, the wounding of the Admiral and
his subsequent assassination; next the stabbing of Loreine, of
Seroune, of Ramus, and of the Schoolmasters, with compre-
hensive orders to kill 'a hundred Protestants' who have been
chased into the Seine, etc. Immediately upon this, for no
reason, so far as we are told, the King himself dies. Mugeroun
is shot a few scenes later; then the Guise is assassinated, and
soon after his brother the Cardinal is strangled; the play
concluding with the dramatic stabbing of the King by the
Friar, and the scuffle between them in which the Friar is
killed by the dying King. This piling up of corpses wearies
and disgusts the reader: it is all too mechanical and lacking
in dramatic plausibility. Only the tough-fibred Elizabethan
audience could so allow its nerves to be played upon while
its intellect remained inactive,—and its nausea quiescent.

Furthermore, we cannot find anything to make us believe
the play to have suffered at the hands of an incompetent
hack, woefully failing to fill in the grandiose conceptions of a
master-mind. It has, indeed, been suggested that Marlowe
merely sketched the main lines of the play, but apart from
the fact that such a statement is supported by no evidence,
there is the added difficulty created by the Marlovian note
of many speeches throughout the play.[1] As Professor
Tucker Brooke says: 'The fallacy of the theory, that
Marlowe left the play to be completed by another is evident
from the indisputable genuineness of the French King's last
speeches (Sc. XXI, ll. 55–71; 91–107), while the final words
of Navarre, with which the play closes, are as convincing
in their swing and melody as the poet's autograph:

And then I vow for to revenge his death,
As Rome, and all those popish prelates there,
Shall curse the time that e'er Navarre was King,
And rul'd in France by Henry's fatal death.'

[1] See, e.g., Sc. II. ll. 34 ff.; VI., 24 ff.; XII., 27 ff., etc.

IV

SOURCES OF THE PLAY

No exact source from which Marlowe drew his material has ever been discovered. During Marlowe's lifetime a vast number of books and pamphlets issued from the presses of England and France, describing the events portrayed in *The Massacre*. Marlowe, as we know, was in France from time to time, and some of these books, many of them little more than pamphlets, may have come his way. Mr. Bullen, for example, in his edition of Marlowe, drew attention to a volume entitled *The Three Partes of Commentaries containing the whole and perfect discourse of the Civill Wars of France*, etc., London, 1574, and to this we may add *Commentaries of the Civill Wars in France and Flanders*, Part IV, London, 1576. In this work, which was written by J. de Serres and translated into English by T. Timme, there are several passages (see, e.g., pp. 182, 186, etc.) which parallel incidents in the play. Again, Professor Tucker Brooke has discovered another work by the same author, translated by A. Golding, entitled *The Life of Jasper Coligny*, 1576. Either of these works might have given Marlowe his information, but nowhere do we get the feeling that he was working with his source before him.

Further, it is clear that the later part of *The Massacre* deals with events that were so comparatively modern that it seems more reasonable to believe that Marlowe learnt about them more by current gossip and rumour, with an occasional broadside to lend support to one or other story, than by means of printed books. We know now of his intimate connection with the system of spying and plotting that formed part of the underworld of Elizabethan politics,[1] so that we may reasonably believe that his knowledge of foreign affairs would be considerably above that of the

[1] See F. S. Boas : *Marlowe and his Circle*, and E. Seaton: *Review Eng. Studies*, July 1929. See also Tucker Brooke, *Life of Marlowe*, 34, n[1].

average Elizabethan dramatist. It was in keeping with his character that Marlowe should try to create a drama from the still seething mass of incident which from day to day had given life and excitement to everyday affairs.

Not much time, however, need be wasted deploring our lack of knowledge of Marlowe's reading for *The Massacre.* Recent investigators, notably Miss E. Seaton and Miss Ellis-Fermor, have made very considerable researches into the sources of *Tamburlaine,* and have been able to show in great detail the materials he had looked over before writing that play. But even so they both emphasise with the greatest force how small a thing this so-called 'debt' really is. Miss Seaton says (*Rev. Eng. Studies*, Oct. 1929) : ' Is Marlowe then reduced to a drudging student, reading and working up a mass of material with the laborious accuracy of a modern historical novelist ? Is his work degraded to a patchwork of gaily coloured scraps of Eastern silks, a mosaic of Oriental stones ? To me rather the impression has been one of admiration for his astonishing ease in handling, and for his imaginative power in transforming, this unwieldy load of learning. . . . He conceals his art, and juggles with his facts so skilfully as to deceive even the very elect. Like every true poet he was transmuting to his alchemic purpose all he could lay hands on of metal worthy and unworthy ' (*op. cit.,* p. 401).

Miss Ellis-Fermor in her edition of *Tamburlaine* in this series thus sums up her impressions (p. 50) : ' The " debt " of Marlowe to his sources is, then, in the nature of things, as small as any poet's. Of all his contemporaries, he can say with most assurance, " I call no man father in England but myself " . . . It is idle to do more in the case of Marlowe than to remark such outward resemblance as his story bears to his original. The process by which he came to his real knowledge is his own, and the possession of information, after the bare, essential outline was gained, had little to do with it.'

V

ACT AND SCENE DIVISION

One of the greatest difficulties facing an editor of *The Massacre* is the division of the play into acts and scenes. The corrupt nature of the text makes this almost impossible, and no editor has tried to make a regulation five act drama of it. Robinson and Cunningham divided it into three acts, but there is little point in this, and here I have confined myself to an indication of the scenes. These are somewhat fewer in number than most previous editors have found necessary, but agree almost exactly with the divisions of the latest editor, Dr. W. W. Greg. The only point at which we differ is in the division of the long massacre scene, and concerning this Dr. Greg writes : ' It is this [scene] that gives the greatest trouble, for no very strict rules can be applied to the technique of the Elizabethan battle piece, such as this is in effect. It has been decided in the present [Malone Society] reprint to treat [it] as a continuous scene, not because the action is necessarily continuous, though it may be, but because the state of the text makes it impossible to determine exactly, how it was represented, and therefore what divisions were intended. At the same time in view of this uncertainty asterisks have been placed in the margin at the points where possible breaks occur ' (*op. cit.* xi.). I have ventured to start a new scene at one of these asterisked points mentioned by Dr. Greg, where the introduction of Peter Ramus in his study suggests to me the necessity for a change of scene. The exact locality of each of these scenes is even more difficult, and I am inclined to believe that no very definite attempt at localisation was made by Marlowe. Very many of them seem to take place in an open space or street in Paris, or elsewhere, and beyond that the author felt no need to be more explicit. In the notes I have tried to indicate more fully the reasons that have led me to indicate changes of scene, but have not ventured to introduce my ideas as to localisation into the text.

THE MASSACRE AT PARIS

DRAMATIS PERSONÆ [1]

CHARLES THE NINTH, *King of France.*
DUKE OF ANJOU, *his brother, afterwards* KING HENRY THE THIRD.
KING HENRY OF NAVARRE.
PRINCE OF CONDÉ, *his brother.*
DUKE OF GUISE,
CARDINAL OF LORRAINE, } *brothers.*
DUKE DUMAINE,
SON TO THE DUKE OF GUISE, *a boy.*
THE LORD HIGH ADMIRAL.
DUKE JOYEUX.
EPERNOUN.
PLESHÉ.
BARTUS.
TWO LORDS OF POLAND.
GONZAGO.
RETES.
MOUNTSORRELL.
MUGEROUN.
THE CUTPURSE.
LOREINE, *a Protestant preacher.*
SEROUNE.
RAMUS.
TALEUS.
FRIAR.
SURGEON.
ENGLISH AGENT.
APOTHECARY.
COSSIN, *captain of the guard.*
PROTESTANTS, SCHOOLMASTERS, SOLDIERS, MURDERERS, ATTEND-
ANTS, *etc.*
CATHERINE, *the Queen-Mother of France.*
MARGARET, *her daughter, wife to the* KING OF NAVARRE.
THE OLD QUEEN OF NAVARRE.
DUCHESS OF GUISE.
WIFE *to* SEROUNE.
MAID *to the* DUCHESS OF GUISE.

[1] The list of *Dramatis Personæ* is not in the Octavo, but was drawn up
by Robinson.

SCENE I

Enter CHARLES, *the French king ;* CATHERINE, *the Queen-Mother ; the* KING OF NAVARRE ; MARGARET, *Queen of Navarre ; the* PRINCE OF CONDÉ ; *the* LORD HIGH ADMIRAL ; *the* OLD QUEEN OF NAVARRE ; *with others.*

Char. Prince of Navarre, my honourable brother,
Prince Condé, and my good Lord Admiral,
I wish this union and religious league,
Knit in these hands, thus join'd in nuptial rites,
May not dissolve till death dissolve our lives ;
And that the native sparks of princely love,
That kindled first this motion in our hearts,
May still be fuell'd in our progeny.
Nav. The many favours which your grace hath shown,
From time to time, but specially in this,   10
Shall bind me ever to your highness' will,

Scene i.

Bullen, Greg : *Act the First, Scene i* Robinson, Cunningham : *omit* O. and Dyce. No acts or scenes marked throughout by Octavo. Localities of scenes indicated by Dyce and Bullen only. *Enter . . .*] Robinson, Dyce, Cunn., Bull. substantially : omit *Margaret, Queen of Navarre* O.

8. *fuell'd*] Dyce : *feweld* Octavo : *fuelled* Bullen : *fuel'd* Rob.

Scene I] The play opens with the conclusion of the marriage ceremony between Henry of Navarre and Margaret of Valois, and from line 18 we see that Charles and others proceed into the church (Notre-Dame at Paris) while Henry and his friends wait without. It is clear, then, that the scene is some open place (perhaps the *parvis* before the cathedral) in Paris. The outer stage would be sufficient.

3. *this union . . . league*] On 18th August 1572 Henry of Navarre (afterwards Henry IV of France) was married to Margaret of Valois, the sister of Charles IX. This marriage secured at least a formal unity—at that time an urgent necessity of state, after years of religious bitterness and quarrelling. Henry, of course, was one of the leaders of the Huguenots.

7. *motion*] inward prompting or impulse. See *Othello,* I. iii. 355 : ' We have reason to cool our raging *motions.*'

8. *fuell'd*] The first use of the word, according to the O.E.D. Here used to mean ' to supply or furnish with fuel '.

13   181

In what Queen Mother or your grace commands.

Cath. Thanks, son Navarre. You see we love you well,
    That link you in marriage with our daughter here ;
    And, as you know, our difference in religion
    Might be a means to cross you in your love.—

Char. Well, madam, let that rest.—
    And now, my lords, the marriage-rites perform'd,
    We think it good to go and consummate
    The rest, with hearing of a holy mass :   20
    Sister, I think yourself will bear us company.

Mar. I will, my good lord.

Char. The rest that will not go, my lords, may stay :
    Come, mother,
    Let us go to honour this solemnity.

Cath. Which I'll dissolve with blood and cruelty.   [*Aside.*
        [*Exeunt all except the King of Navarre, Condé,
        and the Admiral.*

Nav. Prince Condé, and my good Lord Admiral,
    Now Guise may storm, but do us little hurt,
    Having the king, Queen Mother on our sides,

---

12. *Queen Mother*] O., Rob. : *Queen-Mother* Dyce, Bullen. 19–21. As Rob., etc. ; ll. 19, 20 end *rest, think* ; l. 21 reads *your selfe* . . . O. 22. *lord.*] Rob, etc. : *lord*, O. 23. *my lords*] Rob., etc. : (*my lords*) O. 24, 25. As Dyce, Bull. : one line O., Rob., Cunn. 26. *Aside.*] Added by Rob., etc. 26. *Exeunt* . . .] Rob., etc. : *Exit the King, Q. Mother, and the Q. of Nauar, and manet Nauar, the Prince of Condy, and the Lord High Admirall.* O. 27. *Lord*] Rob., etc. : *L. O.*, and so at line 39. 29. *king, Queen Mother*] Broughton conj., Dyce, Bull. : *King, Qu. Mother* O. : *king-Queen Mother* Rob., Cunn. *sides*] O., etc. : *side*, Rob.

18, 25] In Golding's translation of the *Life of Coligny* (1576), sig. F.8, quoting a letter of the Admiral to his wife, dated 18 Aug. 1572, we read : ' It was this day past fower of the clocke in the afternoone, ere the mariage masse was celebrated. While that was a singing, the King of *Nauarre* walked up and downe with certein noblemen of our Religion which followed him, in a certein yard with owt the Churche.' See also the extract printed by Bullen from a volume of 1574 entitled ' *The Three Partes of Com-mentaries containing the whole and perfect discourse of the Civill Wars of France, &c.*'. Book X, p. 9ᵛ.

24, 25] Scanned as one line in Octavo and some editions, but probably better as two. It requires an inordinate amount of swallowing and gabbling to read as anything like an ordinary pentameter, unless we may consider the vocative *Mother* as intrusive.

29. *king, Queen Mother*] In the original printed ' King, Qu. Mother ', while Robinson and Cun-

To stop the malice of his envious heart,   30
That seeks to murder all the Protestants.
Have you not heard of late how he decreed
(If that the king had given consent thereto)
That all the protestants that are in Paris
Should have been murdered the other night ?

Adm. My lord, I marvel that th' aspiring Guise
    Dares once adventure, without the king's consent,
    To meddle or attempt such dangerous things.

Con. My lord, you need not marvel at the Guise,
    For what he doth, the Pope will ratify,   40
    In murder, mischief, or in tyranny.

Nav. But he that sits and rules above the clouds
    Doth hear and see the prayers of the just,
    And will revenge the blood of innocents,
    That Guise hath slain by treason of his heart,
    And brought by murder to their timeless ends.

Adm. My lord, but did you mark the Cardinal,
    The Guise's brother, and the Duke Dumaine,
    How they did storm at these your nuptial rites,
    Because the house of Bourbon now comes in,   50
    And joins your lineage to the crown of France ?

Nav. And that's the cause that Guise so frowns at us,

33.] No brackets in O.   37. *consent*] O., etc. : *assent*, Rob., Cunn.   52.
the] Rob., etc. : ye O.

ningham punctuate ' the king-Queen Mother '. Broughton (MS.) first proposed the change.

sides] Dyce rightly observes that the alteration to ' side ' by some editors is unnecessary, and compares *John*, v. ii. 8 : ' Upon our *sides* it never shall be broken.'

40, 41. *For . . . tyranny.*] i.e. what he does in (the way of) murder, etc., the Pope will ratify.

46. *timeless*] untimely, premature. Used also by Marlowe in 2 *Tamburlaine*, v. iii. 252 : ' Let earth and heaven his *timeless* end deplore ', and cf. *Edward II*, l. 213. O.E.D. quotes *Trag. Richard II*

(1560) : ' 'Ile revenge thy *tymlesse* tragedye '.

47, 48. *the Cardinal, . . . brother,*] i.e. Henry Duke of Guise's youngest brother, Louis, Cardinal de Guise.

48. *Dumaine*] Compare *Love's Labour's Lost* where Dumaine is unhistorically made a friend and companion of Navarre. Shee (*Gent. Mag.*, Oct. 1880) says : ' This is a common Anglicised form of that Duc de Maine, or Mayenne, whose name was so frequently mentioned in popular accounts of French affairs in connection with Navarre.'

And beats his brains to catch us in his trap,
Which he hath pitch'd within his deadly toil.
Come, my lords, let's go to the church, and pray
That God may still defend the right of France,
And make his Gospel flourish in this land.   [*Exeunt.*

SCENE II

Enter GUISE.

Guise. If ever Hymen lour'd at marriage-rites,
    And had his altars deck'd with dusky lights;
    If ever sun stain'd heaven with bloody clouds,
    And made it look with terror on the world;
    If ever day were turn'd to ugly night,
    And night made semblance of the hue of hell;
    This day, this hour, this fatal night,
    Shall fully show the fury of them all.

Scene ii.
Rob., Cunn., Bull., Greg: *omit* the rest.
7. *hour*] O., etc.: *hour, and* Dyce conj.: *hour, [and]* Cunn.

53, 54. *trap . . . pitch'd . . . toil*] Cf. IV. 3, *post.* As *toil* or *toils* signify nets pitched, i.e. set ' so as to enclose a space into which the quarry is driven, or within which the game is known to be ' (O.E.D.), ll. 53, 54, if taken literally, mean that Guise had not only contrived a toil but set a trap within it; but probably the trap and the toil are the same thing. The usual phrase is ' pitch a toil ', as in *Love's Labour's Lost*, IV. iii. 2, ' they have pitched a toil '. Cf. also Dekker, *The Belman of London* (Temple Classics, p. 102), figuratively: ' In this *Forrest* of *Wilde-men*, the safest *Toyles* to pitch is the Irish *Toyle*, which is a net so strongly and cunningly woven together ', etc.
55–57. *Come . . . land.*] These lines give an excuse to clear the stage. Navarre and his friends have ostentatiously remained out-

side the church earlier in the scene (see line 23).

Scene II

Scene II.] Either a room in Guise's house, or possibly again out in the open street or place. The outer stage used.
1, 2. *If ever Hymen . . .*] Compare Ovid, *Met.* x. 1 ff., where is described the presence and actions of Hymen at the marriage of Orpheus and Euridice.

' adfuit ille quidem, sed nec sollemnia verba
  nec laetos vultus nec felix attulit omen.'

The whole passage is much in the Senecan style, with its parallel of sentences and meteorological references.
7. *This day, . . . night,*] The whole emphasis of this line is

Apothecary !

Enter APOTHECARY

Apoth. My lord ?   10

Guise. Now shall I prove, and guerdon to the full,

The love thou bear'st unto the house of Guise.

Where are those perfum'd gloves which I sent

To be poison'd ? hast thou done them ? speak ;

Will every savour breed a pang of death ?

Apoth. See where they be, my good lord ; and he that smells

But to them, dies.

Guise. Then thou remainest resolute ?

Apoth. I am, my lord, in what your grace commands,

Till death.   20

Guise. Thanks, my good friend : I will requite thy love.

Go, then, present them to the Queen Navarre ;

For she is that huge blemish in our eye,

That makes these upstart heresies in France :

---

9. *Enter . . .*] Rob., etc.: *Enter the Pothecarie.* O.   13. *which*] O., Dyce : *which late* Rob., Cunn. : *which [late]* Bull.   16. *good lord*] O., etc. : *lord* Rob., Cunn.   16, 17. As Rob., etc. : divided after *lord* O.   18. *remainest*] O., etc. : *remain'st* Dyce.   19, 20. As Rob., etc. : prose in O.

gained by Marlowe's skilful use of four feet only. Hence Dyce's proposed emendation is worse than unnecessary.

11. *guerdon*] reward, recompense, as in line 32 below.

13. *perfum'd gloves*] The use of poison was one of the favourite devices of the Elizabethan stage. Marlowe uses it again in *The Jew of Malta*—a poisoned nosegay : Webster has a poisoned book in *The Duchess of Malfi*, and a poisoned visor and a poisoned portrait in *The White Devil*, etc. Mr. Percy Simpson refers in a note on Jonson's *Every Man in his Humour*, IV. viii. 16, to Pedro Mexia, *The Treasurie of Auncient and Moderne Times* (trans. 1613), II. xvii. : ' That a man may be impoysoned by Pomanders of sweete smell, Fumes of Torches, Tapers, Candels ; by Letters, Gar-

ments, and other such like things.' Even in Steele's time it was remembered that the innocent appearance of such gifts was sometimes fallacious. Cf. *The Funeral*, I. i. (Mermaid ed., p. 21) :

' The Italians, they say, can readily
remove the too much intrusted,
Oh ! their pretty *scented gloves* '.

15. *savour*] smell, aroma. Used again by Marlowe in *Ed. II*, v. v. 9 :

' I was almost stifled with the *savour*.'

23. *in our eye*] always before us, in our sight, as in *Hamlet*, IV. iv. 6 :

' We shall express our duty *in his eye*.'

24. *upstart heresies*] Protestantism. The Queen of Navarre was one of the leading figures of the Huguenot party.

Be gone, my friend, present them to her straight.

[*Exit Apothecary.*

Soldier !

Enter a Soldier.

Sold. My lord ?

Guise. Now come thou forth, and play thy tragic part.
Stand in some window, opening near the street,
And when thou see'st the Admiral ride by,   30
Discharge thy musket, and perform his death ;
And then I'll guerdon thee with store of crowns.

Sold. I will, my lord.   [*Exit.*

Guise. Now, Guise begins those deep-engender'd thoughts
To burst abroad those never-dying flames
Which cannot be extinguish'd but by blood.
Oft have I levell'd, and at last have learn'd
That peril is the chiefest way to happiness,
And resolution honour's fairest aim.
What glory is there in a common good,   40
That hangs for every peasant to achieve ?
That like I best, that flies beyond my reach.

27. *lord ?*] Rob., etc. : *Lord,*] O.

26. *Enter a Soldier.*] ' The name of him that shot [the Admiral] was diligently kept secret. Some saye it was Manrevet, which in the third Civill War traitorously slew his Captaine, Monsieur de Mony . . . and straightway fled into the enemie's campe. Some say it was Bondot, one of the archers of the king's guard.' *The Three Partes of Commentaries*, etc. (Book X. p. 10). The assassin's name was really Maurevel.

29. *Stand . . . window*] Golding's translation of the *Life of Coligny* (1576) contains a detailed account of the outrage, but says he was wounded in three places : ' For the forefinger of his ryght hand was broken in peeces, and hys left arme shot through with two pellets of brasse ' (sig. F.7ᵛ).   See also below, Sc. III., l. 31.

34. *begins*] O. : *begin* Rob., etc.

37. *levell'd*] guessed at. Compare Lyly, *Euphues* (Arber's edn.), p. 289 : ' Since your eyes are . . . so cunning that you can *level* at the dispositions of women whom you never knew ' ; and *Merch. of Venice*, I. ii. 41 : ' As thou namest them, I will describe them, and according to my description *levell* at my affection '.

38. *peril . . . happiness*] A characteristic Marlovian idea. Quoted, not quite accurately, in *England's Parnassus* (1600), p. 48 :

' Daunger's the chiefest ioy to happinesse,
And resolution honours fairest ayme,

Ch. Marlowe.'

39. *aim.*] course, direction.

Set me to scale the high Pyramides,
And thereon set the diadem of France ;
I'll either rend it with my nails to naught,
Or mount the top with my aspiring wings,
Although my downfall be the deepest hell.
For this I wake, when others think I sleep,
For this I wait, that scorns attendance else ;
For this, my quenchless thirst, whereon I build,   50
Hath often pleaded kindred to the king ;
For this, this head, this heart, this hand, and sword,
Contrives, imagines, and fully executes,
Matters of import aimèd at by many,
Yet understood by none ;
For this, hath heaven engender'd me of earth ;
For this, this earth sustains my body's weight,
And with this weight I'll counterpoise a crown,
Or with seditions weary all the world ;
For this, from Spain the stately Catholics   60
Sends Indian gold to coin me French ecues ;
For this, have I a largess from the Pope,

49. *scorns*] O. : *scorn* Rob., etc.   53. *Contrives, . . .*] O. etc. : delete *and*
Cunn. : *Contrive, imagine, and fully execute*, Rob.   54. *aimèd*] Dyce,
etc. : *aimde* O. : *aimed* Rob.   57. *weight*] Rob., etc. : *wiat*, O.   60.
Catholics] O., etc. : *Catholic* Rob., Cunn.   61. *Sends*] O., Rob., Cunn. :
Send Dyce, Bull.

43. *high Pyramides*,] Here used
as a singular, as the next two lines
show. Cf. *Faustus*, l. 844 ; and
The London Prodigal, III. iii. 212 :
' As I to scale *the hye Piramydies*.'

48. *For this . . . sleep*,] For a
parallel line see *The Contention*, l.
157 :
' Watch thou, and wake when
    others be asleep,
To pry into the secrets of the
    state.'
With York's speech there, should be
compared this entire speech of the
Guise.
53. *Contrives*] plots, as in *Julius
Caesar*, II. iii. 16 :

' If thou read this, O Cæsar ! thou
    may'st live ;
If not, the Fates with traitors do
    contrive.'

53. *Contrives . . . executes*,] The
head contrives, the heart imagines,
and the hand and the sword
execute. The heart is thought of
as the seat of imagination.
61. *ecues*] crowns, from Fr. *écu*—
originally *shield*, so called because
originally it bore on one face three
fleurs-de-lys, like an heraldic shield.
62. *largess*] A gift or dole of
money, generally bestowed by one
of higher rank than the recipient.
Compare *Richard II*, I. iv. 44 :
' Our coffers, with too great a

A pension, and a dispensation too ;
And by that privilege to work upon,
My policy hath fram'd religion.
Religion ! *O Diabole !*
Fie, I am asham'd, however that I seem,
To think a word of such a simple sound,
Of so great matter should be made the ground !
The gentle king, whose pleasure uncontroll'd   70
Weakeneth his body, and will waste his realm,
If I repair not what he ruinates :
Him, as a child, I daily win with words,
So that for proof he barely bears the name ;
I execute, and he sustains the blame.
The Mother Queen works wonders for my sake,
And in my love entombs the hope of France,
Rifling the bowels of her treasury,
To supply my wants and necessity.
Paris hath full five hundred colleges,   80
As monasteries, priories, abbeys, and halls,
Wherein are thirty thousand able men,
Besides a thousand sturdy student Catholics ;
And more,—of my knowledge, in one cloister keeps

76. *Mother Queen*] O., Rob. : *Mother-Queen* Dyce, etc.   84. *keeps*] O. :
keep Rob., etc.

court, And liberal *largess*, are
grown somewhat light.'
   72. *ruinates*] Commonly in. use
in Elizabethan times.   Compare
Titus Andronicus, v. iii. 204 :
' Then afterwards, to order well the
state, That like events may ne'er it
ruinate.' See also *3 Henry VI*, v.
i. 83.
   74. *for proof*] i.e. as a proof (of
my statements).   For the idea cf.
Ed. II, l. 2014 : ' My nobles rule,
I bear the name of king.'
   83. *a thousand . . . Catholics ;*]
An allusion, perhaps, to the
students in seminaries, so feared by
Elizabethan   Protestants.   (See
Scene XVIII., lines 102 ff.)

84. *more,—*] moreover. The line
would be better without *more*,
which might perhaps be an actor's
emphasis addition, or possibly a
printer's error due to the *and more*
two lines below.
   84. *keeps*] dwell, reside.   The
O.E.D. says it was frequently in
use from *c.* 1580 to 1650.   It is still
used colloquially at Cambridge by
University men.   There is no need
to read *keep*, as do some editors ;
keeps is a common Elizabethan
form, and a note on these *s* and *th*
plurals will be found in a preface
to the 3rd edition of Prof. R. H.
Case's *Antony and Cleopatra* (Arden
edn.).

Five hundred fat Franciscan friars and priests :
All this, and more, if more may be compris'd,
To bring the will of our desires to end.
Then, Guise,
Since thou hast all the cards within thy hands,
To shuffle or cut, take this as surest thing,   90
That, right or wrong, thou deal thyself a king.—
Ay, but, Navarre,—'tis but a nook of France,
Sufficient yet for such a petty king,
That, with a rabblement of his heretics,
Blinds Europe's eyes, and troubleth our estate.
Him will we—[*Pointing to his sword.*] but first let's
  follow those in France
That hinder our possession to the crown.
As Cæsar to his soldiers, so say I,—
Those that hate me will I learn to loathe.
Give me a look, that, when I bend the brows,   100

87. *To bring*] O., etc. : *Do bring* Cunn. *the will*] O., etc. : *the whole* Coll.
conj.   88–90. As Dyce, etc. : divided after *cards* O., Rob.   92. *Navarre*],
Rob., etc. : *Nauarre, Nauarre*, O.   96. As Dyce, Bull. : divided after
we—O., Rob., Cunn.   97. *possession*] O., etc. : *procession* Brereton
conj. : *accession* Holthausen conj.

85. *Five hundred . . .*] A characteristic Marlovian exaggeration.
Few medieval monasteries exceeded
a hundred residents among the
professed, but Marlowe was not the
man to trouble about that, and his
imagination bodied forth hundreds
of colleges and monasteries—all full
of fat lazy clerics ! Marlowe's
feelings concerning Franciscans may
be assumed from *Faustus*, i. iii.
(Mermaid ed., p. 183) :
'Go and return an old Franciscan
  friar ;
That holy shape becomes a devil
  best.'
89–91. *Since . . . king.—*]   C.
Crawford draws attention to a
similar passage in *Locrine*, lines
1538 ff. :
' Will Fortune favour me yet once
  again ?
  And will she thrust the cards into
  my hands ?

Well, if I chance but once to get
  the deck,
To deal about and shuffle as I
  would ;
Let Selim never see the daylight
  spring,
Unless I shuffle out myself a King.'

92. *Navarre*] The original edition
reads *Ay, but Nauarre, Nauarre*,
but all editors have considered the
second *Navarre* to be a compositor's
error.   It is, however, just possible
that it was inserted by Marlowe to
emphasise the thoughtful, anxious
consideration Guise was compelled
to give, despite himself, to this
adversary.
97. *possession to*] Brereton objects to this as an unusual expression, and proposes *procession to*.
100–101. *Give me . . . face ;*] A
similar idea is expressed in *1 Tamburlaine*, ii. i. 21–22 :

Pale death may walk in furrows of my face ;
A hand, that with a grasp may gripe the world ;
An ear to hear what my detractors say ;
A royal seat, a sceptre, and a crown ;
That those which do behold, they may become
As men that stand and gaze against the sun.
The plot is laid, and things shall come to pass
Where resolution strives for victory.   [*Exit.*

SCENE III

Enter the KING OF NAVARRE, QUEEN MARGARET, *the* OLD
QUEEN OF NAVARRE, *the* PRINCE OF CONDÉ, *and the*
ADMIRAL ; *they are met by the* Apothecary *with the*
gloves, which he gives to the OLD QUEEN.

Apoth. Madam,
    I beseech your grace to accept this simple gift.
Old Q. of Nav. Thanks, my good friend.   Hold, take thou
    this reward.   [*Gives a purse.*
Apoth. I humbly thank your majesty.   [*Exit.*
Old Q. of Nav. Methinks the gloves have a very strong
    perfume,
    The scent whereof doth make my head to ache.
Nav. Doth not your grace know the man that gave them you ?

---

105. *behold, they*] O., Bull. :   *behold them,* Rob. :   *behold them* Dyce, Cunn.

Scene iii.

Rob., Cunn., Bull., Greg :   *omit* O., Dyce.   *Enter* . . .] Rob., etc.
So substantially in O.

1, 2. As Dyce, etc. : prose in O., Rob.   2. *accept*] Rob., etc. : *except* O.
3. *Gives a purse*] Dyce, Bull. :   *omit* the rest.

' His lofty brows in folds do figure
    death,
And in their smoothness amity
    and life.'

105. *behold, they*] Dyce and others
read *behold them,* but the old reading
need not be disturbed.

Scene III.

Scene III.] The two parties evidently enter by the two side doors,
and the scene is supposed to be out

in the open.   From Sc. II. l. 30,
we know that it is a street some-
where between the Louvre and the
Admiral's lodging.   Outer stage.

2. *accept*] The Octavo reading
except might, perhaps, be left, as it
is sometimes used in the sense of
accept.   See Gower : *Confessio*
Amantis, VII. 2745.

5. *Methinks . . . perfume*] The
Queen is not suspicious, as is
Navarre, since gloves frequently

Old Q. of Nav. Not well ; but do remember such a man.

Adm. Your grace was ill-advised to take them, then,
   Considering of these dangerous times.   10

Old Q. of Nav. Help, son Navarre ! I am poison'd !

Mar. The heavens forbid your highness such mishap !

Nav. The late suspicion of the Duke of Guise
   Might well have mov'd your highness to beware
   How you did meddle with such dangerous gifts.

Mar. Too late, it is, my lord, if that be true,
   To blame her highness ; but I hope it be
   Only some natural passion makes her sick.

Old Q. of Nav. O, no, sweet Margaret ! the fatal poison
   Works within my head ; my brain-pan breaks ;   20
   My heart doth faint ; I die !   [*Dies.*

Nav. My mother poison'd here before my face !
   O gracious God, what times are these !
   O, grant, sweet God, my days may end with hers,

---

20. *Works*] O., Dyce, Bull. : *Doth work* Rob. : *Worketh* Dyce conj., Cunn.

were highly perfumed. Cf. *Much Ado*, III. iv. 58 : ' These gloves the Count sent me, they are an excellent *perfume.*'

10. *Considering of*] A common Elizabethan usage. See Abbott, §178.

11. *I am poison'd*] The historical facts are these : On June 9th, 1572, the Queen, who had come to Court about the middle of May for the wedding of her son, died of pleurisy, after a short illness. For some time after the charge of poisoning was constantly levelled against the Catholics, especially the Queen-Mother. There appear to be no grounds worth consideration for any such charge. ' Joane Queene of Navarre . . . died in the Court at Paris, of a sodaine sicknesse, . . . where, as the suspition was great that she dyed of poyson, and her body being for that cause opened by the Phisitions, there were no tokens of poyson espied. But shortely after, . . . it hath ben founde that she was poysoned with

a venomed smell of a payre of perfumed gloves, dressed by one Renat the Kings Apothicarie, an Italian . . . which could not be espied by the Phisitions whiche did not open the heade nor looke into the braine.'—*Three Partes of Commentaries*, x. 9.

13. *The late suspicion*] The suspicion held by us, of late.

18. *natural passion*] Here used to mean some violent disorder of the body, arising naturally—and not as a result of poison. Compare Boorde's *Brev. Health* (1557), p. 33 : ' In latyn it is named *Ventralis passio*. In English : the belly ache, or a *passion* in the belly.'

20. *Works*] Robinson, for the sake of metre, prints ' *Doth work* ', and Dyce and Cunningham conjecture ' Worketh '. The text is so corrupt that it scarcely seems worth while disturbing it.

brain-pan] Broughton (MS.) quotes *Faerie Queene*, VI. 6, 30 : ' The tempered steel did not into his *brain-pan* bite.'

That I with her may die and live again!

Mar. Let not this heavy chance, my dearest lord,
(For whose effects my soul is massacred),
Infect thy gracious breast with fresh supply
To aggravate our sudden misery.

Adm. Come, my lords, let us bear her body hence,   30
And see it honoured with just solemnity.

> [*As they are going out, the Soldier dischargeth his
> musket at the Lord Admiral.*

Con. What, are you hurt, my Lord High Admiral?

Adm. Ay, my good lord, shot through the arm.

Nav. We are betray'd! Come, my lords,
And let us go tell the king of this.

Adm.   These are
The cursed Guisians, that do seek our death.
O, fatal was this marriage to us all.

> [*Exeunt, bearing out the body of the Old Queen of Navarre.*

32. *Lord*] Rob., etc.: *L. O.*   34, 35.] As Dyce, etc.: as prose O.:
divided after *us* Cunn.   36, 37.] As Dyce, Bull.: as prose O., Rob., Cunn.
37. *Exeunt . . .*] Dyce, Bull.: *They beare away the Queene and goe out.*
O., and subs., Rob., Cunn.

27. *effects*] accomplishment or
fulfilment. The O.E.D. instances
Starkey's *England* (1538), p. 195:
'I thynk hit schold be veray hard
to bryng thys to *effect*', and *Two
Gent. of Verona*, I. i. 50: 'Losing
. . . the fair *effects* of future
hopes'.

30. *Come, . . . hence,*] Since this
scene is in the open, and therefore
on the outer stage, some such
speech as this is necessary to
provide for the removal of the body
from the stage.

31. *As they are going . . .*] 'The
Admirall (as he determined before)
having accesse and opportunitie for
that purpose, moved the Kings
privie Counsell the 22. of August,
which was the fifte daye after the
King of Nauarres mariage, and
spente muche time in that treatie.
About noone, when he was in
returning home from the Counsell,
with a greate companie of noblemen

and Gentlemen, beholde, a Harque-
buzier out of a window of a house
neere adioyning, shot ye Admiral
with two bullets of leade through
both the armes. When the Admiral
felte himselfe wounded, nothing at
all amazed, but with the same
countenance that he was accustomed, he sayde, throughe yonder
windowe it was done: goe see who
are in the house: what manner of
treacherie is this?' (*The Three
Partes, &c.*, x. 10). The soldier
appears on the upper stage, as if
in a window overlooking the street.
See Sc. II, ll. 26–29.

37. *O, fatal . . . all.*] Compare
The Contention, 1. 80:

'Ah Lords *fatall is this marriage*
  cancelling our states,
Reversing Monuments of conquered France,
Undoing all, as none had nere bene
  done.'

SCENE IV

Enter KING CHARLES, CATHERINE *the Queen Mother,*
GUISE, ANJOU, *and* DUMAINE.

Cath. My noble son, and princely Duke of Guise,
Now have we got the fatal, straggling deer
Within the compass of a deadly toil,
And, as we late decreed, we may perform.

Char. Madam, it will be noted through the world
An action bloody and tyrannical ;
Chiefly, since under safety of our word
They justly challenge their protection :
Besides, my heart relents that noblemen,
Only corrupted in religion,   10
Ladies of honour, knights, and gentlemen,
Should, for their conscience, taste such ruthless ends.

Anj. Though gentle minds should pity others' pains,
Yet will the wisest note their proper griefs,
And rather seek to scourge their enemies
Than be themselves base subjects to the whip.

Guise. Methinks my Lord Anjou hath well advis'd

Scene iv.
Rob., Cunn., Bull., Greg : *omit* O, Dyce. *Enter* . . .] Rob., etc. :
*Enter the King, Queene Mother, Duke of Guise, Duke Anioy, Duke De-
mayne.* O.

10, 11.] As Rob., etc. : divided after *honour* O.   11, 12.] As Rob.,
etc. : one line as prose beginning *Knights* O.   17. *Lord*] Rob., etc. : *Lord,* O.

Scene IV.] This scene begins in
an open street in Paris, close to the
Admiral's house. Then at line 50,
the curtain is drawn and the
Admiral is discovered in his bed on
the upper stage. This, rather than
Dr. Greg's explanation (see note on
line 51), seems best to fit the facts.
The scene closes with ' *Exeunt
omnes* ', and the curtains are drawn
to, leaving us in the open street
again, and ready for Sc. v.
1. *My noble son* . . .] ' After
noone the Queene mother led out
the King, the Duke of Aniow,
Gonzague, Tauaignes, the Counte
de Retz. . . . Then she shewed

them, howe those whome they
hadde long bene in waite for, were
nowe sure in hold, . . . Nowe was
a notable opportunitie (saide she)
offered to dispatch the matter.'
(*Three Partes, &c.,* x. 12ᵛ.)
2, 3. *Now* . . . *toil*] See on Sc. I.
ll. 53, 54, above. *Fatal* is used in the
Latin sense of *fated.*
14. *proper*] own. Compare
Tempest, III. iii. 60 : ' even with
such like valour, men hang and
drown Their *proper* selves.'
17. *my Lord Anjou*] The Octavo
punctuates *my Lord, Anioy* and
regards *my Lord,* as a vocative.

Your highness to consider of the thing,
And rather choose to seek your country's good
Than pity or relieve these upstart heretics.   20

Cath. I hope these reasons may serve my princely son
To have some care for fear of enemies.

Char. Well, madam, I refer it to your majesty,
And to my nephew here, the Duke of Guise :
What you determine, I will ratify.

Cath. Thanks to my princely son,—Then tell me, Guise,
What order will you set down for the massacre ?

Guise. Thus, madam.   They
That shall be actors in this massacre
Shall wear white crosses on their burgonets,   30
And tie white linen scarfs about their arms ;
He that wants these, and is suspect of heresy,
Shall die, be he king or emperor.   Then I'll have
A peal of ordinance shot from the tower, at which
They all shall issue out, and set the streets,

28, 29.] As Dyce² : divided after *madam.* O., etc.   32. *suspect*] Rob., Dyce², Cunn., Bull. : *suspected* O., Dyce¹.   33–35.] As Dyce, etc. : divided after *Emperor, tower, streets,* in O., Rob.   34. *ordinance*] O. : *ordnance* Rob., etc.   35. *set*] O., etc. : *'set*] Rob., Cunn.

24. *my nephew*] Used here with some latitude.   It denotes a relative merely, as in *1 Henry VI*, II. v. 64, where nephew = cousin.

30. *burgonets*] helmets.   From the Fr. *bourguignotte*, apparently from *Burgogne*, Burgundy.   The name given to a light steel cap for the use of infantry, as well as to the helmet with a visor.   So in Heywood's *The Foure Prentices of London* (*Works*, ed. Pearson), II. 243 : 'Proofe, Cuiraces, and open *Burgonets.*'

31. *white . . . scarfs*] See note on l. 34, *post.*

32. *suspect*] Dyce, in his first edition, wrote, 'The modern editors print *suspect* ; and so the poet probably wrote : but there is no end to corruptions of the text in the play.'   Hence he printed *suspected* as in the octavo, but in his second edition he corrected it to *suspect,* as do all the other editors.

34. *peal of ordinance*] discharge of guns or cannon.   Compare Hakluyt's *Voyages* (1889), p. 157 : 'The castle discharged a *peal of ordinance.*'   'The token to set upon them, should be given, not with a trumpet, but with tocksein or ringing of the great bel of the Palace, which they knew to be accustomed only in great cases : and the marke for them to be knowne from other, should be a white linnen cloth hanged about their lefte arme, and a white crosse pinned upon their cappes.'—*Three Partes of Commentaries, &c.*, X. 13ᵛ.

35. *set . . . streets*] to beset the streets for the purpose of capturing or intercepting people.   See also below, Scene v, line 55.   Robinson and Cunningham print '*set,* i.e. beset.

And then,
The watchword being given, a bell shall ring,
Which when they hear, they shall begin to kill,
And never cease until that bell shall cease ;
Then breathe a while.

Enter the ADMIRAL'S *Serving-Man.*

Char.   How now, fellow ! what news ? 40
Serv.-M. And it please your grace, the Lord High Admiral,
    Riding the streets, was traitorously shot ;
    And most humbly entreats your majesty
    To visit him, sick in his bed,
Char. Messenger, tell him I will see him straight.
                          [Exit Serv.-M.
What shall we do now with the Admiral ?
Cath. Your majesty were best go visit him,
    And make a show as if all were well.
Char. Content ; I will go visit the Admiral.
Guise. And I will go take order for his death.   50
                           [Exit Guise.

The ADMIRAL *discovered in bed.*

Char. How fares it with my Lord High Admiral ?

36, 37.] As Dyce, Cunn., Bull. : one line O., Rob.   41. *And*] O. : *An*
Rob., &c.   43. *humbly*] Rob., etc. : *humble* (i.e. *humblie*), O.   50. *Exit
Guise*] O. : *Exeunt*, Rob., Cunn., Bull. : *Exeunt Catherine and Guise*. Dyce.
50. *Scene V.*] Rob., Cunn., Bull. : *omit* O., Dyce, Greg.   50. *The Admiral
discovered* . . .] Rob., etc. : *Enter the Admiral in his bed*. O.

49. *I will go . . . Admiral.*] Cf. Golding's *Life of Coligny* (sig. G. iii.) : ' Abowt twoo of the clocke in the afternoone, the King being certified of the Admiralls desyre, went untoo him, accompanyed with the Queene Moother, the Kings twoo brothers,' etc.

51] Dr. Greg (*op. cit.*, p. x) writes : ' Most editors, shocked by the crudeness of the stage device, have begun a new scene here and supplied a previous " *Exeunt* ". But the original is quite explicit in reading " *Exit Guise* ", and the following direction, " *Enter the Admirall in his bed* ", is to be taken literally.   The bed must be supposed thrust out onto the stage already occupied by the other characters.   This is obvious from the fact that no entry is given except to the Admiral, though the King not only speaks himself, but addresses another character at l. [64] ; while the presence of the Queen-Mother appears to be historically accurate.   At l. [71] the

Hath he been hurt with villains in the street ?
I vow and swear, as I am King of France,
To find and to repay the man with death,
With death delay'd and torments never us'd,
That durst presume, for hope of any gain,
To hurt the nobleman their sovereign loves.

Adm. Ah, my good lord, these are the Guisians,
That seek to massacre our guiltless lives !

Char. Assure yourself, my good Lord Admiral,   60
I deeply sorrow for your treacherous wrong ;
And that I am not more secure myself
Than I am careful you should be preserv'd.—
Cossin, take twenty of our strongest guard,
And, under your direction, see they keep
All treacherous violence from our noble friend ;

57. *their*] O., Bull. : *his* Rob., Dyce, Cunn.   64. *Cossin,*] Ed. : *Cosin*
O. : *Cousin*, Rob., etc.

scene closes with the correct direction "*Exeunt omnes*".' But see
note at beginning of scene for a
slightly different interpretation in
part.
  52. *with*] by. As commonly in
Shakespeare, cf. *Ant. and Cleop.*, v.
ii. 170 : ' must I be unfolded, *With*
one that I have bred ? ' etc.
  53, 54. *I vow . . . death,*] Cf.
Golding's *Coligny* (Sig. G. iii) : ' In
the meane season the King of
Nauarre and the Prince of *Condey*
complayned to the King of the
heynowsenesse of the fact (i.e. the
attack on Coligny). To whom the
King answered thus : I sweare by
God whom I take to witnesse, that
I will revenge this fact so severely,
as it may bee an example to all that
shall come after.'
  57. *their*] Robinson, Dyce and
Cunningham amend needlessly to
his.
  60–68. *Assure . . . peace.*] ' The
King answered that . . . he was
fully determined to provide as well
for the Admiral's safetie as for his
owne, and that he would preserue
the Admirall as the ball of his

eye. . . . Therewith the Duke of
Aniow the King's brother commanded Cossin, Captaine of the
King's guarde, to place a certaine
band of souldiers to warde the
Admiralle's gate.' (*The Three
Partes, &c.*, x. 12.)
  62, 63. *And that . . . preserv'd*]
my own security is not greater than
is my care of your security.
  64. *Cossin*] All the editors have
taken this as *Cousin*, both here and
in Scene v., line 20. That this is
wrong is clear from the extract
printed above on line 60, and from
Golding's *Coligny* (sig. G.7), where
the officer is referred to as *Mounsyre Cossins* : ' Then the other
man . . . desired the King to send
sum part of his gard too the
Admirall. Too whom the Duke of
Angeow (Anjou), who was come
thither with his moother sayd :
very well, take Mounsyre *Cossins*
too yow with fiftie Hargabuttes.
. . . Within a feaw houres after,
Mounsyre *Cossins* came to the
Admirals lodging, accompanied with
50 Hargabutters.'

Repaying all attempts with present death
Upon the cursed breakers of our peace.—
And so be patient, good Lord Admiral,
And every hour I will visit you.   70
Adm. I humbly thank your royal majesty.

[*Exeunt omnes.*

SCENE V

Enter GUISE, ANJOU, DUMAINE, GONZAGO, RETES,
MOUNTSORRELL, *and* Soldiers, *to the massacre.*

Guise. Anjou, Dumaine, Gonzago, Retes, swear,
By the argent crosses in your burgonets,
To kill all that you suspect of heresy.
Dum. I swear by this, to be unmerciful.
Anj. I am disguis'd, and none knows who I am,
And therefore mean to murder all I meet.
Gon. And so will I.
Retes. And I.
Guise. Away, then! break into the Admiral's house.

71. *I . . . majesty.*] O., etc. : *omit* Rob.   *Exeunt omnes.*] O. : *Exeunt,*
Rob., Cunn. : *Exeunt Charles, etc.   Scene closes.*   Dyce : *Exit Charles.*
The bed is drawn in. Bull.

Scene v.
Greg : *Scene VI.* Rob., Cunn., Bull. : *omit* the rest.
1.] As Dyce, etc. : *divided after Retes,* in O., Rob.   2. *in*] *on* Rob., Cunn.

67. *present*] immediate, instant.
Compare Bacon's *Essays* (Arber's
edn.), p. 103 : ' Peter stroke
Ananias . . . with *present death.*'

Scene V.
Scene V.] The open street or
place again. The Admiral's dwell-
ing is known from the previous
scene, and it is from the upper
stage that the body is thrown
down (line 33). Then later in the
scene the action takes place at
Seroune's door, imagined to be one
of the side doors—one of the
' threshold scenes ' Sir E. K.
Chambers has demonstrated to be
14

so common in Elizabethan drama.
    1. *Gonzago*] Louis de Gonzague,
Duc de Nevers by his marriage with
Henriette de Clèves. He distinguished himself in the Catholic
party during the Wars of Religion.
    1. *Retes*] Albert de Gondi, Duc
de Retz, an Italian, came to France
with Catherine de Médicis, and by
her was rapidly given advance-
ment. He is said to have been one
of the chief instigators of the
Massacre, and was certainly a
prime favourite, both with Charles
IX and Henry III.
    2. *argent . . . burgonets*]   See
above, Sc. IV. 1. 30.

Retes. Ay, let the Admiral be first despatch'd.   10
Guise. The Admiral,
  Chief standard-bearer to the Lutherans,
  Shall in the entrance of this massacre
  Be murder'd in his bed.
  Gonzago, conduct them thither ; and then
  Beset his house, that not a man may live.
Anj. That charge is mine.—Switzers, keep you the streets ;
  And at each corner shall the king's guard stand.
Gon. Come, sirs, follow me. [*Exit Gonzago with others.*
Anj. Cossin, the captain of the Admiral's guard,   20
  Plac'd by my brother, will betray his lord.
  Now, Guise, shall Catholics flourish once again ;
  The head being off, the members cannot stand.
Retes. But look, my lord, there's some in the Admiral's
  house.

11, 12.] As Rob., etc. : one line O. 14–16.] As Dyce, etc. : two lines
divided at *thither*, in O., Rob. 20. *Cossin*] Ed. : *Cosin* O. : *Cousin*
Rob., etc. 24. *The Admiral . . .*] Dyce, Bull. : *Enter into the Admiral's
house, and he in his bed.* O., Rob., etc., Cunn. substantially. *Scene VII.*]
Rob., Cunn. : *omit* the rest.

11–16. *The Admiral . . . live.*]
The Octavo found this passage
a difficult one to print metrically,
and evidently it has been badly
mangled. The repetition of line 12
below in line 40 suggests some
confusion.

13. *entrance*] beginning or com-
mencement. Compare Coverdale's
Erasm. Par. Philip, I. 5 : ' Ever
since the fyrst *entraunce of* your
profession, even unto this daye.'
And see *The Jew of Malta*, v. ii. 22.

14–19] Professor Le Gay Brereton
suggests (privately) the following
rearrangement : Read (to end l. 14)
Gonzago ⟨go⟩—a very easy omission,
because of the identity with the final
syllable of the name, and rearrange
ll. 15–19 to divide after *house, mine,
corner, me.*

17. *Switzers*] Swiss mercenaries,
to be found serving all over Europe
at this time. Nash, in his *Christ's
Tears over Jerusalem* (ed. McKerrow,

II. 99), says : ' Law, logicke, and the
Switzers may be hired to fight for
anybody.'

17, 18. *Switzers . . . stand.*] Cf.
Golding (*op. cit.*, sig. H. ii.) : ' By
that time Cossins having removed
the chests, and the other stoppes
that were cast in hys waye, brought
in first certein of the *Swissers*
apparelled in long cotes garded
with blacke, white, and greene,
whereby it was perceyued that they
were the Duke of Aniowes gard.'

24. *The Admiral . . . house*]
Here the Admiral is ' discovered '
in a bed on the upper-stage, or
balcony, for a few lines later we
hear Guise ordering those within to
' throw him down ' (l. 33). Gonzago
and others, who went off the lower
stage at line 19, have evidently now
appeared above, and the S.D.
suggests that they are shown entering to the Admiral. Anjou, of
course, remains below.

Thus, in despite of thy religion,

The Duke of Guise stamps on thy lifeless bulk!

30. *Dies.*] Dyce, Bull : *omit* the rest. 31. *Gonzago, . . . dead?*] O., etc. :
What, is he dead, Gonzago? Rob., Cunn. 33. *The body . . . down*] Dyce,
Bull. : *omit* the rest. 34, 35.] As Rob., etc. : prose in O. 35. *'tis*] Rob.,
etc. : *it is* O. 39. *Chatillon*] Dyce, etc. : *Shatillian* O. : *Chatellain*
Rob. 39, 40.] As Rob., etc. : prose in O. 42. *lifeless*] Rob., etc. :
liueles O.

33. *throw him down.*] Both Golding and *The Three Partes, &c.*,
describe this : Golding (*op. cit.*,
H. ii.) : ' The Admiralls bodie being
throwne downe out of a windowe,
was trampled under foote by the
yong Duke of *Gwyse*, and anon
after tumbled into the myre in the
open streete, and mangled and vsed
with all the vilanie that might be,
and a thre dayes after carried out
of the Citie by the furious multitude, and hanged up by the feete
vppon the gallowes of Mount-
falcon.' See also *The Three Partes,*

&c., x. 14ᵛ : ' Then said the Duke
of Guise, our Chevelier (meaning
King Henries bastard) unlesse he
see it with his eyes will not believe
it : *throw him down* at the window.'
38. *He miss'd . . . near*] i.e.
nearly missed him.
39. *Chatillon.*] The family name
of Coligny. Cf. Golding's title
page : ' The Lyfe of the most
Godly, Valeant and Noble Capteine
and Maintener of the trew Christian
Religion in Fraunce, Jasper *Colignie Shatilion*, sometyme great
Admirall of Fraunce,' etc.

Anj. Away with him ! cut off his head and hands,
 And send them for a present to the Pope ;
 And, when this just revenge is finished,
 Unto Mount Faucon will we drag his corse ;
 And he, that living hated so the Cross,
 Shall, being dead, be hang'd thereon in chains.

Guise. Anjou, Gonzago, Retes, if that you three
 Will be as resolute as I and Dumaine,   50
 There shall not be a Huguenot breathe in France.

Anj. I swear by this cross, we'll not be partial,
 But slay as many as we can come near.

Guise. Mountsorrell, go shoot the ordinance off,
 That they, which have already set the street,
 May know their watchword ; then toll the bell,
 And so let's forward to the massacre.

Mount. I will, my lord.   [*Exit.*

Guise. And now, my lords, let's closely to our business.

Anj. Anjou will follow thee.

Dum.   And so will Dumaine. 60
    [*The ordinance being shot off, the bell tolls.*

---

43. *Anj.*] omit Rob. 49. *Guise*] omit Rob. 51. *breathe*] Rob., etc. : *breath* O. 54. *ordinance*] O. : *ordnance*, Rob., etc. 55. *set*] O., Dyce, Bull. : *'set* Rob., Cunn. 56. *then toll*] O., Dyce, Bull. : *and then toll* Rob. : *then go toll* Cunn. 59. *let's*] Rob., etc. : *let us* O.

43, 44. *cut off . . . Pope*] 'Then a certain Italian of Gonzague's band cut off the Admirall's head, and sent it, preserved with spices, to Rome to the Pope and the Cardinal of Lorraine. Others cut off his hands.' *The Three Partes, &c.,* Book X, p. 14ᵛ. See also Mezeray's *Hist. of France* (1646), II., p. 1095, and above, note to line 33.

46. *Mount Faucon*] Dyce writes : ' So in the old ed. ; and so indeed our early authors usually wrote the name. Thus, Sylvester's edn. of Du Bartas, *Works* (1641), p. 517 :

' O, may they once as high as
 Haman mount,
And from *Mount Faulcon* give a
 sad account,' etc.

Montfaucon was the name of a hill near to Paris, on which, it is said, were constructed several gibbets in the XIVᵗʰ century ; and the site became notorious as the place where the bodies of criminals were hung, and allowed to decay. See below, note on Sc. VIII. l. 11.

52. *I swear . . . partial*] It has been suggested by Prof. Tucker Brooke that this line might be made regular by regarding *cross* as a parenthetical cue to the actor, accidentally introduced into the text. ' I swear by *this* ' (pointing to the cross on his burgonet). Cf. Sc. IV. l. 30.

55, 56. *That they, . . . watchword*] See above, Scene IV., lines 33 ff.

Guise. Come, then, let's away. [*Exeunt.*

Enter GUISE, *and the rest, with their swords drawn, chasing the Protestants.*

Guise. Tuez, tuez, tuez !
　　Let none escape ! murder the Huguenots !
Anj. Kill them ! kill them ! [*Exeunt.*

Enter LOREINE, *running ;* GUISE *and the rest pursuing him.*

Guise. Loreine, Loreine ! follow Loreine !—Sirrah,
　　Are you a preacher of these heresies ?
Lor. I am a preacher of the word of God ;
　　And thou a traitor to thy soul and him.
Guise. ' Dearly beloved brother,'—thus 'tis written.
　　　　　　　　　　　[*Stabs Loreine, who dies.*
Anj. Stay, my lord, let me begin the psalm. 70
Guise. Come, drag him away, and throw him in a ditch.
　　　　　　　　　　　[*Exeunt with the body.*

Enter MOUNTSORRELL, *and knocks at* SEROUNE'S *door.*

Seroune's Wife [*within*]. Who is that which knocks there ?
Mount. Mountsorrell, from the Duke of Guise.
Seroune's Wife [*within*]. Husband, come down ; here's one
　　would speak with you.
　　From the Duke of Guise.

61. *Scene VIII.*] Rob., Cunn : *Scene VII* Bull.: *omit* others. *Enter
. . . rest . . . .*] Dyce, Bull.: *The Guise enters againe, with all the rest,* . . .
O., Rob., Cunn. 62. *Tuez, . . .*] Dyce, etc. : *Tue* . . . O., Rob. 62, 63.]
As Dyce, etc. : one line in O., Rob. *Huguenots !*] Dyce, etc. : *Hugonets.*
O. 69. *Stabs . . . dies.*] Dyce, Bull. : *he stabs him.* O., Rob., Cunn. 71.
Exeunt . . . body.] Dyce, Bull. : *Exeunt.* the rest. 71. *Scene VIII*]
Bull. : *omit* the rest. 72, 74. [*within*]] Rob., etc. : *omit* O. 74–76.] As
Rob., etc. : prose in O.

62. *Tuez, . . .*] The same cry,
with the same spelling as in the
Octavo, *Tue*, is found in the *Larum
for London* (p. 64, ed. Simpson).
From the passage in Sc. IX. l. 7 it is
clear that Marlowe pronounced the
word in two syllables.

64. *Enter Loreine running.*] Cf.
The Three Parts, sig. D. iii. :
' Leranne being thrust through
with a sworde, escaped and ranne
into the Queene of *Nauarres*
chamber, and was by hir kept and
preserved from the violence of those
that pursued him.'

Enter SEROUNE *from the house.*

Ser. To speak with me, from such a man as he ?
Mount. Ay, ay, for this, Seroune ; and thou shalt ha't.
                              [*Showing his dagger.*
Ser. O, let me pray, before I take my death !
Mount. Despatch, then, quickly.
Ser.   O Christ, my Saviour !
Mount. Christ, villain !   80
    Why, darest thou presume to call on Christ,
    Without the intercession of some saint ?
    Sanctus Jacobus, he's my saint ; pray to him.
Ser. O, let me pray unto my God !
Mount. Then take this with you.
                    [*Stabs Seroune, who dies ; and then exit,*

SCENE VI

Enter RAMUS, *in his study.*

Ramus. What fearful cries comes from the river Seine,
    That frights poor Ramus sitting at his book !

75. *Enter . . . house.*] Dyce, Bull. : *Enter Seroune.* others. 77. *ha't.*] Rob., etc. : *hate.* O. 80–83.] As Rob., etc. : prose in O. 83. *Sanctus.*] Rob., etc. : *Sancta* O. *he's*] Dyce[2], Bull. : *he was* O., Rob., Dyce[1], Cunn. *he is* Dyce[1], conj. 85. *Stabs . . . exit.*] Dyce, Bull. : *Stab him. Exit.* O. : *Stabs him and exit.* Rob., Cunn.
                    Scene vi.
    Ed. : *Scene IX* Bull. : *omit* the rest.
    1. *comes*] O. : *come* Rob., etc. 1. *Seine*] Rob., etc. : *Rene* O. 2. *frights*] O. : *fright* Rob., etc.

Scene VI.
Scene VI.] Dr. Greg has marked this as a possible point for the beginning of a new scene, although he has not himself so made it in his Malone Society edition. But *Enter Ramus, in his study* seems to me to be a clear indication that the rear stage was used, and since the upper stage has just denoted the lodging of the Admiral, and the side door the house of Seroune, a slight pause to mark a change of locality has its advantages. The scene then is a street outside the house of Ramus, and the curtain drawn back reveals him in his study. Later at line 68, the stage side door is again used to denote a house.
    1. *Ramus*] Petrus Ramus, or Pierre de la Ramée (1515–72), a charcoal-burner's son, was one of the most famous academic figures in France during the sixteenth century. His opinions were so advanced that in 1544 his lectures in the University of Paris were forbidden for a time, but in 1551 he became professor of philosophy

I fear the Guisians have pass'd the bridge,
And mean once more to menace me.

Enter TALEUS.

Tal. Fly, Ramus, fly, if thou wilt save thy life !
Ramus. Tell me, Taleus, wherefore should I fly ?
Tal. The Guisians are
    Hard at thy door, and mean to murder us :
    Hark, hark, they come ! I'll leap out at the window.
Ramus. Sweet Taleus, stay.   10

Enter GONZAGO *and* RETES.

Gon. Who goes there ?
Retes. 'Tis Taleus, Ramus' bedfellow.
Gon. What art thou ?
Tal. I am, as Ramus is, a Christian.
Retes. O, let him go ; he is a Catholic.   [*Exit Taleus.*
Gon. Come, Ramus, more gold, or thou shalt have the stab.
Ramus. Alas, I am a scholar ! how should I have gold ?
    All that I have is but my stipend from the king,
    Which is no sooner receiv'd but it is spent.

Enter GUISE, ANJOU, DUMAINE, MOUNTSORRELL, *and*
Soldiers.

7–9.] As Dyce, etc. : prose in O., Rob.   12. *'Tis*] O., etc. : *It is* Rob.,
Cunn.   15. *Enter Ramus.*] O. : *omit* the rest.   17. *Alas . . . gold ?*] As
two lines, first ending *Alas*, T. Brooke.   19. *Enter . . .*] Dyce, Bull. :
Enter the Guise and Anioy. O. : *Enter Guise, Anjou and the rest.* Rob., Cunn.

and eloquence in the Collège de
France. Ten years later he became
a Protestant, and his life hence-
forward was a troubled one and he
finally fell a victim in the Massacre.
He claimed to have superseded
Aristotle by a new and independent
system of logic. Marlowe almost
certainly heard of him while at
Cambridge, for his new system
caused much disputing in the
University, and an edition in the
original Latin with notes was published at Cambridge in 1584. For
a full account of this dispute see
Mullinger's *Hist. of the Univ. of
Cambridge,* ii. 404–13.

5. *Taleus*] Omer Talon, born at
Amiens, about 1510, was a friend
of Ramus, and sometime professor
of rhetoric at the college of Cardinal
De Moine in Paris. He survived the
Massacre, and died in 1610. His
Rhetorica was entered to M.
Harrison on 6th Dec. 1588 (see
McKerrow's *Nashe,* IV. 334).

Anj. Who have you there ?   20
Retes. 'Tis Ramus, the king's Professor of Logic.
Guise. Stab him.
Ramus.   O, good my lord,
    Wherein hath Ramus been so offensious ?
Guise. Marry, sir, in having a smack in all,
    And yet didst never sound anything to the depth.
    Was it not thou that scoff'dst the *Organon*,
    And said it was a heap of vanities ?
    He that will be a flat dichotomist,
    And seen in nothing but epitomes,
    Is in your judgment thought a learned man ;   30
    And he, forsooth, must go and preach in Germany,
    Excepting against doctors' axioms,
    And *ipse dixi* with this quiddity,

22, 23.] As Dyce, etc. : prose in O., Rob.   26. *scoff'dst*] Rob., etc. :
scoftes O.   28. *dichotomist,*] Rob., etc. :   *decotamest,* O.   32. *axioms,*]
Dyce², Bull. : *actions*, the rest.   33. *ipse*] Rob., etc. : *ipsi* O.

23. *offensious*] A rare form of
'offensive'. The only example
given in the O.E.D.
24. *smack in*] 'A slight or super-
ficial knowledge or smattering ',
O.E.D. quoting, e.g., Lyly, *Euphues*,
ed. Arber, p. 151 : 'atteine learning, and haue *in* all sciences a
smacke, whereby he may readily
dispute of any thing.'
26. *Organon*] A volume of Aristotle's comprising his six writings
on formal logic. Ramus, at one
time, denied the authenticity of
this work.
27. *a heap of vanities*] Ramus in
the thesis for his degree (1536) had
ventured to uphold the view that
'Everything that Aristotle taught
is false '. Then in 1543 he published a criticism of the old logic
entitled *Aristotelicae Animadver-
siones.*
28. *dichotomist*] one who classifies
by dividing a class or genus into two
lower mutually exclusive classes or
genera.
29. *seen in*] versed in. Compare
The Taming of the Shrew, I. ii. 134 :

'a schoolmaster Well *seen in*
music.' And also Lyly's *Mother
Bombie*, II. iii. 56 : 'well *seene in*
cranes dirt.'
31. *in Germany*] Ramus lectured
for a time at the University of
Heidelberg. For his controversy
with Schegk of Tübingen, see note
to line 43.
32. *Excepting*] objecting, taking
exception to ; as in *Twelfth Night*,
I. iii. 7 : 'Sir Toby . . . your
Cousin takes great *exceptions* to
your ill hours.' It was a term much
used in law.
32. *axioms*] This emendation of
Dyce's has much to recommend it,
and seems to bring out better the
intrepid audacity of Ramus than
does the colourless *actions*.
33. *quiddity*] quibble, captious
nicety of argument ; Guise alluded
'to the scholastic arguments on the
quiddity' of things. Compare
Fulke's *Heskins' Parl*, p. 475 : 'He
saith hee will not use the *quiddities*
of the schooles, but plaine examples.'

Argumentum testimonii est inartificiale.
To contradict which, I say, Ramus shall die :
How answer you that ? your *nego argumentum*
Cannot serve, sirrah.—Kill him.

Ramus. O, good my lord, let me but speak a word !

Anj. Well, say on.

Ramus. Not for my life do I desire this pause ;   40
But in my latter hour to purge myself,
In that I know the things that I have wrote,
Which, as I hear, one Scheckius takes it ill,
Because my places, being but three, contains all his.
I knew the *Organon* to be confus'd,
And I reduc'd it into better form :

---

34. *Argumentum* . . .] Mitford conj., Dyce, etc. : *Argumentum testimonis est in arte fetialis.* O. : *Argumentum . . . in arte partialis.* Rob. 36, 37.] As Rob., etc. : prose in O. *sirrah.—Kill him.*] Dyce, Cunn., Bull. : *Sirrah, kill him.* O., Rob. 43. *Scheckius*] Dyce, etc. : *Shekins* O., Rob. 44. *contains*] O. : *contain* Rob., etc.

---

34. *Argumentum* . . .] The term is defined in Cap. xxxi (p. 65) of *The Logicke of the moste Excellent Philosopher P. Ramus Martyr, Newly translated . . . Anno M.D.LXXIIII.* ' The artificiall argumente being expounded followethe cōsequently the unartificiall. The argumēte inartificiall or withoute arte is an argumente which prouethe or disprouethe not of his owne nature, but by the strengthe which it hathe of some argumente artificiall. In civill and temporall affaires, the aucthoritie of the disputer gueeth no little creditte ther vnto yf he be wyse, vertuous, and hath the beneuolence of the auditor : all these by one name maye be called a testimonie.'

36. *nego argumentum*] A term commonly used in disputation in the schools of the Universities of the Middle Ages. Cf. Lyly's *Endimion,* I. iii. 29. Guise in asserting ' Ramus shall die ' is illustrating what Ramus classes as an inartificial argument based on a witness's testimony or assertion. Here, however, it is unanswerable !

Cf. Ramus' *Dialectica,* I. xxxiii, where he says : ' *Testimonium* igitur ipsum in se consideratum, (id est, affirmatio seu negatio testantis de re testata) nihil habet artis aut virtutis arguendi sed fulciri debet *argumentis artificialibus.*'

43. *Scheckius*] The original again confuses and has *Shekins.* Dyce says: 'Concerning Schecius or Scheckius, see letters from Ramus, " Jacopo Schecio, clarissimo Tubingensis Academiae Philosopho "—a letter from Schecius to Ramus . . . in the volume entitled *Petri Rami Professoris Regii, et Audomari Tolei, Collectaneæ, Præfationes, etc., Marpurgi,* 1599, pp. 175, 179, 185, 193, 196, 466.' The letters between Ramus and Schegk were first published in 1569, and Ramus's *Defensio* in 1571 (see on l. 47); the former under the title ' P. Rami et Jacobi Schecii epistolae in quibus de arte logicae institutione agitur '.

44. *places*] Bullen writes : ' Grounds of proof,—in the scholastic sense of τόποι, or loci. " Itaque licet definire, *locum esse argumenti sedem.*" Cicero, *Top.* II. 3.'

And this for Aristotle will I say,
That he that despiseth him can ne'er
Be good in logic or philosophy ;
And that's because the blockish Sorbonnists   50
Attribute as much unto their [own] works
As to the service of the eternal God.

Guise. Why suffer you that peasant to declaim ?
Stab him, I say, and send him to his friends in hell.

Anj. Ne'er was there collier's son so full of pride.

                               [Stabs Ramus, who dies.

Guise. My Lord of Anjou, there are a hundred Protestants,
Which we have chas'd into the river Seine,
That swim about, and so preserve their lives :
How may we do ? I fear me they will live.

Dum. Go place some men upon the bridge,   60
With bows and darts, to shoot at them they see,
And sink them in the river as they swim.

Guise. 'Tis well advis'd, Dumaine ; go see it straight be
    done.   *[Exit Dumaine.*
And in the meantime, my lord, could we devise
To get those pedants from the King Navarre,
That are tutors to him and the Prince of Condé—

---

50. *Sorbonnists*] Rob., etc. : *thorbonest* O.   51. [*own*]] Dyce, etc. : *omit*
O., Rob.   55. *Stabs . . . dies.*] Dyce, Bull.: *kill him.* O.: *Stabs him.* Rob.,
Cunn.   56. *of Anjou,*] O., etc. : *Anjou,* Rob., Cunn.   57. *Seine,*] Rob., etc. :
Rene, O.   63. *Dumaine ;*] O., etc. : *omit* Cunn.   *straight be*] O.: *omit* Rob., etc.
63. *Exit . . .*] Dyce, etc. : *omit* the rest.   64. *And*] O., etc. : *omit* Cunn.

47. *And this . . . say*] See his
*Defensio pro Aristotle, contra J.
Schecium.* Lausanæ, 1571.
  50. *Sorbonnists*] The name given
to students at the Sorbonne, which
was the seat of the faculty of
theology in the University of Paris.
The O.E.D. gives no instance of the
use of this word before Weever's
Funeral Monuments, 1631.
  54. *I say*] This may well be an
actor's interpolation only.
  55. *collier's son*] Dyce quotes
from Theophilus Banosius' *Vita
Rami,* prefixed to *Commentarii de*

Religione Christiana (Francofurti,
1577), p. 581 : ' Carbonarius pater
probri loco illi [sc Ramo] objectus
est.'
  56. *of Anjou,*] Robinson and
Cunningham improve the metre by
omitting *of,* which may possibly be
a printer's error.
  66. *Prince of Condé*] This is the
young prince of Condé, cousin and
friend of the King of Navarre, and
not to be confused (as Marlowe
seems to have done) with the father,
who appears earlier (Sc. I.) in the
play.

Anj. For that, let me alone : cousin, stay you here,
    And when you see me in, then follow hard.

ANJOU *knocketh at the door ; and enter the* KING OF NAVARRE
    and the PRINCE OF CONDÉ, *with their two* Schoolmasters.

    How now, my lords ! how fare you ?
Nav. My lord, they say   70
    That all the Protestants are massacred.
Anj. Ay, so they are ; but yet, what remedy ?
    I have done what I could to stay this broil.
Nav. But yet, my lord, the report doth run,
    That you were one that made this massacre.
Anj. Who, I ? you are deceiv'd ; I rose but now.

    GUISE, GONZAGO, RETES, MOUNTSORRELL, *and* Soldiers,
                    come forward.

Guise. Murder the Huguenots ! take those pedants hence !
Nav. Thou traitor, Guise, lay off thy bloody hands !
Con. Come, let us go tell the king.
                    [*Exit with the King of Navarre.*
Guise.   Come, sirs,
    I'll whip you to death with my poniard's point.   80
                    [*Stabs the Schoolmasters, who die.*
Anj. Away with them both !
                    [*Exeunt Anjou and Soldiers with the bodies.*
Guise. And now, sirs, for this night let our fury stay.
    Yet will we not that the massacre shall end :

67. *you*] O., etc. : *omit* Rob., Cunn.   70, 71.] As Dyce, etc. : prose in
O., Rob.   76. *Guise, . . . forward.*] Dyce, etc. : *Enter Guise.* O. : *omit*
Rob.   79. *Exit . . . Navarre.*] Dyce, Bull. : *Exeunt.* O. : *Exeunt Nav.
and Condé.* Rob., Cunn.   80. *Stabs . . . die.*] Dyce, Bull. : *He kils
them.* O. : *Stabs them.* Rob. : *Stabs the Schoolmasters.* Cunn.   81. *Exeunt
. . . bodies.*] Dyce, Cunn., Bull. : *Exit Anioy.* O. : *Exit.* Rob.   82. *sirs,*]
O., etc. : *omit* Cunn.   83. *that*] O., Dyce, Bull. : *omit* Rob., Cunn.

76. *Guise . . . forward.*] At this
point the Duke of Guise and his
friends come from the back of the
stage where they have remained
during the last few lines. (see line
67 : 'stay you here').
    84,   85. *post   you . . . Rouen*]

' Messengers were sent in post into
all the partes of the Realme, with
oft shifting their horses for hast, to
commaunde all other Cities in the
Kinges name to followe the example
of Paris.'   *Three Partes of Commentaries, &c.,* x. 16ᵛ.

Gonzago, post you to Orleans,
Retes to Dieppe, Mountsorrell unto Rouen,
And spare not one that you suspect of heresy.
And now stay
That bell, that to the devil's matins rings.
Now every man put off his burgonet,
And so convey him closely to his bed.   90

                                                    [*Exeunt.*

SCENE VII

Enter ANJOU, *with two* Lords of Poland.

Anj. My lords of Poland, I must needs confess,
    The offer of your Prince Electors' far
    Beyond the reach of my deserts ;
    For Poland is, as I have been inform'd,

---

85. *Dieppe,*] *Deep,* O.   85. *Rouen,*] *Roan,* O.   87, 88.] As Dyce[2], Bull. :
as prose O., Rob., Dyce[1] : as two lines first ending *bell* Cunn.   88. *matins*]
[*midnight*] *matins* Cunn.

Scene vii.

Ed. : *omit* O., Dyce : *Act the Second.   Scene i.* Rob., Cunn. : *Scene x.*
Bull.   *Scene vi.* Greg.   2. *Electors'*] Ed. : *Electors* O : *Elector's* the rest.

87, 88. *stay That bell . . . rings*]
This fine line helps to conjure up
the violence of this scene, and may
be compared with *the dreadful bell*
which rings in Cyprus on the night
of the quarrel between Cassio and
Roderigo.   Cunningham writes :
' Something was evidently wanting
here, and having the authority of
Dryden for " midnight matins ", I
have ventured to insert the word
[midnight].'

90. *convey him closely*] steal off
secretly.   Compare Hall's *Chronicle,*
1548, p. 56 : ' The citezens . . .
would prively steele and *conveigh
them* selves away,' and *Hamlet,* III.
i. 29 : ' We have *closely* sent for
Hamlet hither.'

Scene VII.

Scene VII.] No clear indication
of the whereabouts of this scene is
given.   It probably followed on in
the open place of the previous scene
on the Elizabethan stage.

1.] ' The Duke of Anjou, by the
means of the nobles of Polonia,
was made king of Polonia . . .
Monluce, Bishop of Valence, had
solicited the matter to the noble
men of Polonia with great diligence,
and with golden sermons.' (*Fourth
Part of Commentaries, &c.,* XI. 86.)
A full account of the secret history
of this affair may be read in
D'Israeli's *Curiosities of Literature,*
New Series, Vol. 3, p. 140 ; which
is based on a narrative of the
events written by the Bishop's
secretary in 1574.

2. *Prince Electors'*] ' The greater
and the lesser nobles and gentlemen,
all electors, were reckoned at one
hundred thousand ' (Disraeli, *op.
cit.,* 145).   I have punctuated the
text to agree with this statement.

A martial people, worthy such a king
As hath sufficient counsel in himself
To lighten doubts, and frustrate subtle foes ;
And such a king, whom practice long hath taught
To please himself with manage of the wars,
The greatest wars within our Christian bounds,— 10
I mean our wars against the Muscovites,
And, on the other side, against the Turk,
Rich princes both, and mighty emperors.
Yet, by my brother Charles, our king of France,
And by his grace's council, it is thought
That, if I undertake to wear the crown
Of Poland, it may prejudice their hope
Of my inheritance to the crown of France ;
For, if th' Almighty take my brother hence,
By due descent the regal seat is mine.   20
With Poland, therefore, must I covenant thus,—
That if, by death of Charles, the diadem
Of France be cast on me, then, with your leaves,
I may retire me to my native home.
If your commission serve to warrant this,
I thankfully shall undertake the charge
Of you and yours, and carefully maintain
The wealth and safety of your kingdom's right.
First Lord. All this, and more, your highness shall command,
For Poland's crown and kingly diadem.   30
Anj. Then, come, my lords, let's go.   [*Exeunt.*

11. *Muscovites,*] O., etc. : *Muscovite,* Cunn.

9. *manage*] a term much used in Elizabethan English to denote expert direction of any operation, or of horses, or men, etc. Compare Kyd's *Soliman and Perseda,* iii. i. 119 : ' wilt thou be our Lieutenant there, And further us in *manage* of these wars ? ' and see *post,* Sc. xiii. l. 2 and Sc. xv. l. 7, etc.

11. *our wars*] Is this a misprint for *your wars,* due to *our* in the previous line ?

11. *the Muscovites,*] Cunningham writes : ' This has always hitherto been printed *Muscovites,* but the word *princes* two lines below proves that like " the Turk " it should be in the singular number.' There seems to be little substance in this.

SCENE VIII

Enter two Men, *with the* ADMIRAL'S *body.*

First Man. Now sirrah, what shall we do with the Admiral?

Sec. Man. Why, let us burn him for an heretic.

First Man. O, no ! his body will infect the fire, and the
fire the air, and so we shall be poisoned with him.

Sec. Man. What shall we do, then?

First Man. Let's throw him into the river.

Sec. Man. O, 'twill corrupt the water, and the water the
fish, and by the fish ourselves, when we eat them !

First Man. Then throw him into the ditch.

Sec. Man. No, no. To decide all doubts, be ruled by me : 10
let's hang him here upon this tree.

First Man. Agreed.

[*They hang up the body on a tree, and then exeunt.*

Enter GUISE, CATHERINE *the Queen-Mother, and the*
CARDINAL OF LORRAINE, *with* Attendants.

Guise. Now, madam, how like you our lusty Admiral?

Cath. Believe me, Guise, he becomes the place so well
As I could long ere this have wish'd him there.

Scene viii.
Ed. : *omit* O., Dyce : [*Act II.*] *Scene ii.* Rob., Cunn. : *Scene xi.* Bull. :
Scene vii. Greg.
8. *and by*] O. : *and* Rob., etc.   12. *They . . . exeunt.*] Dyce, Bull. :
They hang him. O. : *They hang him up, and exeunt.* Rob., Cunn.

Scene VIII.

Scene VIII.] Near Paris, possibly
in a wood as the men decide to
hang up the body here ' upon this
tree '.   According to Sc. v. l. 46,
however, the body was to be hung
on the gallows at Montfaucon, and
there it was visited by the Queen,
etc. (see note to line 11).

8. *and by*] Robinson and all
the editors omit *by* ; but the
sense is clear enough as the passage
stands : the water will corrupt the
fish and by means of the fish ourselves.

11. *let's hang him*] ' The Admiral's body being hanged up by
the heeles upon the common
gallowes of Paris, . . . the Paris-
ians went thither by heapes to see
it.   And the Queene Mother to
feede her eyes with that spectacle,
had a mynde also to goe thither,
and she caryed with hir the King
and both her other sonnes.'—*Three
Partes of Commentaries, &c.*, x. 20.
Marlowe substitutes the tree for the
gallows of Montfaucon despite his
reference in Sc. v. l. 46 : ' Unto
Mount Faucon will we drag his
corse.'

But come,
Let's walk aside ; the air's not very sweet.
Guise. No, by my faith, madam.—
    Sirs, take him away, and throw him in some ditch.
        [*The Attendants bear off the Admiral's body.*
    And now, madam, as I understand,   20
    There are a hundred Huguenots and more,
    Which in the woods do hold their synagogue,
    And daily meet about this time of day ;
    And thither will I, to put them to the sword.
Cath. Do so, sweet Guise ; let us delay no time ;
    For, if these stragglers gather head again,
    And disperse themselves throughout the realm of
       France,
    It will be hard for us to work their deaths.
    Be gone ; delay no time, sweet Guise.
Guise.   Madam,
    I go as whirlwinds rage before a storm.   [*Exit.* 30
Cath. My Lord of Lorraine, have you mark'd of late,
    How Charles our son begins for to lament

16, 17.] As Dyce, Bull. : one line in O., Rob., Cunn.   17. *the air's*] Dyce[2],
etc. : *thair's* O. : *th'air's* Rob., Dyce[1]. 19. *The Attendants . . . body.*]
Rob., etc. : *Carry away the dead body.* O. 24. *And thither*] O., etc. :
Thither Rob., Cunn. 29, 30.] As Dyce, etc. : *Madam . . . storm* one line
in O., Rob.

19. *thow him . . . ditch*] Cf.
Golding's *Coligny* (sig. H. ii),
where after describing the indigni-
ties offered the corpse at Montfaucon the author adds : ' But
within a feaw dayes after, the
Admirall's bodie was taken downe
in the night by certaine horsemen,
and buryed in a secret place.'
  22. *synagogue*] Here used contemptuously by Guise to denote the
assembly of the Hugenots for
worship.
  24. *And thither*] Robinson and
Cunningham omit *And* for the sake
of the metre. Such a weak *and*,
however, before words like *thither*
and *therefore* is common and has
little metrical value. Cf. Sc. x.

l. 36 : ' *And therefore,* as speedily as
I can perform,' which Robinson and
Cunningham print unaltered.
  26. *gather head*] Acquire strength
by collecting forces together. See
Edward II, II. ii. 120 : ' Meantime,
my lord of Pembroke and myself,
Will to Newcastle here, and *gather
head.*'
  27. *disperse*] Pronounce *'sperse.*
  32. *for to lament*] ' From the
earliest period " for to ", like
" to ", is found used without any
notion of purpose, simply as a sign
of the infinitive.' Abbott, *op. cit.*,
§ 152. See also here below, l. 37,
and Sc. XVIII. 93, and XX. 2, etc.
It may be worth while noting that
three of these instances occur in

For the late night's-work which my Lord of Guise
Did make in Paris amongst the Huguenots ?
Card. Madam, I have heard him solemnly vow,
   With the rebellious King of Navarre,
   For to revenge their deaths upon us all.
Cath. Ay, but, my lord, let me alone for that ;
   For Catherine must have her will in France.
   As I do live, so surely shall he die,   40
   And Henry then shall wear the diadem ;
   And, if he grudge or cross his mother's will,
   I'll disinherit him and all the rest :
   For I'll rule France, but they shall wear the crown,
   And, if they storm, I then may pull them down.
   Come, my lord, let us go.   [*Exeunt.*

SCENE IX

Enter five or six Protestants, *with books, and kneel
together. Then enter* GUISE *and others.*

Guise. Down with the Huguenots ! murder them !
First Pro. O Monsieur de Guise, hear me but speak !
Guise. No, villain ; that tongue of thine,
   That hath blasphem'd the holy Church of Rome,

34. *amongst*] O., Dyce: *among* Bull.: *'mongst* Rob., Malone, Cunn.
46. *let us*] Dyce, etc.: *lets us* O.: *let's* Rob.
          Scene ix.
Ed.: *omit* O., Dyce: [*Act II*] *Scene iii.* Rob., Cunn.: *Scene xii.* Bull:
Sc. viii. Greg. *Then . . . others*] Dyce, Bull.: *Enter also the Guise.* O.:
Enter also Guise and others. Rob., Cunn.

practically the same stereotyped
contexts : ' For to revenge their
deaths ' (Sc. VIII. l. 37), ' for to
revenge thy death ' (Sc. XX. l. 2) and
' for to revenge his death ' (in O.,
Sc. XXI. l. 110).
   38–46. *Ay, but, my lord, . . .*]
The opening phrase is closely
repeated in Sc. XI. l. 61 : ' Tush
man, let me alone with him,' and
still more so in Sc. XX. l. 31 :
' Tush my lord, let me alone for
that.' More important, the entire

passage is strikingly echoed in
Catherine's later speech, Sc. XI.
ll. 61 ff.

          Scene IX.

   Scene IX.] The wood outside
Paris, as mentioned by Guise in
Sc. viii. l. 22. The Huguenots enter
first and kneel silently in dumb
show, followed later by the Guise
and others (probably from the
other door).

Shall drive no plaints into the Guise's ears,

To make the justice of my heart relent.—

Tuez, tuez, tuez! let none escape.

                          [*They kill the Protestants.*

So, drag them away.   [*Exeunt with the bodies.*

SCENE X

Enter KING CHARLES, *supported by the* KING OF NAVARRE *and* EPERNOUN ; CATHERINE *the Queen Mother, the* CARDINAL OF LORRAINE, PLESHÉ, *and* Attendants.

Char. O, let me stay, and rest me here a while !

A griping pain hath seiz'd upon my heart ;

A sudden pang, the messenger of death.

Cath. O, say not so ! thou kill'st thy mother's heart.

Char. I must say so ; pain forceth me complain.

Nav. Comfort yourself, my lord, and have no doubt

But God will sure restore you to your health.

Char. O, no, my loving brother of Navarre !

I have deserv'd a scourge, I must confess ;

Yet is their patience of another sort   10

---

7. *Tuez, . . .*] Dyce, etc.: *Tue, . . .* O., Rob.   7. *They . . . Protestants*] Dyce, Bull.: *kill them.* O.: *They kill them.* Rob., Cunn.   8. *Exeunt . . . bodies.*] Dyce, Bull.: *Exeunt.* O., Rob., Cunn.

Scene x.

Ed.: *omit* O., Rob., Dyce, Cunn.: *Scene xiii.* Bull.: *Sc. ix.* Greg. *Enter . . .*] Rob., etc.: *Enter the King of France, Nauar and Epernoune staying him : enter Qu. Mother, and the Cardinall.* O.

5. *complain*] O., etc.: *to complain* Rob.   10. *their*] Cunn., Bull.: *there* O., etc.

---

7. *Tuez . . .*] See note on Sc. v. l. 62.

Scene X.

Scene X.] No very definite location is given to this scene : it may be either within the palace or while he is outdoors that the King is stricken down. Dyce, following history, places it in ' an appartment in the Castle of Vincennes '.

2. *A griping pain . . .*] Charles

IX did not die, as was said ' empoisonné avec la poudre de corne d'un lièvre marin ', but mainly because of his excesses in the chase and by his over-violent exercise. He died on the 30th of May 1574.

10–12. *Yet . . . worse*] On this passage Bullen writes : ' The correction from " *Yet is there patience* " to " *Yet is their patience* " was made by Cunningham, who explains the passage thus : " There are persons

15

Than to misdo the welfare of their king :
God grant my nearest friends may prove no worse !
O, hold me up ! my sight begins to fail,
My sinews shrink, my brains turn upside down ;
My heart doth break : I faint and die.   [*Dies.*

Cath. What, art thou dead, sweet son ? speak to thy mother !
O, no, his soul is fled from out his breast,
And he nor hears nor sees us what we do !
My lords, what resteth there now for to be done,
But that we presently despatch ambassadors   20
To Poland, to call Henry back again,
To wear his brother's crown and dignity ?
Epernoun, go see it presently be done,
And bid him come without delay to us.

Eper. Madam, I will.   [*Exit.*

Cath. And now, my lords, after these funerals be done,
We will, with all the speed we can, provide
For Henry's coronation from Polony.
Come, let us take his body hence.

[*The body of King Charles is borne out ; and exeunt
all except the King of Navarre and Pleshé.*

14. *brains turn*] O., etc. : *brain turns* Rob., Cunn.   19. *there now for*] O.,
Dyce : *now for* Rob., Cunn. : *there now* Bull.   25, 26. As two lines first
ending *now* Bull.   26. *be done*] *omit* be T. Brooke conj.   28. *Polony*] Dyce,
Bull. : *Polonie,* O. : *Polonia.* Rob., Cunn.   29. *The body . . . Pleshé.*] Rob.,
etc. : *All goe out, but Nauarre and Pleshé.* O.

(you yourself, and my Protestant subjects, for instance) from whom I have deserved a scourge, but *their* feelings would never lead them to poison their king ; God grant that my dearest relations may prove to have been no worse than those who ought to be my enemies ", etc.— *Scourge* must surely be the scourge of God. Navarre had said, " God will surely restore you " ; to which the king answers, " I have deserved a scourge ", from God. Before l. 10 a line or more referring to the massacre of the Protestants must have dropped out.'

19. *what resteth . . . done*] The metrical difficulties of this line have provoked many conjectures. See *Text Note.* May it be that we should read *rests* for *resteth* ?

23. *Epernoun*] One of Henri III's favourites, a son of the Seigneur de la Valette. He was one of the earliest members of the League and was created Duke of Epernoun in 1581 as a reward for his military and diplomatic services. Henri employed Epernoun to negociate an alliance with Navarre, but this failed. On the death of Henri III he refused to recognise Henri IV, but was eventually forced to yield. Henri treated him with great clemency.

Nav. And now, Pleshé, whilst that these broils do last. 30
    My opportunity may serve me fit
    To steal from France, and hie me to my home,
    For here's no safety in the realm for me :
    And now that Henry is call'd from Poland,
    It is my due, by just succession ;
    And therefore, as speedily as I can perform,
    I'll muster up an army secretly,
    For fear that Guise, join'd with the king of Spain,
    Might seem to cross me in mine enterprise.
    But God, that always doth defend the right, 40
    Will show his mercy, and preserve us still.
Pleshé. The virtues of our true religion
    Cannot but march, with many graces more,
    Whose army shall discomfort all your foes,
    And, at the length, in Pampelonia crown
    (In spite of Spain, and all the popish power,
    That holds it from your highness wrongfully)
    Your majesty her rightful lord and sovereign.

30. *now, Pleshé*] Dyce[2], etc. : *now, Navarre,* O., Rob., Dyce[1] : *And, Pleshé, now* Dyce conj. 38. *king*] Rob., etc. : *K.* O. 39. *seem*] O. : *seek* Rob., etc. 42. *true*] O., Dyce, etc. : *poor* Rob. 44. *discomfort*] O., etc. : *discomfit* Dyce. 45. *Pampelonia*] O., Cunn., Bull. : *Pampeluna* Rob., Dyce. 46, 47. No brackets in O.

30. *Pleshé*] Philippe de Mornay, Seigneur du Plessis-Marly, was one of the stoutest leaders of the Huguenots, so much so that he was sometimes called ' The Pope of the Huguenots '. He served Henry of Navarre with untiring zeal and fidelity. The Octavo reading *And now, Nauarre,* is probably a compositor's mistake, unless we assume the King to be communing with himself—and ignoring his companion.

31. *My opportunity . . . me.*] Marlowe, in these lines, skilfully suggests that the massacre is recently over and that Navarre is seizing the first opportunity of returning to his kingdom. Thus the dramatic time is made much shorter than the historic time, and two distinct parts of the play are linked together.

34. *Henry*] a trisyllable.

39. *seem to*] I have retained the Octavo reading, since *seem to* is not uncommon in Elizabethan English. Cf. *Macbeth,* I. v. 30 : ' the golden round, Which fate and metaphysical aid doth *seem To* have thee crowned withal.' See also Fenton's *Bandello* (Tudor Trans.), ii. 148 ; *Apocrypha* (Tudor Trans.), 256, &c.

45. *Pampelonia crown*] i.e. Pampeluna, or Pamplona, which was the capital of the kingdom of Navarre. *Crown* is a verb, having for object *Your Majesty* in l. 48.

46, 47. *In spite . . . wrongfully.*] Pampelonia was at this time in the hands of the Spaniards.

Nav. Truth, Pleshé ; and God so prosper me in all,
    As I intend to labour for the truth,   50
    And true profession of his holy word !
    Come, Pleshé, let's away whilst time doth serve.
                                [*Exeunt.*

SCENE XI

*Trumpets sounded within, and a cry of ' Vive le Roi,' two or
three times. Enter* ANJOU *crowned as King Henry the
Third* ; CATHERINE *the Queen-Mother, the* CARDINAL OF
LORRAINE, GUISE, EPERNOUN, MUGEROUN, *the* Cutpurse, *and others.*

All. Vive le Roi, Vive le Roi !   [*A flourish of trumpets.*
Cath. Welcome from Poland, Henry, once again !
    Welcome to France, thy father's royal seat !
    Here hast thou a country void of fears,
    A warlike people to maintain thy right,
    A watchful senate for ordaining laws,
    A loving mother to preserve thy state,
    And all things that a king may wish besides ;
    All this, and more, hath Henry with his crown.
Card. And long may Henry enjoy all this, and more ! 10
All. Vive le Roi, Vive le Roi !   [*A flourish of trumpets.*
Henry. Thanks to you all. The guider of all crowns

Scene xi.

Ed.: *omit* O., Dyce: [*Act II*] *Scene iv.* Rob., Cunn.: *Scene xiv.* Bull.:
Sc. x. Greg. *Trumpets . . . times*] Rob., etc. : *Sound Trumpets within, and
then all crye* viue la Røy *two or three times.* O. *Enter Anjou . . . others.*]
Rob, etc.: *Enter Henry crowned : Queene, Cardinall, Duke of Guise,
Epernoone, the kings Minions, with others, and the Cutpurse.* O.

1. *le Roi*] Reed, etc.: *la Roy* O. And in 11. 1, 11. *A flourish . . .*] Rob.,
etc. : *Sound Trumpets.* O. 4. *fears*,] O., etc. : *foes*, Collier (MS.).

49. *Truth, . . . all,*] An irregular
line which might be regularised by
the omission of *so.* The pronuncia-
tion of *Pleshé* is clearly shown by
l. 52.

Scene XI.

Scene XI.] An open place : the
King going in procession to his
palace fresh from his coronation.
Line 43 shows it to be without the
palace.
    2–9. *Welcome . . . crown.*] Is
this in contrast with the perils of
Henry's previous position as King
of Poland ? See Sc. VII. ll. 9–13.

Grant that our deeds may well deserve your loves !
And so they shall, if fortune speed my will,
And yield your thoughts to height of my deserts.
What says our minions ? think they Henry's heart
Will not both harbour love and majesty ?
Put off that fear, they are already join'd :
No person, place, or time, or circumstance,
Shall slack my love's affections from his bent :   20
As now you are, so shall you still persist,
Removeless from the favours of your king.
Mug. We know that noble minds change not their thoughts
For wearing of a crown, in that your grace
Hath worn the Poland diadem, before
You were invested in the crown of France.
Henry. I tell thee, Mugeroun, we will be friends,
And fellows too, whatever storms arise.
Mug. Then may it please your majesty to give me leave

15. *your*] O., etc.: *our* Rob.   16. *says*] *saies* O.: *say* Rob., etc.   29, 30.
As three lines ending *please, punish, feast.* Bull. conj.

15. *And yield . . . deserts.*]
Robinson prints *our faults*, perhaps
inadvertently. The line is to be
construed with the preceding ones :
My deeds shall deserve your love, if
fortune favours me, and you but
think of my high deserts.

16. *minions*] those specially beloved or favoured by the sovereign
were so described. See *Ed. II*,
I. iv. 87 : ' The king is love-sick for
his *minion*.' Dr. Greg (*op. cit.*, xix)
writes : ' By the king's minions are
probably meant Mugeroun and
Joyeux.'

16-17. *think they . . . majesty ?*]
A reminiscence of Ovid : ' Non
bene conveniunt, nec in una sede
morantur, Maiestas et amor.' (*Met.*
ii. 846.) See also this partially
quoted in *Ed. II*, I. iv. 13.

20. *his bent*] its purpose or intention. Compare Bacon's *Advance-
ment of Learning*, I. iv. § 2 : ' The
whole inclination and *bent* of those
times.'

29, 30. *Then . . . feast.*] Two

alexandrines as the text stands.
Bullen would print as three lines,
inserting *dare* before *profane* in the
last.

29-37.] This episode seems to
have no historical warrant, but
was, perhaps, picked up by Marlowe (or another) from current
gossip. In the ' Merry Passages
and Jests ', collected by Sir
Nicholas Lestrange (d. 1655), and
now Harleian MS. No. 6395, there
occurs the following story. It was
printed by W. I. Thoms for the Camden Society in 1839, in a volume
entitled *Anecdotes and Tradi-
tions*, No. XXXI: 'A gentleman at
a play sate by a fellow that he
strongly suspected for a cutpurse,
and, for the probation of him, took
occasion to draw out his purse,
and put it up so carelessly as it
dangled down (but his eye watched
it strictly with a glance), and he
bent his discourse another way ;
and his suspected neighbour observ-
ing, upon his first fair opportunity

To punish those that do profane this holy feast.   30

Henry. How mean'st thou that ?

> [*Mugeroun cuts off the Cutpurse's ear, for cutting the
>   gold buttons off his cloak.*

Cutp. O Lord, mine ear !

Mug. Come, sir, give me my buttons, and here's your ear.

Guise. Sirrah, take him away.

Henry. Hands off, good fellow ; I will be his bail

For this offence.—Go, sirrah, work no more

Till this our coronation-day be past.—

And now,

Our solemn rites of coronation done,

What now remains but for a while to feast,   40

And spend some days in barriers, tourney, tilt,

And like disports, such as do fit the court ?

Let's go, my lords ; our dinner stays for us.

> [*Exeunt all except Catherine the Queen-mother and the
>   Cardinal of Lorraine.*

Cath. My Lord Cardinal of Lorraine, tell me,

How likes your grace my son's pleasantness ?

His mind, you see, runs on his minions,

---

30. *profane*] O., etc.: [*dare*] *profane* Bull. conj.   31. *Mugeroun . . .*]
After line 30 in O.   38, 39.] As Dyce, etc. : one line in O., Rob. 39.
solemn] O., etc.: *omit* Rob.   43. *Exeunt . . .*] Rob., Cunn. (subs.), Dyce,
Bull. : *Goe out all, but the Queene and the Cardinall.* O.

exercised his craft ; and, having got his booty, began to move away, which the gentleman noting, instantly draws his knife, and whips off one of his ears, and vowed he would have something for his money. The cutpurse began to swear, to stamp, and threaten. ' Nay, go to, sirrah ', says the other ; ' be quiet ; I'll offer you fair : give me my purse again ; here's your ear, take it, and begone.'

41. *barriers*,] See Cowell, *The Interpreter,* 1637 : ' Barriers, commeth from the French (*barres*) and signifieth with us that which the French men call (*ieu de barres. i. palæstrum*) a martial sport or

exercise of men armed and fighting together with short swords, within certain limits or lists, whereby they are severed from the beholders.'

42. *disports*,] entertainments, diversions, as in *The Four Elements* (Hazlitt's *Dodsley*, i. 45) : ' *Disports*, as dancing, singing, Joys, trifles, laughing, jesting.'

46, 47. *His mind . . . himself ;*] Marlowe here summarises the character of Henry in words that would equally well have served for Edward II. We may note, too, the parallelism of l. 46 with *Edward II,* II. ii. 4 : ' And still his mind runs on his minion.'

And all his heaven is to delight himself;
And, whilst he sleeps securely thus in ease,
Thy brother Guise and we may now provide
To plant ourselves with such authority   50
As not a man may live without our leaves.
Then shall the Catholic faith of Rome
Flourish in France, and none deny the same.
Card. Madam, as in secrecy I was told,
My brother Guise hath gather'd a power of men,
Which are, he saith, to kill the Puritans;
But 'tis the house of Bourbon that he means.
Now, madam, must you insinuate with the king,
And tell him that 'tis for his country's good,
And common profit of religion.   60
Cath. Tush, man, let me alone with him,
To work the way to bring this thing to pass;
And, if he do deny what I do say,
I'll despatch him with his brother presently,
And then shall Monsieur wear the diadem.
Tush, all shall die unless I have my will;
For, while she lives, Catherine will be queen.
Come, my lord, let us go seek the Guise,
And then determine of this enterprise.   [*Exeunt.*

54. *as . . . I*] O., etc.: *as I in secrecy* Rob., Cunn.   56. *are*] Rob., etc.:
as O.   68. *lord*] Rob., etc.: *Lords* O.

56. *are*] The Octavo reading *as he saith* is almost certainly a mistake of the compositor: *as he saith* being a frequent locution.

61–69. *Tush, . . . enterprise.*] It should be noticed that these lines are virtually a repetition of the Queen's words in Sc. VIII. ll. 38 ff.

65. *And then . . . diadem.*] A particularly close echo of Sc. VIII l. 41. *Monsieur* is the Duc d'Alençon.

68. *lord*] The Octavo reading *Lords* seems clearly an error, unless the S.D. at l. 43 replaces an earlier one which left several courtiers on the stage.

SCENE XII

Enter the DUCHESS OF GUISE *and her* Maid.

Duch. of G. Go fetch me pen and ink,—
Maid.   I will, madam.
Duch. That I may write unto my dearest lord.   [*Exit Maid.*
      Sweet Mugeroun, 'tis he that hath my heart,
      And Guise usurps it 'cause I am his wife:
      Fain would I find some means to speak with him,
      But cannot, and therefore am enforc'd to write,
      That he may come and meet me in some place,
      Where we may one enjoy the other's sight.

      Re-enter the Maid, *with pen, ink, and paper.*

      So, set it down, and leave me to myself.
                  [*Exit Maid. The Duchess writes.*
      O, would to God, this quill that here doth write, 10
      Had late been pluck'd from out fair Cupid's wing,
      That it might print these lines within his heart!

                  Enter GUISE.

Guise. What, all alone, my love? and writing too?
      I prithee, say to whom thou writes.

Scene xii.

Ed. : *omit* O., Dyce: [*Act II*] *Scene* v. Rob., Cunn. : *Scene xv.* Bull. :
Sc. xi. Greg.
      2. *Exit* . . .] Dyce, Bull. : after *Madam* O., etc.   8. *Re-enter* . . .] Dyce,
Bull. : *Enter the Maid with Inke and Paper.* O., Rob., Cunn. (sub.).
9. *Exit* . . .] Rob., etc. : *she writes* O.   14. *writes*] O. : *writ'st*
Rob., etc.   14–16. *To* . . .] As Dyce, Bull.   As prose in O. : As two lines,
first ending *lines* Rob., Cunn.

Scene XII.

Scene XII.] An interior scene—a table, etc., being obviously required. Presumably played on the inner stage, the locality suggested by the Duches's words in ll. 6 ff.

3. *Mugeroun*] Dyce says that ' the gallant of the Duchess was not Mugeroun (Maugiron), but Saint-Mégrim, another of the King's

" Mignons ".' See Anquetil's *Hist. of France* (1817), v. 345.   The lines in *Arden of Feversham*, I. 98–100, closely resemble lines 3 and 4 here :

' Sweete *Mosbie* is the man that
      hath my hart :
And he usurps it, hauing nought
      but this,
That I am tyed to him by mar-
      riage.'

Duch.   To such

A one, my lord, as, when she reads my lines,

Will laugh, I fear me, at their good array.

Guise. I pray thee, let me see.

Duch. O, no, my lord ; a woman only must

Partake the secrets of my heart.

Guise. But, madam, I must see.   [*Seizes the paper.* 20

Are these your secrets that no man must know ?

Duch. O, pardon me, my lord !

Guise. Thou trothless and unjust ! what lines are these ?

Am I grown old, or is thy lust grown young ?

Or hath my love been so obscur'd in thee,

That others needs to comment on my text ?

Is all my love forgot, which held thee dear,

Ay, dearer than the apple of mine eye ?

Is Guise's glory but a cloudy mist,

In sight and judgment of thy lustful eye ?   30

Mort Dieu ! wert not the fruit within thy womb,

Of whose increase I set some longing hope,

This wrathful hand should strike thee to the heart.

Hence, strumpet ! hide thy head for shame ;

And fly my presence, if thou look to live ! [*Exit Duchess.*

15. *my lord*] O., etc.: *omit* Rob., Cunn.   20. *Seizes . . .*] Dyce, Bull.:
he takes it. O. : *Snatches the paper, and reads it.* Rob., Cunn.   26. *needs*
O. : *need* Rob., etc.   31. *Mort Dieu*] Rob., etc.: *Mor du* O.   *wert*] O.:
were Rob., etc.

16. *good array*] Does this mean
that the recipient will laugh because of the good array, i.e.
the orderly arrangement of the
Duchess' letter in opposition to the
triviality of her thoughts ?

23. *trothless*] destitute of troth or
loyalty. Compare Lodge's *Wounds
of Civil War*, III. i. : ' The trustful
man that builds on *trothless* vows.'

25, 26. *Or . . . text ?*] a metaphor from the scholiasts.   The
gloss or comment on the obscure
text of a classical or sacred author
was one of the greatest occupations
of the medieval scholar.   Cf.
Browning's *Grammarian's Funeral* :

' Grant I have mastered learning's
    crabbed text,
  Still there's *the comment.*'

and see also *Tamburlaine*, v. ii. 81 :

' Where Beauty, mother of the
    Muses sits
  And *comments* volumes with her
    ivory pen.'

31. *Mort Dieu*] *Mor du* in the
Octavo. Compare with *mor du* in
Sc. XIV. l. 28, and with *Mor du ma
vie* in the Quarto of *Henry V*,
IV. v. 3—another ' bad ' text.
32. *Of*] i.e. on.

O wicked sex, perjured and unjust !
Now do I see that from the very first
Her eyes and looks sow'd seeds of perjury.
But villain, he, to whom these lines should go,
Shall buy her love even with his dearest blood. 40
[Exit.

SCENE XIII

Enter the KING OF NAVARRE, PLESHÉ, BARTUS, *and train,
with drums and trumpets.*

Nav. My lords, sith in a quarrel just and right
We undertake to manage these our wars
Against the proud disturbers of the faith,
(I mean the Guise, the Pope, and king of Spain,
Who set themselves to tread us under foot,
And rent our true religion from this land ;
But for you know our quarrel is no more
But to defend their strange inventions,

Scene xiii.
Ed. : *omit* O., Rob., Dyce, Cunn. : *Scene xvi.* Bull : *Sc. xii.* Greg.   6.
rent] O., etc. : *rend* Rob.

Scene XIII.

Scene XIII.] A bare open place to denote open country. Unlocalised further, the audience would probably have imagined it to be in Navarre. Dyce writes : ' I must leave the location of this scene to the reader. I should have marked it La Rochelle, but that a Messenger presently informs the King that a mighty army comes *from France.*'

Bartus] There seems to be strong reason for identifying this character with the well-known poet Du Bartas, so important in English literature. In the *Biographie Universelle* we read : ' Bartas (Gillaume de Saluste Du) né vers 1544 . . . De la même religion que Henri IV, avant qu'il fût roi de France, et attaché à la personne de ce prince, en qualité de gentilhomme ordinaire de la chambre, il fut employé par lui, avec succès, pour ses affaires en Danemarck, en Écosse et en Angleterre. . . . Il se trouva à la bataille d'Ivry, et chanta la victoire à laquelle il avait contribué.   Quatre mois après, en juillet 1590, il mourut, âgè de quarante-six ans, de suites de quelques blessures qui avaient été mal guéries.' I owe this identification to the kindness of Professor R. H. Case.

2. *manage*] See above, Sc. VII. l. 9.
7. *But for*] But since.
8. *But to*] Except to.
8. *defend*] repel, ward off. Cf. 1568 Grafton, *Chron.* II. 17 : ' To withstand and *defend* his enimyes ' (O.E.D.).
8. *inventions*] designs, plans. Here apparently used in the special sense of religious innovations. Compare *Taming of the Shrew*, I. i. 194 : ' and now 'tis plotted. . , , Both our *inventions* meet and

Which they will put us to with sword and fire,)
We must with resolute minds resolve to fight,   10
In honour of our God, and country's good.
Spain is the council-chamber of the Pope,
Spain is the place where he makes peace and war;
And Guise for Spain hath now incens'd the king
To send his power to meet us in the field.

Bar. Then in this bloody brunt they may behold
The sole endeavour of your princely care,
To plant the true succession of the faith,
In spite of Spain and all his heresies.

Nav. The power of vengeance now encamps itself   20
Upon the haughty mountains of my breast;
Plays with her gory colours of revenge,
Whom I respect as leaves of boasting green,
That change their colour when the winter comes,
When I shall vaunt as victor in revenge.

Enter a Messenger.

How now, sirrah! what news?
Mes. My lord, as by our scouts we understand,
A mighty army comes from France with speed;
Which are already muster'd in the land,
And means to meet your highness in the field.   30

---

29. *are*] O., etc. *is* Rob.   30. *means*] O., Rob.: *mean* Dyce, etc.

jump in one,' and see *3 Henry VI*, IV. i. 35. *Inventions* must here be pronounced as four syllables.

14. *for Spain*] on behalf of, as the agent of Spain.

Guise . . . incens'd the king] Note how this tag is again used a few lines later in the scene (l. 32)— possibly a collocation running in the mind of the anonymous reporter of this text. Incensed = incited.

18, 19. *To plant . . . heresies.*] If Spain in l. 19 refers to the country as in ll. 12, 13 above, one would expect *her*, though *his* (i.e.

its) is possible. Probably, however, Spain in this instance means the King of Spain, as the natural opponent of the King of Navarre.

20–25. *The power . . . revenge.*] This passage has in it something of the spirit of *Tamburlaine*. The remarkable metaphor in l. 21; the simile in l. 23 and the alliteration in the last two lines are to be noted. It is not easy, however, to attach any very clear meaning to the passage, and it may be that something has dropped out after l. 22.

Nav. In God's name, let them come !
   This is the Guise that hath incens'd the king
   To levy arms, and make these civil broils.
   But canst thou tell who is their general ?
Mes. Not yet, my lord, for thereon do they stay ;
   But, as report doth go, the Duke of Joyeux
   Hath made great suit unto the king therefore.
Nav. It will not countervail his pains, I hope.
   I would the Guise in his stead might have come !
   But he doth lurk within his drowsy couch,   40
   And makes his footstool on security :
   So he be safe, he cares not what becomes
   Of king or country ; no, not for them both.
   But come, my lords, let us away with speed,
   And place ourselves in order for the fight.   [*Exeunt.*

SCENE XIV

Enter KING HENRY, GUISE, EPERNOUN, *and* JOYEUX.

Henry. My sweet Joyeux, I make thee general
   Of all my army, now in readiness

36. *of Joyeux*] O., etc. : *Joyeux* Rob., Cunn.
Scene xiv.
Ed. : *omit* O., Cunn., Rob., Dyce : *Scene xvii.* Bull : *Sc. xiii.* Greg.

35. *for thereon do they stay*] it is for
this they wait.
   36. See below, Sc. XIV. l. 1.
   38. *It*] The King's decision.
countervail his pains] equal, i.e.
satisfy his 'great suit'. Cf.
Pericles, II. iii. 56 :
'As if the entertainment in our
   court
 Had not a show might *countervail*
   his worth.'

40. *But he . . . couch*] Cf. with
Guise's words in Sc. II. l. 48 : ' I
wake, when others think I sleep.'
Navarre, apparently, is among the
' others '.

Scene XIV.
Scene XIV.] Here both inner and

outer stage seem to be used. The
King is in council, and probably
seated on a raised throne on the
inner stage, while the whole outer
stage is required for the courtiers,
attendants, etc.
   1. *Joyeux*] Anne de Joyeuse, the
favourite of Henry III, had been
advanced step by step to the
highest positions in the realm by
his doting master, and in 1586
was given command against the
Huguenots in Guienne.   During
the operations he was defeated and
slain at Coutras the next year.
(See below, Sc. XV. l. 1.)   A vivid
account of the three brothers
Joyeux is given in Stanley Wey-
man's novel, *The Abbess of Vlaye.*

To march against the rebellious King Navarre ;
At thy request I am content thou go,
Although my love to thee can hardly suffer't,
Regarding still the danger of thy life.
Joyeux. Thanks to your majesty ; and so, I take my leave.
Farewell to my Lord of Guise, and Epernoun.
Guise. Health and hearty farewell to my Lord Joyeux.

[*Exit Joyeux.*

Henry. So kindly, cousin of Guise, you and your wife 10
Do both salute our lovely minions.
Remember you the letter, gentle sir,
Which your wife writ
To my dear minion, and her chosen friend ?

[*Makes horns at Guise.*

Guise. How now, my lord ! faith, this is more than need.
Am I thus to be jested at and scorn'd ?
'Tis more than kingly or emperious :
And, sure, if all the proudest kings
In Christendom should bear me such derision,
They should know how I scorn'd them and their
mocks. 20

3. *against*] O., etc. : *'gainst* Dyce², Bull. 4. *go*] O., etc. : *go'st* Rob.
5. *suffer't*] Rob., Dyce, Bull. : *suffer* O. : *suffer it* Cunn. 8. *to*] O.,
etc. : omit Rob., Cunn. 10-14. As Rob., etc. : prose in O. 10. *So*]
O., etc. : *How* Rob. 14. *Makes . . . Guise.*] Rob., etc. : after line
11 in O. 18. *kings*] O., etc. : *kings beside* Rob., Cunn. 18, 19. Division
after *In* in O. 20. *how*] O. etc. : *omit* Rob.

3. *against*] pronounce *'gainst*, and
so printed by Dyce², and Bullen.
10. *So . . .*] Robinson reads
How, referring to the farewells
immediately exchanged between
Joyeux and Guise. But the Duchess
is not present, and there can be little
doubt that something is missing here.
14. *Makes horns*] This gesture
with the fingers is equivalent to
calling Guise a cuckold. O.E.D.
quotes Pearson's Dekker, III. 9 :
Northward Hoe : 'If a man be
deuorst . . . whether may he haue
an action or no, gainst those that
make hornes at him ? '
17. *emperious*] More usually imperious—befitting an emperor or
supreme ruler, as in *Titus
Andronicus,* IV. iv. 81 : ' King, be
thy thoughts *Imperious.*' Here the
line means ' going beyond the
privilege of king or emperor.
There is great spirit in this speech
of the Guise, and it is one of many
passages in Marlowe which con-
vince me that Sir Walter Scott was
familiar with his writings '
(Cunningham).
20. *mocks*] contemptuous actions
or speech. Compare Hawes' *Pastime of Pleasure* (E.E.T.S. edn.),
p. 181 : ' He . . . called me boye,
and gave me many a *mocke.*'

I love your minions! dote on them yourself;
I know none else but holds them in disgrace;
And here, by all the saints in heaven, I swear,
That villain for whom I bear this deep disgrace,
Even for your words that have incens'd me so,
Shall buy that strumpet's favour with his blood!
Whether he have dishonoured me or no,
Par la mort de Dieu, il mourra!   [*Exit.*

Henry. Believe me, this jest bites sore.

Eper. My lord, 'twere good to make them friends,   30
For his oaths are seldom spent in vain.

Enter MUGEROUN.

Henry. How now, Mugeroun! met'st thou not the Guise
at the door?

Mug. Not I, my lord; what if I had?

Henry. Marry, if thou hadst, thou mightst have had the
stab,
For he hath solemnly sworn thy death.

Mug. I may be stabb'd, and live till he be dead:
But wherefore bears he me such deadly hate?

Henry. Because his wife bears thee such kindly love.

Mug. If that be all, the next time that I meet her,
I'll make her shake off love with her heels.   40
But which way is he gone? I'll go take a walk
On purpose from the court to meet with him. [*Exit.*

---

22. *disgrace*] O., etc.: *disgust* conj. Coll. (MS.).   28. *Par . . . mourra*]
Rob., etc.: *Par la mor du, Il mora.* O.   29. *me,*] O., Dyce, Bull.: *me,*
Epernoun, Rob., Cunn.   39–42.] As prose in Rob.   41, 42.] As Dyce, etc.:
prose in O.   41. *take*] Rob., etc.: *make* O.

28. *mort de Dieu*] Compare the
Octavo reading *mor du* with the
exclamation *Mor du* (Mort Dieu) in
Sc. XII. l. 31, and the note there.
mourra] *mora* in the original.
    40. *shake . . . heels*] repudiate
love. Cf. *Much Ado,* III. iv. 51,
'I scorn that with my heels',
which appears to have been a
proverbial expression. Possibly

there is also allusion to the sense
associated with heels, as in, e.g.,
The Two Angry Women of Abingdon,
Hazlitt's *Dodsley,* VII. 275: 'yea,
foul strumpet, light-a-love, short-
heels!'
    41. *take*] The compositor of the
Octavo set up *make* here by mistake,
his eye being caught by that word
in the preceding line.

Henry. I like not this. Come, Epernoun,

    Let us go seek the duke, and make them friends.

                                               [*Exeunt.*

SCENE XV

Alarums, within, and a cry—' The DUKE JOYEUX *is slain.'*
Enter the KING OF NAVARRE, BARTUS, *and train.*

Nav. The duke is slain, and all his power dispers'd,

    And we are grac'd with wreaths of victory.

    Thus God, we see, doth ever guide the right,

    To make his glory great upon the earth.

Bar. The terror of this happy victory,

    I hope, will make the king surcease his hate,

    And either never manage army more,

    Or else employ them in some better cause.

Nav. How many noblemen have lost their lives

43, 44. As Dyce, etc., prose in O., Rob.   44. *Let us*] Dyce, Bull.: *Let's*
O., Rob., Cunn.

Scene xv.

    Ed.: *omit* O., Dyce: [*Act II*] *Scene vi.* Rob., Cunn.: *Scene xviii*
Bull.: *Sc. xiv* Greg. *Alarums, . . .*] Rob., etc. (substantially): *Alarums
within. The Duke Ioyeux slaine. Enter the King of Nauarre and his
traine.* O.

44. *Let us*] An emendation of the
Octavo *Let's* by Dyce which im-
proves the metre.

Scene XV.

Scene XV.] An open field of battle
again. All necessary indications are
given to the audience by the ceremonial entry of Navarre, and his
first words ' The duke is slain ', etc.
Possibly the death of the Duke was
represented in dumb-show and the
body removed after l. 19 at end of
scene.

    1, 2. *The Duke . . . victory*]
These lines, like those of Sc. xx.
ll. 4, 5, below, are so reminiscent of passages from *The True
Tragedy* and *3 Henry VI* that
some direct borrowing is fairly
certain. In *3 Henry VI*, v. iii. 1–2,

we have ' Thus far our fortune
keeps an upward course, And we are
graced with wreaths of Victory ',
while in *The True Tragedy* they
read: ' Thus farre our fortunes
keepes an upward Course, And we
are grast with wreaths of victorie.'

    6. *surcease*] abandon, give up.
Compare Spenser's *Faerie Queene*,
III. iv. 31: ' The waves . . . their
rage *surceast* ', or Dekker's *Hist. of
Sir T. Wyat* (*Works*, 1873) III. 99:
' *Surcease* your armes, discharge
your souldiers.'

    7. *manage army*] The phrase
manage wars is a favourite one of
Marlowe's. See above Sc. VII. l. 9;
Sc. XIII. l. 2, and constantly in
I Tamburlaine, II. vi. 16, III. i 35,
etc.

In prosecution of these cruel arms,   10
Is ruth, and almost death, to call to mind.
But God we know will always put them down
That lift themselves against the perfect truth ;
Which I'll maintain so long as life doth last,
And with the Queen of England join my force
To beat the papal monarch from our lands,
And keep those relics from our countries' coasts.
Come, my lords ; now that this storm is overpast,
Let us away with triumph to our tents.   [*Exeunt.*

SCENE XVI

Enter a Soldier.

Sold. Sir, to you, sir, that dares make the duke a cuckold,
    and use a counterfeit key to his privy-chamber-door ;
    and although you take out nothing but your own, yet
    you put in that which displeaseth him, and so forestall
    his market, and set up your standing where you should
    not ; and whereas he is your landlord, you will take
    upon you to be his, and till the ground that he himself
    should occupy, which is his own free land ; if it be

15. *Queen.*] Rob., etc. : *Q.* O.
                              Scene xvi.
Ed. : *omit* O., Rob., Dyce, Cunn. : *Scene xix.* Bull. : *Sc. xv.* Greg.

15, 16. *And with . . . lands,*]
Henry of Navarre was constantly in
treaty with Elizabeth for some sort
of offensive alliance between them
against the Catholic forces in the
Netherlands, France and Spain.
See, e.g., *Sir Francis Walsingham*,
by C. Read, III. 17, 34, 37, 85, etc.
    17. *relics*] in what sense here used
is hard to say—objects of super-
stitious worship, remainders of
false ideas or practice (the ' strange
inventions ' of Sc. XIII. l. 8) or the
remainder of their foes. But is it
possibly a misreading due to mis-
hearing : it sounds much like
prelates.

Scene XVI.
    Scene XVI.] From Sc. XIV. lines
41–2, we know this scene takes place
outside the Louvre where Mugeroun
goes to ' take a walk '. Again an
open place is all that is indicated, or
necessary.
    Enter a Soldier] For a discussion of
this important scene, see pp. 253 ff.
    5. *set . . . standing*] This con-
tinues the metaphor involved in
' forestall his market '. The allusion is to the setting up of market
booths for the sale of goods.
    8. *occupy*] Shakespeare alludes to
the degradation of this word, which
was often used in an immoral

not too free—there's the question ; and though I come
not to take possession (as I would I might !) yet I
mean to keep you out ; which I will, if this gear hold.

Enter MUGEROUN.

What, are ye come so soon ? have at ye, sir !   12
          [Shoots at Mugeroun and kills him.

Enter GUISE *and* Attendants.

Guise. [*Giving a purse*] Hold thee, tall soldier, take thee
    this, and fly.   *[Exit Soldier.*
Lie there, the king's delight, and Guise's scorn !
Revenge it, Henry, as thou list or dare ;
I did it only in despite of thee.
          [Attendants bear off Mugeroun's body.

Enter KING HENRY *and* EPERNOUN.

Henry. My Lord of Guise, we understand
That you have gathered a power of men :
What your intent is yet we cannot learn,
But we presume it is not for our good.   20

11. *Enter . . .*] Rob., etc.: after *sir* in l. 12, O.   12. *Enter . . . Attendants.*]
Rob., etc.: *Enter the Guise.* O.   13. *thee this,*] O., Dyce, Bull.: *thou this,*
Rob., Cunn.   15. *dare*] O., etc.: *dar'st* Rob.   16. *Attendants . . . body.*]
Rob., etc.: *Take him away.* O.   17–20.] As Rob., etc.: prose in O.

sense, as in *2 Henry VI*, ii. iv. 159 :
' these villains will make the word
as odious as the word *occupy*.'
For its use see *Hickscorner* (Hazlitt's
Dodsley, i. 174) : ' Like heretics we
occupy other men's wives.'
   12. *Shoots . . .*] ' Mugeroun (Maugiron) fell in a duel : Anquetil,
Hist. de France, v. 344 : but Saint-
Mégrin, the gallant of the Duchess
of Guise, *was* assassinated. " Ils
dressèrent une embuscade à la porte
du Louvre. Comme Saint-Mégrin
en sortait la nuit, des assassins
apostés se jetèrent sur lui, et
l'étendirent sur le pavé, percé de
trente-cinq coups. Il vécut cepend-
ant jusqu'au lendemain. Anquetil,
ibid., p. 347." ' (Dyce.)
16

13. *tall*] brave, etc., as commonly.
  17–20. *My Lord . . . good.*] The
quarrel between Guise and the
King was the subject of several
contemporary English pamphlets.
One is entitled : ' An Advertisement
from a French Gentleman, touching the intention and meaning
which those of the house of *Guise*
haue in their late leuying of forces
and Armes in the Realme of France
. . . Anno 1585. Iune.' (Tucker
Brooke.)
  18. *a power*] forces, as in *Ant. and
Cleop.*, iii. vii. 77 : ' His *power*
went out in such distractions as
Beguiled all spies.'

Guise. Why, I am no traitor to the crown of France ;
  What I have done, 'tis for the Gospel's sake.
Eper. Nay, for the Pope's sake, and thine own benefit.
  What peer in France, but thou (aspiring Guise)
  Durst be in arms without the king's consent ?
  I challenge thee for treason in the cause.
Guise. Ah, base Epernoun ! were not his highness here,
  Thou shouldst perceive the Duke of Guise is mov'd.
Henry. Be patient, Guise, and threat not Epernoun,
  Lest thou perceive the king of France be mov'd. 30
Guise. Why, I am a prince of the Valoyses line,
  Therefore an enemy to the Bourbonites ;
  I am a juror in the holy league,
  And therefore hated of the Protestants :
  What should I do but stand upon my guard ?
  And, being able, I'll keep an host in pay.
Eper. Thou able to maintain an host in pay,
  That livest by foreign exhibition !
  The Pope and King of Spain are thy good friends ;
  Else all France knows how poor a duke thou art. 40
Henry. Ay, those are they that feed him with their gold,

---

22. *Gospel's sake.*] Rob., etc. : *Gospell sake.* O.   27. *Ah*] O., etc. : *Oh*
Rob., Cunn.   28. *Duke*] Rob., etc.: *D.*O.   31. *I am*] O., Rob., Dyce[1],
Cunn. : *I'm* Dyce[2], Bull.   *Valoyses*] O. : *Valois's* the rest.   38. *livest*] O.,
etc.: *liv'st thyself* Cunn.

31. *prince . . . Valoyses line,*]
Compare lower in l. 52, where
Guise more properly describes himself as a member of the house of
Lorraine, and also with Sc. XVIII.
l. 85, where Guise curses Valois his
line. See also his brother Dumaine's
threat in Sc. XX. l. 7.
   33. *juror*] One who has taken an
oath, or sworn allegiance to some
body or cause. The O.E.D. gives
this passage as the earliest use of
the word thus.
   33. *holy league*] The Catholic
League under the Guises was
formed mainly in reaction to the
pacific policy towards the Huguenots adopted by Henry III., as
shown in the ' Peace of Monsieur ',

1576. The League demanded the
re-establishment of Catholic Unity,
and set the religious right of the
nation in opposition to the divine
right of incapable or evil-doing
kings.
   38. *exhibition.*] maintenance or
support, from the Late Latin
exhibitio. Compare *Bury Wills*
(Camden Soc.), p. 65 : ' I will that
. . . oon parte thereof to be applied
. . . to *thexibicion* and sustenacion
of a perpetuall chapleyn.' See
ante, II. 60 ff., in which Guise mentions his revenues from Spain and
the Pope. Cunningham wantonly
proposed ' That liv'st *thyself* . . .
exhibition '.

To countermand our will, and check our friends.
Guise. My lord, to speak more plainly, thus it is:
    Being animated by religious zeal,
    I mean to muster all the power I can,
    To overthrow those factious Puritans :
    And know, my lord, the Pope will sell his triple crown,
    Ay, and the Catholic Philip, king of Spain,
    Ere I shall want, will cause his Indians
    To rip the golden bowels of America.   50
    Navarre, that cloaks them underneath his wings,
    Shall feel the house of Lorraine is his foe.
    Your highness needs not fear mine army's force ;
    'Tis for your safety, and your enemies' wrack.
Henry. Guise, wear our crown, and be thou king of France,
    And, as dictator, make or war or peace,
    Whilst I cry *placet*, like a senator !
    I cannot brook thy haughty insolence :
    Dismiss thy camp, or else by our edict
    Be thou proclaim'd a traitor throughout France.   60
Guise. The choice is hard ; I must dissemble.—
                                        [*Aside.*

    My lord, in token of my true humility,
    And simple meaning to your majesty,
    I kiss your grace's hand, and take my leave,
    Intending to dislodge my camp with speed.
Henry. Then farewell, Guise ; the king and thou are friends.
                                    [*Exit Guise.*

---

46. *factious*] Rob., Malone conj., Coll. conj., Dyce, etc.: *sexious* O.   51. *cloaks*] O., etc.: *clucks* Coll. conj. 54. *wrack*] O. : *wreck* Rob., etc. 61. *Aside*] Rob., etc. : *omit* O.

46. *factious*] The Octavo reading is *sexious*, which the O.E.D. says is ' a nonce-wd. [? for *sectious*, f. SECT. sb + — IOUS] ? sectarian ' ; and then follows this one quotation. All the editors, however, have preferred the safer conjecture of Robinson—*factious*.
  51. *cloaks them*] i.e. the Puritans or Huguenots. Collier (MS.) proposes the bizarre emendation *clucks*, involving the comparison of Navarre with a hen !
  56, 57. *dictator . . . senator*] Another reminiscence from Roman history. Cf. Sc. II. l. 98 ; Sc. XVIII. l. 51, etc.

Eper. But trust him not, my lord ; for, had your highness
   Seen with what a pomp he enter'd Paris,
   And how the citizens with gifts and shows
   Did entertain him,   70
   And promised to be at his command—
   Nay, they fear'd not to speak in the streets,
   That the Guise durst stand in arms against the king,
   For not effecting of his holiness' will.
Henry. Did they of Paris entertain him so ?
   Then means he present treason to our state.
   Well, let me alone.—Who's within there ?

        Enter an Attendant.

   Make a discharge of all my council straight,
   And I'll subscribe my name, and seal it straight.
                  [Attendant writes.
   My head shall be my council ; they are false ;   80
   And, Epernoun, I will be rul'd by thee.
Eper. My lord,
   I think, for safety of your royal person,
   It would be good the Guise were made away,
   And so to quite your grace of all suspect.
Henry. First let us set our hand and seal to this,
   And then I'll tell thee what I mean to do.—   *[Writes.*
   So ; convey this to the council presently.
                  [Exit Attendant.

67–70.] As four lines divided after *lord, pomp, citizens* T. Brooke.
69, 70.] As two lines, first ending *citizens* Cunn. 70, 71.] As Dyce², Bull.:
one line in O., Rob., Dyce¹. 72. *speak*] O., etc.: *speak it* Bull. 73. *the
Guise*] O., etc.: *Guise* Rob. 77. *Enter* . . .] Rob., Dyce, Cunn.: *Enter
one with a pen and inke.* O.: *Enter Attendant,* . . . *ink.* Bull. 79. *Attendant writes.*] Dyce, Bull. 82, 83.] As Dyce², Bull.: one line in O., etc.
83. *royal*] O., etc.: *omit* Rob., Cunn. 85. *quite*] O., etc.: *quit* Rob.,
Cunn. 87. *Writes.*] Rob., etc.: *he writes.* O., after line 86. 88. *Exit
Attendant.*] Rob., etc.: *Exit one.* O.

72. *speak*] Bullen's suggestion
that we should read *speak it* has
much to commend it.
  76. *present*] immediate, instant,
as always in Elizabeth times.

85. *quite*] free, acquit. Compare
Paston Letters, I. 208 : ' We undir-
stande he shall not be *quyte* but
before the Justice.'

And, Epernoun, though I seem mild and calm,
Think not but I am tragical within.   90
I'll secretly convey me unto Blois ;
For, now that Paris takes the Guise's part,
Here is no staying for the king of France,
Unless he mean to be betray'd and die :
But, as I live, so sure the Guise shall die.   [*Exeunt.*

SCENE XVII

Enter the KING OF NAVARRE, *reading a letter, and* BARTUS.

Nav. My lord, I am advertised from France
    That the Guise hath taken arms against the king,
    And that Paris is revolted from his grace.
Bar. Then hath your grace fit opportunity
    To show your love unto the king of France,
    Offering him aid against his enemies,
    Which cannot but be thankfully receiv'd.
Nav. Bartus, it shall be so : post, then, to France,
    And there salute his highness in our name ;
    Assure him all the aid we can provide   10
    Against the Guisians and their complices.
    Bartus, be gone : commend me to his grace,
    And tell him, ere it be long, I'll visit him.
Bar. I will, my lord.   [*Exit.*
Nav. Pleshé !

Enter PLESHÉ.

Scene xvii.

Ed.: *omit* O., Dyce : *Act III. Scene i.* Rob., Cunn. : *Scene xx* Bull. :
Sc. *xvi* Greg.

2. *the Guise*] O., etc. : *Guise* Rob., Cunn.   15. *Enter . . .*] Dyce, Bull. :
after line 14 O., etc.

90. *tragical*] excited with tragic feeling. So O.E.D., but perhaps used here in opposition to *mild and calm*, to refer to Henry's plans against the Guise, which he is determined shall be fatal to that prince (see l. 95).

Scene XVII.

Scene XVII.] Navarre : an open place.

11. *complices*] associates, confederates. The word was largely used in connection with crime in this century, as in 25 Henry VIII, c. 12 : ' Conspiracies . . . of the said Elizabeth, and her other *complices.*' It is a favourite of Marlowe's. Compare *Edward II*, II. ii. 263 : ' Have at the rebels and their *complices* ', and also III. ii. 153, etc.

Pleshé. My lord !

Nav. Pleshé, go muster up our men with speed,
    And let them march away to France amain,
    For we must aid the king against the Guise.
    Be gone, I say ; 'tis time that we were there.   20
Pleshé. I go, my lord.   [*Exit.*
Nav. That wicked Guise, I fear me much will be
    The ruin of that famous realm of France ;
    For his aspiring thoughts aim at the crown :
    And takes his vantage on religion,
    To plant the Pope and Popelings in the realm,
    And bind it wholly to the see of Rome.
    But, if that God do prosper mine attempts,
    And send us safely to arrive in France,
    We'll beat him back, and drive him to his death,   30
    That basely seeks the ruin of his realm.   [*Exit.*

SCENE XVIII

Enter the Captain of the Guard, *and three* Murderers.

Cap. Come on, sirs.   What, are you resolutely bent,

---

21. *Exit*] Rob., etc. : *omit* O.   25. *And*] O., Bull :   *He* Rob., Cunn. :
'*A* Dyce.   31. *Exit*] Rob., etc. : *Exeunt* O.

Scene xviii.
Ed. : *omit* O., Dyce : [*Act III*] *Scene ii.* Rob., Cunn. : *Scene xxi* Bull. :
Sc. xvii Greg.   *Murderers*] *murtherers* O.

18. *amain*] at full speed, as in
Holinshed's   *Chronicles* (1587, I.
176) : ' Then without respect of
shame they fled *amaine.*'
    25. *And takes . . . religion*] The
subject changes from the *aspiring
thoughts* of Guise of l. 24 to Guise
himself.   There is no need therefore
for the alteration to '*A* of Dyce, or
He of Robinson and Cunningham.
    25. *vantage*] opportunity.   Com-
pare G. Harvey's *Letter Book*
(Camden Soc.), p. 2, ' If the *vantage*
had bene presently takin ' (O.E.D.).

Scene XVIII.
    Scene *XVIII.*] A room in the
King's castle—possibly outside the
royal cabinet of l. 27, to which the
King retires with Epernoun in l. 45.
    1. *What*]   An   extra   metrical
word—possibly an actor's insertion
for emphasis.   See also l. 7, where
the   word   *But*   affords   another
example of corruption.
    1. *resolutely bent*] absolutely de-
termined, as in Goldsmith's *Citizen
of the World* (1837), VI. 20 : ' The
youth   seems   obstinately   *bent*   on
finding you out.'

Hating the life and honour of the Guise ?

What, will you not fear, when you see him come ?

First Murd. Fear him, said you ? tush, were he here, we
would kill him presently.

Sec. Murd. O, that his heart were leaping in my hand !

Third Murd. But when will he come, that we may murder
him ?

Cap. Well, then, I see you are resolute.

First Murd. Let us alone ; I warrant you.

Cap. Then, sirs, take your standings within this chamber ; 10
For anon the Guise will come.

All three Murderers. You will give us our money ?

Cap. Ay, ay, fear not : stand close : so ; be resolute.

Now falls the star whose influence governs France,

Whose light was deadly to the Protestants :

Now must he fall, and perish in his height.

Enter KING HENRY *and* EPERNOUN.

Henry. Now, captain of my guard, are these murderers
ready ?

Cap. They be, my good lord.

Henry. But are they resolute, and arm'd to kill,

Hating the life and honour of the Guise ? 20

Cap. I warrant ye, my lord. [*Exit.*

13. *so*] O., etc. : *omit* Rob., Cunn. 13.] Rob., etc., add *Exeunt
Murderers.* 21. *ye,*] O., etc. : *you,* Rob., Cunn. 21. *Exit*] Rob., etc. :
omit O.

10. *standings*] stations. Used in
the plural by Marlowe, as in *1 Tamburlaine,* I. ii. 150 : ' Keep all your
standings, and not stir a foot.'

13. *so*] Omitted by Robinson
and Cunningham, and possibly an
actor's insertion accompanying the
stage business with which the
Captain stations the murderers
' within this Chamber '. Robinson,
etc., add here *Exeunt murderers,* but
they only retire into the inner stage,
and therefore the Octavo rightly has
no such direction. See below on
line 25.

14. *star . . . influence*] For the
supposed influence of the stars
on mortal destinies, compare *The
Tempest,* I. ii. 182, *Hamlet,* I. i. 118
9 : ' and the moist star Upon
whose influence Neptune's empire
stands ', etc.

16. *in his height*] i.e. at the height
of his power.

20. *Hating . . . Guise ?*] a suspicious repetition of l. 2.

21.] The addition of *Exit* by
Robinson is clearly right, for the
Captain has done his part of the
business and does not come on

Henry. Then come, proud Guise, and here disgorge thy
    breast,
  Surcharg'd with surfeit of ambitious thoughts ;
  Breathe out that life wherein my death was hid,
  And end thy endless treasons with thy death.
                        [*Enter the Guise and knocketh.*
Guise. Holà, varlet, hé !—Epernoun, where is the king ?
Eper. Mounted his royal cabinet.
Guise. I prithee, tell him that the Guise is here.
Eper. And please your grace, the Duke of Guise doth crave
  Access unto your highness.

25. *Enter . . . knocketh*] O.: *Knocking within.* Dyce, Bull.: *Guise knocks without.* Rob., Cunn.   26, 28. *Guise*] O.: *Guise [within]* Rob., etc.   26. *Holà, varlet, hé !*] Dyce, Bull.: *Halla verlete hey* O.: *Holloa, varlet, hey!* Rob., Cunn.   29. *And*] O.: *An't* Rob., Cunn.: *An* Dyce, Bull.   29, 30.] As Rob., etc.: prose in O.

again until all is over, as is proved by the Octava direction in l. 87 : *Enter Captaine of the Guarde.*

25. *Enter the Guise . . .*] The S.D.'s here are very perplexing, and all modern editors have solved the difficulties by altering them to suit their own purposes. Thus Robinson and Cunningham read *Guise knocks without,* with which Dyce and Bullen's *Knocking within* is in substantial agreement. This, of course, involves tampering with the S.D. of line 32 (see *Text Note*). I have preferred to leave the original S.D.'s as they seem capable of interpretation. The Guise enters, knocking at the side door of the outer stage, and Epernoun appears from the inner stage where the King and the murderers are concealed : he tells the Guise that the King has ' mounted his royal cabinet ' (i.e. ascended some sort of throne or dais on the inner stage), and speaks through the curtains to the King, who says ' Let him come in '. As Guise approaches Henry says lines 31 and 32 as an aside, and afterwards turns to welcome the Duke. They talk together, moving forward out of the inner stage, and at l. 45 the King goes out, leaving Guise.

From his hiding-place in the inner stage the Murderer emerges (l. 57), and warns Guise not to go forth by ' the next room ' (l. 64). He insists on so doing and is stabbed there on the back stage. There his body lies throughout (see ll. 91, 118 and 137), and remains till the traverse closes at the end of the scene.

26. *Holà . . . hé !*] As the Guise opens the door, on which he knocks, he calls out to the lacqueys in attendance in the ante-chamber *Holà . . .,* and is (perhaps unexpectedly) answered by Epernoun.

27. *Mounted*] i.e. Mounted in. Bullen compares with *2 Tamburlaine,* IV. 3 : ' *Mounted* his shining chariot.' I am not sure that this use of *mounted* here has any more significance than that the King has entered his cabinet, which may perhaps have had a dais or raised platform at the rear of the inner stage to suggest a throne. (See Sc. XXI., note on staging.) There seems little justification for the idea that he *mounted* the upper stage at this point, and converses with the Guise below much as Lancaster and Edward converse at Tynemouth in *Ed. II* (l. 985–95).

Henry.   Let him come in.   30
  Come, Guise, and see thy traitorous guile outreach'd,
  And perish in the pit thou mad'st for me.

           The GUISE *comes to the King.*

Guise. Good morrow to your majesty.
Henry. Good morrow to my loving cousin of Guise :
  How fares it this morning with your excellence ?
Guise. I heard your majesty was scarcely pleas'd,
  That in the court I bare so great a train.
Henry. They were to blame that said I was displeas'd ;
  And you, good cousin, to imagine it.
  'Twere hard with me, if I should doubt my kin,   40
  Or be suspicious of my dearest friends.
  Cousin, assure you I am resolute,
  Whatsoever any whisper in mine ears,
  Not to suspect disloyalty in thee :
  And so, sweet coz, farewell.   [*Exit with Epernoun.*
Guise. So ;
  Now sues the king for favour to the Guise,
  And all his minions stoop when I command :
  Why, this 'tis to have an army in the field.
  Now, by the holy sacrament, I swear,   50
  As ancient Romans o'er their captive lords,
  So will I triumph o'er this wanton king ;

32.] Add *A side* Rob., Cunn. *The Guise comes to the King.*] O. : *Enter Guise.*
Rob., etc. 37. *bare*] O., Dyce. : *bear* Rob., Cunn., Bull. 45. *Exit . . .*
Epernoun.] Rob., etc. : *Exit King.* O. 46, 47.] As Rob., etc. : one line in
O. 51, 52. *o'er*] Rob., etc. : *ouer* O.

32. *The Guise . . . King*] Guise
crosses the stage and passes through
the traverse towards the King.
  37. *bare*] probably a genuine pre-
terite, as Dyce understands it.
But Robinson, etc., print *bear.*
  38. *They were to blame*] See above,
Sc. XVI. l. 17 ff., unless we may
make a distinction between the
Guise's ' power of men ' and his
train at court. But remembering
the King's words in XVI. 95 and a

few lines earlier in this scene it is
obvious that he is merely dissembling.
  46. *So ;*] This word derives its
force from being assigned a line to
itself, and has been so distinguished
by all the editors.
  47. *Now sues . . .*] Note the
dramatic irony of this speech with
the murderers waiting without.
  52, 53. *So will I . . . wheels.*] Cf.
with this *The Contention*, Sc. VIII.

And he shall follow my proud chariot's wheels.
Now do I but begin to look about,
And all my former time was spent in vain.
Hold, sword,
For in thee is the Duke of Guise's hope.

Enter Third Murderer.

Villain, why dost thou look so ghastly ? speak.
Third Murd. O, pardon me, my Lord of Guise !
Guise. Pardon thee ! why, what hast thou done ?   60
Third Murd. O my lord, I am one of them that is set to
    murder you !
Guise. To murder me, villain !
Third Murd. Ay, my lord : the rest have ta'en their stand-
    ings in the next room ; therefore, good my lord, go
    not forth.
Guise. Yet Caesar shall go forth.

56, 57.] As Dyce, Bull. : one line in O., Rob., Cunn.   57. *Duke of*]
O., Dyce, Bull. : omit Rob., Cunn.   *Enter . . .*] Dyce, Bull. : *Enter one
of the Murtherers.* O., Rob., Cunn.   67–70.] As Rob., etc. : prose in O.

l. 6 : ' That ears't did follow *thy
proud Chariot wheeles*, When thou
didst ride in *tryumph* through the
streets.'
    54. *Now . . . about*] i.e. not till
now, when he has an army, could
he look upon him with confidence.
    56, 57. *Hold . . . hope*] Printed
as one line in the Octavo, and also
by Robinson and Cunningham, who
make it a pentameter by omitting
Duke of.
    57. *Enter . . .*] The murderer
comes forward from the inner stage.
    67. *Yet Caesar shall go forth*] This
is an important line for textual
students of the play, for it is
verbatim from *Julius Caesar*, II.
ii. 28 : ' Yet Caesar shall go forth.'
Dr. Greg writes : ' We may suppose that the echoes [see also
pp. 227, 245 for others] were introduced by actors in performance or
by a reporter in his reconstruction
of the play. . . . The borrowing

must have been from the play as
acted . . . [as Julius Caesar] was
not printed till 1623. If the
borrowing was from Shakespeare's
play as preserved, it implies a date
for the printing of *The Massacre*
hardly before 1600 : on the other
hand, it is possible that Shakespeare took the phrase (as he may
have taken ' Et tu, Brute ') from
some earlier play on the subject,
or even that, as some have supposed, an earlier version of Shakespeare's play once existed ' (*op. cit.*,
ix.).   We may add that there are
two other references to Caesar in
The Massacre : see below l. 87 and
Sc. II. l. 98, as well as several
allusions to Roman history (see
note on Sc. XVI. ll. 56, 57), and
further that Wm. Wells, *The Authorship of Julius Caesar*, 1923, and J. M.
Robertson, *The Shakespeare Canon*,
1922, both argue that Marlowe was
the original author of *Julius Caesar*.

Let mean consaits and baser men fear death :
Tut, they are peasants ; I am Duke of Guise ;
And princes with their looks engender fear.   70

First Murd. [*within*] Stand close ; he is coming ; I know
him by his voice.

Guise. As pale as ashes ! nay, then, 'tis time
To look about.

First and Sec. Murderers. Down with him, down with him !
[*They stab Guise.*

Guise. O, I have my death's wound ! give me leave to speak.

Sec. Murd. Then pray to God, and ask forgiveness of the
king.

Guise. Trouble me not ; I ne'er offended him,
Nor will I ask forgiveness of the king.
O, that I have not power to stay my life,
Nor immortality to be reveng'd !   80
To die by peasants, what a grief is this !
Ah, Sixtus, be reveng'd upon the king !

68. *consaits*] O. : *conceits* Rob., etc.   71. *First Murd.* [*within*]] Dyce,
Bull.: I. O.: 2 *Murd.* [*without*] Rob., Cunn.   *he is*] O., etc.: *he's* Rob.,
Cunn.   73. *'tis*] O., Rob., Dyce¹, Cunn.: *it is* Dyce², Bull.   73,74.] As
Dyce², Bull.: prose in O., Rob., Dyce¹, Cunn.   74.] Dyce, Bull. add
Enter First and Second Murderers : Rob., Cunn. add *Enter Murderers.*
74. *First . . . Murderers.*] Dyce, Bull.: *All.* O., Rob., Cunn.   75. *I
. . . wound !*] O., etc.: *I've my death-wound !* Rob., Cunn.

68, 69. *Let : . . . Guise*] These
lines again are reminiscent of
Caesar's speeches in II. ii. of *Julius
Caesar.*
68. *consaits*] an Elizabethan
spelling of *conceits* : here used in
the sense of mental capacity,
understanding.
71. *First Murd.* [*within*]] Within
the inner stage.
73. *As pale as ashes !*] Dyce took
this to refer to Guise, and somewhat
fantastically conjectures that he
must have seen himself in a mirror
as he uttered these words. He was
probably led to this supposition by
his reading in Anquetil's *Hist. de
France,* v. 463 : 'A peine il (Guise)
fut entre, que, soit indisposition
naturelle, soit frayeur, fruit de la

reflection, *il devint pale*' . . . But
as his next words show—'*tis time
to look about*—Guise evidently refers
to the ghastly look of the murderer
(see above, l. 58). For Marlowe's
theory of paleness, due to passion,
see *Tamburlaine,* II. i. 17 ff. The
phrase ' 'tis time to look about '
was evidently common. Cf. *Mucedorus,* I. iv. 1 : 'When heapes of
harmes do houer overhead, *Tis time*
as then, some say, *to looke about*',
and *Lear,* iv. vii. 92.
74.] There is no need for the S.D.
Enter Murderers, etc. (see *Text
Note*). As explained on l. 25,
Guise steps into ' the next room '
where they are in hiding (l. 10).
82. *Sixtus*] Pope Sixtus V was
one of Guise's allies. He excom-

Philip and Parma, I am slain for you!
Pope, excommunicate, Philip, depose
The wicked branch of curs'd Valois his line!
Vive la messe! perish Huguenots!
Thus Caesar did go forth, and thus he died.　　[*Dies.*

Enter the Captain of the Guard.

Cap. What, have you done?
Then stay a while, and I'll go call the king.
But see, where he comes.　　　　　　　　　　90

Enter KING HENRY, EPERNOUN, *and* Attendants.

My lord, see, where the Guise is slain.
Henry. Ah, this sweet sight is physic to my soul!
Go fetch his son for to behold his death.—

　　　　　　　　　　　　[*Exit an Attendant.*

Surcharg'd with guilt of thousand massacres,
Monsieur of Lorraine, sink away to hell!
And, in remembrance of those bloody broils,

---

85. *curs'd*] Dyce, Bull. : *curst* O., Rob., Cunn.　85. *Valois his*] O., etc. : *Valois's* Rob., Coll. conj. (MS.).　86. *messe !*] Rob., etc. : *messa*, O. 87. *died.*] O., Dyce, Bull. : *dies.* Rob., Cunn.　88–90.] As Rob., etc. : prose in O.　90. *Enter . . .*] Dyce, Bull. : *Enter King and Epernoune* Rob., Cunn. : *omit* O.　93. *Exit . . .*] Dyce, Bull. : *omit* O., Rob., Cunn. 96. *And, in*] O., Dyce, Bull. : *In just* Rob., Cunn.

municated Henry of Navarre, and strongly supported both the League and the Armada. See above, Sc. XVI. l. 39.

83. *Philip*] Philip II of Spain was also a strong supporter of the Duke of Guise, to whom he gave a pension of 600,000 golden crowns.

83. *Parma*] Alexander Farnese (1545–1592), Duke of Parma, was the great leader of the Spanish forces who subjected the Netherlands, and one of the most doughty soldiers against whom Henry IV was destined to fight. Cf. *Faustus*, 121 : 'And chase the *Prince of Parma* from our land.'

85. *The wicked . . . line !*] Collier (MS.) would read 'The wicked branch of curséd Valois's

line' and adds 'How absurd to keep *his*, see Sc. XXI. l. 95 [94]'. But see also Sc. XX. l. 7 : 'And root Valoys his line,' etc.

87. *Thus . . . died.*] See above, l. 67. Is there a reminiscence of this scene in Dekker's *The Wonderful Year* (1603), Grosart's ed., I. 146 : 'Like the fellow that described the villainous motion of *Iulius Caesar* and the Duke of *Guise*, who (as he gave it out) fought a combat together'?

95. *Monsieur of Lorraine*] i.e. the Duke of Guise. The house of Lorraine, from which the Guises came, was one of the oldest and most powerful of France. See above, Sc. XVI. l. 52.

To which thou didst allure me, being alive ;
And here in presence of you all, I swear,
I ne'er was king of France until this hour.
This is the traitor that hath spent my gold   100
In making foreign wars and civil broils.
Did he not draw a sort of English priests
From Douay to the seminary at Rheims,
To hatch forth treason 'gainst their natural queen ?
Did he not cause the king of Spain's huge fleet
To threaten England, and to menace me ?
Did he not injure Monsieur that's deceas'd ?
Hath he not made me, in the Pope's defence,
To spend the treasure, that should strength my land,
In civil broils between Navarre and me ?   110
Tush, to be short, he meant to make me monk,
Or else to murder me, and so be king.
Let Christian princes, that shall hear of this,
(As all the world shall know our Guise is dead),
Rest satisfied with this, that here I swear,
Ne'er was there king of France so yok'd as I.

Eper. My lord, here is his son.

Enter GUISE'S Son.

101. *civil*] O., Dyce, Bull. : *cruel* Rob., Cunn.

102. *sort*] a number of persons associated together in some way. Compare Jonson's *Every Man in his Humour*, I. v. 19 : ' I was requested to supper, last night, by a *sort* of gallants.'

103. *Douay*] Douai, in Belgium, was a famous theological college established in 1568, under William Parsons. It was under the patronage of the King of Spain, and in 1578 the insurgents against Spain, urged on by Queen Elizabeth's emissaries, expelled the students from Douai, as being partisans of the enemy. Allen, the principal, moved his students to Rheims under the protection of Guise, and it was here that the Douai version of the Scriptures was begun. The ' treason ' was the hatching of the Babington conspiracy, 1586.

105. *the king . . . fleet*] The Armada of 1588. Collier says that therefore ' we may conclude that it was produced soon after this date '. But Henry is only recapitulating his grievances against Guise.

109. *strength*] O.E.D. gives examples of this, including one from Tusser. See his *Five Hundred Points*, etc., 46 :
' Marsh wall too slight, *strength* now,
     or god night.'

114. (*As all . . . dead*.)] Cf. *The Jew of Malta*, Prologue, 3 : ' And now the Guise is dead . . .'

116. *so yok'd*] so coupled, and therefore curbed. Cf. line 141, *post* : ' Nay, etc.'

Henry. Boy, look, where your father lies.

G.'s Son. My father slain ! who hath done this deed ?

Henry. Sirrah, 'twas I that slew him ; and will slay   120
    Thee too, and thou prove such a traitor.

G.'s Son. Art thou king, and hast done this bloody deed ?
    I'll be reveng'd.   *[Offers to throw his dagger.*

Henry. Away to prison with him ! I'll clip his wings
    Or e'er he pass my hands. Away with him.
        [Some of the Attendants bear off Guise's Son.
    But what availeth that this traitor's dead,
    When Duke Dumaine, his brother, is alive,
    And that young cardinal that is grown so proud ?
    Go to the governor of Orleans,
    And will him, in my name, to kill the duke.   130
        [To the Captain of the Guard.
    Get you away, and strangle the cardinal.
        [To the Murderers.
    [Exeunt Captain of the Guard and Murderers.
    These two will make one entire Duke of Guise,
    Especially with our old mother's help.

Eper. My lord, see, where she comes, as if she droop'd
    To hear these news.

Henry. And let her droop ; my heart is light enough.

    Enter CATHERINE *the* QUEEN-MOTHER.

    Mother, how like you this device of mine ?
    I slew the Guise, because I would be king.

Cath. King ! why, so thou wert before :
    Pray God thou be a king now this is done !   140

Henry. Nay, he was king, and countermanded me :

120, 121.] As Rob., etc. : prose in O. So in 124, 125. 121. *and*] O. :
an Rob., etc. 125. *Some . . . Son.*] Dyce, Bull. : *Exit Boy.* O. : *The
Attendants bear off the Boy.* Rob., Cunn. 128. *that is*] O., Dyce, Bull. :
that's Rob., Cunn. 130, 131.] Stage directions added by Rob., etc. :
omit O. 134, 135.] As Rob., etc. : prose in O. 136. *Enter . . .*] Dyce,
Cunn., Bull. : after line 135 O., Rob.

130. *will*] order. Commonly   ' We will and command ', etc.
used by kings, as in the phrase

But now I will be king, and rule myself,
And make the Guisians stoop that are alive.
Cath. I cannot speak for grief.—When thou wast born,
I would that I had murder'd thee, my son !
My son ! thou art a changeling, not my son :
I curse thee, and exclaim thee miscreant,
Traitor to God and to the realm of France !
Henry. Cry out, exclaim, howl till thy throat be hoarse !
The Guise is slain, and I rejoice therefore :   150
And now will I to arms.   Come, Epernoun,
And let her grieve her heart out, if she will.
                                        [*Exit with Epernoun.*
Cath. Away ! leave me alone to meditate.
                                        [*Exeunt Attendants.*
Sweet Guise, would he had died, so thou wert here !
To whom shall I bewray my secrets now,
Or who will help to build religion ?
The Protestants will glory and insult ;
Wicked Navarre will get the crown of France ;
The Popedom cannot stand ; all goes to wrack ;
And all for thee, my Guise ! What may I do ? 160
But sorrow seize upon my toiling soul !
For, since the Guise is dead, I will not live. [*Exit.*

153. *Exeunt . . .*] Rob., etc. : *omit* O.   159. *wrack*] O., Rob., Dyce,
Cunn. : *wreck* Dyce², Bull.

146. *changeling*] An allusion to the popular belief that the fairies would steal a child at birth, and leave a less favoured child in his place. See *1 Henry IV*, I. i. 87 :

' O that it could be proved
That some night-tripping fairy had exchanged
In cradle clothes, our children where they lay,
And call'd mine Percy, his Plantagenet ! '

and see note on those lines in Arden edn. for many references.
147. *exclaim*] cry out against, proclaim loudly. The O.E.D. gives no other example earlier than 1782, and marks it as a rare and obsolete use of the word.
155. *bewray*] make known, divulge. Compare *Titus Andronicus*, II. iv. 3 : ' Write down thy mind, *bewray* thy meaning so.'
161. *toiling soul*] struggling or striving, either against the wickedness of the world and of her enemies, or perhaps against her own weakness of health, which was to bring her death a few days later on 5 January 1589.
162. *Exit.*] The Queen goes out, and the traverse is drawn, thus shutting off the body of Guise from view.

SCENE XIX

Enter two Murderers, *dragging in the* CARDINAL.

Card. Murder me not ; I am a cardinal.

First Murd. Wert thou the Pope, thou mightst not 'scape
from us.

Card. What, will you file your hands with churchmen's blood ?

Sec. Murd. Shed your blood ! O Lord, no ! for we intend
to strangle you.

Card. Then there is no remedy, but I must die ?

First Murd. No remedy ; therefore prepare yourself.

Card. Yet lives my brother Duke Dumaine, and many moe,
To revenge our deaths upon that cursed king ;
Upon whose heart may all the Furies gripe,   10
And with their paws drench his black soul in hell !

First Murd. Yours, my Lord Cardinal, you should have
said.—   [*They strangle him.*
So, pluck amain :

Scene xix.

Ed. : *omit* O., Dyce : [*Act III,*] *Scene iii* Rob., Cunn : *Scene xxii* Bull. :
Sc. xviii Greg. 6. *there is*] O., Dyce, Bull. : *there's* Rob., Cunn.
8. *moe,*] O. : *mo*, Bull. : *more*, Rob., Dyce, Cunn. 9. *revenge*] O., etc. :
'venge Rob. *deaths*] O., Dyce[1], Bull. : *death* Rob., Dyce[2], Cunn. 13.
They . . . him] Rob., etc. : *Now they strangle him.* O. 13-15.] As
Dyce, Bull. : prose in O., Rob., Cunn.

Scene XIX.

Scene XIX.] We have little to help us to localise this scene. Sufficient indication, however, is given the audience from the previous scene and from the first words ' I am a Cardinal ', for them to be able to provide their own setting —either in prison, or near the Cardinal's palace, etc.—it is of no great importance.

3. *file*] defile, stain, as in Tourneur's *Revenger's Tragedy*, II : ' A word that I abhor to *file* my lips with ', or Spenser's *Faerie Queene*, III. i. 62 : ' She lightly lept out of her *filed* bed.'

8. *moe*] as frequently in Elizabethan literature instead of our word more.

9. *our deaths*] i.e. The Duke of Guise's and his own. Robinson, etc.,

without giving any reason, alter to *our death*.

11. *drench*] plunge or overwhelm seems the necessary connotation here. Compare this passage with *Tamburlaine*, Part II, Act III. v. 21 ff., where Orcanes anticipates the progress of his foe ' to the lake of hell : Where legions of devils . . . Stretching their monstrous paws, grin with their teeth, And guard the gates to entertain his soul.'

13. *amain*] violently, as in Coryat's *Crudities* (1611), p. 215 : ' Two days after it rained *amain*.' See also *The Jew of Malta*, IV. ii. 22. The whole situation and wording of this passage and that in *The Jew* should be noted.

He is hard-hearted ; therefore pull with violence.
Come, take him away.   [*Exeunt with the body.*

SCENE XX

Enter DUMAINE, *reading a letter ; with others.*

Dum. My noble brother murder'd by the king !
O, what may I do for to revenge thy death ?
The king's alone, it cannot satisfy.
Sweet Duke of Guise, our prop to lean upon,
Now thou art dead, here is no stay for us.
I am thy brother, and I'll revenge thy death,
And root Valoys his line from forth of France ;
And beat proud Bourbon to his native home,
That basely seeks to join with such a king,
Whose murderous thoughts will be his overthrow. 10
He will'd the governor of Orleans, in his name,
That I with speed should have been put to death ;
But that's prevented, for to end his life,

15. *Exeunt . . . body.*] Dyce, Bull. : *Exeunt* O., Rob., Cunn.

Scene xx.

Ed. : *omit* O., Rob., Dyce, Cunn. : *Scene xxiii* Bull. : *Sc. xix* Greg.
2. *for*] O., Dyce, Bull. : *omit* Rob., Cunn.

7. *Valoys his*] O. : *Valois his* Dyce, etc. : *Valois's* Rob.

Scene XX.

Scene XX.] An open place : the need for secrecy gives rise to Dumaine's words in ll. 32–3, which close the scene and cause the speakers to retire to some more private place.

3. *The king's alone*] sc. death. The word *it* emphatically repeats the subject : *The king's death.*

4, 5. *Sweet Duke . . . us*] See above, on Sc. xv. ll. 1, 2 ; and compare with *3 Henry VI*, II. i. 68–9 :

' Sweet Duke of York, our prop to lean upon
Now thou art gone, we have no staff, no stay.'

and with *The True Tragedy*, sig. B4 :

' Sweet Duke of Yorke our prop to leane upon,
Now thou art gone there is no hope for us.'

7. *Valoys his line*] See note on Sc. XVI. l. 31.

8. *proud Bourbon*] i.e. Henry of Navarre. He was of the great house of Bourbon, being the son of Antony of Bourbon and Jeanne, Queen of Navarre.

11. *He*] i.e. Henry III. See Sc. xviii. l. 130.

17

And all those traitors to the Church of Rome
That durst attempt to murder noble Guise.

Enter Friar.

Fri. My lord, I come to bring you news that your brother,
the Cardinal of Lorraine, by the king's consent, is lately
strangled unto death.

Dum. My brother Cardinal slain, and I alive ?
O words of power to kill a thousand men !   20
Come, let us away, and levy men ;
'Tis war that must assuage this tyrant's pride.

Fri. My lord, hear me but speak.
I am a friar of the order of the Jacobins,
That for my conscience' sake will kill the king.

Dum. But what doth move thee, above the rest, to do the
deed ?

Fri. O, my lord, I have been a great sinner in my days,
and the deed is meritorious.

14. *And*] Rob., etc. : *His life, and* O.   19. *Cardinal*] O., Rob. : [*the*]
Cardinal Dyce, Bull., Cunn.   21. *let us*] O., Dyce, Bull. : *let's* Rob. : *let us*
[*straight*] Cunn.   23, 24.] Two lines, first ending *am*, Cunn.

14. *And . . . Rome*] The Octavo
line beginning *His life, and . . .*
would make an alexandrine. This
is possible, but all the editors have
agreed that it is most probable that
His life is a printer's accidental
repetition of the words at the end of
the preceding line.

19. *brother Cardinal*] I have
ventured to leave the Octavo reading. It is a perfectly possible
Elizabethan construction, and the
line scans better unamended.

21. *Come, . . . men !*] Cf.
Edward II, II. ii. 98 : ' *Come
Edmund let's away, and levy men.*'

23, 24.] Cunningham spoils the
force of line 23, which well answers
the Friar's purpose of arresting
attention, by tacking on *I am* from
line 24.

24. *the Jacobins*] The friars of the
order of S. Dominic were called
Jacobins, from the church of S.
Jacques, in Paris, which was given

to them and near which they built
their first convent (Littré). Cf.
The Jew of Malta, IV. i. 107.

29. *the deed is meritorious*] Cf. *2
Henry VI*, III. i. 270 : ' Seeing the
deed is meritorious.' There was
evidently much discussion in England about the Pope's justification of
the murder of Henry III. See the
following work, containing an
epistle signed ' R.W.' : ' Martine
Marsixtus. A second replie against
the defensory and Apology of
Sixtus the fifth late Pope of *Rome*,
defending the execrable fact of the
Iacobine Friar, vpon the person
of *Henry* the third, . . . *to be
both commendable, admirable, and
meritorious . . . 1591* ' (Tucker
Brooke). Cf. also *King John*, III. i.
176 ff. : 'And *meritorious* shall that
hand be call'd Canonised and wor-
shipp'd as a saint, That takes away
by any secret course, Thy hateful
life.'

Dum. But how wilt thou get opportunity ?   30
Fri. Tush, my lord, let me alone for that.
Dum. Friar, come with me ;
    We will go talk more of this within.   [*Exeunt.*

SCENE XXI

Drums and Trumpets. Enter KING HENRY, *the* KING OF
NAVARRE, EPERNOUN, BARTUS, PLESHÉ, Soldiers, *and*
Attendants.

Henry. Brother of Navarre, I sorrow much
    That ever I was prov'd your enemy,
    And that the sweet and princely mind you bear
    Was ever troubled with injurious wars.
    I vow, as I am lawful King of France,
    To recompense your reconciled love
    With all the honours and affections
    That ever I vouchsaf'd my dearest friends.
Nav. It is enough if that Navarre may be
    Esteemed faithful to the King of France,   10
    Whose service he may still command till death.
Henry. Thanks to my kingly brother of Navarre.
    Then here we'll lie before Lutetia walls,
    Girting this strumpet city with our siege,
    Till, surfeiting with our afflicting arms,
    She cast her hateful stomach to the earth.

Scene xxi.
Ed.: *omit* O., Dyce: [*Act III,*] *Scene iv.* Rob., Cunn. : *Scene xiv.*
Bull.: *Sc. xx* Greg. *Drums . . .*] *Sound Drumme . . . and enter the King
of France, and Nauarre . . . and Souldiers.* O.
    13. *Lutetia walls,*] Dyce, Bull. : *Lucrecia walles,* O. : *Lutetia's walls,*
Rob., Cunn.

31. *Tush, . . . that.*] A common
form reply. See *supra,* Sc. VIII. l. 38
and Sc. XI. l. 61.

Scene XXI.
Scene XXI.] A Council chamber
again, and the whole stage in use—
Henry seated in the inner stage on
his chair of state.
    13. *Lutetia*] Paris : the old name

of Paris being *Lutetia Parisiorum.*
The original edition's *Lucrecia* is a
misprint.
    14. *Girting*] encircling as in a
girdle. See Greene's *Orlando
Furioso* (ed. C. Collins), I. ii. 369 :
' But trust me princes, I have *girt*
his fort, And I will sack it.'
    16. *stomach*] Used to denote a
proud or haughty adversary. Com-

Enter a Messenger.

Mes. And it please your majesty, here is a friar of the order
of the Jacobins, sent from the President of Paris, that
craves access unto your grace.

Henry. Let him come in.   *[Exit Mess.* 20

Enter Friar, *with a letter.*

Eper. I like not this friar's look :
'Twere not amiss, my lord, if he were search'd.

Henry. Sweet Epernoun, our friars are holy men,
And will not offer violence to their king,
For all the wealth and treasure of the world.
Friar, thou dost acknowledge me thy king ?

Fri. Ay, my good lord, and will die therein.

Henry. Then come thou near, and tell what news thou
bring'st.

Fri. My lord,
The President of Paris greets your grace   30
And sends his duty by these speedy lines,
Humbly craving your gracious reply.   *[Gives letter.*

Henry. I'll read them, friar, and then I'll answer thee.

17. *And*] O. : *An* Rob., etc.   20. *Exit . . .*] Dyce, Bull. : *omit* the rest.
29–32.] As Rob., etc. : prose in O.   32. *Gives letter.*] Dyce, Bull. : *omit*
the rest.

pare *Henry VIII*, IV. ii. 34 : ' He
was a man of unbounded *stomach*,
ever ranking himself with princes.'
There is also a quibble with *cast*,
in the sense of ' to vomit '. Compare *Macbeth*, II. iii. 39 : ' though
he [i.e. drink] took up my legs sometime, yet I made a shift to cast
him '; and cf. North ; Plutarch,
Antonius : ' he, being queasy-
stomached with the surfeit he had
taken, was compelled to lay all
before them ', etc. See for *cast* and
another quibble, Jonson, *Every Man
in his Humour*, I. iii. 54.

18. *President of Paris*] i.e. The
President of the *Parlement* is here
meant. ' Quand les confidents de
son dessein furent bien assurés de sa
(Clément's) resolution, ils lui re-

mirent, comme lettre de recom-
mandation auprès le Roi, un faux
billet en italien *du premier président*,
Achille de Harlay, prisonnier à la
Bastille ' (Lavisse, *Hist. de France*,
VI. i. 299).

20. *Enter Friar*] The murderer of
Henry III was a Dominican, only
23 years of age, by name Jacques
Clément. He was the son of a
peasant, and of a most excitable
nature.

31. *speedy*] hasty, quick-written.
Compare the O.E.D. quotation
from Willis's *Stenographie* (1602),
Aiib : ' Secondly, in *speedie* writing :
For he that is well practized in this
art, may write verbatim, as fast as a
man can treateably speak.'

Fri. Sancte Jacobe, now have mercy upon me !
    [*Stabs the king with a knife, as he reads the letter ; and
       then the king gets the knife, and kills him.*
Eper. O, my lord, let him live a while !
Henry. No, let the villain die, and feel in hell
    Just torments for his treachery.
Nav. What, is your highness hurt ?
Henry. Yes, Navarre ; but not to death, I hope.
Nav. God shield your grace from such a sudden death ! 40
    Go call a surgeon hither straight.　[*Exit an Attendant.*
Henry. What irreligious pagans' parts be these,
    Of such as hold them of the holy church !
    Take hence that damned villain from my sight.
             Attendants carry out the Friar's body.
Eper. Ah, had your highness let him live,
    We might have punish'd him to his deserts !
Henry. Sweet Epernoun, all rebels under heaven
    Shall take example by his punishment,
    How they bear arms against their sovereign.
    Go call the English agent hither straight :　　　50
                 [*Exit an Attendant.*
    I'll send my sister England news of this,
    And give her warning of her treacherous foes.

          Enter a Surgeon.

Nav. Pleaseth your grace to let the surgeon search your
    wound ?

34. *Jacobe*] Dyce, Cunn., Bull. : *Jacobus* O., Rob.　36, 37.] As Rob.,
etc. : prose in O.　41. *Exit* . . .] Dyce, Cunn., Bull. : *omit* O., Rob.
44. *Attendants* . . . *body*] Dyce, Cunn., Bull. : *omit* O., Rob.　47–49.]
As Rob., etc. : prose in O.　48. *his*] Rob., etc. : *their* O.　50. *Exit* . . .
Attendant] Dyce, Bull. : *omit* O., Rob., Cunn.　52. *Enter* . . . *Surgeon*]
Rob., etc. : *omit* O.

42. *parts*] personal qualities or
attributes. See *Much Ado*, v. ii. 64 :
' For which of my bad *parts* didst
thou fall in love with me ? '
43. *hold them*] esteem, consider,
themselves.
48. *his*] The Octavo *their* is probably a mistake due to the word
occurring in the next line.

50. *the English agent*]　Sir
Edward Stafford, the English ambassador to France, had been
called home in March and did not
return until September.　Henry
was assassinated on the 21 July
(O.S.), so the Agent at the time must
have been a deputy.
53, 54. *search your wound*] probe

Henry. The wound, I warrant ye, is deep, my lord.
      Search, surgeon, and resolve me what thou see'st.
                        [*The Surgeon searches the wound.*

                  Enter the English Agent.

      Agent for England, send thy mistress word
      What this detested Jacobin hath done.
      Tell her, for all this, that I hope to live ;
      Which if I do, the papal monarch goes   60
      To wrack, and [th'] antichristian kingdom falls.
      These bloody hands shall tear his triple crown,
      And fire accursed Rome about his ears ;
      I'll fire his crazed buildings, and enforce
      The papal towers to kiss the lowly earth.
      Navarre, give me thy hand : I here do swear
      To ruinate that wicked Church of Rome,
      That hatcheth up such bloody practices ;
      And here protest eternal love to thee,
      And to the Queen of England specially,   70
      Whom God hath bless'd for hating papistry.
Nav. These words revive my thoughts, and comforts me,
      To see your highness in this virtuous mind.
Henry. Tell me, surgeon, shall I live ?

---

   55. *ye*] O., Dyce, Bull.: *you* Rob., Cunn.   60, 61.] As Dyce, etc.:
divided after *wrack* in O., Rob.   61. *and*[*th'*]] Dyce², Cunn., Bull.: *and*
O., Rob.   64. *enforce*] Coll. (MS.), Dyce², Cunn., Bull.: *incense* O.,
Rob., Dyce¹.   65. *lowly*] Dyce, Cunn., Bull.: *holy* O., Rob.   67. *that*]
O., Dyce, Bull.: *this* Rob., Cunn.   70. *specially*] O., etc.: *especially* Rob.
71. *papistry*] O., Dyce, Bull.: *papestry* O.: *popery* Rob., Cunn.   72.
comforts] O.: *comfort* Rob., etc.

your wound, as in *Titus An-dronicus*, II. iii. 262 : ' Now to the bottom dost thou *search my wound* ', or Donne's *Poems* (1633), p. 150 : ' So . . , nice in *searching wounds* the Surgeon is.'

   64, 65. *I'll fire . . . earth*] Dyce notes the similarity of this passage with the lines in *Edward II*, I. iv. 100, 101 : ' *I'll fire* thy crazed *buildings*, and *enforce The papal towers to kiss the lowly* ground.' This may be due to Marlowe, but more probably to an actor's memory proving faulty, and confusing diatribes against Rome which occur in the two plays. In any case the alterations of Dyce (following this passage from *Ed. II*) are necessary to make sense. Collier (MS.) after reading Dyce's conjecture in his first edition, ' Should it be enforce ? ' adds ' Of course. What silly timidity ! '

   68. *practices*] plots as commonly.

Surg. Alas, my lord, the wound is dangerous,
> For you are stricken with a poison'd knife !

Henry. A poison'd knife ! what, shall the French king die,
> Wounded and poison'd both at once ?

Eper.   O, that
> That damned villain were alive again,
> That we might torture him with some new-found
>   death !   80

Bar. He died a death too good :
> The devil of hell torture his wicked soul !

Henry. Ah, curse him not, sith he is dead !
> O, the fatal poison works within my breast !
> Tell me, surgeon, and flatter not—may I live ?

Surg. Alas, my lord, your highness cannot live !

Nav. Surgeon, why say'st thou so ? the king may live.

Henry. O, no, Navarre ! thou must be king of France !

Nav. Long may you live, and still be King of France.

Eper. Or else, die Epernoun !   90

Henry. Sweet Epernoun, thy king must die.—My lords,
> Fight in the quarrel of this valiant prince,
> For he's your lawful king, and my next heir ;
> Valoyses line ends in my tragedy.
> Now let the house of Bourbon wear the crown ;
> And may it ne'er end in blood, as mine hath done !
> Weep not, sweet Navarre, but revenge my death.
> Ah, Epernoun, is this thy love to me ?
> Henry, thy king, wipes off these childish tears,
> And bids thee whet thy sword on Sixtus' bones, 100

75, 76.] As Rob.: prose in O. 78–79. *O,...*] As Dyce, etc.: one line in O.,
Rob. 81–82.] As Rob., etc.: prose in O. So in 83–85. 91.] As Rob., etc.:
divided after *die* in O. 93. *he's*] *he is* O. 96. *may it*] O., Dyce, Bull :
may't Rob., Cunn. *ne'er*] Rob. to Bull.: *neuer* O. 100. *Sixtus*] *Sextus* O.

76. *For . . . a poison'd knife !*] A
touch of Marlowe's own, truckling
to the wishes of his audience.
Henry was seriously wounded, but
his physicians at first assured him
that in ten days he would be on
horse-back once again. In the
evening, however, he took a turn

for the worse, and died on the
2nd August 1589.
100. *Sixtus' bones,*] This may,
perhaps, be taken as an indication
that Pope Sixtus V was dead when
the play was written. He died on
17th August 1590. The reference
to the corpse of the Pope is

That it may keenly slice the Catholics.
He loves me not [the most] that sheds most tears,
But he that makes most lavish of his blood.
Fire Paris, where these treacherous rebels lurk.
I die, Navarre ; come bear me to my sepulchre.
Salute the Queen of England in my name,
And tell her, Henry dies her faithful friend.   [*Dies.*

Nav. Come, lords, take up the body of the king,
That we may see it honourably interr'd :
And then I vow so to revenge his death   110
As Rome, and all those popish prelates there,
Shall curse the time that e'er Navarre was king,
And rul'd in France by Henry's fatal death.

> [*They march out, with the body of King Henry lying on
> four men's shoulders, with a dead march, drawing
> weapons on the ground.*

FINIS.

102. [*the most*]] Dyce², Cunn., Bull. : *omit* O. : *the best* Rob., Dyce¹.
110. *so*] Rob., etc. : *for* O.   111. *As*] O., Dyce, etc. : *That* Rob.

therefore, an anachronism in the mouth of Henry.

101. *slice*] used in the sense of cut, as with a sword, is a favourite word in *Tamburlaine*, cf. IV. ii. 1 ff. : ' Ye holy priests of heavenly Mahomet, That sacrificing *slice* and cut your flesh,' and IV. iv. 41, etc.

102. [*the most*]] All the editors have felt a need to complete this four-foot line by some addition. Robinson proposed *the best*, but Dyce's *the most* has been adopted by both Cunningham and Bullen. It might, perhaps, be argued that there is no absolute need to alter the Octavo reading.

103. *lavish*] In this substantive use, O.E.D. quotes Nash's address *To the Gentlemen Students of both Universities*, prefixed to Greene's *Menaphon*, 1589 : ' with the sweete satietie of eloquence, which the *lauish* of our copious language maie procure.' (Arber's *English Scholars' Library*, p. 8.)

110. *I vow . . . death*] The presentation of Navarre as arch-enemy of the Catholics and leader of the

Protestant forces must have been felt to be infelicitous, after his acceptance of the Roman Catholic faith in July 1593.   Cf. Spenser's rebuke to him as Burbon, in *Faerie Queene*, V. xi. xlix ff.

110. *so to revenge*] The Octavo *for to revenge* was altered by Robinson, and the change has been accepted by all subsequent editors.   *For to revenge*, as we have seen (see on Sc. VIII. l. 32), is a frequent enough construction in *The Massacre*, but it does not sort well with the next line.   Dyce suggested that the MS. read *soe*, which the compositor misread as *for*.   I should prefer to think it a mistake due to the use of *for* with the infinitive running in the mind of either the person who furnished the copy of the Octavo, or of the compositor.   Note that it occurs no less than seven times, viz. for to lament (VIII. 32) ; for to revenge (VIII. 37) ; for to be done (X. 19) ; for to behold (XVIII. 93) ; for to end (XX. 13) ; and XX. 2 and XXI. 110.

APPENDICES

APPENDIX A

THE 'COLLIER LEAF'

NO editor of *The Massacre* can afford to ignore the existence of what is known as the 'Collier Leaf'. This is
a version of Scene XVI which was first printed by
J. P. Collier in 1825. In Volume VIII, p. 244, of his edition
of Dodsley's *Old Plays*, as part of his introduction to *The
Jew of Malta*, he wrote thus :

'A curious MS. fragment of one quarto leaf of this tragedy [The
Massacre] came into the hands of Mr. Rodd of Newport-street not
long since, which, as it very materially differs from the printed
edition, is here inserted *literatim* : it perhaps formed part of
a copy belonging to the theatre at the time it was first acted,
and it would be still more valuable should any accident hereafter show that it is in the original hand-writing of Marlow.
It relates to the death of a character called Mugeron in the old
printed copy, without date, but who in the MS. is called Minion.'
Then follows the transcript.

In 1831, Collier again published his transcript (with alterations), with the following note in his *History of English Dramatic
Poetry* (iii. 133) :

'With regard to this play, I am in possession of a singular
proof, if any were wanted, of the imperfect state in which it
appears in the old printed copy, published perhaps from what
could be taken down in short-hand, or otherwise, during the
representation. I have a single leaf of an original contemporary
MS. of this play, possibly, as it came from the hands of Marlow,
which shows how much was omitted, and how injuriously the
rest was garbled. Even the names of the characters were
mistaken, and he who is called *Mugeron* in the old edition was,
in fact, called *Minion* consistently with his situation and habits.
I will copy the MS. *literatim*.' [1]

Now the two versions as printed by Collier contain a certain
number of variant readings (noted in the transcript printed

[1] When in 1879 Collier re-edited his *History* he reproduced the above
statement, but modified so as to show that he had parted with the original.

253

below), as well as minor variations of spelling and punctuation, and Professor Tucker Brooke was inclined to doubt its authenticity on the grounds that 'the spelling is absolutely different and many phrases are entirely changed, the wording of the expanded passage is very suspicious, and also because the MS. apparently had been seen by no one else.' So far as the last count is concerned it may be dismissed at once, for the fragment was purchased by J. O. Halliwell-Phillips sometime about 1887, and is included in his *Calendar of the Shakespearean Rarities at Hollingbury Copse* (1887), and was in his possession at his death. Some time later it passed into the hands of Mr. M. J. Perry, and from him to the late Mr. H. C. Folger of New York, where it remained and was not available for detailed examination.

The first charge has more substance, but is overstated. There are variants—but not many or serious. They may well be the result of a hasty reading of the original. And, lastly, the 'suspiciousness' of the expanded passage is a very difficult matter to dogmatise about. Each reader will form his own opinion of this. Pending a careful examination of the original, when that becomes possible, the balance of evidence seems to me to be in favour of the authenticity of the fragment.

Scene XVI. as printed by J. P. Collier in Dodsley's *Old Plays*,
viii. 244, 1825.

Enter a SOULDIER *w*th *a muskett.*

Souldier. Now, ser, to you y^t dares make a duke a cuckolde, and use a counterfeyt key to his privie chamber : thoughe you take out none but yor owne treasure, yet you put in y^t displeases him, and fill up his rome y^t he should occupie. Herein, ser, you forestalle the markett, and sett upe yor standinge where you shold not. But you will say you leave him rome enoughe besides : that's no answere : he's to have the choyce of his owne freeland, yf it be not to free, there's the questione. Now for where he is your landlorde, you take upon you to be his, and will needs 10 enter by defaulte. What thoughe you weere once in possession yett comminge upon you once unawares, he frayde you out againe : therefore your entrye is mere intrusion : this is against the law, ser. And thoughe I come not to keep possessione as I wolde I mighte, yet I come to keepe you out, ser.

Enter MINION.

You are welcome, ser ! have at you.   [*He kills him.*
Minion. Trayterous Guise ah, thou has morthered me !

Enter GUISE.

Guise. Hold thee, tale soldier : take thee this and flye. [*Exit.*
    Thus falls imperfett exhalation,   20
    Which our great sonn of France cold not effecte :
    A fyery meteor in the fermament.
    Lye there, the kinge's delyght and Guise's scorne !
    Revenge it, Henry if thou list or dar'st ;
    I did it onely in dispight of thee.
    Fondly hast thou incest the Guise's sowle
    That if it self was hote enoughe to worke
    Thy just degestion wth extreamest shame,
    The armye I have gathered now shall ayme :
    Now at thie end thine exterpatione :   30
    And when thou think'st I have forgotten this,
    And that thou most reposest one my faythe,
    Than will I wake thee from thy foolishe dreame,
    And lett thee see thie self my prysoner.
                              [*Exeunt.*

    The following variants occur in Collier's second version of the fragment
published in his *Hist. Dram. Poetry*, iii. 133, 1831 : 16. S.D. after 17.   18.
has] hast.   19. *thee . . . thee*] the[e] . . . the[e].   *tale*] tall.   20. *falls*]
fall.   26. *incest*] incenste.   27. *if*] of.   29. *ayme :*] ayme
  30. *Now*] More.   *thine*] then.   32. *one*] in

APPENDIX B

A SHORT LIST OF EDITIONS AND AUTHORITIES

[*Note*. This list does not pretend to bibliographical complete-ness. Only the books of chief interest to a student of *The Jew of Malta* or *The Massacre at Paris* are classified. References to works of less general application will generally be found in the footnotes. Notices of the play in general histories of literature and the drama are not included.]

I. FIRST EDITIONS

(a) THE JEW OF MALTA

Entry in Stationers' Register : 1594, May 17. 'Entered for there copie vnder the hand of Master Warden Cawood, the famouse tragedie of the Riche Jewe of Malta' Nicholas Ling and Thomas Millington. VI^d (Arber's *Transcript*, II, 650.) 1632, Nov. 20 'A Tragedy called the Jew of Malta.' Nicholas Vavasour. (Arber, *op. cit.*, IV, 288.)

Title-page : The Famous | TRAGEDY | OF | THE RICH IEW | OF *MALTA*. | AS IT WAS PLAYD | BEFORE THE KING AND | QVEENE, IN HIS MAJESTIES | Theatre at *White-Hall*, by her Majefties | Servants at the Cock-pit. | *Written by* CHRISTOPHER MARLO. | Device [1] | LONDON ; | Printed by I. B. for *Nicholas Vavafour*, and are to be fold | at his Shop in the Inner-Temple, neere the | Church. 1633.

Running-title : The Iew of Malta :

Quarto. A—I in fours, K1, K2. Unpaged.

Contents : Title-page on A2, verso blank. Dedication [by T. Heywood] A3, 3^v; Prologue spoken at Court, and Epilogue ; A4 ; Prologue to the Stage, at the Cocke-pit, and Epilogue A4^v. Text begins on B1, and ends on K2^v.

---

[1] I have been unable to identify this device, which does not occur in Dr. McKerrow's *Printers' Devices*. Dr. McKerrow has been good enough to examine it for me, but can refer me to no other example of its use.

Printer : The printer was John Beale, who had a press at ? Fetter Lane, 1612–1641. Nicholas Vavasour was in business first near the little door of S. Pauls, and from 1623–43 in the Inner Temple. He was made free of the Stationers' Company on 22 March, 1622.

Copies. Nine copies are known. Two at the British Museum (one imperfect) ; at the Bodleian ; in the Dyce collection, South Kensington ; at Trinity College, Cambridge ; Huntingdon Library ; Chapin Library ; the late W. A. Wight's library ; J. L. Clawson's library. The five copies in England present no variations so far as I have observed.

(b) THE MASSACRE AT PARIS

Entry in Stationers' Register : None.

Title-page : THE | MASSACRE | AT PARIS : | With the death of the Duke | of Guife. | As it was plaide by the right honourable the | Lord high *Admirall* his Seruants. | Written by *Chriftopher Marlow.* | Device, (McKerrow, Nᵒ. 290) | AT LONDON | Printed by *E. A.* for *Edward White,* dwelling neere | the little North doore of S. Paules | Church, at the figne of | the Gun.

Running-title : The *Maffacre* | at Paris. (Badly set in the first two sheets. The following pages bear the wrong half of it : A4, A5ᵛ, A6 (A8ᵛ), B3, B4, B5, B5ᵛ, B6, B6ᵛ.) On D3 it reads *ʞv Paris.* A8ᵛ is wrong in the Museum, and Bodleian copies.

Octavo. A—D in eights, unpaged.

Contents : Signature only on A1. Title page on A2, verso blank. Text begins on A3, and ends on D6ᵛ. D7, D8 are blank. (All the copies in England lack the first leaf as well as D7, 8. The White copy is similarly deficient, the Chapin copy has A1 but not D7, 8. The Huntingdon copy alone possesses all three leaves.)

Copies : At the British Museum ; Dyce collection, South Kensington ; Bodleian ; Pepys collection, Magdalene College, Cambridge ; Huntingdon Library ; Chapin Library ; the late W. A. Wight's library.

Printer : E. A. is Edward Allde, who was made free of the Stationers' Company on 18 February 1584 and continued printing until 1628. (See McKerrow, *Dict. of Printers and Booksellers,* p. 5.) Edward White, senior, was in business between 1577 and 1612. (McKerrow, *op. cit.,* p. 288.)

II. LATER EDITIONS

[*Note.* A full general description of these editions has been
given by Miss U. M. Ellis-Fermor in her edition of *Tamburlaine*
in this series, and to that the reader is referred. The following
notes supplement her information in certain particulars.]

A. Collected Works :

  The Works of Christopher Marlowe. [Ed. by G. Robinson.]
    3 vols. 1826.

  The Dramatic Works of Christopher Marlowe . . . by W.
    Oxberry. 1827.

  The Works of Christopher Marlowe . . . by the Rev. A. Dyce.
    3 vols. 1850. 1 vol. 1858, etc.

  The Works of Christopher Marlowe . . . by Lt.-Col. Francis
    Cunningham. 1 vol. 1870.

  The Works of Christopher Marlowe, edited by A. H. Bullen.
    3 vols. 1885.

  The Works of Christopher Marlowe, edited by C. F. Tucker
    Brooke. 1 vol. Oxford. 1910.

B. Selected Works :

  Christopher Marlowe : Historisch-Kritische Ausgabe hrsg. von
    H. Breymann . . . und A. Wagner. 3 vols. Heilbronn.
    1885–89.

  Christopher Marlowe. (The Best Plays of the Old Dramatists :
    Mermaid Series.) Edited by Havelock Ellis. 1 vol.
    1887.

  The Chief Elizabethan Dramatists, excluding Shakespeare,
    edited by W. A. Neilson. 1 vol. 1911.

  Christopher Marlowe. (*Masterpieces of English Drama*) Edited
    by F. E. Schelling. With Intro. by W. L. Phelps. New
    Haven. 1912.

C. Separate Editions :

(i) *The Jew of Malta.*

In Dodsley : *A Select Collection of Old Plays.* 2nd ed. . . .
    by I. Reed. Vol. 8. 1780.

In W. Scott : *The Ancient British Drama ;* ed. by W. Miller.
    Vol. 1. 1810.

In Dodsley : *A Select Collection of Old Plays.* A new edition
    by I. Reed, O. Gilchrist and [J. P. Collier]. Vol. 8.
    1825.

[ed. W. Oxberry] : *The Rich Jew of Malta,* with a biblio-
    graphical sketch of the author ; explanatory notes, etc.,
    by W. Oxberry. 1818.

APPENDICES 259

[ed. S. Penley] : The Jew of Malta . . . with considerable
alterations and additions, by S. Penley. . . . 1818.

(ii) *The Massacre at Paris.*

[ed. W. Oxberry] : *The Massacre at Paris,* with . . . explana-
tory notes, etc., by W. Oxberry. 1818.
[ed. W. W. Greg] : *The Massacre at Paris.* (The Malone
Society Reprints, 1928.)
D. Extracts :
The Dramatic Works of Christopher Marlowe. Selected.
With a prefatory notice by P. E. Pinkerton. (The
Canterbury Poets.) 1885.

III. CRITICAL AND BIBLIOGRAPHICAL

C. V. Boyer : *The Villain as Hero in Elizabethan Tragedy.* 1914.
J. le G. Brereton : *Notes on the Text of Marlowe. Beiblatt
zur Anglia.* 1905.
C. Brennan : *Notes on the Text of Marlowe. Beiblatt zur Anglia.*
1905.
K. Deighton : *The Old Dramatists.* Conjectural Readings. 1896.
K. Elze : *Notes on Elizabethan Dramatists.* Halle. 1889.
E. Meyer. *Machiavelli and the Elizabethan Drama.* Weimar.
1897.
M. Praz : *Machiavelli and the Elizabethans.* Annual Italian
Lecture of the British Academy. 1928.
E. Seaton : *Marlowe and his Authorities.* T.L.S. June 16, 1921.
E. Seaton : *Marlowe's Map.* (Essays and Studies. English
Association.) Vol. X. 1924.
E. Seaton : *Marlowe, Robert Poley and the Tippings.* Review
of English Studies. July 1929.
E. Seaton : *Fresh Sources for Marlowe.* Review of English
Studies. Oct. 1929.
J. Schipper : *De versu Marlowii.* Bonn. 1867.
C. F. Tucker Brooke : *The Marlowe Canon.* (Pub. Mod. Lang.
Assoc. Amer. xxxvii.) 1922.
C. F. Tucker Brooke : *The Reputation of Christopher Marlowe.*
(Connecticut Academy of Arts and Sciences.) 1922.
C. F. Tucker Brooke : *Marlowe's Versification and Style.* (Studies
in Philology, xix.) 1922.
C. F. Tucker Brooke : *The Life of Marlowe and Dido.* 1930.
W. Wagner : *Emendationen und Bemerkungen zu Marlowe.*
(Shakespeare—Jahrbuch.) xi, 73, 1876.

IV. The Jew of Malta

F. de Belleforest : *Cosmographie Universelle.* Paris, 1575.

J. L. Cardozo : *The Contemporary Jew in the Elizabethan Drama.* 1925.

K. Clauserus : *Laonici Chalcocondylæ Atheniensis, de origine et rebus gestis Turcorum Libri Decem, etc.* Basle. 1556.

U. Foglietta : *De sacro foedere in Selimum libri quattuor.* Geneva. 1587.

Gentillet : *Discours sur les moyens de bien gouverner . . . Contre N. Machiavel.* Paris. 1576.

H. Graetz : *History of the Jews . . .* trans. by B. Löwy. 1891.

T. Heywood : *The Captives . . .* edited by A. C. Judson. New Haven. 1921.

J. Kellner : Die Quelle von Marlowe's *Jew of Malta.* (Englische Studien, x.) 1887.

M. J. Landa : *The Jew in Drama.*

S. Lee : New Shakespeare Society's Transactions. II, 158. 1887–92.

M. A. Levy : *Don Josef Nasi, Herzog von Naxos.* Breslau. 1859.

P. Lonicerus : *Chronicorum Turcicorum tomi duo.* Frankfort. 1584.

N. de Nicolay : *The nauigations into Turkey.* Trans. by T. Washington. 1585.

W. Porter : *A history of the Knights of Malta.* 2 vols. 1858.

C. F. Tucker Brooke : *A Prototype of the Jew of Malta.* T.L.S. June 8, 1822.

M. Thimme : *Marlowe's Jew of Malta.* (Studien zur englischen Philologie, 61.) Halle. 1921.

L. Wolf : *Jews in Elizabethan England.* (Trans. Jewish Hist. Soc. Eng. xi.) 1924–27.

J. Ziegler : *Terræ Sanctæ Descriptio.* Argentorati. 1536.

V. The Massacre at Paris

C. Fetherstone : *Sixtus V. The brutish thunderbolt . . . of Pope Sixtus the fift, against Henrie , . . king of Nauarre, and . . . Henrie Borbon, Prince of Condie. . . .* Trans. by C. Fetherstone. [Black Letter.] 1586.

A. Golding : *The lyfe of . . . Jasper Colignie.* By J. de Serres. Trans. by A. Golding. 1576.

M. Hurault : *A discourse upon the present estate of France. . . .* Translated by E. Aggas. 1588.

M. Hurault : *Antisixtus. An oration of Pope Sixtus the fift, upon the death of the late French King, Henrie the third. With a confutation upon the said oration. . . . Trans. out of Latin* by A. P., 1590.

J. de Serres : *The Three Partes of Commentaries containing the whole and perfect discourse of the Civill Wars of France, &c.* 1574.

J. de Serres : *Commentaries of the Civill Warres in Fraunce and . . . Flaunders.* Part IV. 1576.

R. W. : *Martine Mar-Sixtus. A second replie against the defensory and Apology of Sixtus the fift . . . defending the Iacobine frier. . . .* [Black Letter.] 1591.

M. Wilkinson : *A History of the League.* Glasgow. 1929.

The Contre-Guyse ; wherein is deciphered the pretended title of the Guyses. 1589.

INDEX TO 'THE JEW OF MALTA'

INDEX TO 'THE MASSACRE AT PARIS'

A

Abbott's *Shakespeare Grammar*, 191, 211

Act and Scene Division, 178, 184; and *see* Stage Directions, Staging

Admiral's men and *The Massacre*, 169, 170, 171

Allde, Edward, 171, 173, 257

Alleyn, Edward, 170

B

barriers, 218

Bartus (Gillaume de Saluste Du Bartas), 222

Boas, Professor F. S., 176 *n.*

Brereton, Professor J. le G., notes by, 189, 198

Brooke, Professor C. F. T., authorship of *The Massacre*, 175; authenticity of 'Collier leaf', 254; date of the play, 171; emendation of text, 200; nature of the text, 173; sources, 176, 229, 246

Broughton, J., MS. notes of, 183, 191

Bullen, A. H., notes by, 205, 236; sources, 176, 182; textual emendations, 217, 232

burgonets, 194

C

Chamberlain's men, the Lord, 170

Chambers, Sir E. K., 197

Coligny, The Life of Jasper, trans. by A. Golding, 176; extracts from, 182, 186, 195, 196, 198, 199, 211

'*Collier leaf*', The, 174 *n.*, 253–255

Collier, J. P., MS. notes of, 231, 240, 241, 250; MS. fragment of *The Massacre*, printed by, 253–255

Commentaries on Civill Wars in France and Flanders, Part IV, 176, 208

Contention, The, 187, 192, 237

Cossin, Captain of the Guard, 196

Cunningham, F., notes by, 178, 213, 225, 236; textual notes of, 191, 208, 209, 230, 246

D

defend, 222

disports, 218

Douay, 241

drench, 244

Dyce, Alexander, notes by, 200, 205, 206, 220, 222, 229, 239; metrical notes, 185, 191; textual suggestions, 183, 190, 194, 204, 225, 237, 250, 252

E

Edward II, 173, 183, 185, 188, 217, 218, 233, 236, 246, 250

Ellis-Fermor, Miss U. M., 177, 258

entrance, 198

exhibition, 230

F

Faustus, Dr., 187, 189

fuelled, 151

G

Golding, A., 176

Greg, Dr. W. W., 169, 170, 172 *n.*, 173, 174, 178, 193

Gwies, guesse, gvyes tragedy, 169, 170, 174

H

Henslowe, Philip, 169, 170

Henslowe's *Diary*, 169

3 Henry VI, 173 *n.*, 227, 245

holy league, 230

I

inventions, 222

J

Jew of Malta, The, 173, 241, 244]

juror, 230

L

lavish, 252

levelled, 186

M

McKerrow, Dr. R. B., 171, 256 *n.*, 257

Malone Society reprint of *The Massacre* (ed. W. W. Greg), 170, 173, 174, 195, 202, 217, 238